PENGUIN BOOKS

PLAYIN

Nasser Hussain was born in M: to
the UK when he was seven. H   .x in 1987 and
has remained at the county ever s   . his test debut for England
in 1990 and was made captain in 1999. He played 45 tests as captain
before resigning in July 2003. He was acknowledged as one of England's
finest ever captains. He lives in Essex.

Paul Newman was born in Walthamstow, north-east London, and began
his career with his local paper. He has subsequently worked for the *Daily
Mail*, the *Daily Telegraph* and the *Sunday Telegraph* and has collaborated on
previous cricket books with David Smith, Nasser Hussain and Angus
Fraser. He is currently the deputy sports editor of the *Daily Mail* and is
married with two children. He first met Nasser Hussain when he was
dismissed by his googly at Valentine's Park in 1981 and was sent packing
with a torrent of abuse by the future England captain. Their relationship
improved to the point where Newman now godfather to Hussain's first
child, Jacob, and is very concerned that he is being bought up as an
Arsenal fan.

Playing with Fire

NASSER HUSSAIN
with Paul Newman

PENGUIN BOOKS

PENGUIN BOOKS

Published by the Penguin Group
Penguin Books Ltd, 80 Strand, London WC2R ORL, England
Penguin Group (USA) Inc., 375 Hudson Street, New York, New York 10014, USA
Penguin Group (Canada), 10 Alcorn Avenue, Toronto, Ontario, Canada M4V 3B2
(a division of Pearson Penguin Canada Inc.)
Penguin Ireland, 25 St Stephen's Green, Dublin 2, Ireland
(a division of Penguin Books Ltd)
Penguin Group (Australia), 250 Camberwell Road, Camberwell, Victoria 3124, Australia
(a division of Pearson Australia Group Pty Ltd)
Penguin Books India Pvt Ltd, 11 Community Centre, Panchsheel Park, New Delhi – 110 017, India
Penguin Group (NZ), cnr Airborne and Rosedale Roads, Albany, Auckland 1310, New Zealand
(a division of Pearson New Zealand Ltd)
Penguin Books (South Africa) (Pty) Ltd, 24 Sturdee Avenue, Rosebank 2196, South Africa

Penguin Books Ltd, Registered Offices: 80 Strand, London WC2R ORL, England

www.penguin.com

First published by Michael Joseph 2004
Published in Penguin Books 2005
2

Copyright © Nasser Hussain, 2004
All rights reserved

The moral right of the author has been asserted

Typeset by Rowland Phototypesetting Ltd, Bury St Edmunds, Suffolk
Printed in England by Clays Ltd, St Ives plc

Contents

List of Illustrations

76. Joy at completing a hundred against New Zealand at Lord's in his last appearance as a player (Philip Brown)
77. The moment of victory, with a hundred under his belt at Lord's (Winston Bynorth)
78. Walking off with his old mate Graham Thorpe (Philip Brown)
79. Ian Botham is now Nasser's colleague in the Sky commentary box (Winston Bynorth)
80. There are always thousands of England supporters present in a foreign field (Patrick Eagar)

Every effort has been made to trace copyright-holders of the illustrations and we apologize in advance for any unintentional omission. We will be pleased to insert the appropriate acknowledgement in any subsequent edition.

Introduction

I was always nervous when I batted. Always had a fear of failure and a fear of not living up to my dad's expectations. Cricket was never just a game to me, it was far more important than that.

Take my usual working day. If I was faced with the prospect of batting the next day in any cricket match, I was always at my worst, grumpy and miserable. I was never very sociable in the evening if I had to bat the following day. I was never able to change my ways, I just coped with it. The process of batting would start in my hotel room, or at home, the night before, when I would watch videos of the bowlers I would be facing next day and then I would make notes about them, about what they did with the ball and how I could best deal with it. Then I would write down little motivational messages to myself, simple things designed to put me in the right frame of mind for the task ahead.

Even if I was tired I would stay up late because I knew that, once I was asleep, my next waking moment meant that batting time was near. I would normally fall asleep about 1 a.m., having fiddled around with my bat to make sure it felt right for a couple of hours, and then wake up again at 5 a.m., opening one eye in the direction of the alarm clock before thinking, 'God, I'm batting today. What's going to happen? Am I going to nick one early on? Am I going to get runs today?' I always felt nervous as hell. I couldn't eat, couldn't read a paper for fear of seeing something negative, so from 5 a.m. I would lie there, looking at the clock, hoping it wouldn't move so that batting wouldn't come any nearer. Eventually I would get up at 7 a.m., go down to breakfast ahead of most of the rest of the team, always try to eat what I had eaten when I scored two hundred against the Aussies, and prepare to leave for the ground.

I always liked to stay fifteen or twenty minutes away from the ground if I could. It meant I had a bit of time in the car to listen to Radio 2 in order to try to calm myself and get my heartbeat down. Then I would arrive in the dressing room to pick up my bat, a major deal for me. The bat would never feel like it did the night before and I would have to take bits of tape off it, or do something to it, to make it feel right again. My obsession with my gear verged on the unhealthy at times. It was quite a compulsive thing.

Then it would be out to the middle, to visualize what lay ahead. As I moved down the steps of the pavilion, I would imagine Mike Atherton or Marcus Trescothick being out and the applause coming from the crowd as I made my way to the middle. I would hear spectators saying 'Good luck' or the chirps of opposition fielders as I made my way to the crease. Then I would stand at the crease and visualize every opposing bowler running in at me and what they would do with the ball when they bowled it at me. By the time you actually went out to bat for real, you felt as if you had already been there and had got over much of the uncertainty of the start of your innings.

Waiting to bat was the hardest thing. If we had a big opening partnership, I would have used up all my nervous energy in the dressing room. That was why I was always at my best when we lost quick wickets and I could get out there with no one expecting me to do well. After I had received my first ball I wasn't nervous any more. I was always happy in the middle. That's where I was different from someone like Graeme Hick. You could sometimes see the fear of failure in his eyes when he was in the middle, but mine had gone by then.

Whenever I was out, however many runs I had scored, I would always throw my gear around or have a bit of a tantrum in the dressing room. It was how I was. If you failed, you were angry; if you had scored fifty, you were angry you hadn't converted it into a hundred; and if you got a hundred, you were angry you hadn't turned it into a really big one. Even when I scored 207 against Australia in 1997 I was angry, because it was Shane Warne who had got me out and I didn't want it to be him.

Everyone reacts differently, but everybody cares. I calmed down a bit as I got older because I saw other people throwing their gear about and I felt I must have looked a prat when I was doing it, but for much of my career I had to hit something on my return in order to get it out of my system. After half an hour I was fine, but for those thirty minutes after I was out it was best to keep out of my way in the dressing room. A couple of times I bruised my hands punching things and a couple of times I broke my bats, which I always regretted afterwards because I was protective over my gear.

That, in a nutshell, was my career. That was what I went through before and after every innings. It's incredible, really. Quite mad that I should get this way over batting, the thing I was supposed to be good at. I have been through a huge cricketing adventure and have come out the other side happy and content. As I look back now, a few weeks after my retirement from cricket, my overwhelming feelings are of my good fortune at what I have experienced and achieved and the incredible life I had led. I have so many memories and I have been shown such wonderful support from so many people. Now I think of all the letters I have had, walking around the ground at Barbados after we won the series in the West Indies and seeing so many wonderful England fans, remembering how good it felt whenever the man on the Tannoy said, 'Leading out England, Nasser Hussain,' and I think back to my younger days when I was perceived as a bit of a selfish bad-boy. The support and good wishes of the English cricketing public means a tremendous amount to me. And what a way to finish – with a century in a match-winning cause for England in a Test against New Zealand.

I feel humbled by my career. I think back to myself and Atherton playing schools cricket together, and I reflect on the fact that between us we have captained England in around 100 Tests. In this book I have included a picture of myself as a child, standing on the Lord's outfield with a friend whose name I can't remember, because in the background is roughly the same place where my last two shots in cricket were aimed, the first one taking me to a hundred, and the second winning a Test in front of a packed Lord's. How could I possibly have imagined that happening when I stood there during my first visit to the home of cricket, almost thirty years ago?

I have made incredible friendships and have the most amazing memories. I am proud of my career. There are a group of cricketers and management I will always have a special bond with because they were the ones that I, largely, shared my best moments with as England captain. People like Mike Atherton, Graham Thorpe, Alec Stewart, Ashley Giles, Craig White, Darren Gough, Matthew Hoggard, Andrew Caddick, Dominic Cork, Marcus Trescothick, Michael Vaughan, Mark Butcher, Phil Tufnell, Graeme Hick, Mark Ramprakash and Steve Harmison. Then there is coach Duncan Fletcher, the biggest single influence on my later career, and others behind the scenes, like Phil Neale, Dean Conway, Nigel Stockill, Malcolm Ashton and Andrew Walpole. And the selectors, David Graveney and Geoff Miller in particular. They will all always have a special place in my life.

As you will read, I was fortunate to have parents who sacrificed so much for me, to enable me to have the richness of opportunity and experiences I have been given. I was awarded the OBE at the start of 2000, a huge honour and one that is totally dedicated to my parents. As is this book.

Everything I say in this book is my opinion. That doesn't make it right or wrong, and I accept that other people have different ways of doing things and I would never criticize them for that. *Playing with Fire* is a perfect title because I have always played with plenty of passion and with my heart on my sleeve. It is the only way I know. Every innings was critical because of my upbringing, and I fully accept that I have been an abrasive character. Other people have often had to play with fire in their dealings with me, but I like to think I have mellowed over the years. Having a family has changed me, as did the tragic death of Ben Hollioake, which emphasized to me that cricket, in the end, doesn't really matter.

If I have a regret, it is not really keeping in touch with friends from my early days. I have never been very good at returning messages or ringing people for a chat. Maybe now I have time on my hands, I will be better at that. And that's the thing that has struck me most since I retired: I seem to have so much time to do things, the little things that just seemed to pass me by while I was still playing. I am relishing having more time with my family, enjoying them and my house, and doing things that it never entered my head to do when I was a player. I have even been strawberry picking!

I get a feeling of warmth and calm when I look back on my career now. This is why I needed to finish when I did. A lot of my career has been about the support and goodwill of people like those I have already mentioned. The supporters, my team-mates, the coach and selectors. I never wanted to outstay my welcome and lose this support. I like to think I will have it with me for a long while yet. I am so pleased that I have no bitterness or bad feelings about anything that happened. On the first day of the second Test against New Zealand at Headingley in 2004, the first match after I retired, I woke up at 5 a.m., as I have just described here, and started fiddling nervously with my bat handle. Then I thought, 'Hang on a minute, I don't have to do this any more.' It was a lovely feeling.

Now for a new career in the media. Let's just hope I don't start waking up at 5 a.m. and begin to fiddle with my microphone at the prospect of the day ahead. If that happens, as Steve Redgrave almost once said, you have my full permission to shoot me!

Nasser Hussain
Little Baddow, Essex, June 2004

I

I never dreamt that all my hard work at cricket, all the sacrifices of my dad and all my ups and downs would lead me to the top of the game. What was beyond my wildest imaginings was that it would also lead me to the centre of world politics.

Nothing could have prepared me properly for the crisis that engulfed the England cricket team and the world game over our participation in our scheduled World Cup match in Zimbabwe in 2003. It was a time when I found myself making decisions and facing situations that I believed only world leaders were qualified to do. It was a time when I remembered being that little kid from Ilford with few aspirations in my mind other than pleasing my dad. How had it come to this? How could it reach a situation where I, as England captain, felt abandoned, not only by the British government but also and mainly by cricket's world governing body and our own board?

How could a person like me, so lacking any interest in politics that I have never voted in my entire life in any election, be faced with the prospect of crucial meetings with the likes of the South African prime minister, Zimbabwe freedom fighters and even the great Nelson Mandela? And what really amazed me was that the stakes were so high. So high that not only were relationships at government level between Zimbabwe, England and South Africa at stake but also a much more crucial issue: people's lives. And all over a cricket match. It was without doubt the most traumatic time of my life.

What a journey I had had to reach this stage. What a rollercoaster. I arrived in England, as you will read, as a seven-year-old boy, my parents giving up a lovely life in India because they wanted their children to grow up and be educated in England. From that time my dad wanted me to be a cricketer, he pushed me and gave me every encouragement.

My dad's drive, and the ability I clearly had, took me further than I could possibly have imagined: from the early trauma of losing my leg-spin action, to re-creating myself as a batsman, and then a professional career with Essex and England. Ultimately, incredibly and to the immense pride of myself and my family, I became England captain. I knew it would be tough. I knew I would have my ups and downs. But what I didn't expect, after being England captain for three and a half years, was being embroiled in one of the biggest political crises in English cricketing history. And somehow I'd ended up being the key figure.

The suffering of the people of Zimbabwe and the particular relationship that country had with Britain – despite President Mugabe stating that England was his sworn enemy – had started to emerge as a serious topic during our Ashes tour to Australia in 2002–3, but I had so much on my plate at that time that I really didn't have the time to give it serious thought. But the closer we came to the World Cup, my last chance to take part and make progress in cricket's biggest event, the more it became obvious that the issue was to become a major one. Maybe we should have been more like the Australians and just done what we were told. Maybe, like a lot of other things in my life, I thought about the issue too much and over-complicated it.

Towards the end of our Australia tour I met up with Michael Atherton in the middle before a match and I asked him what he thought about Zimbabwe. He told me it was a serious issue and, in his usual forthright way, told me to make sure the players didn't put their heads in the sand, as they usually did, but faced up to what was going on. I told the players that we were going to have to address the whole business, but our difficulty at that stage lay in not knowing what people in

England were thinking and saying about Zimbabwe. We had been away from home for so long, we were out of touch and needed to get up to speed.

While Richard Bevan, our representative from the Professional Cricketers Association, was back in England continuously keeping me informed on ICC, ECB and Zimbabwe politics, Andrew Flintoff and Ashley Giles also became crucial, because they had been back in England, recuperating from injuries, and had rejoined us for the World Cup. They told me that we would have to be careful here because people in England were becoming increasingly concerned at the prospect of their national team playing in Zimbabwe when so much was going on in that country. Crucially, Freddie and Ashley had also seen a Channel 4 documentary on the subject, and they told us about the really shocking events it had highlighted, like people being buried in bunkers on Zimbabwean golf courses and the shocking torture and starvation of the people there. I also received a lot of correspondence on the issue from all over the world. Ninety-nine per cent of it said we shouldn't go. What was very clear was that we had to gather as much information as possible on the topic, and I asked Richard Bevan to help.

By now Zimbabwe was becoming the dominant topic in everyone's mind. Our government had said they didn't think it was right for us to play a game of cricket in Zimbabwe but that they couldn't order us not to go because we lived in a democratic country and everyone had the right to make their own minds up. That was convenient for them, and I guess I could understand what they were saying, but I still couldn't understand why they couldn't have given us a way out of the whole sorry business by telling us not to go.

Maybe I'm naive, but as far as I was concerned our government were representing our people, and our people were now making it clear that they didn't want their cricket team to go to Zimbabwe. After all, playing for England is exactly that:

representing the country. So why couldn't the government make the big decision they were elected to make and say 'Our boys are not going'?

But no. That was not going to happen. To me it just reinforced my belief that many politicians are not worth voting for. So many of them seem to be bluffers to me and so many of them don't keep their promises. I don't think I will ever vote.

So, even at this stage I was thinking, 'Why are we going to Zimbabwe when so many of our people don't want us to?' Then, by chance, I switched on the TV in my Australian hotel room and CNN were showing part of the Channel 4 documentary on Zimbabwe. It looked just as terrible as Giles and Flintoff had told me it was. I mentioned that documentary in the course of a press conference soon afterwards and said that clearly we had some big decisions to make, a move which led to the producer of the programme writing to me and sending me documents relative to what he had seen out there.

Richard Bevan, who has done so much for us and brought so much professionalism to English cricket off the field, continued to keep me up to speed on what was happening at ICC and ECB. At this stage he was confident that, with so much evidence to hand, both we and Australia (who were also due to play in Zimbabwe) would be forced to pull out and that the International Cricket Council would have to move the matches to South Africa. He told me not to worry too much; he was sure we would be playing Zimbabwe in Bloemfontein. To me it seemed the obvious answer – but when did common sense play a part in the big decisions?

All the while the ICC and the ECB were still insisting that the game would go ahead because there was no facility for cricketers to pull out of a fixture on moral grounds, only security ones; we received a blow when it became clear that the Australians were planning to fulfil their fixture after all, by flying in and out of the country as quickly as possible. But what nobody seemed to appreciate (apart perhaps from us modest cricketers, who supposedly have no idea what is going on in the outside world) was that Britain and Zimbabwe have a particular relationship through history and the depth of feelings towards us from the Mugabe regime. Surely the ICC should treat this in the same way as it does problems between India and Pakistan? Sympathetically? Maybe that would be too simple.

We flew straight to South Africa from Australia because we just didn't have enough time for the short visit home before the World Cup that we all craved, and we managed to get a couple of days of golf in at Sun City. But we couldn't enjoy it. There was so much happening, so much talking going on between the players over what was facing us. By the time we arrived in Cape Town, the World Cup, the carnival of cricket, was the last thing on our minds. We were caught up in the middle of a full-blown crisis.

The Cullinan Hotel in Cape Town will always hold a significant place in English cricket history now: it was where we were all holed up while we were faced with the biggest decision of our professional lives and where the world's media were gathered to see what we would do. Suffice to say, I don't think I will ever be going back there for a holiday.

As soon as we got to the place we were whisked straight into a meeting and I had to make sure the players were aware of what was confronting them. I addressed them and said, 'Look, I know sometimes when we are discussing cricket and tactics, some of you fall asleep at the back during my team talks, but that doesn't concern me now. Some of you are going to have to take some serious growing-up pills and take this issue very seriously indeed. I know a lot of you are young and I apologize for putting this on you, but it's looking as though everyone is going to leave us to make some pretty big decisions here.'

We had already requested, through Richard Bevan, that the game be switched to South Africa, but nothing encouraging was coming back from the ICC's technical committee, so we asked for urgent talks with the ICC's Australian chief executive, Malcolm Speed, as soon as we reached Cape Town. All the ICC and ECB were concerned about was security and that that was our only chance of succeeding in having the fixture moved, but to me there was so much more to it than that and we were just not being allowed to talk about the morals and the politics of the affair. Basically, we were not being treated as grown-ups.

Then Malcolm Speed arrived to address the team in the presence of our representatives, Richard Bevan and Gerrard Tyrrell, ECB chief executive Tim Lamb and chairman David Morgan and the ECB's legal representatives. I'd been speaking to Duncan Fletcher, our coach, at length about Zimbabwe because he actually comes from the place and was feeling more stress than anyone about our predicament. Duncan had been speaking to a lot of people in Zimbabwe and he was sure that we would be safe as an England cricket team going there. There was never a big issue with us until later on. But Duncan also told me what the people thought about our visit morally, and it was clear that even he was not sure what we should do. Half the people, Duncan thought, felt we shouldn't go, but the other half wanted us to come in order to highlight their plight and make a gesture of support. So our main link to the country, a man who had captained Zimbabwe in a World Cup, didn't know what to do for the best, which neatly summed up our plight. The plight was not what was best for us but what was best for the people of Zimbabwe and the image and integrity of world cricket, surely a vital part of our role as international cricketers. You might have thought so. But Malcolm Speed, it seemed, was having none of it.

He walked in to what we thought was going to be a very

important meeting at which he would take our views on board and listen to the very real concerns we had about playing in Zimbabwe and the reasons behind our plea to have the fixture moved. How wrong could we be? From the start Speed kept looking at his watch as if he didn't give a damn about what we thought. He said, 'I've got thirty minutes.' No respect. No appreciation that England were in a difficult position regarding Zimbabwe. Now, I had been in meetings with Speed before and I have never been impressed with his style. I don't expect people to bow down at my feet as England captain, but I do think administrators should appreciate and have an understanding of what cricketers are all about and our point of view. Speed always seemed to talk down to us. His attitude was always 'Do what we tell you to do.' He felt he ran the game and it didn't matter what cricketers thought or wanted. In my dealings with the ICC, and Malcolm Speed in particular, I never detected an interest in the spirit and future of the game, the image of it or the legacy they will leave. It seemed to me that the priority was always money.

So Speed immediately got off on the wrong foot and I could see that the players were confused. We were supposed to be getting ready for one of the highlights of our careers and instead we were stuck in a room with Malcolm Speed. There were some players, like Giles and Flintoff, who had already decided they were not going to Zimbabwe even if the ICC tried to force us. Most of the others were worried, confused and incredulous that it had come to this. So I started off by saying to Speed, 'Do the ICC not realize that the British government have stated that they don't want us to go, a couple of our lads have been home and are adamant that the English people do not want us to go? So how can we go against all that and go and play cricket in Zimbabwe when we don't think it is morally right to go?' The moment I said 'morally' he jumped at me. It was the same with Tim Lamb. It was as if you pressed a button with administrators as soon as you used that word and they would immediately tell us that we can't have morals in cricket. Oh no, that would be totally wrong.

I then asked Speed why the situation vis-à-vis India and Pakistan was different, and he said that was because their governments told them not to visit each other's country rather than advising their players, as ours had done. And so it went on. Speed kept looking at his watch and refusing to talk about anything other than safety, which he insisted would be dealt with by the ICC's security advisers. He was so intransigent and inflexible. I had thought we were going into a meeting to get an explanation from the ICC as to why they felt the game should go ahead in Zimbabwe, but all I got was a declaration that we were going to play there, that it was safe to do so and that was the end of the matter. Then, after exactly half an hour, he announced that he was leaving.

It was then that I made my point to him. And this is the honest truth about what I said and did, a truth that can be verified by the minutes of the meeting that are held by the Professional Cricketers Association. And I say this because for some inexplicable reason Tim Lamb, my boss at the ECB, later felt compelled to apologize to Malcolm Speed for what I said next. Unbelievable.

I said, 'You have come here, you have given us half an hour, you are dealing with players who have been in tears over all this and don't know what to do, and I hold you, Malcolm Speed, and the ICC responsible for this mess. We are three days away from the biggest tournament in cricket, you have known about this situation for months and you could have had this meeting with us at any time over those months. You know this is a sensitive political issue for England because of our historical ties with Zimbabwe, but you have fudged this issue. You are supposedly running this game and protecting the image of this game, can't you see the damage that is being done by this and what damage will be done if we play this game?'

8

He just said 'No' and brushed me aside, so I repeated that I held him personally responsible for what was going to happen and what these boys in this room were going to have to go through for the next couple of days before reaching a final decision. I was calm. I never swore and I was never offensive. Yes, I pointed at him, but that was the nearest I got to aggression.

My parting shot was that he had buried his head in the sand by refusing to accept that this was a moral issue and seeing what damage our visit would do. We had been reliably informed, through Richard Bevan's intelligence, that opposition parties in Zimbabwe would hold mass demonstrations if England went there, and it was clear that their government wouldn't allow that and that people would be hurt. Badly hurt. I asked Malcolm Speed if that was what he wanted: people being beaten, arrested or worse, much worse, simply over a game of cricket. He just wouldn't listen to me. Then he was gone, after telling us that we would all have to move into another room, where we would be told about the security details surrounding our visit.

I switched off now. I was so disillusioned. To me it wasn't about our safety. It was about morals and the safety of people in Zimbabwe during the game. And Speed had treated us so dismissively, with such a lack of respect for us and for the image of the game, that I felt deflated and demoralized.

But there was another twist to the tale. Before we went in to meet with the tournament security people, Bevan relayed information to us that we were sure would force the ICC to listen to us. Because Richard now had evidence that our safety would be in jeopardy if we went to Zimbabwe, and as those were the only grounds on which the ICC would listen to our request for the game to be moved, we felt this was a significant development.

Richard told us about a threat that had been made to us by an organization called 'The Sons and Daughters of Zimbabwe' which the ECB had known about for months but, in their wisdom, had decided not to tell us about.* Now, in full and graphic detail, the players were being told that not only they but their families would be at risk if we set foot in Zimbabwe. Clearly this had to be addressed in our next meeting. Surely.

So I tried to switch back on. The meeting was with Patrick Ronan, who was the head of ICC security, Pete Richer, who was a director of Kroll, a huge American intelligence company which had been commissioned by the ICC to look into security at the World Cup, and one of the most amazing characters I have ever seen. His name was Andre Pruis and he was the deputy commissioner of the South African police force. He was a huge Afrikaaner with a deep voice and he reminded me of a *Spitting Image* puppet. He was one scary bloke. Almost like a caricature of a South African copper.

This huge bloke proceeded to show us just what he would do to any demonstrator who tried to get near us in Zimbabwe. He was hilarious. He couldn't help but mimic the action of a horsewhip as he spoke. He went on and on, his arm flicking, clearly enjoying every second, showing how he would hit them and then hit them again, just to make sure they knew they had been hit. And, to be fair, if I was five yards from trouble I would want this bloke by my side. But I was bewildered now. This, to me, was confirming that there would be bloodshed if we went to Zimbabwe, that people were going to get seriously hurt. This presentation was supposed to reassure us that we would be safe and that it was right for us to go, but all it was doing was confirming my worst fears, that in all probability someone would get killed if we played in Zimbabwe. And over a cricket match. I thought to myself, 'This is going to look

* For the complete text of the letter from The Sons and Daughters of Zimbabwe, see Appendix 1, page 445.

really good. We're playing a game and this bloke is outside, beating someone up. That's going to look really good for the TV cameras.' This demonstration was not convincing me I should go. Quite the opposite. In a way I was thinking a little selfishly. While the policeman was talking about how he would airlift us out of Harare in helicopters if something went wrong, all I could think about was me being tarnished as the England captain who took his side to Zimbabwe and had to flee the country while mass demonstrations took place and, possibly, people were killed. How could I live with that for the rest of my life?

It was farcical. The players wanted to know about the death threat that had just been thrown at us, but the ICC bloke and the Afrikaaner both said they had no knowledge of the Sons and Daughters and that it should be completely dismissed as irrelevant, that they got letters like this all the time. But the man from Kroll said he had some pertinent information as to who they were and that they should be treated seriously. One security expert was saying they definitely didn't exist and another that they did. This caused uproar among the players. This meeting was supposed to reassure the players, but the various security forces had differing opinions as to the authenticity of a death threat which had been kept from us for months!

By the end of this second meeting it was really late and we were all very tired and stressed. So I handed the lads a piece of paper each and told them to write down, anonymously, yes or no on whether we should go. They all did, and it was 15–0 against going. I was not surprised.

This was the moment when Tim Lamb's face dropped. And, from that moment, the ECB switched from being totally on our side and supportive about our feelings to turning on the emotional blackmail in an attempt to force us into going. All along I had wanted to speak out about our moral objections to visiting Zimbabwe, but I had kept my mouth shut because the ECB had wanted me to go down the security route, reasoning that we could get out of going on those grounds and would not lose face or any World Cup points. It had made the players look narrow-minded and insular, but I had done it in order to protect the ECB, and now Tim Lamb was turning on the pressure as only he could. Suddenly he was trying every trick in the book to get us to go, picking off the players one by one, ringing people like Duncan Fletcher in their hotel rooms at 3 a.m. and saying things like 'You do know how many of your fellow players will lose their jobs if you refuse to go and we get fined? This will kill the domestic game.' At one point he broke down and cried in front of me. Things were getting worse.

David Morgan, our board chairman, was better. He felt for his players and wanted to resolve the issue in our favour. I have always liked Morgan but right now, in a new job, he was in the wrong place at the wrong time. He was behaving like the head of a company should behave and was taking his duties of care towards his employees seriously. Tim Lamb, a smooth operator whose manner I always found unctuous and whom I neither liked nor enjoyed working with, was, I felt, overwhelmingly interested in finances. Apart, that is, from trying to safeguard his own position – a characteristic all too common in English cricket.

Lamb never seemed to look at the bigger picture. He never gave the impression that he thought highly of the players. Consequently, a number of players and management in our squad took a dislike to him. Whenever we had meetings with him, he would always say the wrong thing. He would get under people's skin. And he certainly got under mine. What annoyed me most was what I thought amounted to emotional blackmail, telling young players without a full understanding of what they were involved in that, if they didn't go to Zimbabwe, they would put some of their mates in the county game out of a job, that sponsors would pull out, that some counties would go bust and that the domestic game, in all probability, would be bankrupt. All because of us.

And do you know what? He got to me. I started listening again. As England captain I always felt I had a responsibility to the game. The last thing I wanted to do was make the wrong decision. What if Lamb was right? Surely, I thought, England wouldn't be ostracized from the world game if we pulled out? I know there has been a shift in cricketing power to Asia away from England, but I also know how much it means, in terms of both prestige and finance, for countries like India to tour England. Surely they wouldn't throw us out of the world game, or fine us a crippling amount of money, for not going to Zimbabwe? But would they? I wanted to make sure my decision wouldn't bankrupt the game.

Then the opening ceremony hit us. It was a break from all the stress and chaos. It was the first time we had been out of that damned Cullinan Hotel since we arrived in Cape Town. It dawned on us that we were at a major tournament. It was a great opening ceremony, staged at a lovely ground in Newlands. I was the most proud and confused I have ever been. I was walking around the ground, carrying the flag of St George at the head of my team, and I could see the players looking around, taking it all in and thinking how great it would be to come back here for a World Cup final or semi-final.

Just before the ceremony a man had come up to me and introduced himself as the producer of the Channel 4 documentary on Zimbabwe which had made such an impact both on me and on people in England. He went through all the terrible things he knew and told me that we were absolutely right not to go, even if it did cost us our one chance at lifting the World Cup.

But it was crystal clear to me now that this was a big cricket thing going on here. I went back to my room in a state of utter confusion, and it didn't take long for my phone to ring. Alec Stewart and Ronnie Irani wanted to have a chat, so at 1 a.m. I was in Stewie's room, talking about whether we really were doing the right thing. Should we go after all and make some kind of gesture or make a statement about how we condemned what was going on in Zimbabwe? It was brave of Stewie and Ronnie to consider going back on what we had decided, and I admired them for it. After the amazing opening ceremony I couldn't help thinking the same thing myself.

Then David Morgan asked us if we could have one more meeting at which he would address all of the players one by one on an individual basis. This worried me. I thought he was going to pick people off, so I asked Richard Bevan to sit in on the chats. After that I met up again with Ronnie, who burst into tears. He said, 'Nass, I think I've changed my mind. This is my World Cup. I've worked my nuts off to get here. I understand the argument against but we should talk more about this.' I told Ronnie, an old friend, that I respected what he was saying and that all I asked was that he explain to everyone the alternative argument when next we met as a team.

So Ronnie was in a bad state about it all, Stewie was wavering; we had a few more meetings and Lamb was playing games, having lots of quiet words with people. When he broke down in tears in front of me, I thought, 'You shouldn't be doing this to me. You shouldn't be putting me in this position.' They knew I was a strong person and that if they managed to get to me and convince me to go, there was a good chance a lot of the others would go with me. I did actually feel for Lamb at this point, but he kept on telling me the moral argument was irrelevant and I just couldn't accept that. I thought, 'No, sport has moved on. You can't separate it from politics. I have asked my players to grow up and it's about time the ECB grew up too.'

At the centre of it all, I was sure, was African politics. Ali Bacher, the tournament organizer, was having nothing to do with us as players but was busying himself trying to get us to go. I was sure South Africa were determined to support Zimbabwe in order to guarantee their support over the South African bid to stage the 2010 football World Cup. South Africa's prime minister was saying we should go, and the position of Nelson Mandela was curious. I kept on reading that he was saying, 'If the authorities think it is right for England to go, then they should go,' but I couldn't understand that. Here was a man who had given up most of his adult life to question the South African authorities because he knew they were wrong, but now he was telling us to do what we were told. I was just hoping he had been misquoted and, in any case, who was I to question Nelson Mandela? I was offered a meeting with the great man and maybe I should have gone in order to hear what he had to say, but there was so much going on at this time that the last thing I wanted was to be further confused by Nelson Mandela. I wasn't sure I warranted a meeting with him – and, in any case, how could he understand what a group of cricketers were going through?

I then asked Ronnie to speak to Andy Flower, a teammate of ours at Essex, to find out what his thoughts were about the whole thing. Ronnie reported back that Andy (a bit like Duncan Fletcher) had been in two minds over what to do all winter, but that he had come up with an idea that at that stage he couldn't tell us about.

Next came another significant meeting. In secret an exiled member of the Zimbabwean opposition to Mugabe was smuggled in to see us, a man who put his life seriously at risk in order to come and talk to us. He told us that he was working with Andy Flower and Henry Olonga and he said they would be wearing black armbands during Zimbabwe's matches, to mourn the death of democracy in their country. He urged us to do the same or to make a similar gesture, and that this would do a tremendous amount of good for his cause. Now I didn't know what to do.

This guy, who must remain anonymous for his own safety, then said he had two people he wanted us to meet. We were led into another room in the Cullinan Hotel, and there were Andy and Henry, waiting for us. They too had been smuggled in and they explained to us what they were going to do; they told us they understood our predicament, that it would be nice if we played the match wearing black armbands but that it wasn't our fight and that we had to do what we thought best. Despite the pressure on him, Andy had the grace to say he was proud of us and of the stance we might be taking. I can't tell you how much I admired them. I was sitting there with an Essex teammate, discussing the most important and weighty of topics; both Andy and Henry admitted they were scared about what they were going to do, frightened for the future, but that they were doing something they had to do. When they left, Duncan Fletcher, who met them with me, shook his head and said, 'There go two incredibly brave people.'

I took this back to the team and, to be honest, the idea of wearing black armbands did not go down too well. I could understand that. The players felt we couldn't just go into someone else's country and make a political protest. They felt we would be making a significant gesture in not going, but that we couldn't make such a big gesture as wearing armbands on the back of a little information about the country's plight. And also that, with a death threat hanging over us, it would just be too dangerous a thing to do. For me, nothing had really changed. Yes, we could go and wear black armbands; it would be the bravest and the right thing to do, and I will always admire Flower and Olonga for such a gesture. But I felt, from the information I was receiving, that if we went, and even if we did that, there would be mass demonstrations and people would get hurt or killed, and I couldn't live with that for the rest of my life. So my mind was made up. The game had taken on too great a significance. It was no longer just a game of cricket; it was literally a matter of life or death, and I didn't want any part of it.

I think, deep in his heart, Duncan Fletcher would have liked us to have gone the whole hog and worn armbands because he is a very brave man who was at my side throughout the whole affair. I might have been isolated by my government, my employers and the sport's governing body, but not by Duncan. I know some people felt that, as a Zimbabwean, he could have made more public pronouncements in support of me, but Duncan doesn't have to make public statements just for effect to do his bit. At no stage did he let me down, even though he had a lot of relatives and friends living in Zimbabwe to consider. The team decided, however, that wearing armbands would be too reckless, too much a case of us sticking our noses into somebody else's business. These decisions should be made by governments and sporting bodies.

It was finally 'make your mind up' time. Ahead of our last players' meeting on the subject I spoke and gave my view as the argument against going. Then I asked Ronnie Irani to speak in favour of going. Ronnie spoke very well, very emotionally, not saying that we should go but making sure everyone fully understood the implications of not going. He asked people to think things through. Should we do what the Australians were doing? Going in there, winning and coming out again. No one was holding the Aussies accountable, Ronnie said.

Then I went round the room, asking each player to give his verdict and explain why. I started with the youngest, Jimmy Anderson, and went on from there, trying to make sure that the young players didn't just copy what the senior ones were doing. I can honestly say they all spoke brilliantly. They all had their own reasons, and not one of them said he wanted to go. Even the two doubters, Ronnie and Stewie, abstained rather than vote to go. I think they wanted us to think things through fully. Some said they didn't want to go for moral reasons, others for safety issues, others that after all this they couldn't be in the right frame of mind to play cricket in Zimbabwe. Others were like me, asking how we could possibly justify the possibility of someone being killed over our being there. It was a game of cricket, like Ilford against Colchester, but it had been transformed into a major political crisis. I still couldn't believe what I was going through.

As we prepared to give the ECB our final decision, Mark Roper-Drimmie, the ECB's lawyer, burst in and said that Interpol had told him that the Sons and Daughters of Zimbabwe were a legitimate threat after all and that the ECB were now confident we would be able to move our game without losing money or points. You couldn't make it up. They had known about this for months and had dismissed it, but the moment we make our decision not to go, they tell us that it was a serious threat after all.

Everyone in the room went white. Some players were upset and some left the room in anger. It was like 'How did we get here? How are Interpol involved in a cricket match?' David Morgan told us that now we wouldn't have to do anything further and he would take this to the ICC technical committee. He felt this was the safety evidence the ECB had always sought. So I said, 'Right. Can you now guarantee we will not be going to Zimbabwe?' and Morgan said, 'Yes, this is it. Don't do anything more. Just tell everybody we are not going for security reasons because of this credible threat to our safety.'

I accepted that. I just felt a sense of relief. The ECB held a press conference and I insisted on being there. They were insistent on saying that we had made our decision purely on safety grounds, but it wasn't like that, not at all. Safety was certainly a consideration – and not just the safety of the England cricketers – but the decision was made overwhelmingly for moral reasons. Suggesting that we were blind to anything but security made us sound silly and insular, especially when measured against the bravery of Flower and Olonga. I'm ashamed to say that going along with that just seemed the best way to make sure we didn't go – the right decision made then, it seemed, for the wrong reasons. Over the previous forty-eight hours I had heard so much about death – death-threats to cricketers, deaths of spectators and the death of English cricket – that this was the only way to make completely sure that none of these possible tragic outcomes (however unlikely) could possibly materialize. What stuck in my throat was that what we were discussing, for public consumption at any rate, was not entirely honest and it trivialized a complex situation.

All through this, as I have said, I had been impressed by David Morgan, but then he let us down. He said we definitely weren't going, but something must have happened, because next morning Duncan told me that Morgan wanted a chat. It was literally ten minutes before the matter was supposed to be being closed and we were going back to training. But twelve hours after telling the boys 100 per cent for sure we weren't going, Morgan said to me and Fletch, 'Look, I want you to go.' Clearly, he had been warned by the ICC that the ECB were still going to be fined, or something like that. I had to do a double take. I said, 'Sorry, chairman, you are fucking kidding me, aren't you?' It was the one and only time I swore in the course of the whole affair. He said, 'You don't have to swear, captain, remember where you are,' but I told him that I was sorry, I did have to swear because he had told me I wasn't going to have to take my team to Zimbabwe and now he was urging me to go. What had changed? He said he just needed me to fully understand all the implications of not going and that the Sons and Daughters were not being treated seriously by the ICC again.

I couldn't believe it. It didn't add up. To this day I don't know the full reasons why David Morgan tried to get me to change my mind, but I lost a lot of respect for him that day. I felt it was unforgivable.

I said it was impossible for us to change now. I had agreed with them to say that we as players were pulling out for security issues, but not now. As I write, I'm no longer an employee of the ECB. I have to set the record straight.

The England cricket team pulled out of the match against Zimbabwe for a multitude of reasons. Yes, for some (especially after the death-threat from the Sons and Daughters) it was for personal security; but for many it was a moral issue and a decision based on the welfare of people in Zimbabwe in general, people at that particular cricket match, and the whole image of the game.

We have been told, as a team, to keep quiet and always mention the word 'security' rather than the word 'morality' as it would ensure that they could avoid the fines. I've toed the party line until now, but the way they behaved over the whole affair shouldn't have earned anyone's silence.

As I write, the whole situation is back on the agenda. England are due to go to Zimbabwe around the time this book is due to be published, and history has been repeating itself, with a pig's ear being made of the situation. An ECB official by the name of Des Wilson tried to make a stand, making a case to the ECB for the legitimate pulling out of tours on moral grounds, but predictably he has been ignored and subsequently he resigned. Zimbabwe have sacked all their white players and their Test status has been suspended, but still England plan to go there for one-day internationals. How can that be right? How can one-dayers be different from Tests? At the moment, in my opinion no England team should go to Zimbabwe for moral reasons and those players who went through the whole saga of the 2003 World Cup and who remain must surely, I believe, feel the same. It will be interesting to see if any of them go.

There was one last footnote to an affair which eventually

cost us our chance of progressing to the World Cup knockout stages. We had moved on to East London, thinking the affair was behind us, when I went online and read a report by Mihir Bose in the *Daily Telegraph* saying that Tim Lamb had been forced to apologize to Malcolm Speed for my behaviour during that brief meeting of ours.

Now I was spewing again just when I thought it was all over. I had kept quiet, acted like the dumb cricketer throughout, and now Tim Lamb, who, I reckoned, had behaved in an unsatisfactory manner throughout the whole business, was apologizing on my behalf? I went to see Duncan Fletcher and told him I had to resign over this. Then I called Andrew Walpole, the ECB's media manager, and told him I had had enough. Two minutes later, Tim Lamb was on the phone, denying it all and telling me not to believe Mihir Bose. I didn't believe Lamb. I thought Lamb behaved abysmally through it all and, while I accept that he did a lot of good work at the ECB, I shed no tears for him when I heard he had resigned from his job in 2004. Ironically, he went on the same day I announced my retirement from all cricket! Lamb subsequently insisted he had jumped rather than being pushed and that it had nothing to do with Zimbabwe. But I couldn't help but feel that there was a connection.

I ended up doing an emotional press conference, denying I had done anything which necessitated an apology from Lamb; but I was finished with the ECB by this stage. It proved to me that my spell as captain was coming to an end. I had a mistrust of the ICC, and now I felt the same with the ECB. Why was I captain in these circumstances? What was the point? It was the beginning of the end.

We carried on in the World Cup, trying to pick up the pieces, about which more later. About a year afterwards, I was sitting in front of my TV at home, having just watched the final of *I'm a celebrity get me out of here!* (sad git that I am), when a special *News at Ten* report came on, highlighting the plight of four lads who had demonstrated against Australia's World Cup match in Zimbabwe. They had been arrested outside, then tortured and raped, and had only just been released. It shocked me to the core. I thought, 'Thank God we didn't go. If that had been England, it would have been ten times worse. How could I have sat here and lived with myself?'

It was that moment in South Africa that crystallized everything for me. That time, when I was sitting in a Cape Town hotel, seemingly at the centre of world politics, when I distinctly remember thinking to myself: 'How did you get here? How could a simple lad from Ilford be making decisions that involve governments, Robert Mugabe, Nelson Mandela, human rights issues and the people of Zimbabwe? Not to mention the small matter of England's whole cricketing future? How could I be expected to make decisions that world leaders were seemingly shying away from and which involved the very real business of life and death? How could that be happening to me?'

It was, in many ways, the end of the journey. A journey that started in Madras, moved on to Ilford and then on to so many more places, incorporating so many memories that I could never have envisaged in my wildest dreams. You see, I never set out with the intention of doing all that, being involved in so much important stuff. Life becoming so public has never sat comfortably with me. I am an introvert, happy in my own company, and I don't mix well – more Jack Russell than Darren Gough! I like the simple life. If I had my own way I would spend the majority of my time with my immediate family in my home environment, where I feel happiest.

I also enjoy my golf, often playing nine holes on my own. I like my own company. I hate crowded pubs. I hated every second of my benefit year because it meant mixing with people in a social environment and being the centre of attention. The only place I have ever felt comfortable with people is in the dressing room.

I have never courted publicity or the limelight. I was never interested in *Hello!* magazine pieces or the whole celebrity thing when I was England captain. Just not my scene. Even this book is something of an intrusion into my own little world, but I am not doing it for celebrity or financial reasons, simply to explain who I am and how I got where I am. At times, my shyness has been misinterpreted as arrogance or indifference, but I can't help the way I am. I am a confused person in many ways and, to use a Ronnie Irani expression, the beans are constantly going in my head, but I like who I am and I am at peace with myself. I guess I am confident in my cricket, but not in very much else and I have never been too bothered what people think of me . . . except one person.

You see, everything I have ever done, everything I have ever achieved, all my ambitions, my drive and fire, have come from just one person and had been, initially, *for* one person. My dad. My father Jawad, Joe to everyone in England, has made me what I am, warts and all. He had the drive and ambition for all his family that made his youngest son become captain of England. A guy born in India called Nasser Hussain, with all the racial connotations and accusations of divided loyalty that has brought. It would have been unheard of not many years ago, but I did it. I achieved it and I am very proud of that. It was down to Dad.

I have always considered myself to be one hundred per cent English. Everything I do, everything I am, my accent, my upbringing, is all totally English. I love the country, basically, and have always considered it my home. But having said that, I've always been very proud of my Indian roots and my dad's culture. Much later in my life, when I toured India with England, I actually fell in love with the place and got a much better understanding of that side of me; but my life and my achievements have been totally down to what England has given me and what my dad instilled in me.

But it has been a life that I have lived, to a large degree, for my dad. I am sitting here now, in a fabulous house with a wonderful family, having had so many wonderful experiences and so many cricketing friendships. Visited so many places around the world. Seen how other people worse off than me have to live and realize how lucky I am.

I have had many people's support and have had the greatest possible honour of having to lead ten other men out behind me as captain of England. And I thank my dad for that. But it has not been easy. There have been times when I have wondered whether it has all been worth it, whether the fact that my whole existence has been geared towards cricketing achievement and proving myself to my dad has really been the best way to live my life. Everything I have done has been done for Joe, and even now I still find myself striving for his approval. I guess it will always be like that.

Don't get me wrong. The positive things in my close-knit, highly driven, highly motivated upbringing far outweigh the negatives and I will be passing on to my children the family values given to me by my Indian father and English mother. It means an awful lot to me that I am so close to my family. But in order to understand me it is crucial to understand what I went through, and for me to be absolutely honest in saying it wasn't all a bed of roses. I am going to tell it how it is and was, with the absolute bottom line that I am totally grateful to my family, particularly Dad, for everything they have done for me.

My early years are something of a blur. I have not got the best of memories for people and places, and in many ways it is a little disappointing that I cannot remember more of my formative times in India. I was born in Madras on 28 March 1968, and therein lies a story that I have only just learnt myself. You see, however close we Hussains are, we have never really talked deeply about personal things. Because my life has been forever entwined with my dad, I feel I have never really talked to my mum, Shireen, as much as I could have done. The love and respect have always been present and we were always there for each other, but not in an open way. Everything in my childhood was based around the family and us being happy, only not in an emotional way. Maybe this is an Asian thing. I was brought up to respect my elders, to be totally devoted to my family and to fight my corner. It was the right way to be brought up so far as I'm concerned.

So it was fascinating for me when my mum, upon learning that I was doing this book, sat down and wrote down a lot of things that I had never known about. She did it in the form of a letter to me, to explain to me certain things that have played such a big part in making me the person I am, even if I was unaware of them.

Most of the contents of that letter will always remain private, but it certainly enabled a lot of things to click into place for me. For I have only just discovered that I was so premature, my parents almost lost me. Indeed, it was only my mum's utter determination to the point of obsession not to lose me that gave me the gift of life.

Mum and Dad already had two boys, Mel and Abbas, before I came along, but they had been through the traumatic experience of losing a daughter to cot death. It is something we have never talked about as a family. But I know now that my parents lost her at six months and this had a profound effect on them, particularly Mum. She plunged into depression and the only way she could cope with it was to try to fall pregnant again as quickly as she could. It is only recently that I have fully understood why my mum has never really celebrated New Year's Eve and has always been subdued around that time. It is because that was my sister's birthday.

So she fell pregnant again, but there were problems. I gather now that the doctors in India told her on several occasions that I had died within her. She was even told, quite brutally, that I would have to be flushed down the toilet. That there was nothing there. The baby had gone. She would have to accept it. But Mum didn't. She refused to accept it. She fought to give me the chance to live, and she now believes that I am the way

I am, a fighter, because of this. Mum fought and I guess I fought, and eventually I was born two months premature but alive and healthy.

Mum says that a lot of people thought she was so determined to have me because she was desperate to have a girl to go with her two boys and because she had lost a baby daughter, but she is adamant that this is not the case. She just wanted another baby after the extreme loss she had suffered and, when I was born, the midwife, or whoever was in charge, said something along the lines of, 'I'm sorry, Mrs Hussain, it's another boy.' But that really didn't matter. My arrival had gone some way towards easing the most awful pain my mum has ever experienced.

And as a result of that I think I was a bit mollycoddled. Maybe that is why I am an introvert. If you're premature there is an increased risk of contracting illnesses, so I was kept in the very tenderest of care during my early months and I think that shaped my personality. When I was younger I believed all that psychology stuff was rubbish and that you shaped your own destiny and became the person you were because of your own beliefs and experiences. But I have changed that opinion as I have found out more about those early days.

I guess a mixed marriage was pretty unusual in my parents' day. Mum and Dad met in Ilford when Dad was a club cricketer, having decided to make his life over here, and Mum was studying in London, having been born and brought up in Cornwall. I gather she was just walking through Valentine's Park with a friend one day; Dad was fielding on the boundary for Ilford, and they caught each other's eye and started talking.

I don't think they have ever had a problem with coming from different races and backgrounds. I guess in the 1950s and 1960s unwanted attention and even prejudice might easily have been directed at them, but they have always insisted that they were always accepted as a couple, not least by their families, and it has never been an issue for them.

I guess my mum's willingness to embrace my dad's culture had a lot to do with that. They decided to make their life in my dad's home city of Madras – my sister Benazir came along soon after me to complete our family – and they had a very nice, middle-class lifestyle. This is where things are hazy for me but I do know that my dad worked in electronics, we had a very nice house with servants and virtually all our time was spent at the Chepauk Stadium, home of the Madras Cricket Club.

Dad was a good cricketer, a combative off-spinning all-rounder who was known, in his time, to get himself into a bit of trouble with umpires because of his fire and his tongue (now why does that sound familiar?). He was good enough to play one first-class match for Madras alongside someone who has always remained a good friend of his, the former India captain and Test umpire Venkat; and Dad was captain of the Madras Cricket Club for many years, bringing, it is said, a much more competitive attitude to the club!

All I can really remember is playing cricket on the outfield with my brothers while my dad was living his whole life at that cricket ground. I am told that the great West Indian cricketer Lance Gibbs bowled to me when he was in town with the West Indies, and my dad talks of a huge party he threw at our house to which all the big West Indian names of that time came along. Dad may be a Muslim by birth but he has always liked a drink and has been a very sociable man, unlike me.

Mum, meanwhile, was very happy. She has dark hair and a dark complexion, so she never really looked out of place among the Indian women. She became a Muslim too (Shireen is her adopted name) and threw herself into the Indian way of life even though we were all brought up speaking English. I only ever learnt a few words of my dad's native language (couldn't even tell you whether it was Urdu or Punjabi) and, even though we prayed as a family, religion just never featured in my life and never has done since.

It was pretty idyllic in every way, which is why it must have been such a huge gamble for them to decide to give it all up and start afresh in England in 1975 when I was seven. It was my dad's decision. Mum wasn't homesick or anything like that. And it was a decision that sums up everything my dad has always stood for. He came to the conclusion that it was in the best interests of his children for them to have an English education, and he was prepared to give up the prosperous life we had in India in order to achieve that. Again, it is something I will always be grateful to him for. It says everything to me. That's a man who said, 'Yes, I've got a great standard of living, but I'm going to risk it all for my family. I want them brought up in England. I want them to respect English ways.' He put everything on the line, and that says a huge amount to me. That is someone who is not prepared just to be content with his lot; that is someone with drive and ambition. I think that rubbed off on all us children and I have never forgotten what Dad and Mum gave up for us. If I dropped something in the house in Madras, there would be someone to pick it up for me. If I wanted to go anywhere, there was a driver outside who would take me. A bit different from the life we were going to lead in Essex.

We came to Ilford, where my dad had played previously (as well as enjoying a stint as a club cricket pro in the north-east), and made our life there, a life that was tough at times and which involved a lot of sacrifices for Mum and Dad. For a start, Dad had to make a living. This was done in many ways, as far as I could make out, and not all of them were necessarily legal.

Then there was the fact that when we first arrived in England we had to live with an uncle on my dad's side, something I found difficult because it meant mixing with people I didn't really know, and I didn't relish that. I was pretty unsettled for a while, until we got our own house in Mayfair Avenue, I went to a nice local school and began to feel more and more English.

It was, in many ways, an old-fashioned life. Mum was the

original wife and mother who made sure she had dinner ready to put on the table, often staying up pretty late to wait on my dad when he came home from the cricket club. My mum is quiet, well spoken and very well brought up, with a love of art and drawing. She went to art school, she is very clever and cultured, and could have done a lot more for herself. But she never has. It's always been for us. I hardly ever remember her getting angry and she was just a rock-solid presence in our lives. She did everything for her kids and formed a particularly close relationship with Benu, my little sister. Dad, meanwhile, seemed huge, even though he wasn't a very big man. He was fiery, emotional and an 'eat when he wants, drink when he wants' sort of person, working hard to earn a crust and give his children the best possible start in life.

Dad is one hell of a character, what we in cricket would call a 'badger'. He's like an extreme version of me in many ways. He is the most genuine man, he would do anything for his family and friends, and he is full of love and emotion. Then he will go and do the maddest of things. He will rant and rave, get into an argument when he's had a couple of drinks and get far too worked up about anything said that is slightly less than perfectly complimentary about me. Dad makes a huge impact on anyone he meets and he can make himself look silly with his behaviour at times, but always for the right reasons.

As in Madras, our whole life revolved around the game, this time at Valentine's Park in Ilford, and the Ilford Indoor Cricket School as opposed to the Chepauk Test match stadium. Which was where some of the confusion that there has always been entered my head, because I never really played cricket because I wanted to do it. I played because I seemed to be good at it and because my dad pushed me into doing it.

I remember clearly when it dawned on me that cricket was going to be a big part of my life. Dad must have seen something in me, either that or people told him there was something in my leg-spin; anyway, I was picked for the Essex Under-11s as a bowler when I was just eight, and from that moment the whole dynamics of our family changed. And they didn't change just for me, they changed for all of us because, while Dad was well into Mel and Abbas's cricket, it seemed that it was my cricket which was becoming all-important.

I don't know why that was the case, because in many ways Mel was the most talented one; everyone who knew us will tell you that. He played for Essex Seconds and was a professional with Hampshire, and he still plays a good level of club cricket – but for some reason I became the focus of Dad's attention and ambition.

I would turn up at the Ilford Cricket School (which my dad would later manage), and it would be like 'Oh, he's here. Who is he going to bowl out today?' There was a buzz about the place when this little kid had a ball in his hand. For my part, I didn't really have a clue what I was doing. I was bowling leg-spin but I didn't know how I was doing it or what I was doing. I just let it go and it seemed to spin miles and, for some reason, bamboozle people at the other end. This was fun. People would crowd round at the back of the net to watch me, and I would be able to get much older kids out. For two or three years it was effortless and life was good.

I guess it changed around the time I was eleven when it became clear that I did indeed seem to have above-average ability with a cricket ball in my hand. That was when the competitive aspect of cricket really began and my performances became the be-all and end-all of our life as a family.

And those days are what have shaped me most as a cricketer and as a human being. Because that is when the good days and bad days started, both for me and for the others. If I had had a good day, got five wickets or bowled like a god down at the cricket school and landed everything on a sixpence, then it would make my dad exceptionally happy. His whole mood would be positive on our way home and we would stop off and get chocolate, or a curry takeaway, for the whole family. And as I was a kid looking for affection and approval from my father, it would mean everything to me.

Then there were the bad days. If I didn't take any wickets, it would be 'What went wrong?' from Dad and there would be no chocolate or curry, only inquests. And not just for me. Mel, Abbas and Benu missed out too. It gave me a fear of failure that is present to this day. Whenever I have been dismissed in a cricket match at any level, it has never been 'What do I think?' but always 'What does Dad think?'

Was I scared of Dad? Hell, yes. If I'd had a bad day every little thing would annoy him and he would get angry with Mum or the others for no apparent reason. I'd be sitting upstairs in my room and I would hear him ranting and raving and would think, 'God, it's because I bowled badly,' or, later, 'I didn't get any runs, so it's my fault.' Equally, when things went well – and, to be fair, there were a lot more good days than bad days – things were great and I felt great because the whole family were getting treats because of me.

There was a lot of pressure on Dad. His whole reason for living lay in giving his all for us, and there were a lot of sacrifices made by him and Mum. There were never any holidays. Never any nice things for them. Despite cricket meaning everything to him, Dad was equally determined that we would have the best possible education, and this meant getting us, somehow, into Forest School, the best private school in the area and one with brilliant facilities, both academic and sporting.

He got me there first. I was given a full scholarship, half for maths and half for cricket, but I was put in the year above my age as much because of Mum and Dad's financial considerations as anything else. If I was fast-tracked it would save a year's money, so I found myself, a fairly bright lad, in with all these geniuses, and I just about got by, invariably at the bottom of a high-achieving class. I found it hard.

Mel came to Forest after me. My oldest brother is probably the most normal and well-balanced member of the family, even though I hear he's been known to exhibit the Hussain temper if things don't go exactly to plan on the cricket field. Mel was the one who looked after us all. He hasn't got a malicious bone in his body and I think that might have held him back as a cricketer. He had all the talent in the world but he didn't relish life on the county circuit, all the backstabbing and brown-nosing that goes on. Mel just wanted to play the game and he would put his foot in it by speaking his mind and not worrying about saying the right thing.

He still loves his cricket, still gets great pleasure out of playing in his forties, but it was quite revealing when I rang him up after I resigned as England captain. I said to him, 'Mel, I don't know if you know, but every time I'm out and after every decision I make in cricket I'm always thinking about Dad and what he'll think,' and he said, 'I'm just the same. I still think that when I get out in a club match.' That was intriguing to me.

I wasn't massively close to Mel when I was young because there was a five-year age gap between us, but I had a huge respect for him. If anything, we have become closer in recent years because he was good to talk to during any bad times I may have had towards the end of my career. Mel was more sympathetic to my feelings than, say, Abbas, who was a little bit 'You bloody realize what you've got, just get on with it and don't you dare give it away.' Mel, on the other hand, was more 'I understand what you're going through, mate. Just do your best. Don't worry about Dad.'

In a funny way I think Mel and I are both envious of each other. I am envious of his balanced life, his success in the City and the fact that he has not had to endure the extreme stress that high-level cricket can bring. On the other hand, Mel knows he had more natural talent as a cricketer than I did and he must regret not going on to be a successful county cricketer at least. For instance, soon after he packed it in, a journeyman called Tony Middleton, who couldn't lace Mel's boots as a cricketer when they were at Hampshire together, went on an England 'A' tour, so Mel wouldn't have been human if he hadn't thought, 'That could have been me.'

Abbas is the tough one. As a kid he was the last to make it to Forest, and I think there was a bit of resentment there for a while that he was at a state school while Mel and I were at Forest. It was like 'middle boy' syndrome; he had to fight to be noticed. Ab would scare me, give me a right hook if he was annoyed with me and would scrap for everything he had.

Ab, two years older than me, as a child was a bit of a jack of all trades, good at everything without excelling at any one thing. He was a good-looking lad with girlfriends and, of all of us, was the slightly rebellious one. It was almost, 'If Dad is that interested in Mel and Nasser's cricket then I'm gonna go off and do my own thing.' And he has. Everything he has done he's done well and now he's very successful in business. There was a big change in him, almost overnight. He went around the world after leaving university, met his wife Sue and got a job with Eli Lilly Pharmaceuticals, which made him much more dedicated – to the point where he's now one of their top people and has lived all over the world at various times. His life will probably end up the reverse of mine!

Benu is the one I'm closest to. She came along five years after me, completing our family, and finally gave my mum another daughter. If Dad was keen to see me succeed, Mum had similar ambitions for Benu, which led her to a place at the Royal Ballet School. As we were close in age I would be the one Benu would turn to if ever she needed an older brother to sort anything out for her, and I liked that. It's something we still have today even though her success at ballet has taken her to a new life in Australia.

I believe, after everything my mum went through after losing a daughter, Benu was always going to have anything she wanted. She was a bit mollycoddled and, perhaps, a bit spoilt too. While the boys went to Forest School, she went to White Lodge ballet school in Richmond Park and has since been hugely successful in her own right, dancing at the very highest level. Whereas I was put under immense pressure from Dad over cricket, Benu was put through the same wringer by Mum in her ballet, so I think we both have an understanding of what the other has gone through to get where we are. When we were younger, her personality would frustrate Abbas a little. If we went round to her for a meal, she would want to drink champagne even if she couldn't afford it, whereas Ab would tell her she really should be less extravagant than that and appreciate the value of money. But we have been successful in four very different fields, and my mum and dad can take great pride in that. It couldn't have been easy to make that big decision to come to England when they had such a good life in India. But I like to think they have been rewarded handsomely for their gamble.

Forest School was great for me. I would have been out of place at somewhere like Felsted in Essex, with all the toffee-nosed stuff that goes with it, and equally I would have struggled in a rough-and-ready school, so the equation of Forest and the fact that it was full of normal people who happened to be quite talented or clever was perfect for me. There wasn't much time for mates, or for things like birthday parties or going to the cinema or whatever, because every spare moment was taken up with cricket or trying to keep up with the clever ones.

I have grown to love cricket, the importance of it to so many people and the sheer intricacies of the game, and the spectacle. But even now I don't love the game as much as I love the Ryder Cup, or a big football match. It was forced into me so much that I could have gone the other way and hated the game. I never really had the ambition for myself that my dad had; for me, it was also a case of just trying to play at the next level and have as many good days as possible so that we could all have chocolate and curry!

It was never the passion for me that it was for my dad. I followed cricket a little bit. I watched the game but it wasn't

35

like 'I want to be David Gower. I want to be Graham Gooch.' I just thought I was doing this until my dad got bored with it, and anyway I was much more interested in golf or football. At school I would look forward to the winters so I could play football, and I would run to the noticeboard each week to see if I had made the football team, whereas I was always in the cricket team, so there was no real thrill there.

I can honestly say it was never my ambition to be a professional cricketer, but I would always do what my dad told me – until the only really traumatic time in our relationship. It was the occasion when I came close to rebelling against my dad's strict regime and, possibly, affecting our relationship in an adverse way for life. I was fifteen. Things suddenly changed and I almost gave up the game that has dominated my life.

3

I never really understood how I bowled leg-spin. I was coached at the Ilford Cricket School by Bill Morris, a tough-looking bloke with a formidable Scottish accent who would act the big disciplinarian but who was basically a really nice guy. All I did was run in and lob the ball up and take great amusement from the fact that nobody, least of all me, knew how I was causing so much trouble for batsmen by spinning it so much.

In those days I was very short, and that seemed to help my bowling. Batting was a very small part of the game for me when I was very young. I would play in representative sides with the likes of Mike Atherton, where we would bowl leg-spin in tandem for over after over, hour after hour. In those days I would come up against young lads who were to go on to have considerable careers in the game. Atherton was considered the northern golden boy, myself and Mark Ramprakash were the southern golden boys and I would play with and against others, like Trevor Ward and Martin Speight, who were huge figures in youth cricket. Graham Thorpe, meanwhile, was a year younger and making an impact.

I remember a very big ambition being to play for England Schools, which meant I could wear the England Schools Cricket Association jumper. A small thing, I know, but I really wanted that jumper with a rose on it, and I think I was awarded one when I was about fourteen.

But I only really learnt about the art of leg-spin much later when, on an Ashes tour, we were given a masterclass by Peter Philpott, the old Australian leggie, who talked us through the many variations in preparation for facing Shane Warne, and I heard all about the spin of the ball, under-spin, over-spin, side-spin and all sorts of other spin. It was an education that might have saved me from all sorts of trauma when I was fifteen.

You see, that's when I had the only real crisis of my cricketing life, one that not only threatened my whole future in the game but caused a considerable strain on my all-important relationship with my dad and almost forced me to rebel against the carefully chosen life Dad had mapped out for me.

It all began when I literally shot up in height. The little kid was a foot or so taller overnight, and it was the beginning of the end of my life as a demon bowler. I guess my bowling success must have had something to do with trajectory. Suddenly the angles were all different, and life was about to change for ever.

There I was, captain of England Schools and being tipped to be England's next leg-spinner. I had had my usual short amount of time off during the winter, when I shot up in height, as I say, and went down to the cricket school to start preparing for another season. But I couldn't hit the cut surface. I was bowling into the side netting, bowling into the roof, bowling deliveries that would bounce three times before they reached the batsman . . . and I just couldn't believe what was happening.

I think you could fairly say that Dad couldn't believe it either. At first he must have thought I was taking the piss, doing it deliberately because I was getting a little older and he thought I was trying to get out of cricket practice. But, God, was I trying – and the harder I tried, the worse it got. This was an absolute nightmare and, as it went on, things grew more and more tense between me and Dad.

One incident summed up what we were all going through and I still shudder at the memory of it. During this phase the bad days were overwhelmingly outnumbering the good ones, and chocolate and curry, not to mention smiles, were in short supply at our house.

Dad would always ask me how I did in any match that he couldn't attend, and in reply I would tend to exaggerate, telling him I'd scored 45 if I had scored 40 or taken four wickets if I'd taken three. Always I hoped he wouldn't check up on me and discover I was actually straying a little from the truth. Usually I got away with it, but there was one time when I told him I'd scored 40 and he checked the scorebook and found out it was 36. God, was he spewing that day.

Then, this other day, I was sitting moping in my room, dreading Dad coming home, after another day in which the leg-spinning king had performed like an absolute pauper. I heard him come through the door and I thought, 'Please don't come up and ask how I did,' but then I heard his footsteps coming up the stairs and I just didn't know what to say to him. Basically, he asked me how it had gone. I told him it had gone badly, he said something to me. I answered back (never a good decision), by saying something like 'Dad, can't you see. I've lost it. I can't bowl any more.' And he gave me a strong clip round the head.

Dad's attitude was 'No you haven't. You can't say that. That's weak. You're not trying. Get on with it. Don't give up,' but it was a horrible moment between us. Of course, next morning, you could tell how guilty he was feeling for being so hard on me, and he said something like 'Come on, don't worry. We'll work it out. You're a great son. Let's go down the cricket school.' And we would work even harder at finding a solution to my problems. Never at any time would Dad have considered letting me pack up the game, or given me a break, or whatever. He was so single-minded and driven.

There was another time when I was playing for Forest School and my batting was beginning to improve. I scored a century in an away match at Westminister, one of the biggest schools in the country, and then I took the first six wickets to fall. Well, I was excited now and, in my keenness to take all ten, I started bowling a bit too quickly and lost my rhythm a bit. In the end another lad got the other wickets, but I was still full of what I had achieved as I walked back to join Dad at his car after the game. But Dad wasn't a bit pleased. He was angry at me for not getting the other scalps. 'This is Westminster School,' he said. 'Can't you see how much it would have meant if you, an Asian kid from Ilford, had scored a century and taken all ten?' I couldn't believe what I was hearing and told him that most dads would have been proud at what I'd just done. Wrong move. All it meant was that there was tension between us all the way home in the car, and what should have been a great day had been ruined.

If I've given the impression that my childhood was a gruelling, joyless affair, then I've done my parents a disservice! It was very far from it. We were a happy family and there were always lots of smiles; but my relationship with my dad is crucial to explaining what makes me tick both as a person *and* as a cricketer. I've never made friends quickly, and that, I'm sure, is because as a child I placed such a priority on trying to win Dad's approval that easy friendships took a back seat.

It was the same with cricket. Graham Gooch once said to me that I seemed to regard every single innings as if it were the most crucial I'd ever played. Coming from Goochie that was high praise indeed, but he called it right. I played every innings, however unimportant the game, driven by the thought of what Dad would say.

That, however, was to be one of my last great days with the ball. Things went from bad to worse. Whatever I tried and however hard I tried, I just could not bowl any more. It was not a case of good days and bad days now, more a question of good balls and bad balls. Many many more of the latter.

I tried changing my run-up. I tried bowling round the wicket. I tried standing still and just bowling . . . bowling without a batsman being there . . . trying not to spin it so much . . . trying to spin it more. I had also tried to develop a googly before this crisis, so maybe that was a factor in the whole thing going haywire, but this was serious. And my dad knew it. And he was not happy about it.

What made it worse was that sometimes I'd bowl well for about ten minutes, bowl like I did before, and everybody would say, 'Nass has got it back. Everything is going to be all right.' But it wasn't. It would go wrong again soon afterwards, and it just seemed as though the magic switch everybody expected me to turn back on just wasn't there.

I lost my whole identity. What I was had changed. Until that time, my habitual weekend routine had involved a couple of hours spent bowling at the indoor school, then down to the Ilford club with my dad for lunch and, while he was having a couple of whiskies, people would come up to me and want to know me, be nice to me and tell me what a star I was going to be.

Now, while my dad was having his lunch and a drink, people were saying, 'Nass is dreadful. He's lost it, hasn't he? It's gone.' And my dad would be angry, arguing with people, and saying, 'No, he'll get it back.' It was, to me, as if I'd lost my arm. Or I wasn't half the person everybody thought I was. To me it was completely perplexing.

I can honestly say that I wasn't really bothered that people didn't seem to think as much of me any more. I've never worried what people think of me. And I wasn't nearly as obsessed with making cricket my career as Dad was. I was just looking at people and thinking, 'Well, I don't know what I was doing right before, so don't look at me as if I've suddenly become a complete idiot.'

The nightmare lasted about six months. A whole six months of Dad losing it, me losing it, all sorts of theories and all the ups and downs. Until finally I gave up. I'd had enough. It was the one time when I wondered what else there was, out there in the big wide world. I was at an age when things like girls and other interests were becoming important and I could see a life out there which didn't involve bowling all the time. I wanted to do something that I was in control of. I wanted something less complicated, less emotional. I was close to rebelling.

I wanted people to get off my case. I was fed up with my cricket determining how my dad was with my mum and with my brothers and sister. I could see all my mates going off to football and having a good time. For the first time in my life I actually disliked cricket. Disliked the game and what it was doing to me and my family. I wanted to pack it in.

But could I really do it? Could I really go against my dad and risk upsetting him so much that it could seriously affect our relationship? Basically, there have always been two voices in my head. One of them, at this time, was telling me to pack it in and go and have some fun, but the other, much louder, was reminding me how much this meant to Dad, how much time and effort he had put into this for my sake, for my future, to give me a chance of really making something of my life. I would think to myself, 'You've got lots of mates because of cricket, you're playing for England Schools, everyone wants to know you, you're getting prizes, your dad loves you, your brothers think you're great.'

The bottom line, when push came to shove, was that I couldn't. I couldn't rebel. I couldn't risk alienating him to that degree. Seriously, I was never going to get away with giving up the game and rebelling against my dad, so I simply decided to become a batsman instead.

I had always batted a bit. Had always batted with my brothers, going back to the days when we would innocently play on the outfield of the Chepauk Stadium; and, because of the pure length of time spent at the cricket school, I had a decent hand–eye coordination and I decided that had to be the way forward.

I think those days of self-doubt really shaped my personality as a cricketer. It was when the fear of failure really took hold of me. It has made me the cricketer I am, valuing each innings as if it was my last and selling my wicket dearly; but it has also meant that I have never really gone the final few yards as a player. For instance, someone like Darren Gough just goes out to really enjoy his cricket, seize the moment and play without any fear of being beaten or failing. I've never been able to perform like that.

There was a time, towards the end of my career in Bangladesh, when I played with a rare freedom, reverse sweeping and things like that. When I was out, for 90-odd (cricketers, with a few rare exceptions, can never tell you exactly what they scored), Duncan Fletcher said to me, 'Why don't you always play like that? You don't need to worry about getting out at this stage of your life. Just play.' I felt like turning round to him and saying, 'I wish I could.' I'd love to be like Goughy or Freddie Flintoff, just turning up for a Test Match and saying, 'Who are we playing today?' Or, when I'm out, being able to say, 'I didn't get any? Never mind. I'll try again tomorrow.' It does free you up if you can think like that, but I find it terribly difficult.

You know, some of the best innings I have played have been when I have come back to Essex after a Test Match and just played naturally, without a care in the world, because I had left all my worries behind with England. I remember particularly a National League game against Glamorgan soon after I resigned as England captain in 2003. As far as I was concerned, I had nothing left to prove any more. I was thinking of packing up the game there and then. I just didn't have the nervousness I always get before batting because it really didn't matter to me whether I was out or not. So what happened? I played like God, scored 160-odd and came off thinking, 'How can I possibly think of giving it all up when I can still play like that?' So then batting became all-important again and I went back to being a nervous basket case before every innings!

There was certainly no sense of freedom back when I was fifteen and suddenly found myself a former leg-spin prospect. The first thing that struck me was that I had better concentrate more on my school work if the cricket wasn't going to be there.

Dad, of course, was equally ambitious in that area and started saying things like 'Let's get you to Oxford or Cambridge.' I was a bit more realistic than that, knowing how clever you had to be to get to those places, and anyhow I had seen Abbas go to Loughborough and enjoy it there, so I was always thinking in terms of aiming for a university like Loughborough, Durham or Exeter, and I started asking people what sort of grades I needed to go to one of those.

Meanwhile I was living off my reputation a bit as a cricketer and somehow I was still captain of Essex Under-16s, so I decided to move myself up the order and see if I could start getting more runs and bowl less and less. Of course it wasn't going to happen overnight. For a while I dropped behind my contemporaries. I could see the Athertons and the Ramprakashes still developing and getting professional contracts. Seeing my contemporaries doing well was a big incentive. I was missing out on a few representative games and tours, and I realized that I did still want it. The fighting qualities that my mum insists saved my life before I was born were beginning to come to the surface.

And my dad was realistic about things too. He had finally accepted that the bowling was gone and instead he was concentrating on my batting now, to the point where it was like we were starting over and I had to learn a whole new skill. And it was different. I think if I had carried on as a bowler, if I hadn't shot up in height so quickly, I might have been a very, very good bowler.

But batting has never been as natural to me as leg-spin bowling had been. Right from the early days and throughout my career, my batting has been like peaks and troughs. It's been, at times, about living off sheer adrenalin, fighting, being determined to make the most of every innings. You make one mistake as a bowler and you can put it right next ball; but make one mistake as a batsman and you're gone. History. Game over. So, if anything, my dad and I became even more intense about my game. There was never the old chant you hear in schools, like 'It's only a game, it doesn't matter, it's about taking part, it's about enjoying it.' It was life and death.

I would have good patches as an emerging batsman but, because my technique wasn't the greatest, I'd have bad patches too. It has always been a roller-coaster ride for me. But it has always been about hard work, and that work ethic was given to me by my dad.

And my dad got it right. Whatever I have said about the demands, the fear, the sacrifices, the trauma, I am totally indebted to my father for making me the cricketer and the person that I am. Cricket is important. It's important to give it your absolute best.

What Dad taught me was that you should do everything to the best of your ability. Never do anything, fail at it, and then say, 'Well, it doesn't really matter.' It's something I will drill into my two boys, Jacob and Joel. If you don't try your hardest at everything you do, then there really is no point in doing it. It is the most important aspect of my personality.

I'm like it in everything I do. I think it's a natural thing within me. I love playing golf, but when I miss a putt I don't just put my club back in my bag and say, 'Oh dear.' I'm like 'Fucking hell' and I kick my club across the green. It does not mean nearly as much to me as my cricket, obviously, but it does matter.

And I have always been like that when I'm out. I can't be like Graham Gooch and just sit quietly in a corner of the dressing room and take my gloves off. I shout, scream, throw my bat down, kick my kitbag and take out all my frustrations at myself, the opposition or the umpire in the privacy of the dressing room while I let off steam. I've never made any apologies for being like that. I don't think either way is right or wrong. It just takes all sorts. People are the way they are.

I often use golf analogies. Look at Seve Ballesteros and Nick Faldo. They're both great golfers. One shows all the emotion in the world, the other shows no emotion. And they're both great. I am the sort who wears his heart on his sleeve on the field, and I think this comes from those early struggles and from becoming a batsman a bit late in life, because I certainly don't like showing emotion away from cricket.

4

My life had always been so carefully mapped out for me by my dad that I guess I was fairly inexperienced in the ways of the world as I prepared to leave school. I had only ever really known family and cricket, never been one to go out a lot with my mates or with girls. But I was about to embark on what I would describe as the happiest times of my life so far.

It started when I spent three months on my own in Madras, a trip organized by Dad, and one that Mel had also undertaken earlier; and it went on for three extremely happy years at Durham University, where I think I grew up and developed considerably as a person. Above all, I had fun. Not wild, drunken fun, but just fun in an environment where I could meet new people, be far more relaxed about my cricket and, above all, not have to endure the good and bad days that came with my childhood performances as a cricketer.

I wanted to have a gap year because I was a year ahead of myself in terms of schooling, and I gained reasonable grades at 'A' level without doing quite enough to get to Oxford or Cambridge. I'm afraid I wasn't clever enough for that, and I only just scraped into Durham, thanks to an admissions tutor by the name of Grenville Holland. But more of that later.

First came a short spell working with Mel at his office, which, at that time, was in Stratford, east London. It was a time when I got to know my brother better but also when I had to undertake the most boring job in the world as an office junior, basically checking computer output and puttings lines under things in places where lines had to go. There were attractions, like watching young ladies walking around the place in sec-retarial gear, and the odd beer at lunchtime, but the sole purpose for me was saving enough to fund my trip to India, and I can't exactly say I went about my work with any sort of enthusiasm. Up until now it was my only real taste of a 'normal' job – and it wasn't one that I particularly relished.

India was different. India was about growing up. As I have said, I can remember little of my childhood in Madras, so it was wonderful to go back there as a young adult, meet relatives and friends of my dad, learn about the place where I was born and find out a little more about the Indian side of me. And certain things flashed back to me a little bit, helping me put a lot of things into place.

Everybody was fantastic from the start. The wonderful family virtues of Asians were made very clear to me, with an uncle I barely knew throwing his home open to me and giving me everything I could ever want or need. I had a servant to myself and a driver to take me anywhere I wanted to go.

Not that I was there to just put my feet up, I was there to play some cricket in India; but I learnt a lot about myself. The whole social scene was based around the Madras Cricket Club, where I would hang around in the evenings, playing a bit of snooker or squash and having the odd beer or two. I had a good friend, Krishna, who would take me around on his moped, get me drunk, and introduce me to people. One night I even ended up in hospital on a drip. We thought it was something I had eaten but it might have been one Bloody Mary too many! It was a rare bad experience.

Basically, I had time for things that hadn't featured in my youth. At the weekends I played for Madras and I learnt so much about playing spin, but I could also lie in bed all morning and watch TV. It was the break from a disciplined routine that I relished.

But, me being me, I also worked hard at my cricket. I have always believed in giving my all to every task I have undertaken, and I was in the nets every day, however hot it was. Even if there was just one little leg-spinner in the nets, I'd be there, batting against him, for hours on end. This was the time when I categorically became a batsman rather than a bowler.

The most important aspect of the whole trip, however, was finding out more about my dad. Everyone had a story about Jawad Hussain. I learnt how loved he was and how respected by his community. I needed some understanding of why he was the way he was, and my trip to Madras when I was seventeen provided that. I realized what he and Mum had given up to come to England, the lifestyle they had had, the friends Dad had had and the fact that clearly they were missing him. And that made me realize that he must be missing them. It made us closer when I returned home. I always respected him and knew deep down that, whatever he did, he was doing for me. This trip strengthened my love for him.

And the stories! What a character. There were so many about the way he captained Madras, the fiery temperament, the incidents, the fights, the laughs, the booze, the card games. My dad was quite a geezer. So I returned, a better cricketer and, more importantly, a more rounded person. And the next step was university.

My grades were not quite good enough for Durham but I was sneaked in by Grenville Holland as much for my cricketing ability as anything else. And I am so glad I was. Because everything about my three years in the north-east was great. Everything was right: the people, the place, the atmosphere, the facilities and the lifestyle. And it was a good university. Dad might have talked about Oxford or Cambridge, but he was very happy about me going to Durham because it was the next best thing and, importantly, it was a terrific cricket university.

From a very early stage I linked up with a group of people who are still among my closest friends today. Both male and female. And they included the lady who was to become my wife. I met Karen Birch in my first week at university (and I have later joked that that was my fun university times out of the window) and we got on extremely well straight away. Karen was studying to be a teacher while my course was in geology and chemistry, and the nicest thing about it was that she had no interest in cricket or what it was I was doing when I disappeared from college for weeks at a time to go on a Young England tour or to play for Essex youth teams. We clicked from the off and got on extremely well. My other mates were the same. They did not want to know me because I was an aspiring young cricketer, just for who I was. It made me feel like a normal person for once.

Even now, there are six or seven of us who get together as often as we can. They have followed my career, but we rarely talk about cricket when we get together. When I resigned as England captain I got cards from all of them saying they were proud of what I had achieved, and that meant an awful lot to me, but when we meet up there's never any cricket talk, like 'Nass, why did you call Muralitharan a fucking chucker?' or anything like that. And it's brilliant.

'Natural sciences' was the official name of my course. The only subjects I was good at at school were maths and chemistry, but to do either of them as a degree course was serious stuff and I wasn't at university for serious stuff. So I did a bit of chemistry, a bit of geology and computing, and I just about got by academically, basically bluffing my way through and learning things parrot fashion at times when I had missed maybe six weeks of work because I was away playing cricket.

The cricket, meanwhile, was great. John Stephenson, who was to become a friend and an Essex colleague, originally recommended Durham to me; I played a lot with him and I got to the stage where I was on the brink of playing for the full Essex side. The first year at university I went on an England Under-19 tour with people like Mike Atherton and Mark Ramprakash and made an impression there, the leg-spin nightmare of my youth now well and truly behind me.

And my early Essex call-ups were quite chaotic. I am not a big one for remembering details about my early senior games and stuff like that, but I do remember clearly one weekend when I was supposed to be preparing for an exam when the college phone that we shared – no mobiles then – rang and some northern guy in my college picked it up and shouted, 'There's some bloke called Keith Fletcher on the phone for you.' I ran along the corridor in my boxer shorts, to be greeted by the distinctive tones of Fletch, saying, 'I've only gone and been hit on the fucking ear by Tony Merrick. Come down to Edgbaston. We might need you.'

So I rushed off to Birmingham on the Saturday, expecting to play my first Sunday League match the next day, getting hideously lost on the way down. Then the next morning Fletch, the Essex captain and legend of the time, appeared with his ear heavily bandaged, announcing that he was fit to play and that I would carry the drinks. Which I did and then rushed back to Durham for my exam. One minute I was doing my geology, the next I was in a dressing room with the likes of Fletcher, Gooch, Border, Pringle and Foster. Quite a contrast.

And I can honestly say that it was only around this time that I really seriously thought about a career in cricket. I know my life had been geared towards it, but in my own mind I never assumed – or even really desired – for it to happen until I started mixing with these people. Then it became a realistic ambition.

By this time I was on a summer contract with Essex and spent the bulk of my time with the Second XI under the guidance of the brilliant Ray East, one of the true characters of Essex cricket. It was good cricket. You would come up against people like Sylvester Clarke, making his way back towards the Surrey first team after injury, and the standards, I believe, were higher then than they are today, particularly the fast bowling I was coming up against.

Ray, meanwhile, was brilliant, a huge influence on my career. He was mad, he made everything fun; he would lose it with people and he could be completely erratic, but we loved him and he gave me the contrast in my life to my driven upbringing. At that stage I wasn't good enough to play first-team cricket and I had really been a specialist batsman for only three or four years, so my batting needed rounding off, and even though Ray was a spin bowler by trade he understood the game and was the perfect coach for me.

As I was a good fielder I would often get called up for twelfth man duty with the first team; spending time around all the stars of what was a highly successful Essex team in the late 1980s made a deep impression on me. And they were all pretty good to me. Fletch, famous for getting names wrong, would call me 'Nasher', and Derek Pringle in particular was very friendly. He would sometimes take the young players, people like me and John Stephenson, under his wing and go out with us in the evenings. Pring was always very argumentative, the leading world authority on any subject you cared to mention, but he was also very friendly, and there was never a superiority thing, or an 'I've played for England' mentality.

Generally, the spirit and attitude in the first-team dressing room was good and welcoming. There was no first-team, second-team, old *v.* young concept, like I gather there was in certain other dressing rooms. The only person I didn't really gel with was Neil Foster, but our problems came more towards the end of his career when his knees went and his England days were over and I think he became a little bit bitter about the game and towards young players who were still excited by it.

Pringle would put a young player in his place if he was a bit lippy, but he would do it in an accommodating sort of way, a classic dressing room banter sort of thing. Fozzy was more like the wizened old pro who would say, 'How many runs have you got?' or 'How many wickets have you got?' if a junior player tried to make a point or have his say. He would put them down. He would bang on about how he had played for England and had been in the Essex dressing room since 1983 or whatever, but my attitude, which I wasn't afraid of expressing, was more 'Get on with it. I'm in the dressing room with you now and it's how we do today that counts, and what we as a team produce in the name of Essex County Cricket Club that matters. Not what you were doing five years ago.'

I was always able to stand my corner. I was quite shy then, as I remain to this day, but I was quite comfortable with who I was, and maybe my total fear of failure gave me an edge that led some people to think I was a bit of a cocky so-and-so. The one thing I did have was an ability to speak well in a dressing room situation, I could argue well or put my point across, and I was normally equipped with a useful one-liner that could put someone down if they were coming over a bit Billy Bigtime.

Consequently, I think the big dressing room characters – the Pringles, Fosters and Topleys – were a little bit wary of me, or maybe they didn't give me that much stick. I certainly relished being there, being among them, as often as possible; a great attraction was that there was less pressure on me as a young player among all these stars, in contrast to my youth, when I had been expected to be the leading man.

I remember my first-team debut at Northampton, must have been 1988 but I'm not a great one for dates, when I got to about 13 and then went back to cut Nick Cook, who had played pretty successfully for England. Wrong move. It skidded on a bit and trapped me lbw. As I was taking my pads off, up came Pring, who has always had the ability to be wise after the event, and said, 'Young man, never cut Nick Cook.' And I was like 'Right. Thanks very much for telling me now. You could have said something before.' Then I bit my tongue; but if he had said that to me a couple of years later, he might have got an earful in return.

Other than that there are not too many memories of early innings, early dismissals. I just have this image of Graham Gooch going out and completely demolishing some of the best bowlers in the game, people like Curtly Ambrose and Winston Benjamin, and looking up to him and Allan Border, our overseas player at the time, with complete respect.

There was this one time, I think it was at Edgbaston, when Border was out, he came back to the dressing room and took all his gear off. People were coming up to him and saying, 'Bad luck, AB, never mind.' After about the fourth person had done this, he just stood up and said, 'Bad fucking luck? You Pommies are all the same. Bad luck? I batted like a busted arse and all you lot can say is bad luck.' Then he stormed out of the room. It really made an impression on me. I thought, 'I like that. I love that Australian attitude.' Ever since then it has always been a bit dangerous to come anywhere near me for a while after I've been dismissed. Anybody who might like to offer any advice, like Pring did at Northampton, or even to offer condolences, is unlikely to be greeted with a cheery smile and a 'never mind' attitude from me. Sometimes I went too far, I realize that now.

I was pretty successful straight away at first-team level. I was always a wristy player, I hadn't been over-coached, and I relished the flatter pitches after being used to bad ones as a schoolboy. There was good competition for places in a good county side, and young players like myself, Stephenson and then, a little later, people like Nick Knight, Nadeem Shahid and Jonathan Lewis were emerging and competing for any precious place that came up in the team.

Timing is everything and I was very lucky in that Keith Fletcher was coming to the end of his career at a time when I was ready to play. He was in his forties and had basically had enough, and he started to leave himself out to make room for me, a fabulous gesture that played a hugely significant part in my early development.

I didn't bat too often with Fletch, but there was one time at Southend when Jack Simmons was bowling at me for Lancashire and the runs had virtually dried up. Fletch talked me through it, I ended up getting a score, and people started really talking about me as a batsman to watch.

Fletch was like God. There he was, leading Essex to all these victories and he just seemed such a nice, down-to-earth bloke to me. He would take things seriously, but not too seriously, and he just played the game absolutely in the right way with the right balance of work and play.

Gooch was another huge figure at this time, and (even though he has never told me as much) he played a massive part in my being selected for England when he was captain and, I suspect, being made captain when he was a selector. Which is why it is sad that I am not as close to Graham as I used to be. At this time Gooch was an absolute legend to me. We travelled together to games, I would soak up every word he uttered, and he had a profound influence on me. I can't thank him enough for what he did for me as a young player, and I can't exaggerate his influence on me. To Goochy, though, cricket is all-encompassing. In many ways he was years ahead of his time when he brought a work ethic to the England side; but he cannot see that there are other ways to do things, other methods to bring the best out of people other than just getting them to work, work, work all the time. But more of that later.

I was still pinching myself at what was happening. I couldn't tell you what my first professional contract was worth, but to a student with an overdraft it felt like a million pounds. I remember Pringle telling me to invest in property with my new-found wealth, which I did in 1990 with Karen, and I was really enjoying my cricket – something of a novelty for me really.

I would change in the dressing room in between Pringle and Don Topley, and that in itself was an education. They bickered like husband and wife. They both thought they were world authorities on everything, but they were totally different in so many ways. On the one side there was 'good old Toppers', down to earth, not the brightest perhaps, but full of energy.

55

Then there was Pringle, the stubbornest, cleverest Cambridge man, at least in his mind, and they would argue about everything. I just sat there in the middle, giggling most of the time but occasionally having my say just to wind them up even further.

Those days opened my eyes to the team ethos. Before then my whole being was about getting to the next level and playing for myself. Now I realized there was more to it than simply good and bad personal days. I would watch and learn. People weren't mentors to me in terms of talking cricket all day or coaching me, but I would learn a considerable amount by watching people and seeing what they did. Socially, too, I was amazed at some of the things that went on. There was this time, early on, when we were at the Scarborough Festival and as soon as it rained quite a few of the boys hit the lager. By the evening they were sliding down the banisters at the hotel and I was like 'Shouldn't we go to bed? We've got a game of cricket tomorrow'. And the senior lads were saying, 'No, it's only Scarborough, and in any case more rain's forecast for tomorrow'. So they would get drunk, wake up with hangovers, get to the ground to be greeted by more rain and be back on the booze by lunchtime. On this particular trip I remember a team outing to every pub on the main road outside the ground, a trip made 'to make sure it was still raining'. I have never been the biggest drinker, so it could often be just as hard work as the cricket!

Other times Pring would get out his *Good Beer Guide* and insist we go to a particular pub in whatever area we were in even if it was a horrible spit-and-sawdust sort of dive just so he could get a good pint of ale. I would go with him, but all I ever really drank was rum and coke so I would sit there, wishing we were in a trendy bar rather than this place, but going along with it as a young player keen to keep the company of England players.

Not that it was all fun. It was a steep learning curve. I

remember Fletch giving myself and Stephenson an almighty rollicking for not batting quickly enough in a game at Lytham St Anne's to earn the last batting point in a championship game. Every point was vital to a team that was usually challenging for and (more often than not) winning the title.

I wouldn't call the environment totally professional. Apart from Gooch, very few of us worried too much about physical fitness, and the training basically consisted of a run round the park in Chelmsford while Ray East and John Lever nipped on the bus and met up with us at the finish. I found what we did do quite hard and I've never been the fittest person, but it was nothing like what we do now, particularly now that Michael Vaughan has got the England side concentrating so much on fitness.

This was the greatest era of Essex cricket and I'm glad I got a small taste of it before things changed. Fletch would get annoyed, as I have said, and call people a 'fucking this' or 'a fucking that'. Pringle and Foster would argue while they were bowling, Pring telling Fozzy he could never hit the seam and stuff like that. But everybody was mates. There were never any real problems between any of us. Unfortunately it's not like that any more.

Back in 1989 I was scoring runs for Essex. I had been part of a Combined Universities side that reached the quarter-final of the Benson and Hedges Cup under Atherton's captaincy and with me shining with the bat. And, remarkably, I was about to be picked by England.

I suppose I had a greater level of intensity than most young players. It manifested itself in little things, like always having a bat in my hand. Pringle, for one, would say to me, 'God, do you ever take that bat out of your hand?' or 'Are those pads stuck to your legs?' because I was so keen on having as many nets as possible. Someone like Alec Stewart can just pick any old bat up and go out and play with it, but people like me,

Graham Thorpe and Mark Ramprakash are perfectionists to the point where, later in my career, I think it has become something of an obsession, like a compulsion.

My bats have to be the right weight and shape and the handle has to be just right. One thing I will not miss is the ridiculous routine I went through before I went out to bat. Like the night before an innings, getting out the sticky tape, sandpaper and scissors and taking them to my bat handle to make sure everything is just right. Because every time you change gloves, every time you change your grip, it gives you a slightly different thickness and then it can feel slightly not right and it's in your mind that all is not well with your bat. Who says batsmen aren't mad?

My intensity and my propensity for a bit of bat throwing and chucking toys out of my pram didn't stop me from getting on with most of the characters in our dressing room. Stuart Turner for one was a bit mad, and I remember him driving me somewhere once and racing round the streets like an absolute maniac. He was a top county cricketer and was not one to stab you in the back or anything like that, but our paths never really crossed and I was quite relieved about that because he had this big hair and big moustache and I thought, 'Stay away from him.'

The only two I never really saw eye to eye with were Neil Foster and Alan Lilley. Fozzie was an excellent cricketer and we have got on fine in later years, but there was this little spell towards the end of his career when injury was bringing his time to a premature end. I would stand at slip to him at times and I could see that he was quality, bowling late swing and cutters. In a way he was a bit like Andrew Caddick as a bowler and I would love to have captained him, but to a young player, as frustration seemed to envelop him, he was difficult. Mark Ilott, as a young bowler, was one who often suffered the sharp edge of Foster's tongue. Ilott was emerging and I think this just highlighted that Fozzie's best days were behind him.

Ramble, as Mark is known because he rambles on about anything, would always speak first and think later, and Foster
would always want to cut him down, asking him how many
wickets he had taken, how many games he had played. Silly,
old-pro stuff like that.

Lilley was just someone I never got on with because I felt
he tried to be all things to all men; and I still do, even now he
is a powerful figure in Essex cricket (too powerful in my book).
Basically I just don't think he was the right man to run Essex
County Cricket Club and worried that it might be a case of
'jobs for the boys'. It is a major problem in county cricket.

Here I go again, getting on my soapbox. Unable to ignore
the negative! In fact this first county side had a huge influence
on me. It was fair, it was professional, there were characters
with attitude. And, in Keith Fletcher and Graham Gooch, two
of my greatest mentors. I relished being part of it.

5

1989 was an amazing year for Essex and for me. While I was featuring in that Combined Universities side which so nearly reached the Benson and Hedges Cup final, Essex were challenging strongly in the domestic competitions, as befitted a side who were still then the best in the country.

Essex lost in the final of the cup when Eddie Hemmings scored a four off the last ball to win it for Nottinghamshire – I didn't play, as I'd featured for the Universities earlier in the competition – and were doing very well in the championship until Southend week, which turned out to be hugely costly for the county but not so bad for me because it helped introduce me as a player of promise to those outside the Essex county boundaries.

I scored a century at Southchurch Park on a wicket which ultimately was to be declared unfit for first-class cricket and which cost Essex a 25-point penalty and, as it turned out, the title as well. But I think that innings played a big part in my being called up for England later that season.

To me, there was little wrong with the wicket. It was like those I had been used to in Durham and elsewhere when playing club cricket. Yes, the odd ball would spit at you and it was very dry and it turned, but nothing too outrageous as far as I was concerned; and it was the start, I suppose, of my ability to score runs on poorer surfaces.

This has absolutely nothing – well, not much – to do with my technique (although playing the ball late helps) and almost everything to do with my fear of failure. There have been times when I've sat in the pavilion as our openers have rattled up runs on a flat wicket, and this has only increased the pressure so far as I'm concerned. By the time I've gone in, there has already been a good total on the board and, to my mind, I've been in a no-win situation, expected to score runs and criticized if I didn't. And the game has already taken its course. Consequently I have often failed when conditions and the match situation have absolutely been in my favour.

It's different, mind you, on bowler-friendly surfaces. I have often been at my best when there has been a good scrap to get involved in, when we have lost early wickets and the bowlers have got their tails up. It takes the fear of failure away from me, or at least certainly lessens it, because if I fail I am only doing what our other batsmen have already done and I am not expected to prosper. This has been a consistent trait throughout my career.

On this occasion in Southend, it made me noticed and I started becoming aware of the odd newspaper article basically saying 'Is it time for Hussain?' and stuff like that, speculation that I can honestly say I totally discounted because I felt I was far too young and inexperienced for anything like that.

But England under David Gower were having a terrible summer at the hands of the Australians and, as so often happens in English cricket, there was a mood for change. I was one of a number of younger batsmen making an impact, like my contemporaries, Atherton and Ramprakash, and, as I have discovered many times over the intervening years, people in English cricket like nothing better than to call for youth when things are not going well.

There was also the matter of increasing speculation that another rebel tour of South Africa was being planned, and Graham Gooch, as captain of a previous rebel trip, was being linked with it. Whether that was playing on Graham's mind I don't know, but he certainly seemed to be stressed and distracted around that time on the many car journeys we shared to Essex games.

As a young player making my way in the game, I was

oblivious to most of it, but I was aware of the South African rumours, and names being linked with the trip, of meetings and phone calls to various players taking place. At Essex, the name Foster kept on coming up as one of the players who might be going and, as it turned out, Neil Foster did indeed go to the republic. But Graham Gooch didn't. Instead, he was about to become captain of England.

First, though, there was the matter of another undistinguished Ashes series to complete. England had lost, the repercussions had begun, and a rebel English tour of South Africa featuring many first-choice players had been announced. English cricket, it seemed, couldn't get much lower.

The call for change grew louder. I had played for a Young England side in a match at Jesmond and had scored runs, but still it came as a complete surprise when I was named in the squad, along with my Essex teammate and friend from Durham, John Stephenson, for the last match of the series at the Oval. To be honest with you, I can't even remember how I found out. I know people are supposed to have this sort of thing burnt into their memory for life, but I honestly can't say whether I got a phone call or saw it on teletext (not unusual in those days). I guess I was stunned at the news.

And it came just before Essex were due to play, of all people, the Australian tourists, so they were able to welcome me to the international scene in their own inimitable way by making various comments to me when I arrived to bat against them for Essex at Chelmsford, Geoff Lawson being particularly vocal, I seem to remember.

That sort of thing, however, has never bothered me and the thought I took most clearly from that game was that I could cope against their bowlers. I still didn't think I was ready for Test cricket, but the bowling of those Aussies was a little less daunting than their batting and I remember driving to the Oval on the Tuesday before the match in my little sponsored Fiesta, feeling a bit less petrified than I imagined I would.

Mind you, I didn't really know what I was doing. I didn't know which gate at the Oval to turn up to, and all I was armed with was a letter I'd received, telling me to report to the dressing room at 10 a.m. on the Tuesday. And what a feeling that was, walking into that room at the Oval. Not only was Graham Gooch there but David Gower, an absolute hero, was waiting to greet me as captain of England. John Stephenson was there, as was Mike Atherton, but most of the others were complete strangers that I was totally in awe of.

I just kept my head down in the corner until Gower came up to me and said, 'Congratulations, young man. You're in the squad. Well done. Good on you. Enjoy yourself.' And then he gave me a bag and walked off. That was it. A white plastic bag, which turned out to be full of things like my shirts, cap, jumper and everything. It was the jumper that caught my eye. I loved it. The England Schools jumper was good, but this was fantastic, three lions on the front. I really did get a tingle then. It was an incredible feeling. And I thought straight away about my dad. Every stage of my cricketing life had been about taking the next step and this, in so many ways, was the ultimate step. It was the most gorgeous jumper of all time. I sat there, thinking about watching Ian Botham bat in it, and Gower, and I desperately wanted to put it on and play in the Test that Thursday.

First, though, came an experience which was more like a pop-music show than a cricket match. I walked out of the dressing room to be confronted by what seemed like a million photographers. Then there were the reporters to talk to, and a joint press conference with Stephenson as the new kids on the block, and what seemed like endless other tasks, before we finally made it to the nets. Before then I was used to just turning up at the ground, strapping on the pads and going for a net. This was a different world.

But it was one I had to wait a bit longer before experiencing myself. I slept badly the night before the game, before arriving

63

at the Oval to be greeted by a very busy Gower. 'Bad luck, you're not playing. We're going with John Stephenson,' he told me before he started rummaging in my bag to take back my cap and jumper! 'Sorry, until you play you don't get these,' said Gower . . . and that was that.

I was philosophical about not playing because, as I say, I felt far from ready, but it really hurt to lose my precious stuff so soon after being given it. And it was the England captain who had taken it back. I just sat there and thought, 'Can't I keep my jumper?' but thankfully the words never actually came out of my mouth. My short Test Match experience was, for now, over and I immediately had to hit the road to Northampton to play for Essex.

Even that wasn't straightforward. I hadn't done much driving at that time – and here I was, in deepest South London, needing to get to Northampton. And to be honest I wasn't in a hurry to get there because I didn't fancy fielding so soon after almost playing for England, so after eventually finding the right road I drove as slowly as possible, before arriving to take my place in a fielding Essex side just before lunch (something that was allowed in those days).

Keith Fletcher, as ever, was the wisest person around. He came up to me and said, 'Bad luck, mate, but, believe me, it's a blessing in disguise.' At the time I didn't know what he meant, but I do now. So often, playing in the last match of the series can be counter-productive to a player. So many times players have been picked for that last match, not done particularly well, and then disappeared without trace. As someone who went on to become a selector, I can now see how it works. If a player hasn't played, the selectors can't hold anything against him, whereas if he has had just a limited chance and not done particularly well, it can be the kiss of death for his chances of going on a winter tour.

Take John Stephenson. He played ahead of me in that game, opened with Gooch, scored 15 or so, and that was it. He never played for England again. Who knows what would have happened if it had been the other way around? Maybe I would have failed at the Oval and never played again while 'Stan' (as everyone in the game knows Stephenson) would have gone on to have a long Test career. Who knows?

As ever, I owed a lot to Gooch. Graham was probably consulted about this, and I wouldn't be at all surprised if he or Keith Fletcher had counselled a little caution about playing me at the Oval and had recommended taking me instead to the West Indies that winter. I don't know for sure because Graham has always kept his cards close to his chest, but he's always been one to give a young player a chance, as I found to my cost in the summer of 2003 when, as Essex coach, he left me out of the Twenty20 side and, at times, also out of the National League one because he wanted to give the young lads a chance.

I know, though, that Graham pushed hard for my inclusion when he became captain of England after that match at the Oval. And the most amazing thing for me was that I was included in the touring party at the expense of David Gower, my cricketing hero and the England captain who had both given to me and taken from me my precious England jumper at the Oval a few weeks earlier! That really added to the pressure on me.

I do remember how I received the news this time. I was at Leicester with Essex and I was a little on edge because I did want to go away somewhere. I knew that there was to be an England 'A' tour to Zimbabwe and I thought that was a realistic aim for me because I expected Atherton to be the young player going to the West Indies. Throughout our youth he always looked like an England player to me, and it was no surprise when he was the first of our generation to be selected, for much of that 1989 Ashes series.

I came down for breakfast at our Leicester hotel and there was Gooch who, in that matter-of-fact way of his, dropped into a conversation the following nugget: 'By the way, Nass, you're going to the Nehru Cup one-day tournament in India and then West Indies after Christmas.' I hadn't even thought about one-day cricket. I was totally thrilled and perplexed at the whole thing.

I rang my dad, who was totally chuffed, and the whole chocolate and curry thing went racing through my mind. This was most certainly a good day. I also just reflected on how far I had come, that a year earlier I was playing for Durham University, was a student who didn't have any money and didn't really know what I wanted to do with my life. Now I was about to go on a tour of the West Indies as a full England cricketer.

I also felt a huge weight of expectation upon me. The news came out soon after Gooch told me and on the morning of our game at Leicester where, of course, a certain David Gower played his cricket. And that was hugely relevant because this tour selection caused one mighty ruction concerning the non-selection of Gower, thank goodness, rather than the selection of Hussain.

When we arrived at the ground, the England party was being named over the Tannoy and I remember thinking that, as well as Gower, there would be people like James Whitaker in the Leicester side looking at me and wondering why I was going, not him, and probably putting it down to the fact that my county mentor was the new England captain.

I was actually quite sheepish about it. I was delighted but I just wanted to get through the season as quickly as possible because there was a lot of attention on me. Not altogether surprisingly, I didn't score many runs that day at Leicester.

All the publicity was about Gooch and Gower, the Round-head and the Cavalier in the eyes of the press. It was all about how the man who was a former rebel was now England captain, and the people's hero, the most attractive batsman in the land, wasn't even going on the trip. But Graham coped well with it all. As I say, he has always been a champion of younger players.

Subsequently, I have seen him talk enthusiastically about how well someone like Ashley Cowan, for instance, could bowl, and that he was ready for Test cricket at a time when others weren't sure. He talks now in glowing terms about Alastair Cook and Ravinder Bopara at Essex – and there is no doubt that they are players of promise – but it would be foolish to get too carried away about them. I know he would have been equally glowing about me, and for that I am eternally grateful to Graham, but I do believe now that this is not the absolute best way to go about things.

Maybe his approach was right for the time, because the game was certainly at a very low ebb. And now we would see what the younger generation could do, because it was a party packed with young players. And, as it happened, we did pretty well. As well as me, there were others on their first tour like Alec Stewart, Angus Fraser, Devon Malcolm, Ricky Ellcock and Rob Bailey. There were others who hadn't been around that long and there was only the odd experienced player.

It worked well for Graham at the time because it suited his personality to impose his ideas on young players. And they were very good ideas on the whole. He wanted people to work, work, work and net, net, net – and he couldn't really understand it if anyone did anything in a different way. For instance, Gower liked the good things in life and would want to get so much more than just cricket out of a foreign tour, but when he would want to go wine tasting or whatever, Graham would expect him to be working on physical fitness. I could see why Graham didn't want David around as he went about trying to build a new England.

The trouble was, the moment a lad stopped scoring runs or taking wickets, Graham would think it was because he liked a drink or didn't train hard enough. Well, I would say, no, not really. It might sometimes be because of that, but if certain players are successful doing it their own way, and in a different way from Graham Gooch, then to my mind you have to accept them the way they are and concentrate on their assets rather than become obsessed with their perceived bad points. Graham, I felt, was too dogmatic about things.

I just don't think you can have fifteen or sixteen identical characters in one touring party. You have to have a balance, and I was fortunate to have had the perfect balance of people in my side during my four years as England captain. There were people who liked to train and work extra hard at their fitness, like Michael Vaughan, Marcus Trescothick and Graham Thorpe. Then there were the netters like myself and Alec Stewart, while Atherton would go off and do his pilates exercises to try to strengthen his dodgy back. But we also had people like Darren Gough, who liked a beer, and Phil Tufnell, who liked many things. Andrew Caddick, meanwhile, was never much of a trainer, but he was successful when we got him to concentrate on what he was good at rather than worry about what he couldn't do.

In the early 1990s the football-like, almost military regime of Graham Gooch and Micky Stewart was perfect for us as a team and, when you consider how much attention Vaughan now brings to the physical conditioning of his England side, you could say that Graham was ahead of his time. Certainly he received a lot of unfair stick for his methods because, whatever I have said about doing things differently, Graham's ideas were rooted in professionalism and that can only be a good thing. He was the perfect England captain for that era.

My tour selection wasn't my only bit of good news. Around the time of the South African rebel tour being announced, people were looking at ideas as to how to protect our younger players and at the same time make the lure of a breakaway tour less attractive. There was a guy around at that time called Patrick Whittingdale, a businessman and a lovely fellow who was a cricket nut with loads of money, who wanted to do his little bit to help. So he went to Micky Stewart, the England coach, and said that he wanted to give some money to a promising young batsman and bowler to encourage them to work at their game and give them a financial boost, the only proviso being that they wouldn't go on any rebel tour.

Micky and Patrick talked, about the time of the last Test it must have been, and, as I understand it, Micky came up with the names of Martin Bicknell and either me or Mike Atherton, finally plumping for me because he felt Athers had a better chance of touring the West Indies than I did, which again emphasizes to me that I owed my place on the trip to Graham. So Bickers and I were announced as the first two Whittingdale boys and were given around £15,000 each to work hard all winter and not go to South Africa, no mention of any tours or anything like that. Excellent!

I felt like a millionaire. It was a similar amount of money to my Essex contract at a period when the game was very amateurish and there was little money to be made by anyone other than England players. And I felt even richer when Graham came along and picked me for the Nehru Cup and the West Indies. Meanwhile, Athers missed out on the Whittingdale money and ended up on the 'A' tour of Zimbabwe and, to this day, I can't mention the name Whittingdale to him without him ranting about the injustice of it all!

My dad, meanwhile, had become my absolute hero, because now I could see what it was all for. The good and the bad days. The work, work, work. The non-stop cricket and the huge sacrifices to get me and the others to Forest School, not to mention coming to England in the first place. At Durham I was a happy, broke student thinking, 'What do I need cricket for?' Now I knew. I was getting paid by Essex for playing in a winning side with a great bunch of lads, I was being given money not to go to South Africa when I would never have gone to South Africa anyway, and now I was about to play for England with people like Gooch, Robin Smith, Allan Lamb and all the others. I remember thinking to myself, 'I get it now, Dad. Thanks.'

And the first stop was to India, the land of my father. And rather than talk about cricket, the first thing Dad said to me was, 'Look, there will be a lot of relatives approaching you out there. If anyone does that, just call them "uncle" and make sure you get them a ticket.' And that became a bit of a running theme during my time in India for the Nehru Cup.

In many ways my attempts to get tickets for relatives and for people who insisted they were relatives was my hardest work of the trip. Because it was something of a paid holiday for me in the company of top cricketers whom I barely knew. When we met up ahead of the tour, a sort of mini-World Cup and precursor to the ICC Trophy, just about everyone was a new face to me. Most of them were legends in my mind, even the younger ones like Alec Stewart. Remember, he was already twenty-seven by the time he was picked for England, and Martin Bicknell had told me what a fantastic player he was, so even the newcomers to international cricket were big names to me.

My worry was that they would all think I was only there because I was Gooch's protégé, but everyone was extremely friendly. I knew Derek Pringle, of course, from Essex and I would go out with him or spend time with others who didn't play in all the games, like Nick Cook, whom I hit it off with straight away. Now, of course, we are all warned about the dangers of sitting in the sun too long, but then it was all about getting the best tan you possibly could; Nick was a sun lover and I would sit with him, talking and enjoying his dry humour for hours.

It was the first time I had really got to know Angus Fraser too. I knew of him, of course, and he and his brother Alastair were known as the big two Middlesex boys who were going to play for England. Gus was the best bowler I had ever faced when I was younger; I just couldn't lay a bat on him in schools cricket, and it was no surprise to me that he became an England player in 1989.

Then there were the two South Africans, Lamb and Smith, who scared me a bit. I mean, they were such larger-than-life characters that I didn't know how they were going to act towards me, but I need not have worried because they were great and people I hugely respect to this day.

I was twelfth man a lot on that trip and I remember Robin would be changing his gloves after almost every over. It intrigued me. I knew it was hot, but I couldn't work out why he was doing it. I would just use the same pair of gloves all day. But not any more. I was soon on the phone to Gray-Nicolls, saying, 'I know I'm not playing much out here but I need more gloves because Robin Smith changes his a lot.'

Little things like that struck me at the Nehru Cup. I also remember how impressed I was at the standard of hotels, because I was expecting the ones in India to be a lot more basic; and I also recall sitting next to Micky Stewart a lot during games and being very impressed with the man. I would just be trying to soak everything up and it was noticeable how Micky would sit during matches, virtually scoring, and making notes about various players, shots and deliveries. Turn the clock fifteen years on, and you see Malcolm Ashton, the England analyst, doing something similar on a laptop, so it's clear to me now that Micky was a bit of a visionary, not to mention being a thoroughly decent bloke. Gooch and Stewart formed an excellent partnership for England. They were years ahead of their time in their approach to the game.

I only played two games. The first was a warm-up against India when a young sixteen-year-old came walking out wearing huge Gooch and Gavaskar type pads and everybody said we should watch out for him. His name was Sachin Tendulkar, and even then he looked better than any of our players. I only scored around 15 or 20, but I have still got a picture of me playing in that game because it was my first for England.

Another significant incident happened when England played Australia. Gooch and Allan Border had a bit of a row in the middle, and it struck me that their friendship and their good relationship as colleagues at Essex had gone completely out of the window when on opposing sides. One was captain of England, the other captain of Australia, and once Border had that baggy green on his head and Gooch had his England cap on, it was a different kettle of fish entirely until they walked off the pitch at the end of the match. I liked that. It shaped my thoughts. It made me believe that friendships should always end when you walk on the field.

So just when I was getting used to sitting on the sidelines and enjoying this great learning experience they only went and picked me for the semi-final against Pakistan. I don't know why. It took me a bit by surprise and I was a little nervous at what lay in store.

These days we have videos and so much analysis of opposing players, but then it was just a question of Micky standing up and saying, 'Abdul Qadir bowls a googly and a flipper.' I didn't even know what a flipper was then and my spin experience was limited to my little spell playing for Madras and facing the likes of John Childs and David Acfield in the nets at Essex!

It was a reduced-overs match because of a bit of rain and I was due to go in at number six, but then Gooch turned round to me and said, 'Lamby's not well, you're in ahead of him.' I was making my one-day international debut, batting ahead of Allan Lamb, who was one of the great one-day players, fresh from smacking Bruce Reid all round the Melbourne Cricket Ground to win an amazing match for England against Australia in the last over. So it wasn't ideal.

As it turned out I went in with about ten overs left, and I wasn't worried about having to try to slog, but I was conscious of the fact that Lamb was coming in after me so I didn't want to waste too many balls. Sod's law, Qadir was bowling and I had no idea what he was going to do with the ball. He had a quick arm and his arms and legs were all over the place. He saw this young lad with no idea, whom he could torment, so of course he went through his full repertoire. Meanwhile, I got 1 off about ten balls – a neat summation of my whole one-day career really – until I decided I couldn't keep Allan waiting any longer and ran down the wicket to his flipper, thinking it was a leg break. I got about half a yard down before it hit me on the pad and, whether I was out or not, I deserved to be out because of the sheer poor quality of that shot and my innings in general. So in some ways I was quite relieved when I was given out, pretty much a rarity for me.

Despite my best efforts, we got a reasonable score and were doing pretty well in the field until Salim Malik came in and spoiled things. In those days I didn't know too much about one-day cricket and I thought we were winning the game when they needed something like eight an over, but Sal, whom I didn't know at that stage, played one of the most incredible innings I had ever seen. He just hit Angus to all parts of the ground, and they strolled home. It was amazing; and I guess that must have been the day when Graham made a note to try to sign Salim Malik, because he became our overseas player two years later.

So that was the start of my England career. Lbw to Qadir for 1, worried that I was wasting deliveries that could be more profitably aimed at Allan Lamb. Then it was back home to prepare in earnest for our Caribbean adventure three months later.

6

Playing in the Nehru Cup was one thing. The prospect of going with the full England side to play a Test series against the mighty West Indies was quite another.

I had grown up watching the West Indies. How they kept on beating England 5–0. How they kept on breaking bones, like Mike Gatting's nose in 1986, something I wouldn't mind doing myself, and how some of the great names of English cricket could never even get close to winning a Test against them, let alone a series. Now, with a couple of months off to consider the prospect, I was going to be in the latest team to take on what was then the dominant force in world cricket.

Not that I was in any way idle in the build-up to departure. For one thing I suddenly had all this money and didn't know what to do with it, so I decided to take Derek Pringle's advice, foolish, I know, and buy a house. The location was easy – somewhere between Ilford (home) and Chelmsford (work), so my mum and I started looking at all these places before settling on this nice little house in Hutton. It was going to be a place I shared with Karen, our first property together, so I went back up to Durham, where she was completing her Bachelor of Education degree to become a teacher, to show her details of the house and arrange for her to come down and see it. It was strange for me, going back to Durham. I was walking around the streets that only a few months earlier I had been using as a student, but now I was an England cricketer and was recognized by a few more people than before.

With the house sorted, it was time to get ready for the serious business of preparing for the West Indies, and the prospect of some net sessions with Geoff Boycott, who had been welcomed back into the England fold as an adviser at the invitation of Graham Gooch. Boycott is my sort of person; I have always liked him. And this goes back to the sessions me and many of the England and England 'A' players spent with him in Leeds in the early weeks of 1990.

I can see why he is not everybody's cup of tea, how he could be a disruptive influence in the dressing room or why some of his teammates would have wanted to run him out. But he calls a spade a spade, tells it how it is, and is a genuine person. I really think he wants England and England players to do well, and on this occasion he was delighted to help us prepare for the ultimate test in cricket.

I don't have much recollection of him as a player but I am fully prepared to believe he was a great one, even if perhaps he wasn't the most attractive to watch at times. I know he must have been great because Fiery, as he is known, told me he was. Several times. As he liked to tell everybody who would listen. And I for one believe him.

The sessions used to take place something like once a week. Goochy and I would drive up the A1 for the day and Boycott would basically treat everybody the same, like schoolboys. He would shout out things like 'Hussain, open face. Cut that out,' but he would treat Gooch and the more senior players in exactly the same way. And it was fantastic practice because he had a lot of young Yorkshire bowlers bowling short at us from fifteen or sixteen yards to replicate what we would be facing in the Caribbean.

It was petrifying. Boycott would be winding the bowlers up, saying things to them like 'My old mum could bowl faster than you' and 'They've picked this young lad from nowhere. He can't bat. Hit him on the head.' Then, when I finally got out of the net, Gooch walked in and he was hit on the arm first ball, then he flicked at a wide one, as you do when your ticker is going, and then he played another bad shot at his third ball, and Boycott screamed at him, 'Gooch. You're crap. Get out of there. Come on. Bailey, you go in,' and I was just in total awe that he could say those things to Graham Gooch, and Goochy would accept them like a meek little schoolboy. As it turned out, these sessions were tougher than anything I was to face in the West Indies.

Then, in the afternoons, we would watch ourselves batting on video, the first time I had seen myself bat, and go through all that Boycott had shown us. The great man would hold court, talking about cricket and batting and his meticulous preparation. It was brilliant for me. I could have listened to him all day. It was like my finishing school. Geoff would tell us how he played quick bowling. About survival, accumulating, and areas where you could score runs. He made it clear we would not be getting anything to drive and could not expect to get 50s in half an hour. He was a back-foot player himself and told us not to lunge forward, to use the depth of our crease and expect to take a few blows. How to ride the ball off our hip. Compelling stuff.

It was noticeable that the senior players weren't there. Only Gooch. This was mainly for the young lads and I couldn't imagine someone like Allan Lamb relishing being told what to do by Geoff Boycott. Lamby had a great record against the West Indies and he did it his way, something that James Whitaker, who was there as an England 'A' player preparing for their Zimbabwe tour, brought up when we were all sitting having a Boycott masterclass. 'That's brilliant Boycs,' James said. 'But all you are talking about is accumulating, leaving the ball, playing it off your hip. Other players have been successful cutting and pulling them.' Boycott appeared to take the point, but next time we were there he had a copy of *Wisden* with him and he said, 'Whitaker. Come here. There's my record against the West Indies. My way is the way to play them.' He had to have the last word.

Boycott tells a story of me bringing what was supposed to be a tape of me batting at Headingley to a session with him –

but instead it was a tape of *Neighbours* which, he claimed, 'your girlfriend had taped over'. It's a good story and, it is true, I did bring the wrong tape with me once. But I think there's a little bit of licence there on Geoff's part! I don't think Karen has ever really been a fan of *Neighbours*!

There were times when I could see why some people don't like him. For instance, Geoff got his big break as a commentator on that tour, as it was the first that Sky were showing live and he had a habit of broadcasting what he had told us in the nets or the faults he picked up on. With me, he was always going on about how I played with an open face, and it was the first time I really became aware of that – as did the cricketing public, because of Geoffrey! And there was this one occasion when I had just got out for zip during the Test series and we returned to the hotel where, as now, there were a lot of Brits about, following the series. Fiery shouted across the lobby to me, 'I've told you about that open face. It got you out today.' And all the supporters could hear every word. I thought, 'Not now, Geoffrey. It's OK telling me these things at a net in Headingley, but not when I've just got out in a Test Match for England.' But still I do have total respect for the man.

We were absolutely written off before that series. It was like playing Australia now. And we were doing it with a bunch of kids, really. Chairman of selectors Ted Dexter said we were going to 'fight fire with fire'. There was still a lot of talk about Gower not going and publicity about England's 'young guns', inspired by Sky for their first tour. It was also the arrival of Tetley Bitter as our sponsor, and the whole thing was like a circus to me, photo-shoots and press conferences. All sorts of things.

It was also an introduction to real touring life. In those days there were three or four warm-up games before the real business began, so there was a lot of practice, a lot of fitness work and a lot of socializing in the evenings. I still remember us all hiring mini-mokes and me driving back from a bar with

Gus Fraser at around midnight in ours, and sneaking back into the hotel before management could see us. I guess it was pretty tame stuff compared to the fun and games that some of our predecessors, the Bothams of this world, would get up to, but it still would be unheard of today.

We certainly gelled as a team very quickly and all got on very well. Virtually the whole team would go out for a meal and we would sit there with some wine, thoroughly enjoying ourselves in the extended preparation time we had before the first Test in Jamaica. Another good idea from the management was getting people to share rooms with different guys at each venue, a small thing but one which helped the bonding process considerably.

Already, though, at this early stage of my career, I was getting a reputation as something of a hothead, a label that had a lot to do with an incident during my first tour match in St Kitts. It was the second innings and we were in a little bit of trouble when I was batting with Rob Bailey. I was facing the left-arm spin of Keith Arthurton when I bat-padded it to silly point, who scooped the ball up, clearly on the bounce, and one umpire gave me out while the other didn't seem sure. I started walking off and Rob saw that one umpire was undecided and said to me, 'Where are you going? That didn't carry,' and he gestured to the umpire to call me back. I didn't know what to do. I know I should have walked off, and it must have looked as though I wasn't accepting the decision, but there seemed some doubt and in the end the umpires called me back. Then, about three overs later, I was given out and left reluctantly, so the whole business looked bad but, to me, it wasn't really that big a deal.

It was just me being competitive. It was how I was brought up: to value my wicket and every innings. In my mind, if, for instance, I nicked one, failed to walk and got away with it, then I could go on, get a big score and it meant curry with my dad that night, or something of that sort. That was more important

78

1. Mum and Dad, soon after their marriage. It could be Benu and Mel!

2. The family in India. Note Dad's similarity to Elvis!

3. An early family photo, with Abbas (left) and Mel (right).

4. An early visit to Lord's with a young teammate. Who would have thought that I would play my last shot in cricket, to win a Test for England, to the area behind us nearly 30 years later.

5. Waiting to bat at Essex, watched by Graham Gooch, who was a huge influence in my early years.

6. The scoreboard on an England Under-19 tour to Sri Lanka, where I scored my first hundred at Kandy. I was to repeat the trick in more difficult circumstances with the full team in 2001.

7. Accepting an award from Jonathan Agnew in my youth. At Lord's in 2002 I was aiming three fingers at him!

8. Starting out. My first season with Essex, 1987.

9. Making an impression with a hundred for the Combined Universities team in their march to the Benson and Hedges Cup quarter-finals in 1989.

10. A nice-looking shot from my first Test innings, against the West Indies in Jamaica in 1990. I scored 13.

11. In the England dressing room with my fellow Test debutant Alec Stewart after our win in Jamaica. Our 'coach' Geoff Boycott, who did so much to help us on that tour, stands by.

12. Celebrating our fantastic victory in Jamaica on my Test debut in 1990. I was much happier than I looked!

13. When I was dismissed, it was best to avoid talking to me for a while.

14. Winning the county championship with Essex in 1992, in the days when the county thrived and I enjoyed my cricket with my home county.

15. Graham Thorpe has probably been my best mate in cricket. Here I am delighted to be with him as he scores a century on his Test debut against Australia in 1993.

16. A proud family group at our wedding in 1993. Left to right: Mel, Shireen, me, Karen, Joe, Benu and Abbas.

17. My first Man-of-the-Match award for England, the 1996 Test against India at Edgbaston that was so important to my England career.

18. On the tourist trail with Darren Gough in Zimbabwe.

19. The third victim of a hat-trick from Zimbabwe's Eddo Brandes on our largely unhappy tour of 1996.

20. Captain Atherton and Vice-captain Hussain discuss a vitally important topic. Probably where to go for dinner that night.

21. There was a lot of respect in the captain–coach partnership of Atherton and Lloyd.

than my conscience telling me I was really out on 40, or whatever. These things definitely even themselves out over the years. Umpires are fallible and you get some good decisions and some bad ones, and you just have to take the rough with the smooth. When I have been out, I have usually responded by questioning the umpire, but, after ten minutes of getting it out of my system in the dressing room, I have usually been able to accept what has gone on. I got away with snicking to the keeper at Edgbaston in 1996 and went on to make my debut Test hundred, an enormous factor in my subsequent career, but I can honestly say I have been on the receiving end of some bad decisions too. It is probably even-Steven.

This occasion early in my career wasn't a huge deal to me, but I was starting to learn the ways of the media and the undeniable fact that they need a story every day, and the sniff of dissent from a young batsman on tour was a good one for them to get their teeth into. A couple of hours later, Gooch went for a walk round the outfield with Lamb, his vice-captain, and I asked if I could go with them. It was just a simple thing. But according to the media it became an official reprimand for me from the captain, who ordered me to come for a walk before bollocking me.

What actually happened was that we talked about a lot of things and Graham said to me, 'You had a point. You had every right to wait while the umpires were sorting it out, but be careful what you say to the media and try to not let it look so bad next time. Always go when you are given out.' To this day I think the press got that one wrong. It was an example of how a story can be embellished on a quiet day and then stick with you for the rest of your life.

Over the years I have got on fine with the majority of cricket writers and I certainly had a good relationship with the press while I was captain. And I have never had a problem with any writer who has criticized me over a cricketing matter or who has said it was time for me to go as captain or anything like that. That is the job, and I know it is something I will have to do now I have moved full time into the media.

Anyway, back to Jamaica 1990. I had done reasonably well in the warm-up games, but I didn't expect both myself and Alec Stewart, the two batting newcomers, to play at Sabina Park. Yet we did, and what followed was one of the most incredible and dramatic weeks of my Test career. We hadn't beaten West Indies for sixteen years and thirty Tests, but we pulled off one of the biggest upsets the game had seen in years.

The night before the match started it really dawned on both Alec and me what lay ahead of us. We were rooming together and were having room service, the immaculate, well-prepared Stewie with his grilled chicken and glass of milk and scruffy me with a curry and a can of Coke. Then, next morning, I went and looked at the wicket – and it was like nothing I had ever seen before. It looked like a sheet of glass. I almost slipped, walking on it, and I panicked a bit because in those days I batted in trainers and I was worried I would slip when batting.

I was pleased that we lost the toss. It helped me, being in the field first, trying to come to terms with the big league. There I was, less than a year after finishing at university, suddenly at short leg and being a virtual spectator as Gordon Greenidge and Desmond Haynes almost strolled to 62 without loss. I was thinking, 'Everyone has been right to question our side. What's going on here? Get Gower back. This is men against boys. This is silly,' because these two greats were basically just playing around with us.

At times, that series was quite surreal for me. It was like watching some of the greatest names in the sport, like being back at home and making sure you rushed home to watch the telly so you could see them bat. Only now I was watching from close up.

And it was just as hard as I expected it to be, until Greenidge flicked it down to long leg and decided to take Devon Malcolm's arm on when he slightly fumbled the ball. Now the one thing

Dev has always been able to do is throw – he can't catch because he can't see the ball, but he can throw. And Greenidge was run out, the start of a truly amazing day for us which saw the West Indies crash to 164 all out.

Viv Richards coming in was the most awesome moment for me. The arrival of one of the best batsmen the game has ever seen. The swagger. Just a cap on his head. Awesome. And it was quite clear he was going to target Dev. I guess it was the sight of a raw Jamaican-born bowler playing for England in the West Indies, but Viv was after him from the start – and all with just a little cap on his head. When I faced Dev in the nets I wore every bit of protective equipment I could lay my hands on, but still, in Barbados, he managed to hurt me. He bowled one that bounced over my head, hit the wall behind me, came back and nipped me up the arse. There was no escaping Dev's pace – but to Viv it was just routine.

Then it was time to think about batting. The fear of failure, the worry, it was all there. Only I was playing for my country now. Alec went in at three and was dismissed for 13 before Lamb and Robin Smith put on a big stand for the fourth wicket, incredible stuff. The waiting wasn't doing any good for me and, as I have said, I have always found the pressure has increased on me when I have had to go in after players who have done well.

I can still remember my first innings as if it was yesterday. Patrick Patterson steaming in from the far end, the noise of the crowd, the inevitable bouncer. 'Welcome to Test cricket, Nasser Hussain,' said Tony Cozier on Sky television. Second ball, bouncer again. You just seem to know when they're coming through instinct, and you duck out of the way. Third ball on my hip, and I hit it for 4. It was such a good feeling. It was like 'This isn't too bad. This is a belter of a wicket. I can do this.' Until that moment I honestly didn't know what was going to happen to me. I wondered whether I was going to be made to look silly, whether it would all be too much for me, like Abdul Qadir had been in the Nehru Cup. But now I felt I could cope. I cut another boundary on my way to 13, the same score as Alec, before I edged Ian Bishop to Jeff Dujon . . . and that was it. I was disappointed. I was enjoying myself. But the most important thing was that England, unbelievably, were moving into a winning position.

We rolled them again and, after a nervous day when it rained, we duly did win, leading to some amazing scenes in the dressing room, the TV cameras, the sponsors, the West Indies players saying 'Well done' and us just enjoying ourselves into the night. It meant so much to the likes of Gooch and Lamb, who had suffered at their hands over the years, but for us young lads it was a dream. For me, everything in the garden was rosy. The most amazing times.

I was trying to learn a few things too. I couldn't get my head round the fact that we were in South America, rather than the West Indies, when we went to Guyana and that there were a lot of Asian people in some parts of the Caribbean. Social history has never been my strong point! Also, it was intriguing to me that some of the people in Guyana and Trinidad actually wanted us to win, and there seemed to be a lot of trouble in the background when Viv talked about his 'African' team.

In Guyana it just rained. And rained. And rained. And rained. We had to do the inevitable sponsor's picture, standing in this lake on the outfield with our wellies on, holding up an umbrella; and just trying to occupy ourselves in any way we could while Gooch and Micky Stewart tried to dream up original ways of keeping us fit and occupied, like more running and even basketball.

And there were some tennis courts at the back of the hotel. We had watched a few of the West Indies guys having a game out there, and one day Phil DeFreitas, who I was rooming with, said, 'Do you fancy a game?' And I don't know why, because I don't like tennis, I don't play tennis, but I said, 'Yes.' It was to prove a very costly decision. I guess I was just so bored. And I did it, really, just to keep my feet moving, to pass away an hour or two in what was clearly becoming a wasted week in Georgetown. We played for a while, and in one of the very last games I went to hit a ball over the net and just ran into the net, sort of flipping my left wrist back as I went. I felt a little bit of pain but not much, and even later when I had a shower I couldn't really feel it. Then, about half an hour after I went to bed, it started really throbbing and aching and it was absolute agony. Next day I asked our physio, Lawrie Brown, to look at it and he thought I had probably sprained it and that we should get it X-rayed just in case. This was Guyana 1990 and their X-ray machine was not the best, but nothing showed up, and Lawrie said we would keep an eye on it and look at it again in two weeks because it might be the scaphoid, and that didn't show up immediately.

Meanwhile the game was abandoned and we went off to Trinidad, still one up, but with me in more and more pain and taking more and more painkillers in an attempt to get through. But it was no good. I had to miss the Trinidad Test and was reduced to twelfth man duties in what was to become another incredible Test. Because we did it to them again. Against all the odds, we outplayed the mighty West Indies again to set up a winning position. Devon took 10 wickets in the match, Gooch and Ned Larkins scored runs and we needed 151 to win with the whole of the last day to get them. Which was when the Test and the whole series reached its crucial turning point.

Gooch was a colossus by now. A huge figure for the whole team. And when he got hit on the hand by Ezra Moseley and looked to be in incredible pain, we knew this was a seriously important moment. We were walking the match at the time. And Graham never reacted to being hit the way he did that day; he never showed pain. He was a legend. He had picked us, the young guns, and we had confounded everybody by being on top against the world's best. And his injury sent a ripple of shock and apprehension through the dressing room because I'm not sure any of us felt, deep down, that we could do it without him.

Off he went to hospital for an X-ray, but we were still in a great position as we had lunch without a cloud in the sky. Then, as I was eating my curry and rice, I looked up at the mountain range over the back at Trinidad and suddenly you couldn't see it through the thick clouds. And nobody had mentioned rain. Yet it rained for the whole session. So we were up against it now. We had thirty overs (there was no extra hour in those days) to get around 100 runs, and their acting captain, Desmond Haynes, slowed the game right down, virtually to eight overs an hour, to try to make sure we couldn't get there and go two up in the series.

To be fair to Dessie, he saw a lifeline and he wanted to grab it. He exploited the rules and I can't really blame him for that, because his side was under a lot of pressure, Viv wasn't fit to play, the whole African-Asian thing was going on and here we were on the verge of another famous victory, and the people of Trinidad, many of whom are Asian, did not like it one little bit.

In the end we were 5 wickets down, in the pitch black, with David Capel and Jack Russell at the crease and 30 more runs needed. And we were in a real dilemma because suddenly the possibility of us losing was entering the equation if we were not careful, and that would have been a travesty after the way we had played.

I suppose with hindsight we showed a bit of naivety. We should have stayed out there, like we did later in Karachi under my captaincy when we won in the dark, and we just got through somehow and would have come off if we had lost any more wickets. But it was a tense and dramatic situation as Gooch, back from hospital with a broken hand that was being kept secret through fear of letting the West Indians get any sort of psychological gain over us, sent me out with a message for the batsmen.

I said to them, 'Look, Goochy says it's up to you. If you can see the ball and believe you can win this game, then stay out here; but if you can't see and we could lose, then come off.' Jack, typical of the fighter he is, said, 'I can see it. I can see it. Let's go for it,' whereas Capel was more circumspect and doubted whether we could do it because the light was fading fast. We gave it another over, but they slowed it right down again and we decided to call it a day and come off with our lead intact – but so near to an unassailable position in the series. We were distraught. At lunch we had it won, but now we were without our captain for the rest of the series and were generally a bit dishevelled, with me hurt also and some of our bowlers, like Fraser, feeling the strain and also missing with a rib injury as we headed for Barbados.

My wrist wasn't getting any better but I was double-dosing on the happy pills, and Goochy said to me that I had to play in the tour match against Barbados to see how it was, otherwise I would have to leave the tour. So it was a big game for me. It still hurt, but I played and I played well, scoring 70 not out, including at one point cutting Malcolm Marshall over point for 6. I was back, I felt in good nick, and I returned for the fourth Test, another highly dramatic and controversial game in a tour full of them.

I guess it will be remembered mostly for poor Rob Bailey being caught off his hip and being given out when he clearly wasn't because Viv Richards, who was back and desperate not to lose the series, started running around with his arm in the air putting huge pressure on the umpire to give him out. Rob is one of the nicest guys you will ever meet and he tried his nuts off for England, but undoubtedly this was a huge blow in his Test career; and it just seemed that this was catch-up time for the West Indies, at their Barbados fortress, and that they were going to make us pay.

In the end, we hung on in there as best we could, with Jack showing immense character and bravery, but Curtly Ambrose blew us away in the final hour, with me getting one that kept a bit low to register my first Test duck, and us losing with barely half an hour of daylight remaining. It was a cruel blow, and I just think we knew, deep down, that the tide had turned.

I was still in pain so I asked Lawrie if I could have another X-ray in Antigua. By this time we had been joined on tour by David Smith as Gooch's replacement, and he was struck on the thumb by Moseley in the one-day international in Barbados and had to come with me. When I heard Smithy was being called up, I was like 'Oh my God, he's supposed to be an absolute nutter.' I'd heard people say, 'Never cross David Smith or he'll beat you up,' so I was incredibly apprehensive of him but how wrong could I have been. While Dave undoubtedly was a tough character – he aimed some colourful language at Moseley after he hit him, even though Ezra was only asking if he was all right – he was fantastic company and a real pleasure to be around.

So there we were: me, Dave and Lawrie driving around Antigua, looking for an X-ray department until we find one; and this doctor looks at Dave's thumb first and obviously he didn't know about Smithy's reputation, because he said, 'What is wrong with you, Mr Smith? Do you not want to face our West Indies bowlers? You are fine. Are they too quick for you? Are you scared?' And Dave was getting redder and redder in the face and Lawrie was starting to hold him back and I thought to myself, 'Doc, you are going to need that X-ray machine for yourself in a minute,' and I was just praying he would move on to me before Smithy killed him. Luckily he did so, and he said to me, 'Yes, there's a crack in your wrist. You've broken your scaphoid, which is a very serious injury. There's no blood supply to the bone, so it takes a lot longer to heal, especially as you've carried on playing with it. You will need it pinning.'

This was not what I wanted to hear. I had been playing with a broken wrist in Barbados so, as far as I was concerned, I would play on with it in Antigua and just take my Ibuprofen

86

and suffer the consequences when I got home. So I played, but, for an England team which had come so far and achieved so much, this was a game too far. We were missing Gooch very badly.

The West Indies were starting to find their form. We were suffering with injuries. Things were going against us. This time it really was men against boys. I remember at one point I was fielding at mid-off and David Capel came on to bowl. First ball of his spell, Greenidge just launched at him and hit him straight over his head for 6. I couldn't believe the shot. As I went to get the ball I could see Capel's face, a look of utter bemusement that he had been treated like a spinner first ball, and for us the game was up. I did OK, scoring 35 and 34 and being one of the last men out both times, but we were thrashed by an innings and we lost the series 2–1. But what an experience! What a tour!

I was on a real downer when I came home. The whole tour had been such a high, such an incredible experience, and now I was facing three months on the sidelines. It was almost a case of what do I do now? While I was away, my mum had completed my house purchase for me, which was exciting but couldn't compensate for the emptiness I felt at the prospect of being out of the international scene just as quickly as I had been brought into it.

The following summer was one of balls with virtually no seams and straw-coloured pitches being introduced to the domestic game. It was the summer of batsmen and of huge scores – and I was going to miss out on it. There's no doubt that wrist injury was a huge blow to my career. I like to think that, if I hadn't decided to pass the time away in Guyana with a game of tennis, I would still have been in the England side to face India at home in 1990 and would have scored runs and been a regular player far quicker than I ended up being. Now I am philosophical about it. I haven't had many injuries since.

As it was, I was about to experience an up-and-down time

in county cricket, punctuated only by a brief return to the England side in 1993, until I came back for good in 1996. It was a time when I was to be suspended twice by my county for disciplinary reasons and one when, at times, it looked as though I was to be unfulfilled as a cricketer, failing to live up to the great expectations my dad had for me. Who knows how many Tests I might have played if I hadn't suffered that broken wrist; but thankfully it was not the end for me at the highest level. The amazing England 1990 tour of the West Indies, when a team of kids so nearly pulled off one of the greatest upsets in Test cricket history, was simply the beginning.

7

I suppose you could call the early 1990s an up-and-down time for me. My wrist injury undoubtedly set me back big time and led to years of good and bad periods in county cricket, three England 'A' tours, which were hugely enjoyable and beneficial to me, and the most frustrating full tour of my England career: a visit to the West Indies in 1994 when I failed to play a Test and, for two years after, seemed as far away from fulfilment and a regular Test place as ever.

I tried to spend my time while away injured wisely, getting the house sorted out and trying to keep in check my huge feelings of frustration as I saw batsman after batsman fill their boots in that 1990 season, while I looked on in awe and total admiration as Graham Gooch scored 333 against India at Lord's. The man was truly amazing.

I wasn't fit until the second half of the season, but I finished quite well and was hoping against hope that I might sneak on to the winter Ashes tour as the final batsman – a forlorn hope, as it turned out – but instead I had the consolation of featuring on the second 'A' tour of the modern age, to Pakistan and Sri Lanka.

I guess it would be easy to say that my subsequent disciplinary problems (ones that I maintain to this day were pretty minor but nevertheless guilty of) may have stemmed from the frustration at being away from Test cricket. Certainly I felt as though I had done nothing wrong, but I seemed to be slipping back in the queue of potential England batsmen simply because I had been unlucky enough to be injured in freak circumstances in Guyana. It was a feeling of helplessness really, but I think it's a bit simplistic to say that it turned me into a raging, angry young man.

I have always been competitive, that goes without saying, but I think any problems I had were rather down to the fact that I was getting older, more rounded, more confident, and I had opinions which I wasn't afraid of expressing. That didn't always go down too well in the insular world of county cricket, where, perhaps, a lot of the senior players were a bit taken aback to discover that a youngster could question the direction their team was going in, even in a happy and successful dressing room like the Essex one.

I was just growing up, really, and forming my own way of thinking, both in life and in cricket. Whether this was the start of me formulating my own ideas as a captain of the future I don't know, but even though we won the championship title at Essex in both 1991 and 1992 (my first major domestic honours), there were certain aspects within the team that I didn't agree with and I wasn't afraid to say so. Maybe I could see that this great county side was beginning to reach the end of an era and that the personnel within it needed to change. A few younger players were coming through, but Essex were starting to lose that magic touch and I could see it happening. There have been successes since 1992, but I think it's fair to say that Essex have never been quite the same force since then, and some of that has been their own fault.

But I was still enjoying the life of a county cricketer. I had a productive time in Sri Lanka with the 'A' team under the considerable presence of Keith Fletcher, who had earlier been unselfish enough to give up his place in the Essex side for me towards the end of his career and who now was taking the first steps on the international coaching ladder. Fletch has been a massive influence on me. He and Gooch did so much in my early years. I scored a big hundred in the final unofficial Test Match in Colombo, where later I would enjoy one of my greatest moments as England captain, and I enjoyed a decent domestic season in 1991 before an injury-plagued 'A' tour of the West Indies, when my tendency to have 'popadom fingers' (they snap easily) started coming to the fore.

As I say, Essex were changing. People like Keith Fletcher, John Lever, Stuart Turner and Brian Hardie, legends throughout the 1980s, were disappearing and a new generation of players were coming through. It was almost as though a younger breed were taking us forward, even extending to the overseas players of the time, notably Mark Waugh and Salim Malik. The first time I saw Mark Waugh, I was so impressed. I just took to him immediately. He was a sublime player, far better than I could ever be; but there was more to him than just being a cricketer and he seemed to be able to keep the game in context with the rest of his life. That impressed me.

People sometimes got the wrong impression about Mark. He would have a bet and a game of golf, go out in the evening and enjoy himself, and people got the feeling that perhaps he didn't care enough, that he didn't have the same degree of dedication and intensity as his twin brother Steve. But, believe me, when he picked that bat up in the morning, he cared, and just because he could make batting look ridiculously easy doesn't mean he was trying any less than the next man.

It was the same with David Gower, a similar player. I remember speaking to him about how you can get pigeon-holed – me the angry young man, Gower and Waugh the elegant players who didn't care enough and gave it away. The truth is a lot more complicated than that, and I will tell you this: you do not play as much Test cricket as David Gower and Mark Waugh without having a lot of dedication and passion for the game.

Salim, meanwhile, who had two spells for us as overseas player in the early 1990s, was a terrific, genuine bloke. No one was more surprised than me when he subsequently went on to face match-fixing allegations. There was never any suggestion or suspicion of anything like that in those days. If I had been asked to make a list of people who I thought could possibly be involved in what was to become cricket's biggest scandal, then Sal would certainly have been at the bottom of it.

For one thing, we so rarely saw him. Sal would do his own thing, stay with his own friends and travel with his own little entourage because he was already a big star in Pakistan and world cricket and he had a lot of hangers-on and people around him. We wouldn't see much of him other than when he turned up to play for us, but he never gave less than his all and was an extremely talented and popular player with us.

He was particularly good for myself and Nadeem Shahid, one of the young players coming through at Essex at the time and a good friend of mine. Not only was Salim good for our batting – and I was particularly struck with how he played spin: late, wristy and nearly always from the crease – but, because of the Asian connection, Sal took to us and would take us out for curries when we were at away matches. Wherever he went, people knew him and the restaurants never expected us to pay, a great bonus for a young player!

So while the likes of Mike Atherton, Robin Smith, Mark Ramprakash and the newly qualified Graeme Hick were playing for England, I was on the outside, but learning from people like Gooch, Waugh and Malik, and featuring in record Essex partnerships for the third, fourth and fifth wickets with Waugh, Malik and Mike Garnham that stand to this day.

I was starting to think about the game a bit more; I didn't like to just stand there in the field when we were bowling and wait for my turn to bat. That's how I got into trouble at Tunbridge Wells in 1992! Essex had made the first (in my opinion) of the mistakes which led them to lose their status as the dominant force in the county game. And that was in choosing as captain the next most senior player in the team when Gooch was away, Neil Foster. Picking simply on seniority is clearly wrong.

I know Derek Pringle had spells in charge of Essex and he was great, but I would have given the whole matter a bit more thought and given the captaincy to someone like John Stephenson or Mike Garnham when Gooch and Pringle were unavailable, because to me Foster was just not cut out for the job, however great a bowler he had been. There was so much anger inside him because of the state of his knees, and he used to take that out on other people and didn't show enough enthusiasm for the role or for the players at his disposal.

By this stage I was offering suggestions on field placings and how I thought we could improve because I believed there was a tendency to take our success for granted. But I saw the incredible enthusiasm Graham Gooch and Keith Fletcher had for Essex cricket. Gooch would play a magnificent innings for England and then come back and spend all day practising at Essex ahead of the next county game. He would fire question after question at me when we shared car journeys to matches about how we had played while he had been away, how we had bowled, why we had done a certain thing, etc., etc. When he was away, I just didn't want us to let him down and I think my spat at Tunbridge Wells was born out of a sense of that and a basic lack of respect for Neil Foster as captain of Essex.

There was never any shortage of banter in our team. We all got on very well, and a lot of the banter emerged from a mutual respect between people like myself and Waugh, someone I could take the piss out of even though I thought he was a fabulous player and someone I really looked up to. So this game against Kent was drifting along and Mark was bowling just before tea. At that time Mark bowled quite fast but he had a bit of a problem with his action and, as he was bowling to Carl Hooper, his head was falling away to the off side and he was firing it down the leg side.

So, after the first ball, I started the banter in an attempt to give Mark a bit of a gee-up, saying from slip, 'Come on, Waughy, Hooper's right-handed you know.' After the second had gone down the leg side I piped up, 'He's still right-handed', and then after the third I asked Mark if there was any chance he might like to bowl on the off side? This time Mark bit and snapped at me, 'Is there any chance of you just standing at slip and shutting the fuck up?' which was all part of the game as far as I was concerned. Then, as we walked off for tea, we had a bit of a go at each other and that was it. He said I was accusing him of not trying, I told him it was nothing of the sort and that it was all banter and that was the end of it. Forgotten.

It was the sort of incident that had happened before and one that I knew would be instantly over. It was the way me and Mark Waugh were. We had a good relationship. But as we were having a cup of tea in the dressing room Foster came up to me – only me, not Mark – and started wagging his finger at me and telling me we were not having any of that sort of thing while he was captain. He made a point of having a go at a younger player in front of the whole team, while ignoring the part a senior one had in the whole business; and I sat there, steaming. I felt like saying, 'Hold on. It was only a joke. Don't blow it up out of all proportion. Who are you telling off? Just chill out. It's just banter, like you've had with Mark Ilott when you've told him to shut the fuck up every time he's opened his mouth, and like the banter exchanged every day between Pringle and Don Topley.' I tried to have my say and tell him not to flex his muscles with me, but Fozzie was having none of it and basically said that youngsters in the side shouldn't be allowed to have their say.

In my frustration I kicked out at my cricket case and it slipped over the wooden floor right on to the bare toes of Ilott, one of my best mates in the side and a bowler who had the habit of taking his clothes off during intervals to cool down; he was sitting there, stark naked, before preparing to go back out to bowl.

Now Ramble has always had a low pain threshold, so he jumped up, screaming at the damage done to his toe, which was already hanging off with wear and tear, and he lost it with me, saying, 'Come on then,' and squaring up to me. Me being me, I responded in kind and got hold of him, before we were separated and sat down. Again, it was over. It happens. Can you imagine grown men having to basically live, eat, work and play together for several months in a close and at times tense environment, like cricketers do? It's not the most natural thing, and tempers inevitably fray from time to time. It's like being back at school, like being in a family. Men get heated, the testosterone's flowing, there's a lot of 'handbags at ten paces' and then you kiss and make up and get on with it. I think that should have been the end of the matter.

And invariably it happens between friends or between people who like and respect each other. There was a time, much later on, when I was England captain in Pakistan, when Graham Thorpe, probably my best mate in the game, dropped a catch in a warm-up game in Peshawar and smiled afterwards. I shouted, 'What the fuck are you smiling at?' and soon afterwards he said to me, 'Don't you dare accuse me of not caring,' and a little verbal spat between us ensued. Within minutes of it ending Thorpey came up to me and said, 'Sorry about that, mate. I was just a bit heated.' I apologized also and, boom, it was over. Duncan Fletcher, being the great man he is, just went up to Thorpey at the end of play and said, 'Are you and Nass all right?' and he said, 'We're fine. We know each other too well.' And that was it. No mothers' meeting. No silliness. No getting it out of all proportion. And that was how the Tunbridge Wells incident should have been handled. But it wasn't.

Driving home that evening, I didn't even think there had been an incident. Ilott is a born worrier and he had already said to me, 'We're OK, aren't we? We're still mates?' and I said of course we were, and it was all over.

Next day I was sitting at home and looking forward to my first game at Durham as an Essex player when Gooch, who had not been at Tunbridge Wells, rang me and said, 'Nass, are you in? I'll pop round for a chat.' I thought something must be up, but I didn't know what until we were having a cup of tea and he asked me what had happened at Tunbridge Wells.

I said, 'Look, Gray, me and Waughy were just messing about and had a few words and I didn't think Fozzie should have embarrassed me in front of everyone.' Graham just said he would take it on board, and I still didn't think anything of it until I got summoned to a meeting after nets at Chelmsford the next day. I can't even remember who was there, but Graham certainly was and probably Graham Saville as chairman of cricket at Essex. Gooch just said, 'After what happened we've decided we can either fine you or ban you from playing at Durham and, as I don't think losing money will hurt you, we have decided not to take you to the game at Durham. I have rung round a few of the players and they have said you were a bit out of order.'

I was so dumbstruck I don't think I said much. Not only did I think it was completely over the top but I also felt let down by my mates, who hadn't backed me up and had let me down a bit. And it did hurt me not playing, it hurt me a lot.

I would like to relate it to something that happened with Ronnie Irani in 2003. We were having nets, at a time when Essex were doing badly, and Ronnie had turned up a little late, which annoyed Goochie, who by now was Essex coach. Then Graham told everybody to bat sensibly in the nets and not to slog it, but, whether Ronnie didn't hear him say it or chose not to listen, I don't know. Anyway, he slogged it all over the place, as Ronnie tends to do in net sessions. Gooch went mad and the pair of them, captain and coach, had a massive row, which ended with Ronnie telling Graham where to go and storming off to the dressing room, where I was already getting changed.

Ronnie was spitting nails; he took his gear off and got on the phone to his wife Lorraine and asked her to come and pick him up. I had missed the row and now asked Ronnie what had happened. He told me the story and said, 'I'm not having him talk to me like that. I'm captain of this club. In front of all the players he's speaking to me like that. Who does he think he is? Don't treat me like that. I try my nuts off for this team. He's questioning my passion and my commitment to this team because I was a bit late this morning, but nobody can question my commitment.' I asked him what he was going to do and he said, 'That's it. If he doesn't want me, if he's questioning my commitment, I'm going home and you lot can have another captain for the match against Lancashire.' I immediately said, 'No, no, Ron. Listen. It's Lancashire. It's your big game. Why are you shooting yourself in the foot? You know what will happen if you go now. You know what Goochy's like. He'll flex his muscles. You'll be axed, you'll be gone and you will be banned. You're captain. You'll lose the captaincy. So be really careful what you're doing here. I've been here before, Ron. It'll be all over the papers and everything, so just think about what you're doing.'

But Ronnie, the stubborn bastard, was having none of it. He stormed out in his cricket gear when Lorraine arrived and told me to tell Goochy that he needed another captain for Lancashire. So I've gone to the nets and said, 'Gray, don't shoot the messenger but Ronnie has just told me to tell you he's gone home and you need another captain for Lancashire.' Goochy just said, 'Fine,' but I thought, as senior pro, I had to try to sort this out, so I went to vice-captain Paul Grayson and said, 'We've got to do something about this. It's Stuart Law playing against us. You know what Ronnie's like. He's a bit fired up. Come on, we've got to do something. We can't just let our captain walk out. You know Goochy won't back down on this. He's already looking at his teamsheet. He won't ring Ronnie up, and Ronnie's gone home.'

'Larry' Grayson just said to me, 'What can we do?' and I replied, 'Well, do something. You're vice-captain. Help the bloke out.' But all he could say was that we wouldn't be able to change Goochy's mind. So I decided to try to sort it out myself and, being economical with the truth, rang Ronnie, saying to him, 'Look, Ron, Goochy desperately wants you back but he's a bit too proud to ask. It's Lancashire, Ron. If you don't go, Stuey Law will say, "Told you so. Told you you had the wrong captain." I'll pack your bags and put them on the coach, Ron. Just please turn up for the bus – it's leaving in an hour!'

So I packed all his stuff up and put it on the bus, and then Ronnie did indeed turn up, got on the bus, patted me on the shoulder and said, 'Thanks,' and that was it. Otherwise Essex could have had a new captain then. I'm not trying to pat myself on the back here and say 'brilliant me', I'm just trying to emphasize that these things happen in all dressing rooms and I believe that if you overreact, like the powers that be did with me at Tunbridge Wells in 1992, then all you succeed in doing is adding fuel to the fire. And I still feel slightly bitter to this day that my teammates didn't try to sort it out for me that day when Graham Gooch rang them to ask what I had done in the changing room.

I've seen so many dressing-room incidents over the years. I've seen things happen as England captain between Darren Gough and Andrew Caddick. I've seen Phil Tufnell get involved in matters almost on a weekly basis: lose things, not turn up, miss the bus, have the dressing-room attendant up against the wall, stuff like that. It happens, and I like to think I have always handled situations like this a damn sight better than Essex did in 1992. It was all over the papers. Hussain was a bad boy and that was it. It has been devilishly hard to change that perception.

And it didn't help my reputation that I again incurred the wrath of Gooch in a later incident at the Oval, when we were playing Surrey – again an incident that I maintain was pretty innocuous. More and more I was getting the impression that other sides were moving on and Essex were relying on traditional methods that had worked for them in the past but which were becoming outdated now. People like John Lever and Stuart Turner could bowl yorkers at will because they had practised and practised them, but it seemed to me that the new generation of bowlers felt they could just turn up and do the same. It's not as easy as that. To perfect any art, you simply must practise and then practise some more.

On this occasion Tony Murphy of Surrey had been bowling some really good yorkers and he bowled me with one; and, as ever when I'm out, I have to have a bit of a curse in the dressing room for a bit to get it out of my system. It's normally fucking this, or fucking that, or fucking umpires, but on this occasion I went into our dressing room and said, 'That's what fucking happens when your bowlers practise their skills.'

Graham came straight up to me and said, 'What did you say?' and I just went for it.

I said to him, 'Did you see that? That's what happens when people practise their skills. This is Tony Murphy, who can't lace our bowlers' boots, but he has gone off, practised his yorkers and slower balls, and that's what happened. He gets wickets.'

Gooch was having none of it and shouted at me, 'Who are you to tell our bowlers what to do? You just worry about your batting, young man. Don't you have a go at other people.'

I felt like having it out with him and, if it had been anyone else other than Graham I would have said, 'No, I've earned my respect. It's not about how long you've been around, it's about what you bring to the team, how you feel the team should progress, areas you think the team should work on, and you should have the balls to say that. You get on with it, you have an argument about it, people can come and tell me what they think I should work on. It's healthy.' I didn't say any of that. I should have done but I left it because it was Graham Gooch, because I had huge respect for him and I couldn't argue with a great man like that. My main failing, especially when I was younger, was that I said things out loud and from the heart because of the emotion I was feeling, but I know now that I should have waited before having my say and then explained my point one-to-one. Fact is, when I was captain, I wouldn't have liked it if some upstarts had done what I did, so I can well understand Gooch's point of view.

The problem was, he was going off to Test Matches and I felt that, when he wasn't there, our skills, practice and dedication were slipping to a lower level, suspicions I think have been proved correct by what has happened to Essex County Cricket Club since those glory years. I was only trying to preserve the standards of the Fletcher–Gooch era which Gooch, in his absence, seemed unaware were slipping. As a young player, though, with no authority, I was unable to influence events without sounding like an upstart.

And as a consequence they left me out for the Sunday League game between the sides. With hindsight I guess I should have waited until the end of the match and quietly made my point to Graham in private, but in my defence I had said in meetings three or four times earlier that we needed to work on our slower balls and yorkers and I didn't feel it was hitting home.

I guess this might have been when my 'love' affair with Graham Gooch started to go a little pear-shaped. I started to feel that you could do things only a certain way with Graham. If you were going to be his golden boy, you could only be 'yes sir, no sir'. He is very unemotional in his attitude to cricket. You play your cricket, work hard, train hard and don't speak out of turn. There's no room for characters with Gooch. This was about the time that Gooch and I went in slightly different directions. For me, there is always room for characters in a side. That's where I was very lucky as England captain. We had Gough, Caddick, Tufnell, talented players – but ones where the powers that be often wanted to concentrate on what they couldn't do, their shortcomings, rather than on what they could do. For me, it should be the other way round. Like the time I was England captain and Mike Gatting was a selector. Now Gatt had a huge downer on Graham Thorpe for some inexplicable reason and he once said, 'What else does he bring to the party except runs?' Excuse me? What else does Graham Thorpe need to bring to the party other than runs? It was always like the first thing that anyone ever put down on paper was what they couldn't do. My attitude was, if someone can play, let's pick them and it will be up to me to get the best out of them and deal with any shortcomings they may have.

Anyway, these were still essentially good times for me even though I was away from the international scene, but the one other big issue from these times at Essex, one that I really should address, is the match-fixing allegations levelled by Don Topley about two games we played against Lancashire in 1991 when we were going for the championship and they were going for the Sunday League title. Don didn't actually make his allegations until a couple of years later, when match-fixing became a huge issue within the game; but it is worth explaining the situation as I know it because it became a big topic and led to Don Topley being unwelcome at the county ground, where he was such a popular and whole-hearted player.

I was a junior player at this time and would not have been involved in any discussions about declarations and such matters, but it was far from unusual in those days for captains to collude and set up some sort of target in three-day games, particularly if they were rain affected. It was one of the weaknesses of three-day cricket. And on this occasion as I understand it, Lancashire were reluctant to set us a target to chase on the last day because the Old Trafford wicket was good and we said, 'OK, set us a target, any target, and we'll rest some of our injured players in tomorrow's Sunday League match.' As far as I'm aware, that was it.

They did indeed set us a target, ran in and bowled properly; we won, thanks to a big hundred from Nick Knight, and then the next day we fielded a weakened side, played properly but lost to them. To me, that is a lot different to match fixing. It was something that was happening every season in county cricket and it was because the Sunday sandwich created the situation where it could happen. I'm not saying it was right or in any way ideal and I believe our performance on the Sunday was not at the level it could have been or should have been, but it was part of the game then; someone like Keith Fletcher would turn the deliberations about how many one side would set the other side into an art form, the gift of his gab undoubtedly contributing to many a win for Essex.

It was a shame Don Topley's Essex career ended with those accusations. He was released when he was very close to being awarded a benefit, and I think Don was bitter about that. He was definitely treated harshly after all he had done for the club. So he went to the papers and, although I believe a lot of what he said was correct, I don't think it was anything like as sinister or wrong as the subsequent match-fixing that did indeed appear to be going on in the early to mid-1990s. I got on well with Toppers. I thought he was a good bowler in certain conditions. He was a good bloke to have around the dressing room. He was almost the likeable idiot. He was clumsy, he would walk across Goochy's feet with his boots on, and he'd break things. But he was popular and it was sad how he bowed out of the county.

He didn't help himself at times, like saying, 'Hello, baldy,' to Graham Saville when the chairman of cricket (and the man, ultimately, who decided whether we were going to be offered new contracts) walked into the dressing room; but the bottom line was that he could bowl, and for him to be released so close to a benefit was cruel. Certainly there have been other people who have received benefits when they have not done as much as Don to earn them and that's another area where Essex have sometimes let themselves down.

8

I wasn't selected for either the England tour of India or the 'A' tour of Australia at the end of the 1992 season. It was crossroads time for me. I had fought back after the setback of missing much of the run-laden 1990 summer with a wrist injury, to score reasonably consistently in county cricket and be selected for two 'A' tours. But I seemed as far away from a return as ever. So it was time for me to make a decision.

Either I could settle for being a decent county player and keep my fingers crossed that, with the vagaries of England selection still resulting in call-ups for large numbers of players, I might yet creep back in, or I could try to take my game to a higher level by working even harder during the winter to improve myself as a batsman.

And that was tricky. It was tricky because Karen and I were getting ever closer as a couple and she could rightly be forgiven for thinking that at last, with my non-selection, we might be able to spend some proper time together over a whole winter. She has always been fantastic in understanding the demands of a cricketer's life and the extra pressure it places on the family, but it was at this time that I really came to know that she was special.

I plucked up my courage, after much thought, to talk to Karen about the situation. I said, 'Look, I've got two options here. I can either say England's gone and just stay at home and become a county player, working hard in the summer, or go the other way and really give it everything to get myself mentally right. The hardest place to play is Australia, and I've got the offer of a job playing grade cricket in Sydney. What do you reckon?' And Karen, being the unselfish person she is, said,

'You're going to have to go. You've got to try to get the most out of yourself and your career that you possibly can.' She turned an incredibly hard decision into an easy one and I was extremely grateful to Karen for understanding my predicament.

I remember going to the ground and someone – I think it was Mark Ilott – said to me, 'What are you doing this winter?' and I replied, 'I'm going to Aus. Sydney. I'm playing grade cricket with Nad' (Nadeem Shahid). He said, 'You lucky bastard. Your missus must be very appreciative of you.' It made me think. As I was driving home I thought to myself, 'Yes, I'm very fortunate to have Karen. She's so understanding. She has sacrificed so much already and we've only been together four or five years.' So I went home, rang Karen, and said, 'Look, it's about time we got married. I can't wait until you come home from work to ask you. But give me your answer at four when you get here.' And she said, 'No, I'll give you my answer now. It's yes.' So that was it. No romantic situation, I'm afraid. No getting down on one knee. We were engaged.

Not that it was a spur-of-the-moment thing. We had been thinking about it for some time, but for us it wasn't a huge deal. Marriage was just like the next step in our relationship, really, but it was definitely the right time and we began planning to get married the following year. And off I went to Sydney for four months, with Karen coming out during the school holidays, as by this time she had got a job as a teacher locally and was doing very well in her own career.

I played for a side called Petersham, who had a terrible wicket but were a great set of lads, and Nadeem was there too, along with another English pro, a character called Ed Giddins who would go on to play under me for both England and England 'A' and who became a good friend, even if he was slightly more of an extrovert than me!

It was a very profitable four months. The three of us would get a lot of coaching at the SCG and I met people like Michael Slater and Adam Gilchrist, who were starting off their careers with New South Wales. I was surrounding myself with cricket and cricket people, and for me it was about completing my knowledge of the game. It was a different culture, an exciting cricketing culture. I became more aware of fitness, of technique, of front-foot rather than back-foot play, of every innings being important (music to my ears after my upbringing) because in grade cricket that's the way it is. The real intensity of the game, the camaraderie between the players, and the winning is everything mentality. It was fantastic, and far better than a short spell I spent playing grade cricket in Adelaide before the 'A' tour of Sri Lanka. That hadn't gone so well. This was everything I hoped it would be and it justified the tough decision I had made to be away from Karen when I didn't have to be.

It was also a good time in my relationship with my dad. I'm sure he was disappointed that I hadn't been picked for a representative tour, but when I went away to Australia it was simply a case of 'Nasser's away playing grade cricket' and there wasn't the scrutiny of my game or my scores that I'd still get at home. So whenever I saw him that winter, there was almost an absence of the pressure I would invariably feel. There was no 'good boy' or 'bad boy' sort of thing, just a nice family environment, and I relished that.

Of course, whenever I went round to Mum and Dad's for a curry, the subject would eventually get round to cricket and Dad would say things like 'You keep fighting. Have you seen the scores of the England players this winter? They're not as good as you. April's very important to you. Make sure you're ready.'

And in a way I still needed that. Because it wasn't just me who needed to be strong in going away again that winter and deciding to give my all to my cricket. Dad had to be too. It would have been easy for him to say, 'Boy, you've worked hard. Enjoy your life for once. Enjoy being with your girlfriend. Have a winter off.' The sort of things I can imagine me saying to my boys when they are older. But Dad was absolutely sure that I had to keep working, had to do everything I could to fulfil my potential. And he was right. I needed that reassurance at various times throughout my career and Dad never wavered from giving it to me. I really do owe him everything.

The other thing that was beginning to kick into my life was golf. I had played a little bit at university, but it became a bigger hobby as time went on and I needed a release from cricket and family life. And I was getting used to my Essex teammates having benefit years when they would need your support. Whoever's benefit it was would often give you the choice of going to a dinner or a golf day, and for me the golf was always the better option because it's such an insular, one-on-one game and I didn't have to socialize so much as if I went to a dinner. That suited my personality!

It was a game that began to fascinate me. The hand–eye coordination required suited me, as it tends to suit cricketers; and I'd watch a lot of golf on television and read books about the mindset required and stuff. Seve Ballesteros became a real hero, for his character, his fieriness and the little mind games and psychology he would employ in the Ryder Cup. Seve is still a hero to this day but I have never met him – and I'm quite glad about that because they say it's never a good idea to meet your heroes in case they disappoint you or are not very friendly. If you caught them at the wrong time, it could leave the wrong impression and spoil everything, and I don't want that.

I started at around an eighteen handicap and it's down to about ten or twelve now, but I don't think it will get any better: it's the level I'm at, and I don't think I want to put in the work required to get any better. I have spent all my life working at cricket, and golf is a game I just want to play for fun and not get too worked up about the odd bad shot.

So the winter went well and I knew the next summer was going to be crucial for my hopes of getting back into the England side. Australia were going to be in town, and I knew that, being Australia, there would be a big turnover of England players and it would be up to me to get runs so that my name would come up again. It was like the Australian venture had set me up for the summer and I had got up off my arse and done something about my cricket. It was like 'Yes, you do still want to be an England player and you're doing your best to make it happen.' To me, that gave me an extra five per cent more than some other candidates.

It's like Andy Flower once said to me. It's not the work off the field that he does which is important, it's just the knowledge that he is going on the field having done more work than his opponent. It puts him in good mental condition.

It certainly put me in good enough shape to make my England comeback in the 1993 Ashes series, even though it didn't come until Australia had won the first two matches of the series heavily. I was recalled for the third Test at Trent Bridge, and my first in England, to bat at number seven in a new-look side, still under the captaincy of Graham Gooch, but which included debuts for Mark Ilott, Mark Lathwell, Martin McCague and one Graham Thorpe, who had got his chance after four successive 'A' tours. It really was a mass clear out, and we did pretty well in that Test, with me scoring 71 and an unbeaten 47 when I was at the crease while Thorpey scored a second-innings hundred on debut to save the match for England.

But the next Test saw an era come to an end. England were beaten at Headingley, the Ashes were lost again and Graham Gooch resigned as England captain. In a way it took me many more years before I knew what he was going through at that time, how big a thing it is to pack up the England captaincy.

Graham has always been an honourable man and he believed in doing things the right way. In the past he had asked to be dropped by England when he didn't feel he was playing well enough, and I just think on this occasion he felt that the Ashes had gone, he had had four years at the job and it was time for someone else with fresh ideas to have a go.

I don't remember any big speech to the players by Graham. In fact, I don't think he even told us he was going to quit before we saw him appear at a press conference, so it all went above my head a bit, to be honest. I was only just back in the side, I hadn't done particularly well at Headingley and I certainly didn't feel any of the emotion that hit me when Mike Atherton resigned in 1998. I felt for Graham as someone I knew so well from Essex, but I didn't really know what to say to him. There just seemed to be a general air of acceptance about the place that this is what Australia did to England captains, and Goochy was simply the latest victim. To me it seemed obvious who was going to take over. There was only one man for the job: Mike Atherton.

Athers duly did get the job, and I could sense a real opportunity for me and others to stake a claim for a regular place in his new-look side. I could sense straight away that Athers wanted to mould a team of promise around a few experienced players, the perfect blend, and I was optimistic that I was going to be a part of that.

We lost at Edgbaston in Ath's first game in charge, before turning things around to win spectacularly at the Oval – a little glimpse, we hoped, of a new England. I had faded a bit as the series went on and got bounced out by Merv Hughes for a duck in the second innings, an unusual mode of dismissal for me and one that made me think, 'God, I hope I've done enough to get to the West Indies.' I had. Just. And I looked forward to a new era under Ath, starting off back in the Caribbean, one of my favourite places to play and the scene of my dramatic first tour as a full England player. It all seemed perfectly set up. But it turned out to be my worst England tour and it plunged me back where I was before that grade cricket trip had catapulted me back to the England team.

9

I felt quite at home in the England side as we prepared to tour West Indies, early in 1994. I knew I wasn't an established player. Knew I wasn't a definite in Atherton's side, but I quite liked that. It suited me to have to work for my place and I was full of anticipation as I got ready for the Caribbean with some net sessions at my dad's cricket school. There was also the considerable matter of my wedding to Karen, a fairly quiet affair in Essex with just our families and closest friends, but a wonderful thing to do and a hugely significant event in my life away from the game. I knew I had found the girl I wanted to spend the rest of my life with. When Karen had finished at Durham, she wanted to come down to Essex (originally she is from Lancashire) and set up home here and teach locally.

It can't have been easy for Karen. She was making a new life in a part of the country she didn't know, living with a cricketer who wasn't there half the time; and it was the way she reacted to that situation that made me confident that the marriage would work. You see, cricket is not a real life. We lead such a weird existence that it is no surprise that the divorce rate is so high among cricketers. I can't blame any woman for not being able to deal with the lifestyle, or becoming disillusioned with it. We spend more time with our teammates than we do with our families. It's especially hard when children come along. Can you imagine what it's like to say to your partner, 'Right, I'm off to the West Indies for three months. Good luck with the kids.' A lot of couples in our game don't fully understand what lies ahead of them in the early stages of their relationship, and it's no surprise to me when so many go wrong.

I've been lucky. Not only is Karen incredibly understanding, she is strong and can cope with most things. We are pretty similar people in many ways – another reason perhaps why we have worked. When Karen puts her mind to something, she likes to do it well; and I like people like that. We sometimes play golf together and she wants to win, wants to do the best she can. We've always hit it off, always been the best of mates, and even now when we go out to dinner we can chat all evening. There's always something to say.

I think we were lucky in meeting each other at the age of eighteen. We've grown together with the lifestyle and I think the old saying of absence making the heart grow fonder has been true for us. Because I've been away so often we haven't got stale, and whenever I come back from a tour or a Test there's always a spark between us. We don't get under each other's feet.

It can be weird, coming home after being on tour. You have to sort of retrain your brain to being with your family and get in tune again with how they live, because when you are away you really have only yourself to worry about. A touring cricketer has to be strong – I've seen people like Graham Thorpe and Darren Gough in tears when they've had to leave their children – but your partner has to be ten times stronger, in my opinion. Karen never once said to me, 'Why are you going away again?' Towards the end of my career I was always expecting her to say, 'You've done enough. I've put up with enough. Is there any chance of you acting like a normal husband and father and being here with us for a change?' But she never has. She's always been totally supportive of my career.

To give you one example: when I toured Sri Lanka in my last winter away as an England player, I found my place in the side for the third Test being questioned at management level for the first time in years. I was a bit upset, and I rang Karen. 'I've just had my place questioned for the first time since 1996,' I said to her. 'I feel really down about it. Do you think I should do the right thing and pack it in?' And she said, 'No, don't you dare. You fight, you make sure that when you're old you're not sitting around thinking you did the wrong thing in packing up too early.' I guess she did it a little bit for herself too. I'm sure she didn't want to encourage me to retire, and then for me to hold it against her when we're older if, with hindsight, I felt I'd gone at the wrong time. But she mainly did it for me, as she did when I went away that winter to Sydney and as she has always done.

I used to bring my cricket home with me. In my early years if I wasn't getting any runs I'd go home and sulk a bit. When I'm having a bad time I tend to go into my shell, and there were times when Karen would be looking forward all day to me coming home and I would just sit there quietly, not in the best of moods. And she would put up with that.

As I've got older I've grown more philosophical about the ups and downs of the game and have been able to switch off a lot more at home. I think the turning point was that Test in 1996 when I flicked one down the leg side, was given not out and went on to score my first Test century. That piece of luck kept me in the side for another eight years, so I've tried to get things in a better perspective since then, although I'm sure some of my teammates will laugh when they read this. They have still seen plenty of flashes of my famous temper in the intervening years!

As you get older, you learn all about the fine lines in the game. And as you travel the world, you see what other people have to cope with. When you're young, you think every dismissal is the end of the world, but as you get older you appreciate how lucky you are. The knack is, as Alan Knott once said, to realize how important cricket is to you and to other people but to approach every innings as if it's not important. It's not easy. The best piece of advice I ever received came from Graham Thorpe when he told me to not get too high when I'm doing well and not to get too low when things are going badly. It's like treating the twin impostors the same, staying on an even keel. I think Thorpey's been able to put that into better practice than me on a cricket field over the years, but it's something that has always been in my head.

Karen doesn't even really like cricket, and that suits me fine. I wouldn't like it if she asked me lots of questions about the game, like how did you get on, why is so-and-so playing, what did you do that for? Or ringing me in Brisbane and asking why I had put Australia in to bat. Thankfully, she never asks anything like that. Sometimes she won't even know a Test has started. I would ring her up at the end of a day's play, and not only would she not know how many I'd got but she wouldn't even have realized there was a game on. I like that. It's healthy. It means the game doesn't consume our private lives.

Anyway, back to the West Indies as a married man. I love the West Indies. I have spent so much time there as a cricketer. In a way it doesn't suit my game because I am addicted to net practice and, with the exception of Barbados, the net facilities in the Caribbean are not the best, but I just made up for that with more practice at home before I left.

My first ever hundred was in Barbados, on an Essex Schools tour when I was about seventeen or eighteen, and that was the time when I realized, after my leg-break trauma, that I could bat. Tony Cozier, the great West Indian broadcaster, tells me he was there and that he remembers it. I also had very fond memories of the 1990 tour, when we had come so close to victory, so everything was set up nicely.

But for some reason I struggled to get any sort of rhythm in the early weeks of that 1994 tour. I found the wickets were getting tired and not as quick and bouncy as I remembered from four years earlier and I just couldn't get going as the first Test in Jamaica approached. I also had the feeling that it was between me and Matthew Maynard for the final batting place in the side. Now I probably didn't get on too well with Maynard at this stage. He was a sort of Stuart Law character to me, immensely talented as a batsman but someone who enjoyed life and was much more sociable than me. As time has gone on I have grown to appreciate Matty more, as Duncan Fletcher enabled me to understand him, but in 1994 you would have people like me, Thorpe and Ramprakash, the 'brat pack', going round together, whereas Maynard was closer to someone like Robin Smith in personality.

And I wasn't surprised when Matty was picked ahead of me. I had no grumble with that at that stage because I knew I wasn't playing well, and perhaps I was unfortunate in that I had Atherton as captain and Keith Fletcher now as coach and they were two people who perhaps knew me better than anybody and could sense I wasn't in touch. If anybody had asked me, I would have said, 'I'm ready to play. You know me. Once I get into a Test Match I'll hit them well,' but the truth of the matter is that they were right to leave me out, and so I was reduced to the role of spectator, something I've always been terrible at.

When I'm not playing I really do switch off, which is very bad of me, I know. When you are playing, you expect those not in the side to rally round and do everything to support the team; but, while I was always happy to do my job and get people drinks and stuff like that, I'm afraid I slip into a mood of 'What am I doing here?' when on the sidelines. On this occasion I can't tell you much about what went on except that we lost in Kingston and Atherton came through a really fierce spell of bowling from Courtney Walsh which was clearly intended to rough up the new England captain.

Ath came through it very well, as I would expect him to do, but nevertheless it was important for him to show he had guts and what it takes to lead England. I think any team wants to see their captain show a bit of character and fight and, while Ath had nothing to prove to the rest of us, who respected him hugely already, this was the start of Atherton showing the rest of the world that he would be a tough nut to crack, the beginning of his 'over my dead body' sort of stubborn image that he was now trying to create. It's a bit like Steve Waugh being an 'iceman'. I think it helps your batting once you have an image like that. You almost play up to it.

Walsh also targeted Devon Malcolm in that match, which a lot of cricket people thought was unacceptable as Dev was such a hopeless tail-ender, but we didn't mind one little bit because when Dev was fired up he was often twice the bowler he was when he was calm and contented!

I played in a couple of one-day internationals but, as you may have guessed already, they don't feature too prominently in my memory; and as I think back over my career now, there are barely half a dozen one-dayers that register at all with me. Maybe it's because I was never a great one-day player, or because I played fewer of them; but my overwhelming recollections from this 1994 trip were my continuing absences from the Test side. What I do remember is making a century in the warm-up match in Guyana before the second Test, but not being too surprised when I wasn't picked for it, another match we lost, even though Ath's stock as captain was rightly rising as he scored a big century.

When you are out of the side on tour, you go into something of a downward spiral. As I say, the nets in the Caribbean are not the greatest and I remember us having to wander over the road somewhere, possibly Georgetown, in our pads and going to play on a field which was like the Fives and Heronians Third XI pitch with goats on it. And when you've got pretty useful local bowlers running in at you and bowlers like Alan Igglesden, who was out of the side, also running in at you with a new ball, doing his best to prove his point and get in the team, your form and mental state go from bad to worse.

I had a chat with my dad on the phone about this time and I remember him asking what was going on and why I wasn't in the side. I was trying to be philosophical, telling him there was nothing I could do and I just had to wait my turn. All the time, though, I knew that when my chance did come I would probably be out of nick, and I was also aware that a few of our batsmen were not getting that many runs and my chance could come at any time. It was a case of sitting on my bum, enjoying the social side of things and trying to be as ready as possible when my chance finally came, as it inevitably would.

And then came Trinidad. This was a match we actually played well in, but it will always be remembered as the Test where Curtly Ambrose just blew us away for 46 in our second innings when we had a realistic chance of winning, or so we thought. We dropped some slip catches in that match, particularly their left-handers, which is one area where I think we have always been behind the likes of Australia throughout my career. I've no real theory for it, but we have not had the greatest of slip fielders during my time as an England player. The only possible reason I can think of (and it's a pretty feeble excuse really) is that we practise a lot of our catching in March and April on cold mornings with hard balls, and it's easy to get into bad habits in those sort of conditions. The Australians practise in the warm with soft Kookaburra balls, and they get into good positions and develop good techniques, but at Essex in April you take eight slip catches and your hands feel as though they are going to fall off. So you tend to throw your hands at the ball and your only instinct is to avoid being hurt rather than your technique in catching the ball. It is why, as my career progressed and my popadom fingers were broken more and more, I tended to field at slip only for the spinners rather than the pacemen.

In my time Graeme Hick, Nick Knight and Andrew Flintoff were probably our best slip fielders, but in Trinidad this match Hicky was culpable and there were all sorts of press theories as to why he would drop left-handers but not right. Our fallibility in the field meant we had to chase 194 to win, and

I remember the dressing room being very tense as we got ready to bat. So, after doing my twelfth man bit with the drinks, I decided to take myself off for a little walk round the Queen's Park Oval to get myself a chicken roti. It was only a hundred-yard walk, but every two minutes there was a roar from the crowd and I kept looking up to see another of our wickets had fallen. By the time I got back to the dressing room, we had lost four wickets for next to nothing and I just sat there in a state of disbelief.

Everyone could tell the wicket was playing some tricks, but Jack Russell was out to an extraordinary shot and then I vividly remember Graham Thorpe being out. Ambrose went round the wicket, the ball kept low and it just shattered Thorpey's stumps. He didn't even look back, just walked off with this amazing, almost glazed look on his face and I thought, 'What on earth is happening here?' To all intents and purposes we were gone by the close that night, even though the match hadn't been fully wrapped up. The dressing room was distraught. If we had stayed on for longer that night, we would have been all out for even less, and it was one of those occasions when one of our most spectacular collapses met with one of their irresistible spells of bowling. Every ball looked like taking a wicket.

How good was Ambrose that day? Awesome. Just incredible. His accuracy from such a height was a wonder to behold and the great man was at his very best that day. We have a thing in the dressing room where we are constantly telling bowlers to hit the top of off stump because all players will struggle if you can consistently get it in that place, but nobody did it better than Ambrose, particularly in Trinidad 1994. The ball with which he got Atherton, lbw to one that nipped back to trap the England captain half forward off the first ball of the innings, was a classic of its type and became a familiar mode of dismissal for Ath as the years went on. He would either get out lbw or scissor it to slip – but that's not meant to be in any way a criticism. It was just so difficult to know how to play bowling like that on an up-and-down wicket. Someone like Geoff Boycott might say that you have to get forward, but how can you lunge forward to someone like Curtly Ambrose in those circumstances?

What was Curtly like? Well, in common with a lot of West Indies players he didn't mix too much with us off the field. All of them were very friendly around the dressing room, but that didn't extend to getting to know us very well. When they were with each other, they could talk for the world and I remember, as I was sitting around a lot on that tour, trying to listen to the conversations their fast bowlers were having with each other, when they would be sitting there, talking so fast and discussing who they did and didn't rate. Alec Stewart was included in their World XI, I seem to remember, which was some tribute.

For a young batsman, Ambrose was a frightening prospect. I never really got to know him because he didn't say very much to me, but I had enormous respect for him. He was never too intense. You could see he enjoyed his cricket but that he wasn't going to let it dominate his life. He liked his music and his fishing and he was just a great character and cricketer. For some reason I never feared him as someone who would consistently get me out because I saw him as a 'straight line' bowler and I could line him up a lot better than someone like Courtney Walsh. Glenn McGrath and Allan Donald were the same. Great bowlers, but you sort of knew where it was going and I never dreaded facing them or felt intimidated by them. Walsh was different.

Walsh was the most difficult bowler I ever faced because I just couldn't line him up. He was all arms and legs and would bowl from wide of the crease so you thought it would be coming in at you, and then at the last moment it might hold up on you. That for me was the most difficult because I always got my head a little offside of the ball, which meant I could be opened up a bit and the number of times Walsh would turn me into an S shape was embarrassing. I never felt 'in' against Courtney Walsh.

Meanwhile Trinidad was a huge setback for what Atherton and Keith Fletcher were trying to create and I think, really, that defeat was the beginning of the end for Fletch. You just know what sort of headlines are going to be written after something like that. You know that people in England will be calling for all of us to be sacked, to be sent to the moon, and get another lot in.

You need to have a thick skin at times like this and I could sense Keith Fletcher was really hurting. He would read all the papers, he took most of the flak and was in the thick of all the inquests that were going on. I think one paper might even have printed his phone number and encouraged people to ring him up and complain about us, a cheap trick played on a decent and knowledgeable man. There were many inquests. Everything in the dressing room was starting to be questioned. Take someone like Robin Smith. Fabulous player. Should have played a hundred Tests for England, should have scored eight or nine thousand Test runs. He had the ability. He had the character. He practised hard. I don't know who or what was at fault, but someone messed up badly in not getting the best out of Robin Smith for England, and I don't think it was the man himself. But when things are going wrong, everything is questioned and on this tour Robin's lifestyle came under the microscope. Yes, he liked a drink and yes, he had a few commercial things going on; but I'm convinced they were not at the expense of his cricket and, as ever in England, it was a case of concentrating on negatives rather than the many positives that Robin Smith brought to the game. It was Keith Fletcher who mentioned that Robin might have been distracted on this tour, but this was not done in an unpleasant, undermining way, more because Fletch wanted Robin to make the very best of his ability. But of course it was all interpreted in the most negative way possible.

My overwhelming feeling after that debacle was that I had to get in the nets. We were three down, the series was gone, none of our batters looked in any sort of nick, and we had just been dismissed for our second lowest score in history. I had to be given a chance, or so I thought. But first we had a match in Grenada, not the best place to try to get back into any sort of form. I was desperate to get into the nets, but this place was like an under-developed holiday island and a lot of our bowlers were understandably keen to rest up a bit before the fourth Test. So it wasn't easy to get back in form. And I was aware that the press were starting to ask whether I would be back in the side for Barbados. It was becoming an issue, and I could understand it because I was thinking exactly the same thing. To the point of obsession.

My tour, however, was about to get even worse. I was desperate to score runs in Grenada. I have never given my wicket away lightly – possibly one of the reasons why I was never a great one-day player, because there are times you have to slog it and give it away, and that just wasn't in tune with the way my dad brought me up. But I was accused of throwing my wicket away in this tour game. I was facing the leg-spinner Rawl Lewis and I had just cut him for 4 when he threw in a googly. I just didn't pick it, went to cut it and got bowled. Yes, it looked an average shot. It was an average shot. But the last thing I was doing was not trying. I just hadn't picked the wrong 'un. As I walked off, I was furious with myself for not getting a big score and forcing my way back into the Test side – but I was not prepared for the phone call I took from Dad. 'What's this about you having the wrong attitude and giving your wicket away?' he said. 'The papers are saying you were so angry about not playing, you haven't tried.' I was totally perplexed and, as far as I was concerned, nothing could have been further from the truth.

Whether or not Ath and Fletch started to believe the press I don't know, but Ath came up to me before Barbados and said, 'You're not playing,' something he subsequently admitted was a difficult call for him to make, and one that I found hard to take. But I didn't lose it with him, not at that stage. I said, 'Hold on. We've been bowled out for 46, and I can't get into the side? What are you trying to say to me here, Ath?' But he insisted they wanted to give Ramprakash another chance. It was difficult for me, but I could see his point of view; and now, with hindsight, I can see that Ath was right. He was only doing what I tried to do much later as captain and give everybody a fair chance before discarding them. It was almost a case of saying to the batsmen, 'You got us in this mess. You get us out of it.'

And they did. Or, rather, Alec Stewart did. He scored two centuries in the match as England, remarkably, became the first visiting side to win a Test in Barbados. Alec couldn't have picked a better Test to achieve what he did, with all the British supporters there and us needing to stop the possibility of a blackwash. I knew he was a good player of quick bowling, and this wicket was made for him. It was quick and bouncy, like the old-style West Indian wickets, and they kept on bowling short at him with three men on the hook, and he kept on hitting them for four. It was fantastic stuff. I did a bit of fielding and picked up a couple of catches, and the whole two weeks summed up English cricket – 46 all out in one Test, and then an incredible victory at the fortress of West Indian cricket in the next. Maddening inconsistency, but dramatic Test cricket.

Ramps, meanwhile, again didn't get too many and I could sense that he was over-theorizing somewhat, like I tend to do at difficult times. Mark's dad came from Guyana, and Ramps was a real fan of West Indian cricket. All his heroes were West Indian, like Desmond Haynes and Viv Richards, and by this stage of the tour he would do things like go down to the beach and play beach cricket with the locals to try to get used to quick bowling. He was almost in awe of the place and the people.

It's a tremendous shame Mark Ramprakash has never ful-filled his potential as an England player. He has magnificent natural talent, much more than the likes of me and Atherton. He was a world-class player, or should have been. Ramps had it all: the technique, the shots, the aggression, the discipline. In his training and his healthy eating he was very like Stewie, and they got on well because they were so similar, but Alec was very straightforward in his attitude to batting: he just went and did it. Ramps was more like me, with theories, nervousness, bat handle obsession and stuff like that. Maybe we had similar upbringings, similar dads. But Mark Ramprakash should have achieved more in the game, should certainly have played more Tests than me, and it's a great shame he didn't. I just hope it doesn't eat at him. It doesn't seem to bother him now, for he still achieved a lot, still had a good career in cricket, with England, Middlesex and Surrey. It just shows you what a thin dividing line there can be between the great and those who under-achieve.

It was in Antigua that I lost my temper. We were having fielding practice the day before the final Test and I sensed Atherton walking towards me, the dreaded captain's walk to tell someone they wouldn't be playing. I know England had won in Barbados, but I really thought my turn had come. Especially as Ramps hadn't got many in the series. Nothing against him; he was and still is a mate, but I'd been working all winter to try to play a Test and there was a real finality to being told that I wasn't even going to feature in the last match.

So I turned round to Ath when he told me and I said, 'You're joking.' The conversation became heated. I told him that all the other batsmen had had chances on this tour and it was about time I had one. I reminded him that I had finished the previous summer in the side, a winning side at the Oval against Australia, and while I could appreciate the loyalty he was showing players now, where was the loyalty at the start of the tour when I had been in possession of a place?'

It was a futile exercise really because I have never known a captain change his mind after telling a player he wasn't playing, and I knew it was hard for Ath because we were so close, but I had to get it off my chest. The best thing about it was that I knew it would make no difference to my relationship with Mike Atherton because he was the sort of man you could have an argument with and it was all forgotten the next day. That's the sort of character I like. And we're still good friends now, so it clearly didn't affect our relationship. Mind you, it might have done if that had proved to be the end of my Test career, as seemed possible over the next two years when I didn't get a look in. As it turned out, it was the last time I was to be left out of an England side on form or selection grounds, because after I got back into the team in 1996 I stayed there for the rest of my career – apart from when injuries, and my famously fragile fingers, got in the way.

Antigua was a belter of a wicket. That made me feel worse. And I couldn't believe it when Ramps went down with a stomach upset at lunch on the first day and I had to field for him as the West Indies took advantage of that perfect surface. As it turned out, it was a blessing in disguise because it meant I was on the field for a day and a half, watching one of the most incredible innings of all time.

Brian Lara was awesome that Test At the time I thought I was watching perhaps the best innings of all time as he reached an amazing 375 – but little did I know that, ten years later, I would be back, still playing and in the field at the same St John's Recreation Ground when Brian topped it and took the world record individual Test score to 400 not out. At the time when he scored 375 I thought this had to be about as good as it got. I realized this was how you were supposed to bat. He was just in a different world from the likes of me. Brian was just taking the mickey out of the bowlers. Ath would move a fielder and Brian would place the next ball where the fielder had just been. He was an absolute genius.

What made me feel really humble was that this was a lad I knew well from under-19 cricket; I had been out for a drink with him in Adelaide during the Youth World Cup. He was a good friend at that time. There is no doubt that Brian changed after that innings and his 501 for Warwickshire, a few weeks later. He became more wary. He didn't know who he could trust and who his real friends were any more, and I sort of drifted away from him. I suppose in that knock in Antigua he went from mere mortal to the greatest batsman in the world and it was bound to have an effect on him.

He was on about 250 when Ramps was well enough to return to the field and reluctantly I had to watch the rest of the innings from the dressing room. I'd never seen anything like what happened when Lara broke Gary Sobers's record and passed 365. He pulled Chris Lewis for the decisive boundary – Lewey was a good mate of his too – and almost trod on his stumps as he did it. Can you imagine the disappointment if he had hit his own wicket at that stage? Sobers came on to the pitch and all hell broke loose, with the game being held up for something like ten minutes, spectators doing cartwheels on the pitch and umpire Darrell Hair ordering some bloke to get off the wicket until he realized it was the groundsman, desperately trying to restore order. There was definitely a feeling of being involved in something special. In those days there wasn't anything like the big scores being made today, and it was just something that nobody expected to happen between two major sides. And Brian was a fairly young lad too. He was only just established. Amazing.

There was chaos that night. You could see our money-oriented boys hovering, lads who were determined to get anything they could lay their hands on signed by Brian so it would raise money when their benefit year came along. The English mentality of 'what can we make out of this?' was drifting in a bit and Brian must have signed about ten or fifteen shirts he supposedly wore during that innings. It must have been closer to two or three! To be fair to Brian, he signed everything, and I just said, 'Well done', and hurried away. He had moved on to another level.

10

I came back from the West Indies disappointed, disillusioned and wondering what would come next. I returned to domestic cricket out of nick, and I struggled to get back into form for the whole of the 1994 season. It was quite humbling really. It wasn't as traumatic as when I lost my leg-spin bowling as a kid, but it made me realize how much the game meant and how important it was to me.

But it was never a matter of being plunged into depression or anything like that. It was just a normal loss of form that any cricketer goes through and one of the downs that I have periodically had to cope with throughout my career. I have never been a genius. I've always had to work hard for my runs and, however hard I worked in 1994, they just wouldn't come.

It would be easy in those circumstances to just return to the comfort zone, to slip back on to the treadmill and enjoy an easy life in county cricket, and I must admit that the fact I wasn't listening particularly hard for England selection announcements and getting worried by them did ease the pressure on me a bit. At times that season I actually enjoyed leading a less pressurized life. I've seen some cricketers who have enjoyed the material aspects of getting to the top, the money, the good gear, the fact that everyone wants to know you, but they haven't actually enjoyed the pressures and dedication that go with playing international cricket. I could see why that year. I could see how easy it might be to say, 'Well, I've got a good career in county cricket. I earn forty grand a year, I get winters off, I don't have to make any sacrifices, and it's a good laugh.' So they take the easy option; and that's another problem unique to English cricket, because there is no comfort zone in other Test countries. Players have to work hard to earn any sort of money from the game, and the fact that our system is different has definitely been to our detriment as a Test country.

There is no doubt that there is a bloody good life to be had from not being an international cricketer, but in life there are people who take the easy route and there are those who take the hard yards, and I have always fallen into the latter category. So I had only a brief flirtation with the easy life, realized I would have to score a shedload of runs if I wanted to get back into the England team, virtually wrote off the summer as England tackled New Zealand and South Africa, and started thinking what I could do in the winter to improve my game.

Again, Graham Gooch was good to me. I didn't have anywhere to go that winter, so I asked Goochy for his advice and he recommended Cape Town, where he had contacts. I'm not sure if I desperately wanted to go somewhere different, but maybe in the back of my mind I felt a little apprehensive about going back to Australia to play grade cricket after such a poor English summer. If I had still been out of form I could have really suffered in Aus, and I didn't want that. I wanted somewhere where I could get my confidence back and, I guess, an easier winter. Working quietly on my game somewhere where they had a good climate, good nets and the chance for me to take stock of where I was as a cricketer. So, once again I left Karen in Essex teaching, to spend three months in South Africa.

While I was there I met Dean Headley, who became one of my closest friends in the game. A real honest tryer with a big heart and someone I loved playing cricket with. I wish I had captained him for England, but I never got the chance because of his back injury. I started off at the Primrose Cricket Club, where the people were great but the facilities were poor, and it was clear to me very quickly that I wasn't going to gain much from a full winter there. The turning point was the festival of

Ramadan. My club was Asian and didn't play then, so, at the suggestion of Neil Burns, the old Essex and Somerset keeper, I took myself off to Stellenbosch University where I was told I would find some good nets. Well, I absolutely fell in love with the place. It was like being back at Durham – only stinking hot. Karen came out, I met some great people, including South Africa's Omar Henry; people like Zola Budd were always on the athletics track and it was just a brilliant sporting place. So I ended up staying there and hardly ever went back to Cape Town.

And the most important development during my whole time in South Africa came off the cricket field. I'd known Neil Burns since Essex Under-11s and he was always a big one for a theory. I was talking to him one day about eyesight, as I had always had a problem with my left eye not being as good as my right one. And I told him about my visits to opticians, how I should have worn glasses at school but never had and how, whenever I asked opticians whether contact lenses might improve my batting, they had always discounted the idea and said that my right eye was strong enough and my brain automatically dismantled the bad vision and relied on my right eye. Neil told me to visit a guy called Ken West, an optometrist and sports scientist who was based at the university.

Now Ken was a different sort of character. A bit weird. He knew little about cricket but he knew a lot about the body and the eyes and biomechanics, and he had worked with people like Jonty Rhodes and Daryl Cullinan on little things that had improved their cricket. Not only did Ken help my eye situation, he also had a nice line in little gimmicks that would help my hand–eye coordination and, as a consequence, my cricket. In a funny sort of way it was exactly what I needed at that stage in my career. I needed a new angle, something to stimulate me and get me out of the rut I had slipped into. Ken immediately told me that Graham Gooch shouldn't retire at forty because he could improve his eyes, and I thought, 'I'll have some of that.' Ken said I should have a contact lens in my left eye and that he would retrain that eye to make it as strong as my right one. It was a very precise process, involving lots of visits to the opticians, but it worked. Then we would work at running between the wickets. Don't laugh and say I couldn't have been listening! Ken would have his stopwatch out and time the way I turned and grounded my bat and he gave me various suggestions to save milliseconds.

It was all very theoretical, but I took on board what I wanted to and was constantly aware of the fact that I didn't think Ken knew too much about the game. The most interesting times were those spent in a lab at the university, full of hand–eye coordination games. There were balls flying around the room that you had to stop and catch. A machine where lights would flash on and off and you had to point to the light; and there were eye charts to get you focusing on different things in different parts of the room. He said to me, 'The eyes are muscles, and a lot of muscles around the eyes don't get used and don't get trained. You'd go to the gym and pump weights and everything, so why not train the muscles in your eyes?' I also became more aware of the importance of the eye to batting. I thought about someone like Ronnie Irani, who has a poor technique but always watches the ball right on to the bat, and that's how he scored his runs. Same, to an extent, with Steve Waugh. Not a great technique but a fabulous eye for the ball and great hand–eye coordination. I worked for about a month with Ken West and it was extremely beneficial. Not only that, it started something of a trend because he came over and worked with Lancashire, and I could see a difference in their running between the wickets and I saw their players with their eye charts and things, training the eyes like I had.

Whether it made a difference to my batting I don't know, but it certainly made a psychological difference. I felt as if I'd prepared well for the season and I felt more confident with that contact lens in my left eye. For some time I wouldn't have been without it, but over the last three or four years of my career I went back to how I had been and didn't wear it, starting when I ran out of supplies in Sri Lanka one morning when I was batting. I thought, 'Sod it, I'll just go and bat,' scored a century and then wondered if I needed a contact lens after all, and didn't bother again.

In 1995, however, I was prepared to believe it had made all the difference to me. These were changing times at Essex. Paul Prichard was now the captain after Gooch stood down, having been preferred to John Stephenson, who decided he would be better off at Hampshire. Players I grew up with and was close to, like Nadeem Shahid and Nick Knight, had moved on in search of greater opportunities, and we were nothing like the force we had been. Meanwhile, the international scene seemed like a different world to me. New England stars had emerged like Darren Gough and Dominic Cork, and I remember playing against Lancashire when Mike Atherton was in their side. I thought, 'God, Ath has moved on so much. Here I am, a county player, and he's been captain of England thirty-odd times.' It was like we were inhabiting different worlds then, but the thing that kept me going was that I was scoring lots of runs for Essex and doing my utmost to get back in the frame.

England had done all right in Australia, with Goughy taking the country by storm. And I was saddened by the departure of Keith Fletcher as England coach after another losing Ashes series. The story went that by the end of his reign Fletch was still hitting catches in the air and the players, tired and beaten, were rebelling against what they saw as outdated methods. Fletch lost it with them, as he could do from time to time, and apparently said, 'I've got a five-year contract, but some of you will be out of jobs when we get home.' A few weeks later, they sacked Fletch and put Ray Illingworth in charge.

I've always viewed Keith Fletcher as one of the most knowledgeable and caring people I have ever met in cricket. He doesn't over-coach, he doesn't over-complicate things. He just dispenses words of wisdom in his own quiet way and he has a great understanding of the game. The fact that he wasn't successful as England coach after so much success at Essex is a huge disappointment both for Keith and for all those who know him and rate him so highly. He definitely had it in him to be a lot more successful than he was but, whether it was because he didn't have that thick skin you need, or that some people felt he didn't communicate as well as he might have done at times, I don't know. Certainly the impression at the time was that Keith had had a raw deal in the rush to make the chairman of selectors a supremo with responsibilities for coaching. But Keith is a very loyal person, and even now I don't think he would say a bad word about Illy.

I didn't have much to do with the bloke myself. I remember bumping into Illingworth once around this time when he was chairman and I had scored runs, but he just walked past me and said, 'All right, young lad,' which left me a bit deflated because it seemed to me that the chairman of selectors didn't know who I was. And it was clear, viewed from the outside, that Atherton was having problems. Ath had been trying to build this young team around the nucleus of players who went to the West Indies in 1994, but Illingworth came along and brought back Gooch and Gatting for the following year's Ashes tour and left out Angus Fraser, a selection that caused problems between Atherton and Fraser because they were so close.

There were more problems the following winter when Illingworth took the team to South Africa and surrounded himself with his old mates in Peter Lever and John Edrich as bowling and batting coach. Some of the stories I heard from that trip were from a different world. There were players from one generation being coached by three people from a bygone age and it just didn't work at all. There was the infamous clash with Devon Malcolm which was, perhaps, just the most notorious example of discontent. Apparently every fielding session was like 'Let's get this over with because we're going to play golf,' and the three of them would leave Ath to virtually run the show on his own. How Atherton had the energy to score that 180-odd during the series is beyond me because he was doing everything.

It must have been a very difficult time for Ath because he wanted to do one thing and his chairman and coach (the same person) wanted to do it a completely different way. This is where I was very lucky in having Duncan Fletcher as coach when I was captain because, purely by chance, we got on extremely well from the start and we had very similar views. There's no question in my mind that I wouldn't have survived as England captain if I had been in Ath's position and had had to deal with Illingworth and all the other changes and inconsistencies that were going on at that time. The TCCB were becoming the ECB, all sorts of weird and wonderful characters were involved in selection or selection committees, and basically Ath was just not allowed to pursue his vision, the one he had tried to implement so soon after taking on the job in 1993.

Yet he was still able to keep his true feelings to himself and soldier on. I'm much too emotional for that, I'm afraid. Like when Ath was in trouble over the whole 'dirt in the pocket' saga in 1994, he just took himself off to the Lake District for a week to think about things. Whereas my reaction in that situation would have probably been, 'I've done nothing wrong. If you don't agree, then tough. I'm off.'

I was so detached from the England scene when all that business was taking place that I was just like any other member of the public, intrigued by what was happening to England's young captain. I must confess when I saw it, I wasn't sure what the laws were on the matter; I bet if you challenged a lot of people who subsequently passed judgement on Ath, they wouldn't have been sure either. The only time when I felt he did anything wrong was when he was economical with the truth to the match referee. That was the only time I feared for him as a friend. But some of the outrage and the comments that were flying around were extraordinary over something which – let's face it – was pretty innocuous on the field. I know Ath was hurt and, I get the impression, he still feels some disappointment towards his most vocal critics at that time, like the BBC's Jon Agnew.

The success of Dominic Cork pleased me. I had got to know Dom pretty well when we were together on the England 'A' tour to the West Indies in 1992, when I broke my finger and poor old Dom had to pack and unpack my bags for me wherever we went because I was protecting my dodgy digit! I really got on with Dom, in fact I liked everything about him. He was abrasive with the opposition. He was in your face. But as a teammate he was great to have in your side. If you had a difficult situation in a match, he was one person you would always throw the ball to, or send in to bat, like at Lord's in 2000 when we beat the West Indies; and he would invariably come through for you. Yes, he got on people's nerves at times, but I didn't mind that. He reminded me of myself.

I've always preferred that sort of character to someone who just plays the games in order to be liked. I have watched someone like Paul Grayson at Essex talking to the opposition before a day's play, then talking to the square-leg umpire when we are in the field, and I hate the mateyness of it all. For me you are in the game to win, simple as that. And I know people who have hated Dominic Cork, really hated him, when they have been in opposition to him but have loved the bloke when he has been on their side. A bit like Paul Nixon. I like those sort of cricketers.

Nixon could really wind you up if you were batting while he was keeping. He was one of the few blokes I ever saw Graham Gooch get angry with on the field, and there was one cup final when I was scoring runs against Leicestershire and he shouted, 'Come on, let's get the most unpopular bloke in English cricket out.' I thought, 'Who do you think you are?'

but when he came on an England tour with us, I loved the bloke.

For that period Dominic Cork was a true international cricketer. Later on he lost the art of swing and just tried to live off his bravado and antics, which is all very well in county cricket but doesn't work in the international game; but for a while he was the best bowler in England and I was delighted when he took a hat-trick against the West Indies at Old Trafford and did so well that summer.

And for the first time in two years I was beginning to think I might be close to joining Dom in the England side. With my contact lens in place I had a terrific summer in 1995 and I started paying attention to the speculation about who was going on tour at the end of a good series against the West Indies. The day of the tour announcements came and I was in London with Karen listening to the radio as Ray Illingworth read the names out for the main tour to South Africa. That was how you used to find out in those days.

He started reading his list, and when he got to Richard Ilingworth I knew I was gone. We had moved past H and I wasn't there and I felt very low about that. Then they came to the 'A' tour of Pakistan and they read my name out as captain. I was still thinking about my omission for South Africa, so it didn't really register too clearly, apart from me thinking about papers like the *Sun* calling me a bad boy, and I wondered what they would make of me being captain. Then my brother Abbas rang me and said, 'Don't worry too much. This could be a blessing in disguise. Go to Pakistan, have a good tour, use it as a stepping stone and see how it goes.' It was very astute of him.

Again, I was very lucky in my management team because I was thrown together with three people I didn't know at all but who were fabulous to be with on what turned out to be a crucial tour in my career. Obviously I knew of John Emburey but I didn't know him to talk to, and he turned out to be an excellent coach. Then there was Mike Vockins, the manager, who was an absolute gent, and Dean Conway, a tremendous physio and confidant to the players.

I looked at it in two ways. England hadn't toured Pakistan since the Mike Gatting–Shakoor Rana affair of 1987, so there was a lot of pressure on us and I thought they might have picked me as captain because of my surname, as someone called Hussain was bound to go down well in Pakistan. But against that there was my 'bad boy' reputation to consider on a tour in which diplomacy would be paramount. Did they really want me going out there and causing another incident, I thought.

Yet I have always believed that you behave differently when handed responsibility, something I tried to get through to Lord MacLaurin and David Graveney when they interviewed me for the main captaincy, a while later. They said to me, 'People have said you're selfish, look after your own game and get too angry when you're out,' but I replied that you behave very differently as a player from the way you do as a captain. It was almost automatic to me that I had to react differently as captain than I would as a player. I was now a captain, an ambassador for my country, the figurehead of the side. That 'A' tour of Pakistan was the first time I could show people that I could behave, that I could be aware of my responsibilities and, above all, that I could be a good captain.

I had a good set of lads at my disposal. There was Dean Headley and Ed Giddins, whom I knew from trips overseas. Nick Knight and Ronnie Irani were there. Others I got to know and like, for instance Dominic Ostler. And we were up against a good Pakistan side, led by Asif Mujtaba and including people like a young Shoaib Akhtar and Mohammad Akram.

We played some good cricket and I scored runs. We behaved impeccably and I was the original poacher-turned-gamekeeper in emphasizing to the boys that they mustn't show any dissent when given out and that we were there to build bridges and had to be on our best behaviour all the time. I think they could accept it, coming from someone like me. They knew I had been there and done the things I was now telling them not to do. They could relate to me because I was only human and had made some mistakes. It is why, I think, sometimes the greatest players, the Tendulkars and Laras and even the Gooches, don't always make the best captains, because they can't relate to the bad boys or to those who can't necessarily do the things they can.

We would all play cards a lot and we talked a lot of cricket. Emburey was brilliant; he was still playing at that stage, so someone like Jason Pooley, who knew him well from Middle-sex, would sometimes swear at Embers and I would have to say, 'Be careful. He may be good old Emburey, but he's our coach out here. Let's show him a bit of respect,' and then Emburey would come into the coach, effing and blinding at no one in particular. I think you really gel on 'A' tours and make friends who stick by you afterwards. And it means that when you later play at full England level with these guys, they know and understand you and you can relate to them more easily. Like when I captained Ed Giddins at Lord's I could see some of our players looking at this bloke, who immediately started talking about his sex life, and thinking, 'Who on earth is this badger?' But I knew Giddo and knew what made him tick and I know he thought it was a nice gesture that when I handed him his England cap when he made his Test debut I said, 'This is a long way from Sydney grade cricket, isn't it, Giddo.'

I never thought of the tour as a test of my full captaincy credentials. It was simply a stepping stone back to Test cricket so far as I was concerned. I can honestly say I had never even thought about being England captain until I went for my first interview when Ath resigned. I just wanted to bat and score runs for England. A lot of people assumed it was a big ambition of mine to become England captain, but I can genuinely say it wasn't.

Pakistan, meanwhile, was such an eye-opener, the people were so warm and friendly. We had a big card school going and it would basically take the form of me winning and Ed Giddins refusing to pay up, but I managed to extricate sufficient rupees to have enough money to go out and buy some carpets and maybe a nice leather jacket for myself. So I would go round these markets, and everywhere I went people would know me and would say, 'Hussain, are you Muslim?' They said it in a very friendly way, but it was a difficult one for me to answer because I'm not really, but I suppose I am nominally. I didn't know what to say for the best because I didn't want to offend the locals, so I would end up smiling, and saying, 'I should be.' This appealed to them because I think quite a few of them thought of themselves in the same way, especially the ones who liked a little drink or whatever now and then.

It even happened when we were up near the Khyber Pass when we were in Peshawar and, in among all these guys selling guns in the middle of nowhere, someone said to me, 'Hussain, are you Muslim?' It made me understand the enormous passion for cricket in the sub-continent as much as anything else.

It was a great trip, but it was one with a disappointing ending for me. John Crawley was injured playing for England in South Africa and it became clear that a replacement would be needed. The word was that it was going to be either me or Jason Gallian, who was on our 'A' trip, and after what seemed like an eternity Jason got the call-up instead of me. I was devastated. I had nothing against Gallian but I really thought I had done enough to get on that trip. I really thought someone must have decided I wasn't up to it any more, whether it was Illingworth or even Ath. It was like I'd had my go and wasn't up to it and now he can captain the odd 'A' tour but he's not going to play Test cricket again.

While England were completing their shambolic tour of South Africa and going on to an even worse World Cup campaign in India, I was left with the distinct impression that I wasn't wanted as a Test batsman any longer. But there was to be one further and decisive twist to the Hussain tale.

11

The South African tour as organized by the ECB was a complete shambles. As was the World Cup that followed in India and Pakistan. Their attitude, as ever, seemed to be about making as much money as possible from any tour or world cup, and then let the captain and coach take the blame when inevitably it went wrong on the field. No planning. No forward thinking.

Some years later, when England won the rugby World Cup, the differences between the two sports were made clear. We, as the England cricket team, had a talk from Martin Johnson, the rugby winning captain, and it became obvious that nothing was spared in terms of paying attention to every detail which could give their side an edge. And they went on to win their cup in Australia. So the ECB encouraged us to take rugby's lead. We listened. So, in wanting to pay attention to detail, we asked for a masseuse to tour the West Indies with us, and the ECB turned round and said they couldn't afford one. In the end the players' union said that in that case they would pay for her, and that shamed the ECB into stumping up some of the cost. Typical.

Early in 1996 it just seemed that the ECB had no idea what lay ahead of them in terms of preparing for a World Cup in the sub-continent. Hadn't given it a moment's thought. It was as if there was still a mentality of 'We're England. We invented the game. We will show them how cricket should be played.' But of course the game has moved on and countries have moved on with it. Except England. Poor Atherton was asked to lead a World Cup campaign along with coaches from a different era, with no innovation or modern thinking whatsover.

Again, if I'd been in charge, I'm sure I would have walked away from the job. Ath deserves a medal for hanging on in there.

Everywhere you looked, there were strange selections. Like Neil Smith pinch-hitting at the top of the order. Good county player and all that, but pinch-hitting the likes of Wasim Akram on the sub-continent? No way was that going to be a success. Then, at one point, came the sight of Phil DeFreitas bowling off-spin to Sanath Jayasuriya, who was then emerging as the most destructive batsman in the game. Unbelievable. Talk was that there were problems between Alec Stewart and Ray Illingworth behind the scenes, and it was little surprise that England's whole World Cup campaign never got off the ground, four years after Graham Gooch's side reached the final and were unlucky not to win the World Cup against Pakistan in Melbourne.

It was inevitable that the calls for change would increase and heads would have to roll. But Illy somehow held on to the chairman of selectors role while having to hand over the coaching reins to David Lloyd. I was a bit wary of Bumble, as Lloyd is universally known. I'd never met him but everyone said he was a bit loop the loop. He'd been an umpire and was always friendly enough to players on the field, but it was clear he was pretty scatty. Mind you, at that stage I wouldn't have cared who was coach because I was picked for the first Test against India at Edgbaston and my fears that it was all over for me, with Jason Gallian being preferred as a tour replacement a matter of months earlier, had proved unfounded.

The thing that petrified me the most was being selected to bat at number three. England hadn't had a settled three for ages and I felt at that stage that it was the most difficult place in the order to bat. You come off the field and put your pads on while the openers are facing the new ball and everybody out on the field is in the same boat, the bowlers needing to loosen up while the batsmen play themselves in. Whereas at three you could be facing the new ball or sitting there for ages awaiting your turn. I'd always thought that the number three had to be the most technically accomplished member of the side and I thought of myself as a decent player of spin who was better off down the order a bit where my technique couldn't be exposed. But I was scoring runs at three for Essex, so in I went at three for my big comeback.

The build-up was a bit nerve-racking. We were playing India, so of course that meant everything to Dad, and for me it felt like a fresh start. The team had been through hell over the last year or more, so it wasn't as though I was joining a successful team — always harder, as you had to live up to the standards the others had set. There was a new coach and some new faces in the side and I was a bit relieved when we lost the toss and ended up in the field, so I could acclimatize a bit before the serious business of batting was upon me. Ath asked me to field at cover point, somewhere I've never relished being, but the captain told me to go there and I went there because at that stage I would have done anything he said just to be back in the side.

I don't like cover point because the angle is different. When you field in most positions the game is in front of you, but at cover point it is sideways on and the ball comes out of the crowd to you when the batsman cuts it. This is sounding like an excuse, isn't it? And I needed one after dropping an absolute sitter from their left-handed debutant opener Rathore, early in the game. He sliced it to me at cover, I lost it in the crowd (hadn't been used to a crowd over the previous three years) and down it went. My heart virtually stopped for an hour. I was thinking to myself, 'I've waited three years to get back in the side. This is my chance and I could have already blown it.' When you do something like that, or winning the toss at Brisbane and inserting the opposition, or dropping Graeme Smith at Lord's on his way to a double century, it not only ruins your day, you fear it could ruin all five days. Because you know you will be under even more pressure when you bat, and you stand there watching the drop being shown again on the big screen and you know they will be talking about it on the television.

I wasn't exactly suffering from nerves but I was slightly taken aback by being on the big stage again. It was only my eighth Test, six years after I made my debut, and there was a big Edgbaston crowd with a lot of Indian supporters present. What I was after was a nice, quiet, relaxing couple of sessions in the field, have a few throwdowns before we batted, and I would be a Test cricketer again. The last thing I needed was for something like that to happen, but the fortunate thing for me was that we got the bloke out soon after, because if they go on to make a big one after you drop them, every run is like a dagger through your heart.

My mood improved when Ronnie Irani, on his Test debut, got Mohammed Azharuddin out to a blinding catch by Nick Knight and we dismissed them for a little over 200 before the main event loomed for me. I've always liked Edgbaston even though I hadn't got many runs there before this game. There's just always a nice feel and a nice atmosphere about the place. But the ball was doing a bit when I started batting and there were a couple of nervous moments until, on 14, came one of the most significant moments of my career. Javagal Srinath went round the wicket to me, I gloved one to the keeper, no question, and the Indians all went up for the catch. I gloved it. Definitely. But I wasn't going to walk. When you nick it with your bat you just know the umpires are going to give you out, but it's harder to give when it's a glove and I could see umpire Darrell Hair almost trying to look round me to see if I had touched it. Srinath had gone round the wicket. Hair was unsighted. The finger hadn't gone up. Was he waiting for me to walk off? I wasn't going anywhere. The longer it went on — and I know we are only talking split seconds here — the more I thought I might be getting away with it, and then Darrell just looked down. I couldn't believe my luck. Their players were spewing but they were quite a young side and there wasn't much sledging. Perversely, the incident seemed to relax me. The pitch got flatter, I became more confident and I was starting to enjoy myself.

It never takes the gloss off a hundred if you know you have actually been 'out' during the innings as far as I'm concerned. You get so many good and bad decisions over a career that they even themselves out and you end up around level par. Doesn't spoil it at all. But it has always got me thinking what might have happened if a certain decision hadn't gone my way, a bit like that film *Sliding Doors*. At the time, any decision seems small, but they can have such an effect on your life that you do wonder how things would have ended up if you had received a different rub of the green at certain times.

Edgbaston is a quick-scoring ground, so you can cut and pull and you don't have to run many, and it suited my game as a touch player. My game is sort of based on timing the ball through the covers for four, which you can do at Edgbaston, and it's certainly what I did on this occasion. They peppered me a bit because I think the theory was I couldn't get my hands out of the way of the short ball, but I cut and pulled pretty well and dealt with Kumble, the big threat, as well as I could have done. Sure, I was a little nervous in the nineties, but it went like a dream and I reached my maiden Test century as we moved into a commanding position.

It was a big moment. Big for me and especially big for my dad. I knew he would get so many phone calls from India, so many congratulatory messages. It would be like 'Jawad Hussain went off to England and now his son is scoring Test centuries for them.' That's a really big thing, especially to Dad. Even now I'm not absolutely sure he was there to see it. My dad always asked for tickets from me, especially if we were playing India or Pakistan, but I was never sure if they were for him or whether they ended up with his friends from the cricket school. He's just such a nervous watcher. Generally, I think he used to

143

watch when we were in the field, but he would prefer to be back in his little office at the Ilford Cricket School watching the telly on his own when I was batting. Mum was supposed to be coming to that match, but she didn't then and never did subsequently. I just don't think she could face the prospect of three hours there in the car with Dad smoking and then a tense three hours back if I hadn't scored many. It must be hell for a father to be so committed to his son's career as a cricketer like Dad was. It's probably why I never want to go through it with my boys. Dad even used to sit there at home watching Ceefax if I wasn't on TV, waiting for the scores to be updated and hanging on every mistake I made. No wonder he likes a drink and a fag. It must drive any parent mad.

Afterwards I had a feeling of relief. I had a Test hundred and nobody could take that away from me. More importantly, I now knew I could score a hundred at that level, and once you have done something once you feel you can do it again. Also, a hundred gives you a bit of breathing space, you know you are going to be in the team for a few games after that, and you know you have an extended opportunity to prove yourself and establish your permanancy. That innings relaxed me, and later on in that series I got another one, one of my quickest and most fluent Test hundreds, at Trent Bridge.

Every time I see Darrell Hair now I think of that day and how important his wrong decision was to me. I've always liked him. And not just because he could conceivably have saved my career. Who knows what would have happened to me if he had upheld that appeal? The pressure would have been really on in the second Test, and that match was played on a damp pitch at Lord's, so things could have turned out very differently for me. Darrell is a good umpire (the odd lapse over missing a glove down the leg side notwithstanding) and is not afraid to make a brave decision. If he felt Muralitharan chucked it, he called him and he did it not because he was trying to make a name for himself, simply to do his job to the best of his ability.

It was good to win that series against India through the victory at Edgbaston that came along with my first Test 'Man of the Match' award. There was a feeling that England were getting back on something like the right path and that Ath now had a coach he could work with. He and Bumble were clearly very close, and that was important. And I think Ath was finally getting something like the team he wanted around him, younger players developing together as a unit. I loved playing for David Lloyd. All he ever cared about were his boys in his team. He was a huge character who wore his heart on his sleeve and, like Atherton, nothing was ever done for show. He just wanted England to do well. Bumble, meanwhile, was an enthusiastic, caring coach with modern ideas.

I had a huge amount of time for Ath as a captain. Apart from the odd bout of stubbornness, he had very few failings as a leader. Whether it was because I went back a long way with him I don't know, but I saw him as someone I was desperate to do well for and would always fight for because he gave so much and would fight so hard for his team. And I got on very well with Bumble as a coach. He was so much for you as a player, a real player's coach. He would stick up for you even if it made him look silly and, one of my big hang-ups, would never do anything just to make himself look better. Yes, he was eccentric and sometimes he would lose it. He lost it with me and the team at times, like when we were going up in a lift one day and he announced, 'I wish I'd picked the whole Lancashire side instead of this lot. They're much better,' but you couldn't help warming to the man.

Bumble had his failings, like all of us. He appeared to have his favourites; while others, like Ronnie Irani, struggled to make an impression. But Michael Atherton and David Lloyd simply wanted England to do well. They weren't in it for the money or the glory, or to make themselves look the great captain and coach. And I wanted to play for them.

The rest of the 1996 summer wasn't the greatest. I broke

one of my popadom fingers while scoring that century at Trent Bridge and I faced a race against time to be fit for the first Test of the series against Pakistan, leading to the curious occurrence of being placed in an air bubble to hasten my recovery. It was the idea of our Essex physio, James Davis – a top man and friend, but another big theory man with a lot of letters after his name – and the biggest thing about it was that it involved me wearing a kind of mask to enable me to breathe in there. To get this thing over my beak was most uncomfortable, and I put up with it for about a week before telling James what he could do with his mask and his air bubble.

Experience has told me, as the king of broken fingers, that they take four weeks to heal if the injury has gone into the joint, whatever you try to do to them. That's what nature intended and you just have to put up with it. So I missed the Lord's Test, and it soon became clear that Pakistan would be a very different kettle of fish from India in that their attack contained bowlers of the quality of Wasim Akram, Waqar Younis and Mushtaq Ahmed, all at around their peak. They defeated us comfortably, I returned and got a couple of half-decent scores; but the most important thing was that it felt like a new chapter for English cricket. People like myself, Thorpe, Caddick, Gough, Knight and Cork had become established and I think our arrival and the promise the team generally offered gave Ath a bit of heart to carry on. Not that he was to have a particularly good winter.

Our tour of Zimbabwe and New Zealand got off to a bad start and only really recovered when we got to New Zealand. We had a meeting after selection and it was announced that wives and families were to be completely banned for the whole trip. Evidently people weren't happy with the situation in South Africa the previous winter, when it was felt that the focus had left the tour when the families joined in, towards the end. But the decision was a bit extreme. Instead of trying to find a solution and discuss when the best time for wives to come out might be, the powers that be (whether it was Ath, Bumble or Illy who made the decision I don't know) decided we would be better off on our own for a tour which lasted getting on for four months.

People were not happy about this. And it was difficult for me because I had been made vice-captain for the first time and I had to be loyal to Ath and the decision that had been made. Darren Gough, in particular, was very angry, I remember Graham Thorpe being particularly unhappy, and we had one players' meeting at which things got pretty heated. It was causing huge problems and, even though I agreed with the boys who were upset, I sat there, keeping quiet, out of loyalty to Ath. For possibly the only time in my life, I kept my gob shut and sat on the fence, and luckily the lads didn't quiz me on it because I would probably have agreed with them. From a personal point of view, I've always played my best on tour when Karen has been there because she takes my mind off the cricket in the evenings.

Thing is, we were all old enough and ugly enough to know our own minds and how things like this could affect our cricket. It was up to the individual to decide, I thought, whether it was better or worse for his cricket if his kids were running about at night in his room. At that stage the ECB wouldn't pay for families to have additional rooms, so Ath's argument was that we should go away as a young team and not have any distractions from the cricket, but it was tough for everybody concerned. And now Ath's a family man, I couldn't imagine him putting forward the same argument because I know how hard he finds it now to be away from his boy.

So we were off to a bad start, made worse when Zimbabwe, who were supposed to be the warm-up for New Zealand, took us by surprise by swinging the Kookaburra ball round corners. James Kirtley, then an emerging pro, took wickets against us in a warm-up game, Ath was struggling with his back and the pressure was starting to build.

Really, the pressure should have been eased by the way we played in Bulawayo. I scored a century, the team were on top, and it came down to a run chase of 205 in 37 overs, which we just failed to complete, Nick Knight taking 2 off Heath Streak's final ball instead of the 3 we needed, to leave it as the first drawn Test with the scores being level. It should have been remembered in a positive light, but it wasn't. Instead this was the 'We flipping murdered 'em' Test. That was the comment made by Bumble in the post-match press conference, referring to the wide bowling which Zimbabwe had resorted to in order to stop us from winning the game. They didn't do anything wrong. They just exploited to the limit the laws as they stood at that time by bowling as close to wide deliveries as they could get away with to stop us scoring. Any team would have done the same. I would have done it! But, Bumble being Bumble, he wanted to back up his players and he saw that we were geting frustrated by it all on the sidelines and decided, not for the first or the last time, to speak up in our favour. If our coach had just said, 'We played the better cricket for much of the game,' nothing would have been said, but as Bumble had got quite emotional it caused a bit of a furore, to say the least, and added to our problems as Zimbabwe had much the better of the rest of the tour. (And I'm sure it is one of the reasons why Duncan Fletcher keeps so quiet!)

We drew the second Test, but they won the one-dayers and I was the third victim of a hat-trick which propelled Eddo Brandes, alias the chicken farmer, to international fame. I hadn't even known it was a hat-trick ball because the other two had been taken at the end of the previous over and when I was out I was amazed at the roar from the crowd. I thought, 'I know I got a hundred in Bulawayo but I'm not that good a player. Anyone would think they'd just got Lara out,' until someone shouted 'Hat-trick' at me on my way out and I realized what had been going on.

All the good work of the previous summer – the new dawn,

the fresh start – was in jeopardy now. We had failed to beat Zimbabwe and in some quarters were being described as the worst team in the world. Our captain, meanwhile, was in agony with his back, out of touch with the bat and coming under increasing pressure. We made the long flight direct to New Zealand and, with the jet lag meaning we weren't ready to sleep even though it was 2 a.m., headed straight for a bar where a few of us stayed for a few hours and, yes, had a few drinks.

Next morning Ath was in a totally dishevelled state when he faced the press and immediately had to walk into a barrage of questions from a news reporter who was querying his fitness to captain England. Meanwhile, one tabloid at home was depicting Atherton's face on a sheep's head on the back page, *à la* Graham Taylor and the turnip. It was time for us to rally round. Time for us to support our captain.

As his vice-captain I was at the forefront of that and fully backed up the management in the decision to end the tradition of having a Christmas party with the press because I felt they weren't being fair towards our captain; that caused a stink, as did getting caught up with other dramas on tour, like the situation with Ronnie Irani. Ronnie had had back problems in the build up to that tour and had become involved in the best way to recover from them with the likes of Ian Botham and our Essex physio, James Davis, both of whom had very strong ideas as to the best course of action for Ron to remodel his action. Meanwhile, Ron would talk to me about his problems and I would try to stick up for him with Ath and Bumble, who I always thought had a downer on him. Whether it was over the way Ronnie left Lancashire for Essex, I don't know, but Irani was never their sort of character.

I can actually imagine what Ath's reaction would have been to Ron when he first joined Lancashire. It was probably along the lines of 'Who the hell are you, with your shellsuits, shades and Man United coffee mug?' because Ron has never exactly been backward in coming forward. Ronnie was accused of bringing an injury on tour with him, Craig White was called up, and Bumble later accused me of being in a clique with Ronnie, Graham Thorpe, Dominic Cork and Phil Tufnell that wasn't conducive to team spirit. Not surprisingly, I didn't see it that way. If I spent more time with those players than with some of the others, I would consider that fairly natural because they were the players on the trip I knew best, and if I sometimes put Ronnie's case to management, or other matters, then that was part of my job as vice-captain.

We were in the situation whereby we couldn't have our wives on the trip, and then we were being told that we shouldn't spend too much time with our mates as well. In what other business or walk of life would that happen? This apparent clique seemed to me to consist of half the team and I make no excuse for wanting to spend time with friends within the team on tour. Having said that, Ronnie did push things a bit far with Bumble at times, and there were occasions when he really should have remembered that Bumble was the coach; he had a big say in Ronnie's future and Ronnie should have treated him with a bit more respect.

We certainly had a couple of interesting incidents on what was otherwise a very successful trip that helped reinforce Ath's position significantly. For a start, there was Tufnell being accused of smoking a joint in a bar in Christchurch. Then there was the (I believe) previously undisclosed affair of the England player who mooned to the public out of the window of our coach as we left Auckland. Now, even though the Kiwis are very friendly people, their young supporters can be very abusive, and on this occasion we were getting a lot of stick. So one of our number, in his wisdom, decided to flash his bum out of the back window at them, and wild horses wouldn't drag the name Phil Tufnell from my lips.

But it was over in a flash, so to speak, and I hadn't even known it had happened, as the Goody-two-shoes vice-captain sitting at the front of the bus, until two days later when there was a knock on my door and I opened it to see John Barclay, the tour manager, standing there. Now 'Trout' is a lovely man, everybody thought he was great, but he was perplexed. 'Nasser,' he said, 'we've had a complaint. Someone says an England player mooned at them out of the coach window and we think it was Ronnie. Can you sort it out?' If it wasn't potentially serious it would have sounded funny, because the concept of someone mooning just didn't sound right when spoken of in John Barclay's posh tones; but off I went to Ronnie to ask if it was him, because in management's eyes at that stage everything that went wrong was Ronnie's fault. 'Oh, it's got to be me,' said Ron. 'They think I've done everything. It wasn't me but, go on, tell them it was me. I'll take the rap if it makes it easier.' And he did. Ronnie took the blame to make sure his friend Tufnell didn't get in trouble and that was a measure of the man then, something that has made my subsequent falling-out with him all the tougher to comprehend.

Elsewhere, there was the saga of Dominic Cork. Dom had been allowed to join the tour late because he had been going through a marriage break-up, but when he arrived he clearly wasn't in the right shape for an England tour, mentally or physically, and came close to being sent home again. It was all go!

And the cricket? Well, Auckland will be remembered as the game when Danny Morrison, who had more ducks to his name than anyone else in Test cricket, held out for hours on the final day to earn a draw for New Zealand in the first Test when victory for us seemed assured. Earlier that match, we had been treated to the spectacle of David Lloyd at his vintage best when Alan Mullally, in particular, had made a poor start with the new ball in helpful conditions. When we came back to the dressing room at lunch, we expected a bollocking for not taking advantage of winning the toss, but Bumble was nowhere to be seen. Instead we could just about see the shape of this figure, pacing around at the back of the ground and shaking his head. It was

Bumble. He was too angry to say anything to us at lunchtime and went for a walk. I loved him for it. For me, it was like going back to my Essex Second Team days and having the eccentric Ray East in charge. It was the sort of thing I would do. How someone like Duncan Fletcher remains calm, sits down and analyses bad sessions with us I will never know. Bumble was always a great admirer of Alex Ferguson, but I suspect that if Man United were three down at half-time to Leeds Fergie might not have reacted by walking round an empty field on his own! We knew we had to put it right, and we did so until Morrison intervened; and the youth of New Zealand, bless them, decided to taunt us afterwards with 'Morrison, quack, quack, quack'. For their troubles they were greeted with the sight of Phil Tufnell's arse (or was it Ronnie Irani's?) smiling at them from our coach window.

We're very similar to New Zealand as a team and we have had some good, close series with them. And this one went our way, with victory at Wellington and then a nail-biting successful run-chase at Christchurch which could easily have gone the other way. We had to chase 307 to win, which is a big score batting last, and everyone contributed, notably our captain, who was emerging from his bad patch and scored runs in both innings in Christchurch. Towards the end, when John Crawley and Dominic Cork were edging us closer to home, it all got very tense and myself, Tufnell and Thorpe were glued to the dressing-room sofa, unable to move in case it tempted fate and led to one of our batsmen being out. I even had a cigarette on, and I never smoke.

It was smoke that caused the last controversy of the tour. But whether there was fire to accompany it I just don't know. Phil Tufnell was accused of smoking a cigarette of the illegal type in a bar in Christchurch but was cleared of any wrongdoing, despite the stink it caused back home. Tuffers is one of the biggest characters to have graced English cricket during my time in the game, and I always wanted him on my side. He's a good friend and I make no apologies for that, whatever anyone else may think about him! I would have him in my side simply because he was the best English spin bowler I ever faced, a proper spin bowler, and he was one of the last of the breed in that respect. He was an artist and he knew his art. But I also loved having him around because he made life more enjoyable. He was a huge presence, and you need people like that around. Yes, he has a self-destruct button and he has been known to flirt dangerously with it at times, but whenever there has been an incident involving Phil Tufnell, it has been resolved very quickly, he has been sorry instantly, and it has been over.

For a captain, Phil was insecure, but a great team man. He had a great knowledge of cricket, sometimes an underestimated quality of his, and I would often speak to him if I needed any advice during a game. If he hadn't been a lunatic he would have made a great vice-captain. In the end he drifted out of the England side, not really through people becoming fed up with his behaviour but rather because the game had moved on and, as a spinner, you needed that element of mystery to prosper. Or be an all-rounder who can offer more with the bat than Phil ever could. Towards the end of his career, Tuffers would watch people like Murali, Warne or Harbajhan spinning it further than he ever could and he would say, 'What's going on here? This bloke's making me look like an idiot,' and it was tough for him to take. And he was never going to make up for his shortcomings by endearing himself to the coaching staff or working hard at his batting and fielding. If Phil Tufnell had played ten years earlier, he would have earned a lot more Test caps, but as it turned out he was remembered as much for his personality as for his bowling, and it's lovely that he has cashed in on that by making a great career for himself on the celebrity circuit. I'm delighted that Phil's life has taken off in such a positive direction after winning *I'm a celebrity, get me out of here!* He is a very likeable, genuine bloke, and you want good things to happen to people like that. Tuffers would never be two-faced.

If he didn't like you or didn't agree with something you'd done, he would tell you, and I could talk cricket with Tuffers all night, asking him about any situation because Phil had seen them all. He'd had ten lives by the time I met him, so God knows how many he's had now.

Towards the end of his career I guess I was the only selector who really wanted him in the side. There was a time that Darren Gough talks about when we were in South Africa and Tuffers was being very half-hearted in a fielding drill being operated by Duncan Fletcher and I shouted at him, 'I got you on this trip, don't let me down,' and that was certainly how I felt at times towards Phil. But he remains one of my closest friends in the game, and I don't care what the truth was about his apparent misdemeanour in New Zealand or anywhere else. The game (and the dressing room) needs characters, and Phil Tufnell is certainly that!

I 2

Essex had some good times in the mid-to-late 1990s – but nothing like the domination of county cricket, which ran out in 1992 after something like thirteen years of pretty much unbroken success. When I look back at those years now, I'm afraid that much of what happened to me and to Essex is a bit of a blur, such was my total focus on international cricket.

Looking at it in summary, I can say I played in three domestic finals (always a highlight in a cricketer's career), winning two of them but being embarrassed in the first, in 1996, by Lancashire. I can also say that I was there when Graham Gooch finally decided to retire, aged forty-four, in 1997 and that I became Essex captain in 1999, my benefit year. Yet that is not nearly as big a deal as it really should be, because by that time international cricket was all-enveloping and I was very much a part-time leader of Essex, especially since I became England captain in the same year.

Those were the highs, but there were certainly lows, like finishing bottom of the championship in 1998 and seeing Paul Prichard, Gooch's successor, resign the captaincy before they asked me to take on the job, a sad time for a man I have known since I was a kid and a bloke who really should have achieved so much more in the game.

At the centre of everything in these years at Chelmsford, though, was Stuart Law, who arrived as our overseas player in 1996. He was an Australian who was little known to those who followed only international cricket, but he went on to become one of the most successful foreign batsmen in the club's history. Stuey was – still is – a great player. He may have played only one Test Match (for reasons of personality as well as the vast amount of talent at Australia's disposal), but he could really bat and he dominated county attacks as mercilessly as anyone else who has played the domestic game in modern times.

We were never really that close, and later we were to clash quite vitriolically, but I guess that was because we were different in so many ways. Stuey was a 'let's go and have a beer', matey sort of bloke; outwardly abrasive, he liked a good time and was typically Australian in much of what he did. I was inwardly abrasive, yes, but much more insular than Stuey, and while we were both intense about our cricket we could never be said to be friends. We just had a mutual respect.

Paul Prichard was very close to Stuey. Prich was someone I knew from way back. He had played with my brothers, was something of a hero figure to me early on, and (while I know this is a big call) I would say he was the most talented batsman to come through Essex Schools in the last thirty years. Prich got double-hundreds for fun at schoolboy level. He had tremendous natural ability and everybody was sure he would be our next great batsman when he first came into the side, but by the time Prich inherited the captaincy from Graham Gooch it was clear that those hopes would never be fully realized.

I remember getting a call from Graham Saville, our head of cricket, when Graham Gooch packed it in, telling me that, while I was a candidate for the job, it was probably going to Prich ahead of the other obvious choice, John Stephenson. I had no problem with that. I had a tremendous amount of respect for Prich. Derek Pringle later told me that he had recommended me as captain then, but was told by the Essex hierarchy that he was mad to even think about it, such was the mistrust of my temperament in those days by some people at the club; but I was so consumed with England that I never really aspired to the job at county level anyway.

Essex always worked to a 'who's next in line' policy. They are a family club, have never wanted to do anything radical, and have always looked after their old players. That's fine to an extent, even hugely admirable in many ways, but in my opinion it has also been a massive factor in the county's underachievement in the last few years. The easy option is not always the best. And much as I was pleased for Prich when Saville told me he was getting the job, I couldn't help but think that Stephenson might have been a better choice. It was just a gut instinct. I certainly knew 'Stan' Stephenson would be hurt not to get it. He really wanted it. He is an intense guy, and maybe that counted against him, but, in the same way that people weren't sure how I would react to the responsibilities of leadership, they could have taken a punt on Stan and been pleasantly surprised.

So upset was Stephenson at this development that he took himself off to Hampshire on the promise of succeeding Mark Nicholas as captain, and he wasn't exactly a roaring success at the helm there; but it might have been different at his home county. Not that I begrudged Prich his chance. It was clear by this stage that he wasn't going to play for England, so it was a nice honour for an outstanding Essex player. Paul has always been a 'happy with his lot' sort of person. He never really pushed himself too much. That was his problem, really. He was almost too nice. Just satisfied with nice forties and fifties when he should have gone on to much bigger scores on a more regular basis. And that personality, together with a serious finger injury when at his peak, was why Paul Prichard didn't achieve as much as it had looked as if he would when he was breaking all sorts of records at school, but you really can't hold that against him. We are all as we are, and Prich is an extremely likeable bloke, something I'm sure is as important to him as any achievements on the field.

It is important to realize that everyone has a different character and priorities in life. Not everyone had my intensity and not everybody wanted to be like me. The last thing I want to do is to say that what worked for me would work for everybody else and that I am somehow better for being driven. Each to their own, and there was an awful lot of merit in Prich's approach to life.

When things were going OK on the field for Essex, Prich was an efficient captain. It was only a bit later that he struggled. He wasn't great tactically, so Keith Fletcher, then the coach, would virtually run the team from the sidelines. We would come in at lunch and Fletch would sit Paul down and tell him which bowlers to use at what times, something that I didn't think was healthy because the buck really does need to stop with the captain when things are not going well. At least in Keith Fletcher we had one of the great tacticians pulling the strings behind the scenes.

But Prich was a good calming influence in the dressing room and, because he got on so well with Stuey Law, the Australian was quickly integrated into the team, and the pair of them flourished at the top of the order. And they flourished off the field too. Later on, Prich and Stuey were to get annoyed with me for mentioning in the press that they liked a drink, but they had completely misconstrued what I was trying to say, which I will explain later. I had no problem with the pair of them having a drink in the evenings. It worked for them. One of my biggest things is being able to integrate all sorts of personalities into the team framework and concentrating on what they could rather than couldn't do, and I would have been more worried about Paul Prichard and Stuart Law if they had gone to bed at 9 p.m. rather than have a few drinks after close of play.

Yet what you have to be careful of is the influence you can have on younger players. We had some impressionable young guys coming through and, while it would be harsh to say we had a drink culture in the side, there were certainly a few blokes who felt that, if Prich and Stuey could have a drink, then why couldn't they? The problem came when they couldn't cope so well with that lifestyle and it would affect their game. Someone like Danny Law was often on his last warning for going out too much, but if he was bollocked by Prich he would start muttering, 'How can he have a go at me. He was out with us!' and problems started to creep into our side.

Fletch would ask Prich not to go out so much, Prich would start sneaking out, and the whole thing snowballed a bit. The difference is that people like Prich and Stuey – and others like Robin Smith and Matthew Maynard – can lead a busy social life and it has no effect on their cricket at all. But what other, younger players have to realize is that this doesn't mean they can do it and turn up and score hundreds and take wickets the next day. It's weak of players to follow the crowd that way and just expect success; but if you are going to hand out the bollockings as captain you have to be a little whiter than white and that's where Prich let himself down somewhat.

The biggest setback he had was when an accidental Allan Donald beamer shattered one of his fingers at Chelmsford earlier in his career, no question; but I never saw him really push himself on the field. He would do enough to stay in the Essex side and that was his choice, but with a bit more hunger he could have achieved so much more.

The biggest disappointment of our 1996 NatWest final capitulation to Lancashire was that it was Graham Gooch's last big day at Lord's. He hadn't announced his retirement by that stage, but it was becoming clear that even he couldn't go on for ever and it was a huge shame that he went out on a ground he had graced so often, with us being all out for 57 in my first domestic final. Graham was seventh out for 10, scored in 20 overs, and I could see that many of our lads were wondering if that was to be their only taste of the big time, that they had blown their opportunity to shine in the spotlight. For me, I was concerned that Graham had gone out on such a low at Lord's, a place he loved (and which I later came to love in a similar way). He didn't deserve that.

But we were back, stronger, the following year, this time without Graham Gooch, during a period when perhaps I had my best times as a one-day player. Essex would feel confident about chasing any total. We didn't have the strongest bowling attack but we had a couple of good swing bowlers in Mark Ilott and Ashley Cowan, and we would be confident that we could keep teams to a par score and then just unleash Prichard and Law on them. They would get us off to a flyer and then I would come in and finish the job off, along with people like Ronnie Irani and Robert Rollins, our young wicketkeeper who, but for injury, would have achieved more in the game.

In 1997 we played very well in reaching the NatWest semi-final, where we came up against Glamorgan and (I only discovered recently) one Duncan Fletcher as their coach; his presence that day had completely passed me by because I didn't know him at that stage. I captained our side in Prich's absence and it turned out to be one of the most explosive cup ties in years, notable for a shoving match between Mark Ilott and Robert Croft and verbal confrontations featuring Stuey Law, Ronnie Irani and Darren Thomas. This was also the start of Ronnie's love–hate relationship with Glamorgan and, in particular, Matthew Maynard, and the whole thing was quite comical in many ways, as well as being very serious at the time.

It was a televised game and it was getting very tense. When he was batting I could see Ronnie's eyes had gone with the adrenalin flowing and, when he was given out lbw, he just started running down the wicket, to be met by the bowler Darren Thomas who turned and, in celebration, caught Ronnie with what looked like a right hook. Certainly there was a double take in our dressing room, like 'Has he just punched Ronnie?' Then there was the Thomas beamer at Stuey, and by this time some of our lads, like Ilott, were getting so wound up by it all that they almost jumped off the Chelmsford balcony to get involved!

By the time Mark was batting, the light was very bad and he did the right thing in appealing against it. Glamorgan, meanwhile, were on a roll and wanted to carry on, and there was this silly pushing thing between Ilott and Robert Croft, good friends whose wives were watching together in the crowd, and it made the BBC news and all the morning papers! I know it looked bad, cricketers involved in physical contact, but when you know the characters involved it becomes much more amusing. Those two are the original 'handbags at ten paces' merchants and I know they were both distraught about it afterwards; they were ringing each other up to apologize for weeks! We did go off for bad light in the end and then, apparently, the umpire David Constant, an emotional man, went into the Glamorgan dressing room, evidently to make a big speech about how he had never seen anything like this in cricket, but he was quickly told to go away by Duncan Fletcher and left in tears! Some game.

We won a dramatic semi-final the next morning by one wicket, with Peter Such, who didn't know one end of a bat from the other, hitting the winning boundary; and we cruised to victory in the final against Warwickshire, a game that had lost a lot of its glamour as it had been postponed a day because of the funeral of Princess Diana. For us, though, it was a cup final win at Lord's, and they will always be stored away in your memory bank as career highlights. Ilott and Cowan bowled really well and then Stuey Law took Allan Donald to pieces, he played like God. And I was there, batting at the end too, which was a nice feeling and one that made up for the previous year's embarrassment. That was our motivation all along.

Earlier that summer we had finally said goodbye to Graham Gooch, the end of the career of one of the greatest players the English game has known. As usual with Graham it was low-key. We were at Northampton and he just asked me if I wanted to have a walk round the ground and an ice cream. He bought me a 99 and just said, 'I'm packing it in, thought I'd let you know before it becomes public.' And that was it. Graham announced his decision in a paper the next day and he played one more game before retiring. He really did leave a massive hole in both Essex and England cricket.

It was one that, despite our one-day success, we struggled to fill. We won the Benson and Hedges Cup in 1998 but by that time the cracks in Paul's leadership were starting to show. I guess I was emerging as a credible alternative and had actually led the side most of the way to Lord's that season, as Prich was injured before he came back to captain us to victory in the final against Leicestershire. Basically, he had lost the dressing room. Firstly, he just wasn't running the show and was thought of as a bit of a puppet, and secondly, because of his wholehearted approach to life off the pitch, he was finding it hard to crack the whip with any sort of credibility.

At least he had one more big day in charge – even though, at the time, it rankled with me a little bit that I wasn't captain at Lord's after being in charge for most of the cup run. I got runs against Leicester and I think one of the reasons for that was that I was used to playing for England and was pretty relaxed in the build-up to the finals. I had a curry with Karen the night before the match and barely thought about the game, something I wish I could have repeated over the years when playing for England. I have always been better when I haven't been too worried about failing, but it's not proved easy to switch that mentality on over the years!

In the end I think the powers that be had a little word in Prich's ear and told him they really thought he should concentrate on his batting from now on. He resigned and I don't think he felt too resentful about it; Prich is far too nice a guy to bear grudges. And I was asked to become Essex captain. I'm afraid I can't tell you who asked me or what the circumstances were. My memory is terrible on some things. England was everything and, unbeknown to me, I was about to become captain of my country, a development that was to nip my spell at the helm of my county rapidly in the bud. But before that were two of my best years as an England player, featuring the best innings I have ever played. Not in a county match, or even a normal Test; it was against Australia in the first match of the 1997 Ashes series that I scored a double century. To this day I have never played as well as that again.

13

It is the biggest series of them all. And form is irrelevant. You can win five Tests in a row before taking on Australia in an Ashes series, and it will make no difference to the task in front of you. It's a one-off and you have to perform there and then to the very best of your ability to have any chance of matching them.

Looking back, the 1997 Ashes series in England was my best chance of being on the winning side against the great enemy. They were hardly a poor side, far from it, but perhaps they were not quite as strong as others I have faced, and certainly not as good as the side we played in 2002–3, which arguably was the greatest Test outfit in history. We were entering the summer of 1997 on the back of our good win in New Zealand and there was a mood of optimism about the country, with people like Christopher Martin-Jenkins writing that he believed we would win the Ashes.

I think we approached the series in a realistic frame of mind. Certainly we weren't getting carried away because of anything that had happened in New Zealand, but there was definitely a settled look to our side, and the mood was improved when England won the one-day series 3–0, thanks in part to the emergence of the Hollioake brothers. Ben, in particular, made a huge impact, playing the Aussies off his legs at Lord's as well as anyone ever has, and I remember watching him on TV and thinking, 'God, this lad can play.'

I wasn't there to see it in person. I had been left out of the one-day squad – and rightly so, because I couldn't tell one end of my bat from the other during the early part of that season, I just couldn't buy a run. The real low point for me came during a game at Gloucester, just before the first Test, when I was out for a low score and I remember saying to Keith Fletcher, 'God, Fletch, what am I going to do? I've got the Australians this summer and I'm in the worst form of my life.' The wise old sage just turned to me and said, 'You'll be all right, mate. You're thinking about it too much. Next week's a Test Match. Completely different. Just go in there with a clear mind, and you will be fine.'

It meant a lot to me because I respected him so much, and it eased the panic I was feeling about having to play against the likes of McGrath, Warne and Gillespie, bowlers I hadn't had to face often at that stage. I never thought my place was in jeopardy because I had played well in Test cricket during the winter, but I had an anxious few weeks before the first Test of the summer at Edgbaston.

This was the start, really, of my proper preparations for playing Tests. I decided I had to go about things in a thoroughly professional way. I told myself to treat the Test as my first match of the summer and to get some videos of the opposition's bowling attack. So the concierge at the Swallow Hotel in Birmingham received an unusual request from one of their guests at the start of Test Match week, 1997. I asked for a big TV and video to be sent to my room, and they just placed it in the middle of my room and for three days I watched nothing except tapes of their bowlers over and over again. I just left the TV on all the time, and I got annoyed when sometimes I would return to my room to find that someone had turned it off. I watched them all, even people like Steve Waugh and Michael Bevan, who might not bowl much. With Bevan it was a case of which way was he spinning it, what was he doing with the ball, because left-arm wrist spinners are so unusual.

It was also the start of me visualizing what might happen in the middle. I went out to the wicket in the days leading up to the Test, looked down it and imagined Shane Warne bowling at me. And then McGrath. And then Mick Kasprowicz, who was in the Australian side at that time. I'd imagine them sledging me, different match situations and what the ball was doing from all of the bowlers. In the evenings my teammates would barely see me. I just wanted to stay in on my own during the build-up to the match. It's something that became a habit after that game, really, and something that I may have overdone in the subsequent years. Sometimes it would have been more healthy for me to go out from time to time in order to clear my mind and get away from it all, but it became a routine part of my preparation to get myself a room service curry and think about the task ahead.

My mates in the side would ring me up and say, 'What are you doing tonight?' but I would always just do my own thing from 1997 onwards, and in the end they stopped ringing me. I found a good Indian takeaway in Birmingham who would deliver to my room and I just started to enjoy the time alone. It has worked for me. Maybe as I got to the end of my career I should have gone back to how I used to be, been a bit more sociable. Mike Atherton used to tell me I needed to enjoy myself a bit more during a Test. He told me I should get a life because if I just sat in my room thinking about cricket, playing cricket then doing it all again at the next venue over and over without a break, I wouldn't actually enjoy being an international cricketer. I just couldn't bring myself to do it. And the reason I couldn't bring myself to do it was because my new-found professional preparations (not that I had exactly taken the game lightly before) worked for me at Edgbaston in 1997. And worked in such a spectacular way that I didn't want to change anything afterwards.

That's the problem with the mind games you play with yourself. It's not just about being in the zone, it's getting yourself *into* the zone that matters. It's a complicated business. You can prepare in so many different ways, and quite a few of them work. So you try to stick to a routine that works. This one worked for me.

It was an amazing Test. It was the start of an Ashes series that people thought we could actually win, and the atmosphere at Edgbaston was fantastic. Mark Taylor won the toss and decided to bat, as was his wont, even though it was a humid morning. And we just rolled them. It was just the most incredible day in the field. Everything worked. Everything stuck. Everything went to plan. Darren Gough and Andrew Caddick bowled exceptionally well. Some of the Australians did not relish Caddy at all, and they were already a little wary of Gough because he had done well against them before.

Gough's body language and aura were amazing that day. At one point he got Greg Blewett out with a no-ball, but he was unmoved and just said, 'I'll have to get him next ball.' And he did. Caught by me. As if it was all part of the script for that match. At one point they were 54 for 8 and I couldn't believe what was happening. Warne hit a few and got them up to 118 but, even so, it was a great performance by England's bowlers and one that got the batsmen fired up and ready to try to do our bit with the bat.

Mark Butcher was making his debut in this Test. It's funny. Butch was someone I wasn't sure about, but he went on to become one of my best friends in the side, a sure sign that you should never assume in advance what a person is like. When we played against each other as young players, we didn't get on because I thought he was an arrogant so-and-so and he thought the same of me. He was one of the Surrey strutters. He had to have his shades on and his cap the wrong way round. He had a real natural swagger to him and I used to think, 'Who the hell do you think you are?' We laugh about it now. When I met Butch properly, that summer, I realized he was a genuine, calm, relaxed man who knew his game, was very talented and was very much a team man. I learned so much from him about how to bat with a relaxed mindset and low heartbeat. That's why we batted well together. I made him concentrate more than he wanted to, and he made me relax more than my drive let me!

More importantly, he became a true friend on and off the field. He'd always ring me up in my room to see if I wanted to come out for a drink with him, even though most of the times I'd say, 'No, thanks, I'm having a curry takeaway and watching a video of an opposition bowler.' He'd laugh and tell me I should get out more, but he never stopped ringing. That we could be so different in our approach to life and yet become such a good partnership on and off the field underlined that there was more than one way to become a successful cricketer – a fact I always tried to remember as captain.

It was a great Test in which to make your debut, even though Butch didn't score too many. I was batting at four and had visualized every possibility ahead of me. So much so that when Butch was out and I found myself joining Alec Stewart at the wicket, with us 2 wickets down for not very many, I was up for it and was ready to receive my first ball from Kasprowicz, who had spent the season at Essex with us in 1994.

Whether time has distorted this memory or not, I don't know, but I went out to bat in the most incredible zone I have ever experienced. As Keith Fletcher had said to me, you are only ever a couple of shots away from being back in form, and Kasper bowled a couple to me I could clip away; and I felt good from the start, all my early-season problems virtually forgotten immediately. Whether their bowlers were not at their best I don't know. But Glenn McGrath had lost a bit of his nip and I remember thinking, 'This is like facing Angus Fraser.' Kasper was trying to swing it but couldn't find his swing and Jason Gillespie had a bit of pace but bowled me a few short ones, which I successfully pulled. I thought, 'I can handle all of these.'

The big hurdle was still to come. Shane Warne. I had faced him occasionally in 1993 but not too much, and I remember thinking, 'I hope I'm not on strike when he comes on in case I get a Gatting ball.' History has a way of repeating itself. Shane was right at his peak then, probably between the years 1995 and 2000. He was brilliant and a major threat to us. But the thing that gave me more confidence was that Edgbaston is not the greatest place to bowl spin. OK, it turns a bit, but it comes on nicely. When Shane came on, the drift was awkward – but, again, I thought he was a little under par. Either that or I was in the form of my life. Probably a bit of both!

I was just relishing the whole battle. Everything I hit seemed to go for 4. I hardly had to run any 2s or 3s and the outfield was very quick. Then I became determined to cash in. Everything seemed to be in my favour, including the arrival at the wicket of Graham Thorpe, who I always enjoy batting with. We know each other so well that we never discuss things too much. We just have a little chat. Like, on this day, it was 'Is it swinging? Is Warney spinning it or just drifting it? Are you picking him? What pace is Gillespie?' Those sort of things. The remarkable thing thereafter was that our scores were virtually identical. We put on a big stand, and we always seemed to be around the same figure all the way up, until he beat me to a hundred.

Australia were getting distinctly agitated in the field. Their body language was not the same as it usually is. Mark Taylor was under a lot of pressure because of a poor run of form and, even by his standards, he was quiet. Steve Waugh was almost sledging his own side, saying, 'Come on, we're playing for Australia here,' and, to make things better, Gillespie went off, injured. That meant the introduction of Justin Langer as substitute, someone who has never been short of a word. At one point Justin sledged me, he said something and I said to him, 'Look, I don't mind this lot chirping me, but you've just come on. You're just the fucking bus driver of this team, so you get back on the bus and get ready to drive it back to the hotel this evening.' I was really pumped up. Even Mark Waugh gave me a little smile after that one. I think he found it amusing.

Even now the memories are vivid. At no stage did I feel tired or lacking energy. I just wanted it to carry on for ever. At the end of the first day I was on 80 not out and I received a lot of phone calls, from people like Graham Gooch and others, telling me to carry on and that the job wasn't finished. Atherton said to me, 'For the first time in a long time we've got them by the balls. You keep going and make sure you keep Thorpey going too.' At that stage the little man had a reputation for getting out between 50 and 100, but everything just felt so right I was sure he wouldn't do that this time.

I was really calm that night. Unusual for me! I was wanting more. I was completely in control. When I've batted for a long time my sleep pattern changes. If I'm not batting, I tend not to be able to sleep until two in the morning and then I wake up early. But if I'm batting and have got runs, because of the concentration and the mental side of things I just fall asleep early. That night I had half a glass of wine and was asleep by eight. Trouble was, I was awake again at twelve and just had fitful sleep for the rest of the night as I started thinking about McGrath and the new ball. I can think of better dreams to have!

As a player I used to over-complicate the game. That was definitely a failing in me. My fear of failure didn't let me get in the zone as often as I should have done. I was too much of a thinker, constantly worried that I wouldn't get many runs. I used to look at people like Darren Gough and think that it seemed so natural to him. That's a great asset to have; it's like you need to do all your thinking before you go out on the pitch in the morning, and then completely switch off. I know it sounds weird, but that's the perfect mental state to be in. When you're waiting to bat, you have to try to get your heartbeat down, to stop yourself going at 100 miles an hour. John Crawley was the worst at waiting to bat. Every five minutes he would light up another fag and go to the loo. Never stopped. Mike Atherton always seemed to get in a good, relaxed state. He would sit there with his *Racing Post* and look to have not a care in the world. Yes, he was interested in racing, but it was more to do with switching off from the cricket. The preparations were done and it was time to relax in the build-up to batting.

The reason I mention all this is that none of my usual worries affected me at Edgbaston in 1997. I was not worried about failure. I was able to switch off and keep my heartbeat down. It all came so naturally. And do you know the funniest thing? I have rarely been able to do it again since. Rarely been able to replicate my state of mind or the zone I was in at that time. I have come close, but things have never quite been the same, and that is a great mystery to me.

I have always known exactly how many runs I have got during any innings. Again it goes back to my dad and every run being vital. I have never needed a scoreboard to tell me what I was on. So I didn't need anybody to tell me when I hit Michael Bevan for 4 to go from 99 to 103. It was a very special feeling. Then it was a case of remembering what Gooch and Atherton had said, and trying to bat for as long as we possibly could. We couldn't let those bastards back in the game. We just needed to kill them.

Thorpey went for 138, Crawley was out cheaply and I was in with Mark Ealham as the runs kept coming. I remember going past 150 and then setting myself the target of 197 because that was my top score for Essex then. Warne was bowling. I was on 188 when Shane bowled me a loopy one on leg stump which was almost a yorker, and I clipped it to mid-wicket for 4. Then he bowled me a flatter one and I hit that for 4 too. The next one was almost a carbon copy but it was stopped in the field. Now came the big moment. Shane bowled me a flipper and I picked it straight away and played it accordingly. It raced for 4 and I didn't know what to do with myself. Mark Ealham has always rucked with me because I didn't go to him for a hug but, let's be honest, I knew I would probably never get a double-hundred against Australia again and I just wanted to savour the moment on my own. I made sure I took my helmet off and acknowledged all the crowd. Mark Waugh, or 'burger arse' as I called him in those days, came up to me and said, 'Well played, but we've seen enough of you now, so fuck off back to the pavilion.'

It was my finest moment as a cricketer. I hadn't got 200 against any side before, and here I was doing it against Australia in the biggest match I'd experienced so far. The Australians were very good about it, as they always are, and to have someone like Shane Warne saying, 'Well played, mate' meant a lot. My whole game is about targets but I didn't have one left after reaching 200. I knew that the declaration was about an hour away so I went for my shots and in the end I nicked one from Shane to Ian Healy on 207. If I had played it straighter instead of trying to turn it to leg, I would have been all right, but I could hardly be unhappy with myself. In fact, it was the nearest I've ever come to being completely contented with an innings. I'd hit 38 fours, apparently a record for an Ashes innings by an Englishman, and I couldn't believe what was happening to me.

I get very down when I fail, but success has never really affected me. Dad was great. He rang and said, 'Well done, and can I have some tickets because I can relax and watch, now you're out.' He had been too nervous to watch my innings at the ground. I knew I had played a world-class innings, but I also knew I wasn't a world-class player. I obviously hoped I would continue in that vein but I never expected it. Yes, I've scored quite a few other Test Match hundreds and at times came close to playing that well, like maybe at Christchurch in 2002, but I quickly went back to the same fears of failure and technical problems. Alec Stewart said to me afterwards, 'I didn't know you could bat that well.' Nor did I!

We went on to win the Test, I was Man of the Match and people really thought we could then win the Ashes. I was even pleased for Mark Taylor when he scored a hundred in their second innings. I've never really known Mark, only had about half a dozen words with him in my life, but I've always had a high regard for him and the cerebral way he's led their side. This time that innings saved his bacon, and I think it was the only time I've ever been really pleased for an opposition player when he has scored a century. It was the perfect Test Match!

For the next two weeks I was inundated with requests and demands on my time: photo shoots, all sorts of things, which I tried to keep down to a minimum. In some ways it was my fifteen minutes of fame (at least until I became captain) and a lot of people wanted a piece of me. I remember being down at Sussex and doing an interview with Brough Scott for the *Sunday Telegraph* and then it was a question of 'No more. I've got to get on with my cricket now.' It became quite difficult off the field for a while, but in a way which you accept because it is as a result of you doing something special.

And it was not that easy on the field either. There was a lot of rain at Lord's in the second Test, but it was most notable for the fact that Glenn McGrath found his form and hit back at us in the strongest possible way. He had clearly lost his nip at Edgbaston and there was even one point in that match when I saw Mark Waugh talking to Mark Taylor and I could tell from their hand signals that they were talking about McGrath and how he wasn't getting his wrist behind the ball. It was quite revealing and they were clearly worried about him. Not for long!

McGrath bowled us out for 77 at Lord's and I got out to him the first ball after a rain break, which was particularly annoying because I wasn't properly focused on the ball, something that has always been unforgivable to me, even after a rain delay. We scraped our way to a draw, but the worrying thing was, they had got their momentum back and McGrath was bowling really well again.

Old Trafford for the third Test was really damp but Taylor took the brave decision to bat first to try to ensure that Warne was bowling last on it, and only a hundred from Steve Waugh saved him from a bad call. I swear we had Waugh first ball. I can see it now, how Caddick bowled him a yorker and it hit him stone dead in front, but it wasn't given. Of course, Steve made us pay for that.

I hate Old Trafford; I've never done well there. The people are nice but the ground is never full, the weather is always terrible and the ground looks so run-down and old. The square is always tired and sandy and the outfield is bumpy. One year, their chief executive, Jim Cumbes, even suggested that the England team should come up and try to drum up support themselves. Well, I'm sorry, mate, our job is to turn up and try to win a Test Match for England, and I think we'll leave the marketing to you. If you can't fill your ground, there are other places emerging which probably can, like Riverside and the Rose Bowl.

As usual I didn't score many in this third Test, and the bad vibes I get in Manchester were compounded by the controversy over a catch I took in the second innings to dismiss Greg Blewett. He prodded forward to Robert Croft and nicked it and I dived forward at slip with my head up and fingers down. I felt the ball bounce on the front of my fingers and then up into my hands. Then and now I have no idea whether I caught that ball cleanly or not. I am one hundred per cent certain of my uncertainty. Yet it caused a hell of a stink.

People said then that cricketers always know if they have caught a ball cleanly, and I know in a perfect world it would be lovely if you could always take the word of a fielder over a catch, in time-honoured cricketing tradition, but I can honestly say that there are some catches about which you are never sure. It can be to do with your head position, you can hear a thud, but when the ball is in front of you it's difficult to tell at times. I didn't start celebrating. Our players came up to me to congratulate me but I said, 'I don't know if I caught that.' Blewett was looking at me, the umpires were

22. I was always to be found at the back in any team run, even when I was captain. My fitness has never been the best.

23. The innings that makes me most proud: a double hundred against Australia at Edgbaston in 1997. To this day I don't know how I batted so well. I was never able to reach those heights again.

24. The big moment. A double hundred against Australia in 1997.

25. Mike Atherton was an inspiration and role model for me as England captain.

26. Beating Australia at the Oval under Atherton in 1997.

27. Waiting for the umpire's decision as Australia celebrate. My policy was never to walk.

28. Dismissed by Shane Warne in a one-day final in Sydney, the moment that looked to have cost me my World Cup place.

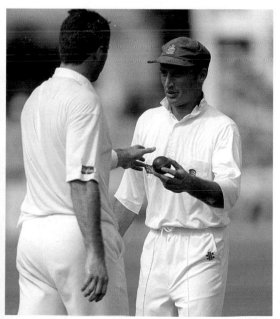

29. Handing Ronnie Irani the ball during my brief spell as Essex captain.

30. Duncan Fletcher has been the most significant figure in England's improvement since 1999. It was my pleasure and good fortune to have him at my side.

31. A proud moment. Sitting with the England team for my first game as captain, against New Zealand at Edgbaston in 1999. We won the match but lost the series.

32. My biggest fear for English cricket is what happens next after Duncan Fletcher goes.

33. My only bowl in Test cricket! At Durban against South Africa at the end of 1999, bringing back memories of my leg-spinning formative years! I took two first-class wickets for Essex: Stuart Lampitt and the great Viv Richards!

34. Darren Gough accepts South African congratulations after scoring the winning runs in the discredited Test in Centurion. Hansie Cronje walks off, deep in his own thoughts.

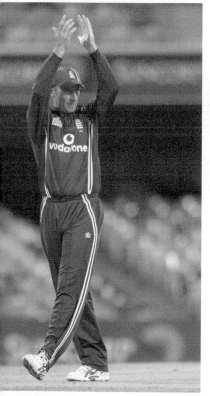

35. An early victory with the one-day side.

36. Walking off in the dark in Karachi after winning the final Test.

37. Taking it all in, in the aftermath of our dramatic win in Karachi, late in 2000.

38. Leading the singing after winning in Karachi.

39. Returning with the trophy from our momentous win in Pakistan.

40. Lifting the Wisden Trophy at the Oval in 2000. By that stage, the England captaincy had become more important to me than life or death.

41. I will always remember being captain of an England side that won four Test series in a row. Here I display our silverware with, left to right, Marcus Trescothick, Alec Stewart, Andy Caddick and Graeme Hick.

conferring and I said to them, 'Look, I think I've caught it but I'm not sure.' They gave him out, but the Australians were not happy.

For the rest of the session until lunch I was watching replays of the catch on the big screen and even in slow motion I don't think it was possible to tell if it was clean or not. It looked as if the ball had bounced on the grass but I think it bounced on the ends of my fingers and into my hands. That's not how the Aussies saw it. I'd had a bit of a taste of their sledging before then, but nothing like this. They really let me have it. When I batted again it was 'Let's get this cheat out' and worse. Not that it contributed to my failure. I never get runs at Old Trafford, and this time was no different. But after the match, as I was driving home, there were phone-ins about my honesty and the whole question of whether a cricketer knows when he has caught a ball.

In our dressing room all the lads thought it was clean but I'm sure in theirs everyone was saying, 'It bounced, it bounced.' That's human nature. I would have been exactly the same in Australia's position. I still get reminded about it at times now, like when Greg Blewett's wife came up to me in a bar on my last Ashes tour and said, 'You're the one who cheated my husband out.' Some people have long memories, but I didn't cheat. I was just not going to be all sporting and tell him to stay put when the bottom line was: I wasn't sure I had taken it, so if I'd said, 'No, I didn't take it,' and had then looked at the replay and seen that I had, I'd have been in serious trouble with Bumble.

It even led to a change in the rules later on that year when it was decided that the third umpire could be used for disputed catches and I was pleased because that took the onus away from the fielder. It is, however, a far from perfect system and I think it's about to be changed again. Until we have cameras covering every possible angle, you will never be a hundred per cent sure about things like this, but I'm happy to leave any decision to the umpires. If they had turned round to me at Old Trafford and said, 'You're not sure so we won't give it,' I would have accepted that. But they must have been pretty sure it was clean, and that was good enough for me. It should always be that way in cricket.

We lost the match, and by now the Ashes were starting to slip away. At Headingley Mike Smith made his debut (he never played again), and went wicketless after Graham Thorpe dropped Matthew Elliott off his bowling. Elliott made the small matter of 199, and in the dressing room afterwards Atherton tried to lighten the mood by paraphrasing a famous Douglas Jardine quote. 'Mr Thorpe, you've just lost us the Ashes,' said the captain. It went down like a lead balloon. Ath the cricketing historian was trying to be funny, but it went straight over everyone's heads and you could see people thinking, 'That's a bit harsh. We're all in this together. You can't blame Thorpey.' I scored a hundred in the second innings, which was unusual for me because I'm normally at my best earlier in a game when you are fighting for the initiative; but I like Headingley. I like quicker surfaces, even if they are poor ones, and it's usually quick in Leeds, with an outfield to match. It's a good sighting ground and the people love their cricket.

But this time my first second-innings Test century was in a losing cause. We were 2–1 down now, and it quickly became 3–1 at Trent Bridge, where the Hollioake brothers were introduced but to no avail. The Aussies were on a run and were proving impossible for us to stop. The Ashes were gone after such a promising start to the series for us and we just didn't make the most of the opportunity we had that summer.

There were certain moments which we had to seize and we didn't grab them. Like when Steve Waugh came in at Old Trafford with the Australians struggling, or when Graham Thorpe dropped Matthew Elliott at Headingley. The Aussies put this down to their mental toughness and them having a hoodoo over us, but I think it's more to do with the fact that we have always struggled to take 20 wickets in a Test against Australia. Many of England's current batsmen have good records against Australia: Thorpe, Butcher, Vaughan (even I've had my moments!); but how many bowlers have really performed against them? Gough, possibly. Bowlers win you matches, especially against a batting line-up as formidable as theirs. Perhaps Steve Harmison is the answer, but who's going to back him up, particularly in the spin department?

At least we managed to pull the score round to 3–2 with a thoroughly enjoyable win at the Oval in the last match, when we bowled Australia out for 104 when they were chasing just 124 to win. It was their over-confidence in the last match of a series getting to them again, something of a habit in those days; but it was also great bowling from Caddick and Phil Tufnell, who had returned for us on a turning wicket and enjoyed one of his greatest moments as an England bowler.

All in all, it was quite a summer. It started with an innings that changed my life, went on to be an all-too-familiar tale of Australian dominance and ended on a massive high for us at the Oval, a bit like in 1993. We had made progress, but it wasn't quite good enough; now, with hindsight, I can say we blew the best chance the likes of me, Atherton and Stewart had of winning the Ashes. Ath must have known it because he subsequently said he wanted to resign the captaincy after this series but was talked out of it by David Lloyd.

As an England captain you know you are basically going to be judged on how you did against the Australians, and I'm sure Ath would have thought that was the best time to move on and only the win at the Oval stopped him in the end. You need just one good game to think that maybe you should stay on after all, together with the support of your coach, like Ath had with Bumble. It was the same for me when we won in Sydney in 2003.

On this occasion Ath decided, against his better judgement,

to stay on, but we were all very happy about that because we rated our captain so highly. We were off again to the West Indies, where, I hoped, I might get a game this time!

14

I think Mike Atherton had decided that if he couldn't beat the Australians, the time had come for a new England captain but he was persuaded to carry on by his close friend, David Lloyd, and instead went on to enjoy and perhaps endure one last tour, another eventful trip to the West Indies.

It started off all right. In fact, it started off very pleasantly indeed as we were put up in a new, all-inclusive resort in Antigua for a training camp which, with Phil Tufnell on board, was always going to be eventful. There was a real holiday atmosphere about the place and we had to wear these wrist-bands which entitled us to all the food and (in some cases more appropriately) drink we wanted! The only thing that spoiled it was the constant rain which hit the island and in the end forced us to leave early for Jamaica when it became clear that the only practice we were going to get was bowling and batting on concrete paths, so wet had the island become. I still have this image of Robert Croft bowling in a road to John Emburey while bemused American holidaymakers wandered around in their Bermuda shorts, looking at us and wondering what on earth we were doing.

We got into trouble with one of them. One night, a few of the boys got drunk and, to relieve the boredom that was kicking in by this stage, started to throw fruit from one of our rooms at this big yacht across the harbour. Next morning, one very annoyed rich bloke was demanding to know why his lovely boat had been pelted by rotten fruit, and a few of the lads were dragged in by management and carpeted for it.

In many ways it was the last of the old-fashioned tours, with a fairly slow, relaxed build-up before the serious business began

– or was meant to begin – in Jamaica after a little stop at Montego Bay on the way. It was all going swimmingly until, as vice-captain, I decided to go to Sabina Park with Ath to have a look at the wicket as the first Test loomed. It was where I made my Test debut and I was remembering it all fondly as we started to walk out on to the ground, and in the distance I could see a strip of land which looked nothing like a cricket wicket.

Surely that's not it, I thought, as we walked towards the square. It looked like a corrugated-iron roof. And when we arrived in the middle, our worst fears were realized. Some wickets, like Perth, occasionally start with some cracks in them, but this one was incredible. We went up to the groundsman and said, 'That's not the Test wicket, is it?' Calm as anything, he said, 'Yes. We've had a few problems. That's the wicket.'

All sorts of thoughts rushed through my mind: memories of the 1995 wicket at Edgbaston when the first ball from Curtly Ambrose ballooned over Atherton's head; suspicions that the wicket had been prepared to suit their fast bowlers; all manner of things. It changed the atmosphere of the whole tour. This was definitely not the sort of surface you wanted to play the West Indies on.

Word quickly spread through our camp that the wicket was a bit dodgy, but we tried to play down any fears the boys may have had and prepared as usual. The next day, one day before the series started, we went back again and, to be fair to the groundsman, he had done an incredible job in papering over the cracks. I don't know if he rolled it, used grass cuttings or simply got the Polyfilla out, but it looked a lot better, while still being far from perfect. We awaited the start of the match with bated breath.

Jack Russell still gets stick for falling ill on the morning of the match. This is a man who is so fastidious about his diet that he can go through a three-month tour of the sub-continent without any sign of stomach problems, but he chose this game to go down with something and, dressing rooms being dressing rooms, he received no sympathy and an incredible amount of stick for being unable to play on the wicket from hell.

Enter Mark Butcher, as we decided to play an extra batsman. Thanks, Jack, thought Butch, and into action we went. I had spent the whole of the previous evening trying to put extra protection on my equipment, particularly my gloves, to take any precaution I possibly could, and when we won the toss Ath decided we had to bat first because this strip could only get worse. The tension was unmistakable. It was Brian Lara's first match as West Indies captain and it was on the home island of the man he replaced, Courtney Walsh. There had been a lot of talk and controversy in the West Indies about that, and I think Brian was as apprehensive as we were, even though he had far more firepower than us to exploit the conditions.

Butch went in, and came back out again after receiving a brute of a delivery first ball, and by this time Tufnell was becoming hysterical in the dressing room. He was running around, trying to find every piece of equipment he possibly could while shouting, 'I'm not going to bat on that. No way.' Not exactly a confidence boost to us batters waiting to go in.

Now, I have never been scared on a cricket field. I can honestly say that no bowler has physically frightened me at any time, and I guess it's because a cricket ball has never really hurt me that much. Yes, I have had broken fingers and been hit on the helmet a few times, but you have so much protective gear these days that I trust it and feel I can face anybody without too much concern. This time, though, I was apprehensive because I had never seen anything like this, and the only fear I had was the fear of losing my wicket very cheaply.

It was simply a case of trying to survive out there. I have never played Courtney Walsh well, and this time I couldn't lay a bat on him. It really was the minefield we'd feared. Luckily I had the perfect batting partner in Alec Stewart, whose street-wise qualities were never more in evidence. He was overreacting to everything. Every time I got hit, he was like 'Stay down, take your time, get the physio on.' Then, as I was receiving treatment, he would be staring at the wicket, tapping it down and shaking his head. I don't think an abandonment was in his mind, but he just wanted to demonstrate to everybody just how tough it was out there and what we were going through. It would have been like 'It's not our fault we're struggling out here. Have you seen what this wicket is doing?'

I was quickly dismissed, but the misery went on. Graham Thorpe took a couple of blows. Alec himself was being hit, and I think for the first time the thought of a cancellation was in people's minds. But not in Lara's. That was the last thing he wanted. First, he had the fast bowlers who could bowl us out cheaply, and, secondly, he was under pressure as Walsh's successor, playing on Walsh's home patch. Brian had the chance of a crushing victory on his captaincy debut and there's no question that if the match had carried on he would have achieved it, almost certainly within two days.

We were sitting in the dressing room in a state of disbelief. People were saying, 'We could get a day off here. We're going to have to come back tomorrow on a different wicket.' Tufnell was still panicking and praying. I was sitting there, gutted that I was out for 1 – and the next thing I knew, they were walking off. The only abandonment in Test Match history and all within an hour of the start of play. I think Venkat, who was umpiring in that match, was a decisive figure and he had taken the brave and correct action. Truth is, it was dangerous out there. Certainly with their bowlers bowling on it. Maybe if we had bowled first, there wouldn't have been such an extreme reaction and the course of history would have been different, but who knows?

It was surreal, a very strange feeling. It was a huge call by the umpires and I think Lara was worried he might be lynched, but it was correct and we were all in a state of shock. By now everything was buzzing. The press were running around, British spectators were wondering what was happening to their holidays, and the enormity of an abandoned Test Match was beginning to hit us. Particularly the money boys among our number, who were busy getting tickets signed up as a highly lucrative benefit-friendly souvenir of this historic occasion.

Then it was like 'What do we do now?' Bob Bennett, our tour manager, was running around like a headless chicken, talking to various board officials and asking questions like 'Do we come back tomorrow?' 'Is it now a four-Test series?' Meanwhile, selfish old Nass was saying things like 'Does that innings count? . . . Is it going to affect my average? . . . Surely it won't.' Then, my biggest complaint was that my 1 run on an unplayable pitch in an abandoned Test was going to count against me, but as time went by and I was inching towards 100 Tests I was actually rather grateful for the extra cap it gave me!

Me and Butch had the hump. Alec was determined that his 9 not out was going to count. And the most delighted man in the ground was Phil Tufnell, who announced that that was the easiest Test Match he was ever going to play and now he was off to enjoy himself. He said, 'I wish every Test was like this!' His mood was slightly spoiled when it became clear that we were going to have to fit in an extra Test in Trinidad to compensate, which meant the (at that time) unusual event of back-to-back matches, which was and still is very tough. And what an eventful two matches they were.

We should have won both matches in Port of Spain. That is my overwhelming memory. At that stage their batting was basically Brian Lara, Carl Hooper and the rest, and they were hitting us with people I'd barely heard of; but it was Hooper who played the decisive innings as we lost a very close game by 3 wickets. Hooper batted brilliantly that day. He was in such good nick. I remember in that series watching from slip and there were balls from Tufnell that I would have played a forward defensive to and Hooper was just whipping them for 6. He didn't run down the wicket or anything like that. He just played Tuffers expertly from the crease and showed what a great batsman he could be. Angus Fraser had a tremendous match on his return to the side, apart from putting down a hard caught-and-bowled chance from David Williams on the final morning that was crucial to the outcome, and I had a reasonable game; but our overwhelming feeling was one of desolation that we had let a fantastic opportunity pass us by. And we were back at the Queen's Park Oval three days later.

It was just as dramatic a Test, just as eventful, but this time we won by 3 wickets. It was a low-scoring match on another terrible pitch, and one of my biggest memories was being trapped lbw by a ball from Hooper that rolled along the ground. But it didn't matter in the end. Fraser had another terrific match and we ended up creeping home with a good little stand from Mark Butcher and Dean Headley.

It should have set us up nicely for Guyana, but it didn't. We lost heavily in Georgetown but redeemed ourselves in Barbados, where we had the best of a draw, and Mark Ramprak-ash, finally and gloriously, scored his maiden Test hundred. The joy on Ramps's face when he reached three figures will stay with everybody who saw it for the rest of their lives. It really should have been the breakthrough for Mark. He really should have had a great Test career, he is such a talented player. But, for whatever reason, it was not to be. From my point of view I was starting to feel a little out of nick, and it did me good to get an unbeaten 46 in the second innings as we set up a declaration. We went to Antigua, still looking to square the series, but it all went horribly wrong.

Athers had been featuring in the press again for reasons that he wouldn't have relished. West Indies had picked these two openers in Clayton Lambert and Philo Wallace who basically came in and slogged. No respect for the bowlers at all. It was so unusual that it wound us all up, particularly Atherton. There he was, fending off Ambrose and Walsh, and when it was the West Indies' turn to bat, these two bruisers would come in and try to thump our bowlers back over their heads first ball for 6. And they often succeeded.

There was a bit of tension about, and when we got Wallace out in Barbados Ath just flicked a little V-sign at him, forgetting that there are a large number of gentlemen around called photographers who watch the England captain's every move. One man caught it on film and Atherton got some criticism for it. This is where the press annoy me at times. OK, he shouldn't have done it, and a photographer caught him in the act, but it really would have ended there if two or three of the English reporters hadn't gone up to the match referee and brought it to his attention. It was like 'Atherton's done this. What are you going to do about it?' and to me that is trying to get your own captain into trouble. Whether they had it in for him because he was never the most open in press conferences I don't know, but I just can't understand that mentality.

So Atherton was under pressure in Antigua and we ended up having one of my most disappointing Test Matches, simply because we folded on the last day when we should have drawn the match easily. A 2–1 defeat by the West Indies in the Caribbean is disappointing, but 3–1 is so much worse. And it was the end of the Atherton era.

It was damp, we started late and we lost a hugely important toss. They were very difficult batting conditions. We were rolled over, and then Lambert and Wallace went berserk as they got plenty. I remember Mark Butcher bagging a pair, having turned down the chance to have a nightwatchman in the second innings, and then myself and Thorpe put on a big stand on the last day with me getting a century. It should have been enough to earn us a draw. Certainly the West Indies thought so. At tea we were 4 wickets down, and as we came back out after the break I saw Ambrose and Walsh had trainers on rather than their bowling boots.

'They've had enough,' I thought. 'They're not going to bowl in this session.' And I really don't think they had any intention of bowling again until Thorpe ran me out. I guess in a way it was payback time for all the people I ran out during that spell of my career when I seemed to have got a reputation for it. I was spewing. Thorpe immediately took the blame for it and apologized to me, which speaks volumes for the man, but I know, as well as anyone, that these things happen.

What really annoyed me was that, as I walked off, I was overtaken by Ambrose and Walsh sprinting off to put their bowling boots on. They had the whiff of an unlikely victory in their nostrils and they grabbed it as we collapsed. The last image of that game was Tuffers backing away and fending the ball off to slip, then practising a perfect back-foot defensive with his body behind the ball as the delighted West Indies supporters dashed on to the pitch. All the hard work we'd done ruined by a stupid run-out. We had played well for much of the tour but had ended up losing 3–1. Even 2–1 was slightly harsh on us, but it was a lot better than 3–1.

I was feeling low. But worse was to come. As the West Indies celebrated, Atherton said he had something to tell us and we all followed him into the dressing room. He simply said, 'Look, I've taken this team as far as I can. I'm giving up the captaincy.' We were distraught. I was in tears. Angus Fraser was in tears. It felt so much like we'd let him down. At the time you think it's that last session that had led to our captain resigning. Later, I came to appreciate that it was four years of effort, often in vain, that led to Athers calling it a day; but at the time you feel responsible as a team.

I was thinking, 'God, we've let you down here. If we'd drawn, maybe you would have carried on. You're my mate and I really want to keep on playing for you, Ath. I've enjoyed playing under you and you've been a good captain. Maybe you've not always managed people brilliantly, but you've never done anything just to make yourself look good. You've always done all you can for England and with the team's best interests at heart. You have been our rock. You have always told the opponents that they would have to beat England over your dead body and we have all tried to follow your example. And we have let you down.' It would have made a good speech, but unfortunately all these thoughts were just swirling around in my head rather than coming out of my mouth. I don't think I was capable of articulating anything at the time.

We were all very emotional. I regret now not telling Mike Atherton exactly what I thought at the time because I would have liked to, but there just never seemed a proper chance. I do know that there were a lot of people who felt exactly the same as me, like Angus, Alec and Thorpey. Ath was our captain; before him, we just played under whoever was the captain. There is a subtle difference. I think, as I experienced later, that you know deep down when your time is up as a captain. I'm sure Ath knew that this was the right time for him to step down. He has subsequently said that he wished he had gone after the previous summer, as he originally intended. At the end of the day you listen to various people's opinions, but you have to make your own mind up; I don't think Ath was in any mood that night to talk to people about his decision or to give anybody the chance to try to talk him out of it. His mind was made up.

Later on, when Ath retired, I heard Charles Colvile on Sky saying that Atherton wouldn't be remembered as a great player because he didn't average the magic 40, but people who haven't played the game don't understand. To me, whether you average 38, 40 or 42 is largely irrelevant. It is what you do for your team as a player and a captain that is far more important than statistics, and that's why to me it is people like Atherton, Gough and Thorpe whom I respect the most. It's how someone responds to the demands of the battle when they cross that line that matters; how they've been when you've looked them in the eye in a pressure situation and responded for you and the team. Have they been there for you?

You would want Mike Atherton to bat for your life, and to me that is far more significant than his average being under 40. Just think of the number of times he went out to bat for us in difficult situations. You just always feared we would collapse once he was out, and that pressure was always with him, as he often carried the hopes of the nation. He would talk to you as a captain, ask your opinion and he never talked down to anyone. Socially, he is a very rounded person. Cricket was important to him, but not in a Graham Gooch 'the game is everything' sort of way. He would discuss cricket at length but he would always know the right time to say, 'Right, that's enough. What are we going to do tonight?'

If there was any Englishman who provided an example of how I would want to captain a side, it was Mike Atherton. I think that's because I like to compare myself to someone who had more to him than just the game of cricket. Because at the end of the day, and I know it's a cliché, it is just a game. You know that famous Bill Shankly quote, about football not being a matter of life and death, it's more important than that? Well, that's a load of rubbish. And it is particularly true of cricket. Really, it is an absurd little game, based on fine margins of luck, involving a bit of wood hitting a bit of leather. If the ball misses your bat by a tiny margin, you can score 207 against Australia, and if it just touches it, you can get nought. And you go from hero to zero.

So it is only a game. Mike Atherton never forgot that. Through all his ups and downs he never lost that perspective, and that remained the case when he resigned as captain and later when he retired as a player. There was none of the 'I want to make myself look good. I'm going to wave my arms all around and look important. Look at me, this is my last game. Haven't I been good.' With Athers it was more important to know what his teammates thought of him, how many friends he still had in the game, whether, when he turned up as a media pundit at Lord's, those old teammates would still greet him as a friend and a colleague. Everyone who played with Ath respects him and admires him. No one who played cricket with Ath will say in the years to come, 'There's Michael Atherton. He's a great man because he averaged nearly 40.' They will say that he's a great man because of his duel with Allan Donald, because he always stuck to his guns, because he would say the same thing to your face as he would in a selection meeting. Make no mistake, he was a very fine batsman. The number of Test runs he scored is right up there with the greats. He is probably one of England's top five batsmen of all time, and that is an awesome achievement.

While towards the end of his career he developed a habit of swinging the bat down from point or gully in a sort of scissors action against bowlers who nipped it back at him, this isn't how he should be remembered. Technically he was the most correct batsman of his generation. He was also England's rock. And he was often in pain because of his chronic back condition. As a captain? Well, he was pretty rounded and had most of the attributes leaders have in equal proportion. Some captains, like Keith Fletcher, were particularly good tacticians. Others were very good at man-management, and some led by example, like Graham Gooch and Alec Stewart. I just think Athers led with all the various compartments filled up virtually to the top. Perhaps he wasn't great at any one discipline, but he was good tactically, good in the dressing room, very professional, and he wouldn't ask his team to do anything he couldn't do.

The only thing remotely critical I would say is that he could be stubborn, so if you crossed him a bit, like Ronnie Irani and Andrew Caddick did, he really wouldn't want to know you again. Once he'd made his mind up about someone, it was pretty well made up. As captain, you have to be flexible. For instance, I didn't rate Ashley Giles very highly when I first became captain. I was more of a Phil Tufnell fan. But he proved me wrong and went on to become a crucial figure during my captaincy years. As a cricketer and as a person I would always have Ash on my side, he's so mentally strong. He has to be. When you are bowling orthodox spin nowadays, it's easy to become demoralized but he never does. His self-belief means he's able to contribute to every aspect of the game: bowling, batting and fielding. Ash proved me wrong and I became a fan. But Ath would say about someone, 'No, he can't play,' and he wouldn't be moved.

His lack of public relations skills, and his virtual contempt for the press, in a funny sort of way made you want to play more for him. If we had a bad day, he would stick up for us in public and we appreciated it, but I know that his attitude towards the media did add to the pressure on him and it was something I was aware of when I became captain. My attitude was that I had to try to get on with the press. I knew they had the capacity to dictate how I felt and how I would be judged. I know how sensitive I am and I just couldn't develop a thick skin like Alec Stewart's, for instance, and just ignore them. Every word that the press say or write gets back to you somehow, even if you try to ignore them, so it does affect you and it does affect your decision making.

I tried to keep the press on my side, whereas Athers decided, particularly after the dirt-in-pocket episode, that they were going to write bad things, so why give them anything? There are two arguments in the dressing room. Some people say, 'They're the press, they've got a job to do. We are ambassadors for the game. We need to help the press for the good of the game.' Then there are those who say, 'Hold on a second, we give players for the press to interview every day, we do whatever they want, and all they do is slag us off, they're always trying to catch us out.' I think Ath was in the latter camp to a large extent and he decided he wasn't going to give them any more than he had to. His stubbornness was a sort of thick-skinned characteristic, but he was hurt by things. I've got great respect for the man and I know a lot of people who played with him feel the same.

15

I did not really have a sense that I might be a candidate for the England captaincy when Athers went. I had been brought up on an England and Essex culture of seniority and, to be honest, even if I was the official vice-captain, Alec Stewart was still very heavily involved with a lot of things. Alec was still very much the senior man in the dressing room, with a lot of respect and a lot of control over certain aspects of our team. And I can honestly say I never wanted the job desperately.

I was living my ambitions by playing for England and, while I would happily have accepted, had the job come my way, I never went out of my way to push my claims or anything like that. The most important part of being a vice-captain is being loyal to the captain. That's why I made Ronnie Irani my vice-captain at Essex. At that stage he was an extremely loyal bloke who wouldn't stand any backchat or knifing of you behind your back, and that was very much my intention when I was made Ath's vice-captain.

Even with regard to things like the 'no wives' policy in Zimbabwe and New Zealand. I didn't necessarily agree with it but I backed Athers up because there is nothing worse than a captain doing one thing and his vice-captain going the other way. So I didn't see being second-in-command as any sort of opportunity to push your claims for the main job or any guarantee that I would get the captaincy when it next became available.

There was obviously a lot of press about the situation when we returned from the West Indies and, while Mark Rampra-kash's name was mentioned, it was considered by the majority to be a choice between Stewart and Hussain. And I always expected Alec to get it. My dad would ring me up and say, 'Go for it,' or 'That Stewart is a real street-fighter. Make sure you match him.' It was almost like electioneering talk from my old man. My preference was to sit quietly and see what happened.

Then I got a call asking me if I would go and see Lord MacLaurin, the chairman of the ECB, to talk about the job. I didn't know much about him at that time, and I know there were certain things about him that a lot of people didn't like, like the fact that he always seemed to be there when we won. Later, I got to know Lord MacLaurin pretty well. He loved cricket and he genuinely wanted to improve the English game. His business background meant that he brought fresh eyes to the game's set-up. However, his initiatives were frustrated by the fact that the single most important change that needed to be made to enable all subsequent reform was the abolition of the First Class Forum. And those particular turkeys were never going to vote for Christmas! I was always impressed by his treatment of the England team and of me in particular; he always wanted to know what he could do for us.

At this stage, though, I was wary of him and I went to see him and David Graveney, the chairman of selectors, with some trepidation. Grav was the bloke I would argue with about my place in the one-day side, but he wasn't someone you either trusted or mistrusted. He wasn't someone who'd make his own mind up about something, he was more a man who would listen to other people before doing anything. I also knew that Lord MacLaurin was big on discipline, and I wondered if I was his sort of character.

There was the time in New Zealand in 1997 when Dominic Cork was going through a rough time at home, and he had lifted his shirt up above his head, as was fashionable in football, when he took a wicket. Later, as vice-captain, I was dragged into a room by the coach, David Lloyd, where he read out a note from his lordship. 'I just don't want this sort of thing,' Bumble read out. 'Please remind Cork that he is playing for

England and if he does this sort of thing again he will be sent home.'

As Mike Atherton so memorably wrote in his book, beware a man with shiny shoes and a perma-tan. Lord MacLaurin had both. Now, to my mind, the only man in our dressing room with shiny shoes and a perma-tan was Alec Stewart, so I felt very much the outsider in the captaincy race. There is nothing shiny about my shoes, nor can I really say that I have got much of a tan, even though, being half-Indian, I am naturally dark. So I was up against it.

I could just tell from my interview that they were concerned about the way I would behave as captain because of the way I had sometimes behaved as a player. There was my tantrums and the way I threw my gear about when I was given out. Clearly I had a reputation for just looking after myself, as the one who would stay in the nets for as long as he could and then get as many throwdowns as he possibly could. And I make no apology for staying behind and doing extra work on my game. Just because I didn't throw to anybody else didn't make me a bad person, my argument went. Yes, I was obsessed with my own game and I always wanted to work at it, but my theory was that if everybody had the same attitude towards their game as me, then we wouldn't go far wrong. Apart, maybe, from having a shortage of people to provide the throwdowns.

So I just soaked up the interview and in the end I said to the pair of them, 'Look, I'm not going to argue with you. Yes, this is how I have been as a player. I've always tried to get the best out of myself. I've always been fiery and worn my heart on my sleeve; but that's how I behaved when I was a player. You have to look at how different I was when I captained the "A" tour to Pakistan. You behave differently. You have to realize that someone, when you give them the responsibility, has it in them to behave differently.'

It was the right way to go about the appointment. It was a very professional and correct procedure. I wish all of English cricket was carried out like that: a proper examination of the credentials of various candidates for any given job before making a measured and well-informed decision.

I can't help comparing it to Essex. It's just not done like that there. Any sort of appointment is just done on seniority and with no consideration of what anyone else might be able to bring to the party, as Duncan Fletcher might say. Just look at Alan Lilley again. Here's a bloke who, over ten years in the game, was known to everyone in the Essex team as 'Cement-head'. Now he's virtually running the club!

I would love someone at Essex to sit him down one day and say, 'Right, Alan. What do you bring to this job? What have you done to deserve running a major company like Essex County Cricket Club?' Experience was what Lord MacLaurin brought to the England and Wales Cricket Board and I think he had a certain amount of success because of it.

I agreed that the England team had to have a clean-cut image. I could see where he was coming from, trying to introduce business procedure to the game. It's very presumptuous to think that, just because someone has played cricket, they can run the game, and I'm afraid that in a lot of cases we cricketers are the last people who know what's best for our game in a business sense. Cricket is not the real world.

I thought my captaincy interview early in the summer of 1998 went fine. At no stage did I think I'd made a prat of myself. It wasn't a life-or-death thing for me. But if I had had to make the decision at that time I would probably have chosen Alec Stewart as captain of England. It was a non-gamble. He knew how to behave. Me? At that stage I could have gone either way. I could have let the country down by behaving stupidly and telling an umpire where to go or stuff like that. That was certainly not what England wanted. But there was also the chance that I could have been a better captain than Alec, a more imaginative leader. I wasn't sure myself, so I couldn't blame Lord MacLaurin and David Graveney for not knowing. They took the only option they could take at that stage, really.

I don't really know why I was vice-captain ahead of Stewie if they didn't think I was the best choice as captain, but I do know that they are different jobs. For instance, I appointed Marcus Trescothick as my vice-captain because I thought he had a good cricket brain and was a very loyal person. But he didn't get the main job when I resigned either. That's the way it goes sometimes.

The one thing you could say is that Alec was a more permanent fixture in the side than me; my form was always going to be a bit more variable. I don't know who Athers recommended for the job, but I wouldn't have been surprised if he'd said that he thought I might make a good captain but that he couldn't be sure how I'd react in certain situations. Which was a pretty fair summary.

I was a bit disappointed when I got the call to say it wouldn't be me. The first person I thought about was Dad. I knew he was hanging on every word of every newspaper article and would be more disappointed than me. But I didn't ring him when I heard. It was all announced very quickly and I didn't really know what to say. The one person I did ring was Alec Stewart, and I said to him, 'Well done, you have my total support.' He told me that he knew he would have my support and that we would work well together.

Alec made a point of making it very clear to people that I was his right-hand man. He wanted to make sure people knew we hadn't fallen out or anything like that. The vice-captaincy is never official at home, but it was obvious I was still expected to do the job, and that suited me fine. I just wanted us to win and for me to score runs. And we had a big series ahead against South Africa.

Alec Stewart as a captain was exactly the way everyone expected him to be. He was a good captain. There are a lot of things, as I have said, that go to making a good captain, and Alec's strength clearly was leading by example. He was immaculate and he would expect us to do things in a certain way. We all knew that he would not expect us to do anything he wouldn't do. Like, if he told us we had to shave or be at a meeting at a certain time, we knew he would always be clean-shaven and be first at the meeting.

16

I will give you an example of how I differed from Alec Stewart as captain. The one thing that Duncan Fletcher told me he didn't like when I was captain was how I was always at the back, struggling, when we did our morning lap of the field before a day's play. He felt that the captain should be up at the front, leading the troops and setting an example.

But the thing was, that was so not me. My argument was that it would look false if I was suddenly transformed into this character who was up the front, sprinting along with my chin up and saying, 'Come on, lads.' To me, the morning lap was low on my list of priorities, as running always has been. I just knew that people like Darren Gough and Andrew Caddick would be saying to me, 'Nass, come on. It's us you're dealing with. Get up the back where you belong,' if I tried that. So I would stagger along at the back, thinking about the day ahead, whether I would choose to bat or bowl, and trying to get my mind on my batting rather than putting anything on for show. Alec was different. It was not 'for show' with him. He naturally would be at the front, immaculate, chest puffed out and leading the way.

And that does have an effect on a team, it has to be said. It was a very good quality of Alec's. He made us disciplined in our approach and our appearance. But he did have failings. He was a bit Gooch-like in not really being able to understand people who were a bit different, like Caddick and Phil Tufnell. They barely played under him, if at all, and that was to the detriment of English cricket. Alec didn't appear to have time for people who maybe needed more careful handling but who, on their day, could be match winners for us.

There was the time in the West Indies, when Mike Atherton was captain, when Alec and Caddick had a bit of a barney in front of the boys; and that, really, summed up their relationship at that time. Thankfully it got a bit better later. We had had a bad morning and Dean Headley, one of my closest friends in the game and a top bowler in his short time with England, immediately put his hand up and said, 'I've bowled terribly. I'm sorry.' That's the sort of bloke he was. Caddy went the other way, as was his wont. He said something like 'When I'm at the end of my mark I feel my team aren't supporting me and I don't think that anyone is encouraging me. When other bowlers are bowling I hear a lot of "well bowled, well bowled". I don't get that.' Everyone in the room was thinking that he was being a bit of an idiot and making excuses, but the thing to do with him is to play mind games. When he was complaining about bowling at a particular end as captain I would say to him, 'Yes, I know it's rough, Caddy, but Goughy won't bowl at this end. What can I do? I really need you to carry the load.' Complete nonsense, of course, but it tended to work. On this occasion Alec had had enough.

'Hold on, Caddy,' he said. 'What are you on about? We always support you.' Then they had a bit of a head-to-head. I don't think they disliked each other, I just think Stewie couldn't understand how this person with so much ability was making so many excuses and was just so apprehensive of getting out there and bowling like we all knew he could. My point is, everyone is different and as human beings we have to make allowances for each other.

Andrew Caddick is a lovely bloke who will do anything for anybody, but he just had this uncanny knack of saying the wrong thing at the wrong time. If, for example, you were not getting runs, the last thing you would want is someone coming up to you and saying, 'You're not doing very well at the moment, you must be under a little bit of pressure,' or 'You're not looking very good at the crease, you know, have you noticed?' Caddy would come out with things like that. There was the famous time at Lord's in 2000 when Darren Gough had again narrowly failed to get a 5-wicket haul and his name on the famous honours board, something that is a huge regret in Darren's career. Caddy just started taking the piss out of Goughy over it, and you just think to yourself, 'Not now, Caddy.' That time Duncan and I had to have a quiet word with him about it, but Caddy hasn't a malicious bone in his body – he just sometimes says the wrong thing at the wrong time.

If Alec Stewart had a fear of failure, like the rest of us, then he hid it incredibly well. I just never saw it in him, and that was a feature of his leadership in 1998, when we had a fabulous series win against South Africa. It was an eventful summer. We played brilliantly at Edgbaston in the opening Test, with Atherton looking as if a huge burden had been lifted from his shoulders. We had the better of the match and it was only rain, really, that stopped us winning. But we have had, over the years, a capacity to squander the initiative, and we did it again at Lord's in the second Test, when we allowed South Africa to recover from 46 for 4 to 360 all out, which proved a match-winning score as we batted badly and they won by 10 wickets. I remember Allan Donald bowling at the speed of light in that game, us letting Jonty Rhodes off the hook as he got a hundred and me scoring my first Test century at Lord's in the second innings.

To be honest, it's not something I look back on particularly fondly because it always seemed likely to be in a losing cause, but I hadn't scored many runs at Lord's at that point and the wickets there were going through a bit of a phase in which they did a bit and the groundsman was under a little bit of pressure. Graham Gooch always told me how much he loved batting at Lord's, and now I know what he meant; but it can be a tricky place until you learn to understand the slope and not fall over, which is easy to do as a right-hander at the pavilion end. This was the first time I'd been able to crack it at Lord's, and it left me with mixed feelings afterwards.

There was a certain amount of criticism of me by some people that I'd celebrated the landmark too much, as it was clearly in a losing cause, but I do not accept that at all. You must always be allowed to celebrate a hundred with an England badge on your helmet. How many times is that going to happen to you? It's not like it comes along every day. To my mind, if your side has batted badly and then one of your teammates scores a century, you as a team have let him down and he has every right to celebrate his achievement. It can act as an incentive. The rest of the team can then say, 'Lucky sod. I want a bit of that. I want to be able to acknowledge the crowd and take the plaudits. It's up to the rest of us to make sure it's not in vain.'

There was a similar case involving Andrew Flintoff in 2003, again against South Africa. Freddie hit a superb century in a losing cause and celebrated it in a subdued manner, presumably through fear that people would accuse him of being selfish and milking the moment. I say, Test centuries are special, especially at Lord's, and they need to be enjoyed. I enjoyed my century in 1998, but of course the overwhelming feeling was one of disappointment that we had lost the Test. It hit hard because at the time I didn't get on with the way they seemed to go about their cricket. I know this will sound bad, especially as there are some nice guys in their team, players like Shaun Pollock, Gary Kirsten, Allan Donald and Jacques Kallis, but there's often an air of self-righteousness about the team's attitude since they were re-admitted to Test cricket that wound up the England dressing room. That was then, though, and the two teams are much closer now.

Old Trafford was a key Test. As ever, it was a very hard wicket to read. It looked as if it was going to be a dust bowl and that we would need two spinners, so Ashley Giles came in for his debut, but Old Trafford can be very deceptive and, after we had lost the toss and batted, it became clear that it was an absolute belter. It was like the Ilford Cricket School: rock hard, and it wasn't going to turn. We desperately needed to win, we had picked the wrong team, and South Africa scored 552.

But even then there was a sense they may have gone on a bit too long. Wily old Atherton was, for once, wise before the event and, while they were moving towards their declaration, he said to me, 'They are being too careful here. This is their chance of wrapping up the series. They are batting on a bit too long.' I was like 'Whatever, Ath. I just want to get off this field!' Yet when we did get off the field it became a bit of a nightmare. Donald bowled really fast, I had my usual Old Trafford failure, and we were all out for 183, and following on.

I don't know why I bother turning up at Old Trafford. I have tried everything. I have got changed in every corner of both dressing rooms they have there. I've visualized walking down the stairs and scoring runs there. I've stood in the middle and imagined being 20 not out, imagined it was Lord's or Chelmsford, just to get a start there. But it never made any difference.

I failed again in the second innings. But Alec Stewart didn't. He led from the front and played brilliantly for a big hundred, his ability to play fast bowling so well proving perfect for the occasion. Thank God he did, because the rest of us were struggling. This was also the game when Graham Thorpe was suffering really badly with his back and bagged a pair, which added to our problems.

Now Graham, the little genius, is one hell of a fighter as a cricketer and you would always back him to come through for you in a tough situation. But the one thing he doesn't fight well is injury. If Thorpey has a bad back, you can rule him out for a month; it's a double stress fracture for him. Similarly, if he has a bruised finger, it's a multiple fracture. In all seriousness, I think he, in common with someone like Mark Ilott, just feels pain a bit more. Whether it's a blood pressure thing I don't know, but Graham has been known to faint when he has been hit on the hand, and on this occasion his back was really hurting. So, being a sympathetic team to one of our number's suffering, we plastered him up, virtually pushed him out of the door and said, 'There you go. You're struggling with your back. Go out there and face Allan Donald bowling at ninety miles per hour.'

Poor Thorpey was out straight away and he walked back, looking like a very old man. That's all we saw of him for a while. Another defeat and another lost series looked inevitable, but we found an unlikely saviour in Robert Croft and, latterly, Angus Fraser. It turned out to be the turning point of the series. And it proved to me how valuable it was to have depth in your batting – not that Angus exactly gave us that. Crofty was not known for his ability to play fast bowling well, but he showed great character and bravery that day. Somehow, against all the odds, we hung on for a draw which felt like a 'get out of jail' win, and now suddenly the tables were turning. We knew that we normally ended series well and we went to Trent Bridge in good heart for a team that were one down and had been largely outplayed throughout the series.

What a great nip-and-tuck game that was. Fraser bowled brilliantly, I recall, and I think there were a few of the usual bad umpiring decisions. Keith Fletcher had warned me about the quality of New Zealand umpires early in my career, and I have to say that I shared his lack of enthusiasm. Thankfully, these days Billy Bowden is improving the reputation of that country's umpires a great deal.

A cracking match came down to us chasing 247 to win, and me and Athers were at the wicket after Mark Butcher had gone fairly early. What happened next has gone down as one of the great passages of play in Test cricket history. Cronje brought Donald back, with us getting more and more established and them needing a wicket badly. A.D. was working up a head of steam when, with Athers on 27, he obviously gloved one down the leg side to Mark Boucher. It was out. Donald kept on running. I almost gave it out at the non-striker's end. But Steve Dunne turned it down. Incredible, really. South Africa were in a state of utter disbelief. You have to remember that we were still heavily reliant on Atherton at that stage and could collapse like a pack of cards once he had gone.

The South Africans were fuming, people like Boucher and Daryl Cullinan in particular. They couldn't believe the decision. Meanwhile, I found the whole thing hilarious. I knew that we (and any other team, for that matter) would have reacted in exactly the same way, which made it all the more amusing that it was them who were suffering and not us. I was hoping they would be as angry and indignant as possible and would lose it with Athers, because I knew that would play into his and our hands.

It was very heated for a while. Donald said a few things and made it perfectly clear that he was after Atherton's head. Cullinan walked by and said something to Ath, but he just told him to fuck off. It was terrific stuff because it meant that Donald, on a flat wicket with an old ball, summoned up even more effort and bowled tremendously well to produce some compelling cricket. So much so that it has become known as the classic Atherton–Donald duel of Trent Bridge. It was a great spectacle and I had the best seat in the house – I was the bloke at the other end! I can say he bowled pretty ferociously at me too, and, while it was Athers's day, I feel pretty proud about my involvement in the victory. I don't think the bowling was quite as hostile as when Atherton faced Courtney Walsh in Jamaica in 1994 or when Alex Tudor was hit by Brett Lee in Perth in 2002, but what made this so significant was how much hostility Donald was able to produce on such a flat surface.

There was another twist in the tail when, soon after the furore over the Atherton 'edge', I nicked one from Donald straight to Boucher. He had gone round the wicket and I should have left it, but I just sort of prodded half forward with my bat and nicked it. I didn't even look back. Boucher's a good keeper, to be fair. Whether they were so het up and ready to charge at the fall of the wicket I don't know, but Donald almost jumped past me, and I waited for his roar at getting me out. But the only roar that came was an aggrieved 'What have you done?' kind of noise as Boucher spilled it. Amazing.

It was clear that Boucher was really upset, I mean distraught. He is a player I have liked playing against. He is a tough competitor, the sort of bloke you want on your side. And I was impressed that he wasn't coming up with any excuses. Donald was good, too, running up from fine leg to give Boucher a tap of encouragement soon afterwards when he could see how upset he was. That's what being a teammate's all about. A.D. didn't do that for show. He meant it. That's far more important than providing throwdowns or stuff like that.

Meanwhile, me and Ath were laughing uncontrollably by now. There is nothing that Mike Atherton likes more than someone else's misfortune. He might deny it, but he loves having a giggle at someone when they have made a cock-up. And I was happy to join him on this occasion. When Boucher walked past us at the end of the over, I said to him, 'You should try to concentrate on your keeping a bit more, rather than your sledging.' He muttered something and carried on walking. As I say, I have never minded Boucher or people of his ilk. There was some talk that he had aimed a racist comment at Butcher during the Headingley Test, and it is true that Butch heard something from behind him when he was batting, but I think it was exaggerated in the press. It made for a good story, especially with South Africa's history, but I don't think it was anything that offended Butch and he certainly wasn't fazed by it. It takes a lot to upset Butch.

I was hugely disappointed to get out when I did, soon after, on 58, with the job not quite done. It would have been nice to have seen it through. As it was, Alec came in and played like God, smacking it around and winning the game, with Ath finishing unbeaten on 98. Important point to make here. Atherton wouldn't have been worried about not getting his century. He didn't really care at the time, and I'm sure he doesn't now. He's a winner, and personal milestones mean less to him than to most. Donald, to his credit, came in and had a beer with Ath, and that's the beauty of cricket. They both knew, as we all did, that the rub of the green didn't go South Africa's way on this occasion but it could easily turn the other way next time. That's why the best players shout and scream at the unfairness of it all when they get a bad decision but they know deep down that these things tend to even themselves out, and you need to keep them in perspective. Well, that's the theory anyway.

We were so desperate to win this series. So the final Test at Headingley was huge for us, probably my tensest week as a Test cricketer prior to captaincy. We hadn't won a major five-Test series for donkey's years. We had looked down and out at Old Trafford a few weeks earlier. And at no time during the final Test was it certain which side was going to win, until Darren Gough hit Makhaya Ntini on the pads on the final morning of the game.

It was hell. I can't remember sleeping much at all during that match. Especially the night before the final morning, when they needed 34 to win with 2 wickets left. I stayed up late and had a few rum-and-Cokes that night, simply because I just couldn't rest. I wanted to know the outcome of the game. I wanted someone to tell me what was going to happen the next morning – and, of course, nobody could. Most times you know as a player, but it was so in the balance this time.

Most of that game is a bit of a blur to me now. Gough was brilliant and was in the wickets in both innings. There were some poor decisions around again. And I played what I suppose you could say was one of my best and worst Test innings in the second innings as we desperately tried to bat ourselves out of their reach. It was doing so much that I was literally just putting my bat there and hoping the ball would hit it. I played and missed quite a lot and I played the ball down to third man quite a lot. A typical Nasser Hussain innings, you could say. I was so convinced I wouldn't survive very long that, in a funny sort of way, it relaxed me. As I have said before, when I am relaxed I can play at my best.

It was one of my best innings, however, because I scored 94 in really bowler-friendly conditions when I was under so much pressure. But I was heart-broken to get out. Not because I was so close to a century but because the job wasn't quite done. I knew that chasing anything around 200 or 220 would be very difficult for South Africa, but when I was out we were nearer 170 ahead and not many batsmen to come. I was devastated. If I had stayed another hour, it would have made all the difference – that's how I viewed it at the time. I was almost in tears as I walked off. I had put in all that time, but I hadn't quite produced the innings that defined the game. It meant that it was hold-your-breath time throughout their second innings.

Within 15 overs South Africa were 27 for 5, thanks mainly to the brilliance of Darren Gough, and I thought, 'Here we go.' But then Rhodes and Brian McMillan came together, and the story changed completely. They put on a big stand and the game was running away from us. Stewie came up to me and said, 'What do you reckon?' For the first time in the match two batters were looking well set, so I recommended bringing on Dominic Cork to bowl bouncers and yorkers and really get under their skin. Until that point all the bowlers on both sides had to do was put the ball in the right place, but not now. I thought that the big South African McMillan would be unable to resist the temptation of going after Corky and would consider ducking out of the way as an affront to his manhood.

Stewie agreed and, after hitting Dom for a couple of 4s, McMillan went to pull and hit one straight up in the air for Stewie to take the catch. A huge wicket. Then it was back to line-and-length to try to finish off the job, but even then they would have a little partnership here and there to put the game back on a knife edge. It was getting late and the light was closing in. There was some confusion, actually, over the extra half-hour and whether we or they could or wanted to claim it. And, to be honest, I wanted us to claim it. I didn't want to go through another evening of hell, not knowing who was going to win the series. But Alec wanted to come off and quickly headed for the dressing room before South Africa had a chance to complain. With hindsight, you have to say Alec was right to regroup and let our bowlers have a breather, but at the time it was torture because the game was so in the balance. Of course, in the dressing room everybody was talking about who was going to win. Goughy was telling everyone we would be fine. Others weren't so sure. Others were asking whether Ntini could bat, because we didn't know much about him at that stage.

I was up by five on the concluding morning. I knew I wasn't going to bat. I knew I wasn't going to bowl. But I could be needed in the field, so I had to do a bit of catching practice. Then I just wanted to get on with it. When I got to the ground at 8 a.m. there was hardly anyone about, but by the time Gough bowled the first ball of the morning there was virtually a full house. It was like the first morning of the Test. Fraser got rid of Donald to ease our nerves, but it looked as though Ntini could bat, which made us all the more edgy. Not for long. Gough hit Ntini's pads, Javed Akhtar's finger went up, and we had done it. I know it's been questioned since, but to this day I remain convinced that Ntini was out. He went across his stumps a long way, Gough is known for bowling stumps to stumps and, in my opinion, it would have hit middle-and-leg.

I think South Africa were more aggrieved about earlier decisions in the series rather than that one, to be honest. Yes, we had the rub of the green in that series but that's the way it goes. I know the anti-corruption people were raising questions about Akhtar later on – although these were strenuously denied and no charges were brought – and I just so hope that there was nothing untoward with that victory. It's sad that there's been a seed of doubt, however unfounded it is. The theory was that there had been some corrupt outside influence making the umpires give as many decisions as possible, but personally I don't think that was the case. You are always going to get a lot of lbws at Headingley. Average umpires were under a lot of pressure in that series. And when you are in that situation, human nature can kick in. It didn't spoil anything for me. For the first time as an England player I was a winner in a major Test series. And it felt good.

17

There was a moment, while England toiled at the Oval in the one-off Test against Sri Lanka at the end of the 1998 summer, when Michael Atherton and I could be found, sitting outside a rather nice Chelsea bar in the King's Road with a caesar salad and a glass of Chardonnay, asking passers-by if they knew the cricket score.

Neither of us could play, Athers because of the back and stomach problems he was suffering, which were compounded by his constant diet of painkillers, and me because of the first real muscle injury I had had in my career. If you could call a hernia a muscle injury. Towards the end of the final Test against South Africa I had begun to feel pain in my groin quite badly, but I really wanted to play against Sri Lanka and tried to give myself every possible chance of making it.

A specialist told me I needed an operation which would keep me out of cricket for two months, so this really was the best time to do it, with an Ashes tour looming; but we had just beaten the second-best team in the world, the sun was shining and the Oval wicket looked a good one. In the end, after feeling a lot of pain running around the ground, I decided I had to miss out – hence our little trip into Chelsea to stop us cluttering up the dressing room with sulking, injured players.

In a way it was a great shame we had to play that match. We should have headed to Australia on the high of our South African triumph rather than the low of controversial defeat to Sri Lanka. It was quite a Test. As so often with England, we prepared a wicket that couldn't have been better suited to the opposition if we had asked them to specify their requirements; but it looked as if we were going to get away with it after centuries from Graeme Hick and John Crawley, who were competing for one Ashes tour batting place, took us to 445 all out. Then things changed quite suddenly.

Sanath Jayasuriya thumped a double century, Sri Lanka raced to 591, and then we ended up losing by 10 wickets after being skittled out for 181. It was not the game itself that caused the controversy but the comments of our coach, David Lloyd, when he was asked to give his opinion of the contribution of one Muttiah Muralitharan, who had taken the small matter of 16 wickets in the match. If memory serves correctly, Bumble was reacting in an interview to a comment by the BBC's Tony Lewis which alluded to how much Murali turned it. 'Well, he would do, wouldn't he?' said Bumble, leaving no doubt in anyone's mind that he was suggesting that Murali chucked it.

We all loved Bumble. He was so passionate and supportive of his players that what he was doing at the Oval was basically reflecting the general view of the dressing room that the Sri Lankan off-spinner, at that time not as well known in England as he is now, was indeed a chucker. In particular, Bumble was backing up Robert Croft (whom he was close to) because Crofty had a big thing about Murali and how he was getting so much turn when Croft, with his classical action, couldn't come close to competing with him.

There are a few things to say here. First, it strikes me now that our batsmen had been given no specialist coaching in how to deal with Muralitharan before that Test. Surely we should all have been sat down and taken through videos of him with advice on how to play him because he was so unique. Secondly, there was Bumble. He had gained even more support within the dressing room for addressing the Murali issue on TV, even if his comments were fairly tame, but he had succeeded in putting more pressure on himself just eighteen months or so after the 'we flipping murdered 'em' business in Zimbabwe.

This is why Duncan Fletcher can be so reticent in press conferences. I know his reluctance to say too much publicly does not go down well with the press but Duncan has seen what happened to Bumble and others, and he doesn't want to be treated the same way. All too often when you try to be honest, outspoken and helpful with the press, it can rebound on you if you are not very careful.

We will come to the question of Muralitharan in a little while, but I will say this now: instead of concentrating on the comments of the England coach, I would like to have seen another pertinent question posed by the press. If his action is legal, why can't we encourage loads of youngsters, at my dad's cricket school in Ilford and all over the country, to come up and bowl/throw just like him? Because the biggest single problem in my time as England captain was the lack of a mystery spinner. And, at the time of writing, we are no closer to finding one who can go through Test batting line-ups on good pitches the way Muralitharan, Shane Warne and others of that ilk from other countries seem able to do.

Anyway, it was a real shame we didn't play Sri Lanka on a seaming wicket at Headingley, or a quick one at Edgbaston, rather than a dust bowl at the Oval. Because much of our momentum was lost as we prepared for what was going to be my first Ashes tour. I guess I was at my peak as a batsman and I was hugely looking forward to the trip, even if I was a little apprehensive. For a start, I could still feel my groin at the start of the tour, and you are never quite sure what awaits you on an Ashes trip.

But I made a good start. A young fast bowler called Matthew Nicholson was being talked up as a good prospect and he took wickets against us for Western Australia in our opening first-class match, but I got a century and batted well. One thing that struck me was the Kookaburra ball and how quickly it changes. For the first ten overs it swung round corners, and after that there was a period when it did nothing, until there was a hint of reverse swing later on. It means, as much as anything, that bowlers who grow up using it on good Australian pitches have to learn to make things happen either by being incredibly accurate or by bowling quickly or really spinning it. They can't just rely on the ball to do the work for them, hence the development of players like Warne, Stuart MacGill, Brett Lee and others, bowlers who would make all the difference to us if they were English.

The warm-up matches were not without incident. An unusual sight greeted me at breakfast during our match in Cairns, before the first Test in Brisbane. We were all expecting Cairns to be some holiday paradise, but it turned out to be quite a rough place. I was certainly a bit wary of it and hardly went out. Unfortunately, some of our other lads did. And one morning I was sitting there, as ever the early riser, having breakfast with Bumble and Ath, when John Crawley arrived. Nice lad, John; I've always got on well with him. Someone you always want in your side. Should have played for England more, really. Good cricket brain. Never gets himself into any trouble .... or so we all thought. But he sat down and it was like a double take. He sat next to Bumble so that the coach could only see one side of his face, but I had a full-on view and he looked terrible. In the end I had to say something and asked him if he was all right. He looked as if he'd gone fifteen rounds with Mike Tyson. Then he came out with this story: 'I came in last night and fell over.' Bumble just looked at him and said, 'What, you fell over twenty times, did you? And you managed to hurt both your eyes?' John didn't say anything, but it was clear something had gone on.

Later it came out that John and Dominic Cork had rung the physio late the previous night, asking for his help because John had 'fallen over'. So, as vice-captain, I found myself walking round the ground during play later that day with Dom and Graham Gooch, our manager on that trip, asking what had happened. Corky was desperate not to land John in it and was also feeling bad that it had happened while he was with him, but eventually the truth came out that they had been walking back from a bar to the hotel, not too late, when John must have looked at the wrong bloke at the wrong time, and suddenly a group of them were piling into him. When you think about the way David Hookes died in a similar incident, it really does show what can happen, and John was really badly beaten up. Dom ran for help and got him out of there; and I think our players were simply in the wrong place at the wrong time; but it really shook John, and it shook the rest of us. Bumble and Goochy handled it very well and we got on with the tour, but I don't think John fully recovered from that on this trip. He was withdrawn for a long time afterwards.

Meanwhile, I was learning on my feet in Australia and picking up things that would be useful later on when I became captain. For now I had enough on my plate as a player. Shane Warne wasn't able to play because of his shoulder operation, but the Aussies were able to hit us with another quality leg-spinner in Stuart MacGill. Make no mistake, MacGill was a real threat. He turned the ball more than Warne and his googly was much trickier, but he was still only about three-quarters the bowler Warne was, as much in character as anything else. MacGill had only a fraction of Warne's character, and that's why Australia were much the poorer for Shane Warne's absence. But clearly not that poor! Only a spectacular thunderstorm saved us in the first Test in Brisbane, before we were humbled in Perth in a Test which lasted only two days and two sessions before we were beaten by 7 wickets.

This was where Alex Tudor made what should have been the first of many Test appearances for England, but at the time of writing he looks to be in danger of suffering a career of unfulfilled promise. Tudes bowled really well on his debut. He has so much natural talent. People have told me that Alex thinks I have a downer on him because of comments I have made about him, but nothing could be further from the truth. If I have ever said anything negative about Alex Tudor (and nothing comes to mind), then it is simply out of frustration that he hasn't gone on to be the player he should have been for England and the one I wanted him to be. The guy has an incredible amount of talent. He is one of the nicest people ever to have played the game, a genuine man who cares about others and doing the right thing, a well-brought-up guy. A credit to his family.

Tudes really should have been the new Dominic Cork, a genuine bowling all-rounder, which is what England have lacked in my time. He was someone I wanted to look after when I became captain, just like I tried to look after a lad called Ricky Anderson, who upset me when he left Essex for Northants after I had taken him under my wing.

So it's unfair to say that I have a downer on Tudes. But it is fair to say that some of the things he has done have disappointed me. First, he is injury prone, and I think that has as much to do with his body shape as anything. Alex has a fantastic upper body, but it is more like a boxer's than a cricketer's, and his legs are disproportionate to his torso; they are like matchsticks. He works at the wrong things in the gym and he has been told that by people he gets on with, like Alec Stewart. Alex has been told to work on his legs and his aerobic fitness, but to my knowledge he didn't do it half as much as he should have done. Secondly, Tudes was almost too nice. He didn't have that ruthless, almost selfish streak that you really do need to have as a cricketer. His natural ball, quite quick and back of a length, would have people in all sorts of trouble in county cricket, but I would stand there in the field and see Tudes bowl the same ball at the Australians and watched them rock back and pull it for 6.

That's normal in a way, and it's how the young bowler responds to that step up in class which matters. One thing I can do in life is read people and, when he was hit, I would look in Alex Tudor's eyes and I could almost hear him saying, 'What the fuck do I do now? That ball has always worked in the past.' It's a heart and character thing as much as anything else. You need to be mentally tough to take that step up in class, and Tudes wasn't strong enough.

Move forward two years, and England are in the nets, preparing to play Australia at Trent Bridge. Tudes is not sure if he is fit or not, not for the first time. Duncan was getting angry with him. Dean Conway, the physio, was getting angry with him. So, in front of everyone, I had a right go at him. I said, 'Tudor, we've all had enough. You're either fit, you stay here and you bowl for half an hour to prove you're ready to play tomorrow. Or you tell us right now that you're not fit for this Test Match, you get in your car and you piss off.' He looked at me and I could see him thinking, 'God, what do I do now? Why are you putting me under this sort of pressure?' But to my mind he needed that. He was looking for sympathy, for someone else to make the decision for him. He wanted someone to say, 'Bad luck, Tudes, you're injured, you can't play.' So Alex bowled, declared himself fit and went on to take wickets in the Test. I really thought we had cracked it. I thought we had got over this mental hurdle with Tudes and that he would move on. But it hasn't happened.

Maybe there's still time for Alex Tudor. He is just the sort of player Duncan loves, a front-line bowler who could provide depth to our batting. He could be a poor man's Shaun Pollock. Or even a rich man's Shaun Pollock. But he's in danger of disappearing without trace, and that's very sad, not least for the lad himself.

So, defeat in Perth, and we moved on to Adelaide. The thing to remember about Adelaide is that it is hot. Really hot. And our preparations for that game made me realize that, at times, I am quite 'old school' in my approach to certain matters.

For instance, we had a fitness consultant then called Dean Riddle, and at times I really thought he just didn't understand the demands of cricket. In Adelaide the Australians would just do a few light stretches, conscious of the fact that the temperature is often in the forties in South Australia, whereas we were out before the match for about forty-five minutes, doing cone work, sprinting and other drills designed to warm us up. Why we had to warm up in that sort of heat is beyond me, and this was one area where, later, I used to have rare disagreements with Duncan Fletcher.

Duncan was a big believer in this sort of thing and he almost gave too much power to the non-cricketing people. He would tell me that even footballers would be out before a match with their cones, doing sprint work and things like that, and we ought to follow their example. Well, my view is that footballers know exactly when they are required to start running around and playing. As a cricketer, I could do my warm-ups but then be sitting in the pavilion for much of the day, waiting to bat. There's a real danger you can leave your energy on the field before the match has even started. I would prefer to spend my preparation time in the nets, and then do my warming up in the covers when we start fielding. Maybe I'm starting to sound like an old-fashioned ex-cricketer already, but I know the Australians found our preparations hilarious. They were sitting there with their high-energy drinks, watching us doing sprints!

Dean Riddle is a nice enough bloke, but he was pretty military in his approach and he clashed with people. There was the time we were at a sort of training camp and Dean asked us to do this drill which Graham Thorpe didn't understand and kept on doing wrong. Riddle called Thorpey dumb, which wasn't the most sensible thing to do, and Graham told him where to go and then he walked off.

Then there was the time Riddle complained to David Lloyd that Mark Ramprakash wouldn't do what he told him to do. Ramps was as fit as anyone, was well toned and did his own weights. His attitude was, 'Look, mate, I know what's best for my body. I know what I'm doing. Leave me alone,' and I could understand that point of view.

I scored a few runs in Adelaide, as I had done in Brisbane, but we were heavily beaten. It didn't occur to me until we lost that match that the Ashes were gone again. I hadn't done the simple mathematics. I was just getting into a series against Australia when I realized that the best we could possibly hope for now was a drawn series. It was the first time, I believe, that the destiny of the Ashes had been decided before Christmas in a series in Australia and we weren't even halfway through our tour.

It was a sobering thought. And the best antidote to being sober was to have a few drinks. What made that particular inquest more significant, though, was that I had my first and, really, only proper chat with Steve Waugh. We went out to a few bars that night and I found myself having a fascinating conversation with a man who had always kept his distance from us. Even when we had written a joint Ashes diary in 1997, I had never properly sat down with Steve Waugh and talked cricket. It wasn't in the man's nature to do anything which might help the Poms. On this occasion I asked him how Australia did it, how they could be so good. He told me that a lot of it was simply down to body language. He felt that we weren't a bad side at all but that we didn't have enough confidence about us or enough mental toughness. Waugh said, 'A lot of my batting is about bravado. I go out there and let the bowler and everyone know that I'm there, rushing to the wicket and sticking my chest out.' I felt like saying, 'There's a bit more to it than that, Steve,' but I knew what he meant. He was imposing himself and his authority on the opposition and, as cricket is such a mental game, he was halfway to winning the battle before he had even started in most games.

Rock bottom on our Ashes tour was reached before we managed to regain some pride; and it was reached in the unlikely setting of Hobart, where we had to play an Australian XI before the fourth Test in Melbourne. Alec Stewart, as captain, wanted a rest and it was decided to rest me as well because I was among the runs and we wanted to give someone else a game. So, in the absence of captain and vice-captain, Mike Atherton was asked if he would lead the side, a task he reluctantly agreed to do. I think Ath was happy to do it if we really wanted him to, but he would have preferred someone else to do it, as his time as leader had gone.

And we were on a hiding to nothing because Australia put out an incredible side. They clearly wanted to beat us with their second team as well as their first team. Adam Gilchrist was the captain and the side included others like Matthew Elliott, Greg Blewett, Darren Lehmann, Stuart Law and Michael Bevan. Not exactly a weakened opposition.

When you are not playing in a tour match, the best thing to do is have a net and then get out of there because you need some time away from the cricket and it also gives you a rare chance to see a little bit of the country. So I had a nice time. There was a bit of sightseeing, a bit of golf, a bit of lunch with Stewie, and then down to the ground to see how the match was going.

It was fine at first. Ath got a double hundred and Graeme Hick scored a hundred. It was a three-day match on a flat pitch, and the Australians helped themselves to some runs before Mark Butcher hit a hundred in the second innings and it came down to the last day. In situations like this the touring side have to decide how best the game can serve their needs. Do you need bowling or batting practice? Worrying about a positive result is not usually part of the equation. But Ath, being Ath, decided to do a little bit for the good of the game and set them a last-day target. He probably also thought that our bowlers needed a bit of a run out before the Melbourne Test. Big mistake. The Australians murdered us on the last afternoon, absolutely blasting to 376 for only 1 wicket.

Being cheapskates, Stewie and I had gone to the ground on that final day for a bit of free lunch, but the tension was already rising in our dressing room as our bowling was dispatched to all parts of the ground. It got worse as the afternoon went on, with the Australians loving it and milking the fact that their second team was thrashing us for all it was worth. It was carnage.

You could cut the atmosphere with a knife afterwards. Darren Gough, who also wasn't playing in the match, turned up dressed as Father Christmas and said he had a present for Angus Fraser – new bowling figures. Gus didn't see the joke and lost it with Goughy. Then Atherton got involved and Gus lost it with him, one of his best friends. And so it went on.

What a night we ended up having as we headed for the airport to fly to Melbourne, spend Christmas and get ready for the fourth Test on Boxing Day. All the bowlers were incredibly hacked off because they had gone at 6 an over. None of the senior players was talking to one another. Bumble was walking around, threatening resignation. We were sitting in the airport departure lounge while Bumble was elsewhere in a café, writing out his goodbye speech. The shit had well and truly hit the fan. It wasn't a bad game to miss.

Ath wasn't sheepish at all. He's so stubborn he would probably insist to this day that the declaration was the right thing to do. But he wasn't happy at the time because suddenly no one was talking to him because of a decision he had made as captain of a side he hadn't really wanted to lead. Thankfully, Christmas helped us. The mood was improved when Wayne Morton, physio at the time, handed out some funny presents, including lager for Cork because he wasn't bitter (Dom was feeling bitter about his exclusion from the one-day side at the time), and that improved our mood a bit. Meanwhile, Ath and Stewie talked Bumble out of resigning!

The Melbourne Test was memorable. As so often happens, we improved once the Ashes had gone, but Australia were still formidable opposition. They outplayed us in the first innings, and I got out twice to the debutant Matt Nicholson, which really annoyed me because I was desperate for a hundred on Australian soil and thought I was playing well enough to register one. The Aussies bowled us out cheaply in our second innings and they really should have won the game, only having to chase 175 to win.

Whether it was Australian bravado in taking the challenge too lightly or wanting to win the game too quickly I don't know, but they have had problems chasing small targets. Maybe they just wanted to make us look silly by winning in 20 overs or something like that. But we took a couple of early wickets, and then up stepped Dean Headley to show what I already knew from captaining Deano on an England 'A' trip – that he had a huge heart to go with his undoubted ability.

Dean had perhaps only 75 per cent of the ability of Alex Tudor, but you could throw him the ball in Melbourne and say, 'Right, you've got to bowl for three hours against the Australians here. Can you do it?' He could. Deano could bowl long spells, Alex couldn't. It was a moment when we needed someone to stand up, and Dean Headley stood up. Where he got his energy from I don't know, but Dean kept on steaming in, even when the day went into an extra half-hour, and he bowled us to a quite magnificent victory.

It was important, too, as the series, if not the Ashes, was still alive, and we held our catches to win by 12 runs. It was Dean Headley's finest moment. I've always been a fan of his and the sheer courage and commitment he showed that day emphasize why. When you looked Dean in the eye, he always wanted to bowl more. So many people are not like that. When I was on the 'A' tour in Pakistan, the contrast between Headley and Ed Giddins was pronounced. Whenever I asked Ed if he wanted another over, he had to know if Dean was having one, because he felt he had to do what his supposed rival for a Test place in the future was doing. Headley didn't care what anyone else was doing. He just wanted the ball. It's a tragedy that injury stopped Dean playing a bigger part for England.

Steve Waugh got a bit of stick after that match for finishing not out and somehow being able to be at the other end while the fireworks were flying, but I would have to defend him on that one. On 80 per cent of the occasions when he has been in that situation, he has marshalled his tail to victory, as much by giving them responsibility as anything else. OK, here it didn't work, but in general his policy of trusting his mate up at the other end has served him well.

You also have to remember that Steve Waugh's whole life has been about not giving his wicket away. He would rather be 99 not out than 100 and out. You can't say to Steve Waugh, 'Sorry, mate, you've got to slog it up in the air and be unselfish now because nine, ten and jack are in.' It's just not in his nature. It's what made him the number one player in the world, so you can't expect him to change for the sake of appearances. His view was, 'I'll carry on valuing my wicket, but I'll also make sure the bloke at the other end knows I think he can bat, and between us we'll get through this.' I don't think you can knock him for that.

So we went to Sydney, still with a chance of squaring the series. And we almost did it too. A score of 2–2 wouldn't have been a fair reflection of the series, to be honest, but we could easily have achieved that, and we might well have done had Michael Slater been run out, as he should have been, at an early stage of his match-winning second innings 123.

Basically, Peter Such was obscuring the view of the third umpire when he watched the replay, and this showed up the problems with technology and affected us hugely in the match because Slater was definitely out, and it left us chasing around 50 too many in our final innings, especially on a turning pitch with Shane Warne back in their side.

Yet we came out of that game with our heads held high. Darren Gough recorded a fantastic hat-trick, I got a few runs again, but in the end we had been beaten once more. A 3–1 score flattered the Aussies a bit, but they deserved to win the Ashes. That has been the story of my career, and I can't see it being any different for a while.

That wasn't quite the end of our Australian tour. I had been in and out of England's one-day side for most of my career up until this point and, as you can see, I haven't really talked about the limited-overs game in any great depth because it has never meant as much to me as Test cricket and I have never been as good at it as at Test cricket. But there was a World Cup in England coming up and I wanted to play in it, so I was pleased to make our one-day squad for the triangular series against Australia and Sri Lanka that ended our tour. But you would never have guessed that a World Cup was in the offing. We were nowhere near settled on our side. One match we would play Vince Wells, then it might be me or someone else.

Yet I was just happy to be in the side, I got some runs in Sydney to start me off, and I then enjoyed a pretty good time with the bat as the series went on. As did England, until we endured one of the most eventful and controversial games in one-day cricket history. Adelaide and the Sri Lankans, of course, is the game everyone will remember from that time. In the build-up to the match we had heard that the Australian umpire Ross Emerson was planning to call Muralitharan for chucking but we didn't know for sure that it would happen. When we batted, we were just sitting there waiting for it to happen and it duly did happen within two overs of Murali being brought on to bowl. Well, people like Bumble and Robert Croft were on their feet in our dressing room, shouting, 'Yes, yes, go on,' because they felt vindicated in their views on the guy. The rest of us were wondering what on earth was going to happen next, but I don't think any of us expected the sheer drama of the scenes that followed.

Arjuna Ranatunga, their captain, simply said, 'OK, it's my bowler, it's my ball, if you're not going to let him bowl we're going off.' Murali meanwhile was behaving like a spoilt brat and whingeing about what had happened to him. Ranatunga, the clever street-fighter, was being much more canny and was quickly on the phone, ringing Sri Lanka and his lawyers and all sorts of people. We thought it was the end of the game but after what seemed like an eternity we all trooped back on, and we ended up scoring over 300 with Murali bowling at Emerson's end so he couldn't call him and Ranatunga insisting that the umpire stood very close to the stumps so he couldn't see what was going on.

Then the real fun started. It was like the beginning of our love–hate relationship with the Sri Lankans which has been short on love. I do enjoy them, though, in a funny sort of way. They play tough and, on the whole, they don't whinge. Ranatunga toughened them up considerably and for such a small island they have produced some fabulous players. And all their toughness was on show here as the match degenerated into a totally bad-tempered affair, with Stewie clashing with Ranatunga, Roshan Mahanama barging into Gough and Gough feigning a head-butt at Mahanama. Surreal stuff. As was the ending, when I missed a run-out chance that would have won it for us and, of all people, Murali hit the winning runs as they successfully chased over 300!

We couldn't believe it. We really wanted to beat them. Nothing to do with the chucking incident. It was simply all the aggro that had gone on in the rest of the match. Sri Lanka were full of it. It was noticeable earlier that we never saw them after matches in which we'd defeated them, but on this occasion they were more than happy to come into our dressing room and try to shake hands with us after beating us. That didn't impress Alec Stewart. He didn't like the inconsistency of it all. I think he refused to shake hands with them that night. I, meanwhile, couldn't help but have a grudging respect for Ranatunga. He had made them so much harder to beat and was prepared to use any trick in the book to get what he wanted. There is something I can't help admiring in that attitude. Certainly Sri Lanka haven't been so well led since he has gone.

Anyway, that defeat didn't stop us reaching the finals of the triangular series against Australia where, in the first of the best-of-three games, I had my worst moment under the reigns of David Lloyd and Alec Stewart. I really did (and still do) have a lot of respect for the pair of them, but they didn't know me as well as I thought they did for them to blame me for our defeat in that final, which they did. We were chasing a reasonable Australian total at the SCG and a few people around me had failed. I was battling, like I had done in the Ashes series, and I got to 50. Throughout my innings I was having a few words here and there with Shane Warne, as I did throughout my career, and he said something to me and I told him to fuck off. Nothing unusual in that.

It was also not unusual for me to use my feet against the spinners and try to hit them back over their head, I have done it all my career. Indeed, David Lloyd had been saying to us that Shane had been bowling a bit more slowly since his shoulder operation and encouraging us to use our feet against him. Even now, on Sky TV, Bumble is always going on about how there is plenty of room back over the bowler's head and that's where people should try to hit the spinners.

I tried to hit Shane over a big gap at wide mid-off, missed the ball and was stumped. I was disappointed. Of course I was. But I had made a decent score and we only needed around 30 to win off ten or so overs with 7 wickets in hand when I was out. But we collapsed and couldn't finish it off. That, to my mind, didn't mean that I had lost us the match. As I have said, part of my failing in one-day cricket was not having the confidence to think I could finish a game off, that there was always someone waiting to come in who could finish games off better than me. So I'm afraid I often got out between 30 and 60, and that was the case on this occasion.

My point is, you could have accused me of taking the weak option and getting myself out because I thought someone like Adam Hollioake or Neil Fairbrother could finish the game off better than me, but please don't accuse me of losing the plot, allowing Shane Warne to get in my head and throwing it away in a huff. Which is what I seemed to be being accused of. Of course Shane milked it and said afterwards, 'I got into Nasser's head, he played a terrible shot, I got him out and we won the game.' It really, honestly, wasn't the case at all. He got me out because tactically I felt he was the bloke we had to get after before Glenn McGrath came back into the attack. I made a misjudgement and got out. Yes, I should have seen the game through, but it was also a game we should have won anyway.

When I came back into the dressing room you could cut the atmosphere with a knife. Bumble was storming around. I went into the back room, to find that he had basically trashed it, including kicking Alan Mullally's ghetto blaster. He was the England coach and he was passionate, and I have no problem with that. It is the sort of thing I have done at times. He cares. But I just felt it was unfair that I was apparently being singled out as the villain of the piece. Other people had failed. At least I had got a score and taken us to the brink of victory.

When we lost the second match, to hand Australia the series, a few of us got into a lift with Bumble, and he stood there and went through the whole Lancashire side before saying, 'I'm going to bring them all in and get rid of this lot.' We just stood there, remembering how much we'd all given over the last four months for him, our country and ourselves in the toughest of all countries to tour. What really hit me was the realization that my lapse against Shane Warne had annoyed the people who matter. If Bumble had come up to me quietly and said that I should have seen the game through, I would have understood and taken the rap; but this was much more, and the silence being displayed by the powers that be towards me was deafening. It looked as though it was going to cost me my World Cup place.

18

There was a lot of tension around as we awaited the naming of the 1999 World Cup squad. Not least in me. I had a gut feeling I wasn't going to make it, even though I had played well for most of the winter. I knew I wasn't the greatest one-day player in the world but I thought I was a good squad player, a decent batsman and good fielder who could come in and do a job during the course of a tournament. What I couldn't accept was that my dismissal against Shane Warne in that one-day final could possibly undo all the good work of an Ashes winter; yet that seemed to be the case, as the squad was picked and my name wasn't in it.

It was a big disappointment to me. There was to be a World Cup in England and I wanted to be in it, I thought I should be involved. Soon afterwards I went to a function which was attended by Alec Stewart and other senior people, and it was awkward for all of us because I was sure I must have been the next name on the selectors' list. I just decided that all I could do was keep my head down and get on with it.

And I had a major distraction to throw myself into. It was my benefit year, an occasion I was both looking forward to, because of the obvious security it can provide for you, but also absolutely dreading. In fact I was dreading it above all else. Because the whole concept is alien to my personality and I just knew I was going to find it a year-long ordeal.

I hadn't prepared properly for it at all. Just hadn't got things signed or done all the necessary work that makes a benefit year a success. Benefits are not really for people like me, Mike Atherton and Alec Stewart. In all honesty we don't deserve them and don't absolutely need them. They should be for the cricketers who have worked hard all their career, serving their counties for very little material reward. We've made our money from international cricket and have got out of the game much more than we have put in, really. I have never played the game for money. I know it's a cliché, but the money is just a consequence of what you are doing. You try to ensure you get as much as you can, you look at what others are earning and try to get the same deal for yourself, but I don't think most cricketers have a clue how much they've got in the bank at any one time or are genuinely driven by the financial rewards on offer – which only recently have been good for international and, in some cases, county cricketers.

But to me, my benefit was the chance to earn in the region of £200,000, or maybe even more, tax free, the kind of sum that a lot of people spend much of their lifetime making; and if that opportunity is there for you and your family, why not take it? And work at it to the best of your ability? Many of us don't relish the system but I've yet to see someone turn a benefit down, and understandably so. The downside for me was that the whole thing was completely and utterly against what Nasser Hussain is all about, because it put me in situations where I was very uncomfortable.

It was the whole social thing, mainly. It can be summed up by me thus. Basically, I had to ring people up and, translating my words into simple English, say to them: 'I don't know you. I've never met you. Probably, being the way I am, I have walked past you sometimes at Chelmsford, blanking you and spewing because I've got out for 20 that day. You have probably tried to say hello to me or just exchange a few pleasantries with an England cricketer, and I've told you to piss off or completely ignored you. Now I'm ringing you up because it's my benefit season and I'm asking you for money even though I've already probably got more of it than you.' Very weird. Lacking in dignity. And it's false. And I hate being false. It's something I just have never done.

I was fortunate. I had a very good committee. People who knew me and were friendly with me and who knew what they were getting with me. People like my chairman, Graham Staples, and others, like Paul Lucas, Paul Vater and Malcolm Field. Top man, Fieldo. He was a very popular and very diligent Assistant Secretary at Essex for years under the late Peter Edwards but some thought he was forced out by the David East–Alan Lilley regime, a huge loss for the county.

There were also people on my committee who I didn't really know that well. People who serve most beneficiaries and love being involved. I wondered at times why on earth they wanted to help me, but I was grateful to them. It's almost as if they expect to be there, doing their bit, and would be very upset if you didn't ask them to be involved.

So I was lucky. Really, the whole system should be replaced by a good pensions system, and the Professional Cricketers Association are doing a lot of work to help on all this; but it would take a brave man to come along and stop benefits because, whenever you abolished them, there would always be some very worthy cricketers just about to be awarded theirs. And that could have an adverse affect on people's lives.

Some people really milk it. Benefits approaching £500,000 are not uncommon now, but I was never going to be like that. You have to be so organized and so thick-skinned, and I was neither. You also have to rely an awful lot on the support of players, and I look back now and think how amazing it was that so many players would give up their valuable spare time to support me on various ventures, like my trip to the Isle of Wight, and one to Dublin.

I know some people have their own reasons for supporting others. They are making contacts for when their time comes. And fair enough. Someone like Mark Ilott would enjoy a benefit day more than he would a day's cricket, it seemed to me. He loved making contacts in the City, charming people and planning for the future. Ronnie Irani was like that too. They came to nearly all my benefit functions and I was very grateful to them. But they also had their own motives.

I think my benefit had a positive effect on my cricket in 1999. When I was out on the field it was like a release. I was so grateful to have escaped from ringing people up to get them to functions or meeting people who could help me that the cricket was a joy!

I hated every moment of the year, to be honest. But that's not to say I'm not extremely grateful to everyone who supported me and my family and helped me have such a successful benefit. It also furthered me as a person. It gave me a glimpse into the real world and how to organize events. It also encouraged me, I guess, to make a few new friendships, something I hadn't gone out of my way to do much since leaving university.

People like those I've mentioned and others, like Caroline Byatt and Colin Richardson, are Essex through and through. They're genuine cricket lovers and good people who want to see Essex and Essex cricketers doing well. There is a real 'no strings attached' feel to their motives, and I like that. There are a lot more like them out there and they are among the most important people in cricket.

I'm terrible at keeping in touch with people. I have to admit that. Over the years I have been awful at returning people's phone calls, keeping in touch with those who helped me so much in 1999. This again is the bad side of Nasser Hussain. The unsociable side of me. I can be so introverted and private. I'm happy that way. I don't know why. So to all those people who have done so much for me, I say: sorry you haven't had much in return while I have either been playing cricket or worrying about playing cricket.

I think these people and the genuine supporters of Essex cricket have been let down by the club in recent years. There are so many good things about the club, so many nice people, but there's a real lack of business acumen, in common with so many of the counties. The main purpose of county cricket has to be to produce England cricketers, especially as so much of their money comes from the ECB. But do you really think, to take my county as an example, that David East and Alan Lilley had much interest in producing England cricketers? No, they're too busy with the short-term priorities of running Essex County Cricket Club, saving money, looking after ex-players and, it has to be said, their own survival. It's understandable, perhaps, but the tragedy is that, irrespective of whether or not it's good for England, it's not even good for Essex in the long run. The club is full of ex-cricketers doing non-cricket jobs which would probably be better filled by people with experience of running a successful business. Even on the coaching side, that attitude can be damaging, like Terry Charrington being moved sideways to accommodate ex-players when, in fact, he's a better coach than some of those who are replacing him.

While 'jobs for the boys' can offer security and appears to be a good way of maintaining a friendly, family feel to a club, at the same time it limits its potential. Look at the success of outsiders like John Bracewell at Gloucestershire or Duncan Fletcher at Glamorgan. Without new blood, there are no new ideas. And without new ideas people don't see a bigger picture. They slip into the comfort zone, and there's no successful future in that.

The whole system is about the preservation of the status quo, and that's why there is so much negativity in our county set-up. In Australia everything is geared towards aiding the national team. Their aspiring players are not interested in state cricket. All they want to do is play for their country because that's where the prestige, the honour and, yes, the money is. Whereas in England too many people just want to do enough to earn themselves another county contract and hang on long enough for a benefit. There's always a safety net, and that just doesn't make for hungry, dedicated cricketers.

So my benefit took up a lot of my time while I came to terms with being left out of the World Cup. But there was a twist in the tail. Mike Atherton was struggling with his back. Really struggling. In the end I got the call to replace him. I felt desperately sorry for Ath. Our careers have run in tandem for so long. I respect him so much. But I was delighted. I really wanted to be there, and now I was to get my chance. I flew out on my own to Sharjah to join the boys in the build-up to the tournament and, to be honest, I felt a bit on the outside. Didn't feel completely part of it. But that didn't bother me. I was realistic enough to know that I probably wasn't one of the best eleven one-day cricketers in England, but I did feel I was worth a place in the squad and had told David Graveney so when the chairman of selectors originally rang me to tell me I had been left out!

Yet even though I was still easing my way into the World Cup squad I could see that there was a sub-plot building up. There was a problem with contracts, and there was a lot of talking going on, much of it acrimonious. Most of it was passing me by. For my part, I was just relieved to be there and I was prepared to accept any money they wanted to give me for being there.

But feelings were running high and meetings were going on with various ECB officials, including one Simon Pack, a military man and a friend of Lord MacLaurin, who had been brought into the ECB as, if I remember rightly, the international teams director.

He really was the wrong man in the wrong job at the wrong time. He just knew nothing about cricket and the mindset of cricketers, who were much more down to earth and streetwise than him. Pack had made his first huge mistake before the West Indies tour of 1998 when, in his wisdom, he sat us down and gave us a talk about the Caribbean that seemed very out of touch with the sensibilities of the late twentieth century.

He had people there saying things like 'The locals are lovely people but not the brightest,' and 'Be careful if you go out at night.' You could see the guys with West Indian heritage in our team bristling and taking real offence at it all. As did the rest of us.

Now Pack and the ECB were at it again and we had a heated meeting in Sharjah. Others there were much closer to the ins and outs than me, but we were being given a small basic contract of something like £5,000 a man; but if you played in every game and we progressed as a team, better rewards would follow. At this stage we had no real help from the PCA and were left very much on our own to deal with disputes like this, and the whole thing was completely unsatisfactory.

It was hoped that the tournament would generate millions and we were only going to see a tiny percentage of it. At this stage, financial considerations were not at the top of my agenda, but when I became captain I played a leading role in getting the whole structure looked at and dealt with more professionally, players being properly represented by our own commercial organization.

The 1999 World Cup débacle was the last in which the players just had to accept what they were given, and for a while there was a very real chance that the team was not going to accept it at all.

It was a difficult time for Alec Stewart. My impression was that he and Simon Pack had earlier come to an agreement over figures, but that Stewie hadn't taken into account that there were a lot of commitments involved in a World Cup other than just the games and that, for a lot of our players, this was their one big chance to earn a decent amount from cricket. It was the first time, I think, that anyone started questioning what Alec Stewart was doing and was the beginning of the end of his time as England captain.

Until then everyone had seen Stewie as our leader but now there was the first inkling of discontent, that Stewie had agreed to a pay deal that would favour people like himself who were going to play in every game, but not necessarily the whole squad. I'm not saying Alec did anything wrong. I can sympathize with him. Particularly as, later, I was in exactly the same position as captain. It was very hard being the captain in Alec's situation. That's why I took the decision to bring someone else in to do our negotiating as an England team. The World Cup had proved a watershed as to how these things were done, and the players wanted to question the ECB, question how much money was going to them, and have a direct relationship with the TV companies and the sponsors who had started putting huge sums into the game.

Most of the anger in 1999 was directed towards Simon Pack and Tim Lamb, the ECB chief executive. Times were changing. At that stage our main wages still came from the counties, and anything we got from England was just like a handout, a bonus. That's why the advent of central contracts was such a huge step forward. We needed to feel like England players first, county players second. It's not a money thing; it's making you feel like an international cricketer. Even up until the 1999 World Cup we felt like county players who every now and then got a call-up to go and play for another side. Now it's the other way round. We are England players first, and that is how it has to be.

It's amazing what that subtle change has done for us. I'm not sure that people like Michael Vaughan and Marcus Trescothick would have fulfilled their potential under the old system. They would still have been playing for Yorkshire and Somerset and just being picked for England and getting a couple of grand each time for the privilege. Same with many others. But now they feel like international players, and the mental advantages of that are tremendous.

Things that happened in 1999 wouldn't happen now. Like the Graham Thorpe incident in Canterbury. We were in a training camp before the World Cup and we had worked our socks off all day and were feeling knackered. The whole pay thing had been swirling around. We had been told to go to lots of functions and were feeling like pieces of meat, just being tossed around by the ECB at the whim of any old dodderer who wanted to plaster his function with lots of England players.

On this occasion I was rooming with Thorpey and we were both lying on our beds after a hard day's work when I realized what the time was and started getting ready for yet another function. I said to him, 'Come on, Gray, we've got to go. You know there's this function.' He just turned over and told me he wasn't going. I thought he was joking. But he told me that he felt he had done his bit and that it didn't say anything in his contract about this function, that he was working his nuts off getting ready for the World Cup and that he wasn't having anything to do with it.

Thorpey put up quite a convincing argument and I agreed with much of what he said, but the bottom line was that, unless you're Graham Thorpe, you don't put two fingers up to the ECB over something like this because effectively you're putting two fingers up at the team. It was a question of 'If we all have to go, then, Graham, you should come too.' We all knew that we were being paid only for the games that we played in, but we were putting up with everything else because we all wanted to play in the World Cup and had, eventually, put up with the contracts that were on offer to us.

I tried to convince him but he's as stubborn as they come, so in the end I just said to him, 'Look, what do you want me to say?' and he told me to tell the powers that be that he wasn't feeling very well. So I got on the team bus and up at the front was Graham Gooch, manager at that time, the coach David Lloyd and Stewie. I was last on because I'd been trying to persuade Thorpey to come, and they immediately asked where my mate was. Well, I don't know if my lie was unconvincing, but a lot of people didn't want to go to this function and they immediately saw through me and marched off the bus towards Thorpey's room when I said he wasn't well.

He never did make the function but the next day he was dragged in to face the music. Stewie had told him to apologize and he would make sure he was OK. Thorpey was having none of that. He went in there and told it like it was. He said, 'I'm here to play cricket and I will win you World Cup games but don't expect me to go to every function when I'm not being paid for them and I'm trying to rest.' As ever, the little man made a lot of sense, but it didn't stop him being fined. It was a small incident which epitomized a terrible build-up to such a huge event like the World Cup. I don't think it affected our performances in the end, but it didn't do us any favours, or any good for the image of the game in this country.

19

Despite all the distractions, I felt I was batting well in the early part of 1999, mainly because I had had a full pre-season with Essex and was used to the green wickets and the sideways movement that had to be a factor in a World Cup taking place in England in May. The rest of the World Cup party had spent a bit of time in Pakistan and Sharjah and, to be honest, I felt my preparation was better.

Meanwhile, Nick Knight, a regular fixture at the top of our order for the previous two years, was struggling – at precisely the wrong time for him. Around this time, David Graveney was quite indiscreet with me a couple of times, and he told me there was a perception that Knighty was playing for himself. That's Grav for you! When I was captain, he was paranoid about me leaking anything to the paper I wrote for; but the truth was, he used to leak far more himself about selectorial matters and who favoured who during meetings. I have always been a big one for collective responsibility and never passed on anywhere near as much as Grav seemed to fear.

Anyway, Grav seemed to think that Nick felt his World Cup place was secure and that he had been a little selfish on the one-day leg of our Australian tour. But to me, it goes back to what I believe about any person who reaches the top in cricket: they have to have a bit of a selfish streak. It's like accusing Steve Waugh of playing for himself. Well, yes he did, but look at the end result. And yes, at times Knighty did make sure that he got his runs first, but he ended up being one of our best one-day batsmen.

I know Duncan Fletcher felt that Knighty's style put a bit of pressure on his opening partner in later years because he was very much a 'four or nothing' sort of person, and his partner might end up with only one ball or so to face an over to make an impression in the first fifteen overs. There was also confusion occasionally over whether Knighty should pinch hit or play normally, because he was much more than just a pinch hitter, and he became a sort of poor man's Sanath Jayasuriya. And, around the time of the World Cup, sides had worked out that he wasn't a great cutter or puller, so they packed those areas and tried to stop him producing his get-out-of-jail shot: running down the wicket and hitting over the top. So his run rate and strike rate had dropped a bit, but he was still a valuable part of our armoury, even though there was some talk about his place in the side in the build-up to our first game against Sri Lanka.

I just kept my gob shut and got on with it, but I really didn't expect the knock on my door at our hotel in Kensington after practice at Lord's, the day before that opening match. It was Alec Stewart, telling me I was going to open the batting. I hadn't even been in the original squad, and I had never opened the batting at that stage in any professional match. Yet here I was, the day before the showpiece opening game of the 1999 World Cup between the holders and the hosts, being told that I was to replace one of the mainstays of the England side.

All I knew of it beforehand was that some sections of the press were mentioning it as an option and Bumble had talked about me as a possible opener during a Sky interview, but I never really expected it to happen. One of Duncan Fletcher's many strong points is that when he believes a player is good enough to succeed at Test level he will not be swayed from that viewpoint. He stays strong if they have a couple of bad Tests because he is sure they can play. And I don't think my selection for that World Cup would have happened if Duncan had been around. And he would have been right.

In all honesty, having invested so much time in Knighty,

they really should have given him the chance to succeed in a World Cup. They really should have gone with him. The selection panel then were just not strong enough, and a lot of that has to be put down to David Graveney. He would listen to anyone, be influenced by too many people. He would ask Ian Botham who he felt should be in the England side. He would ask Bob Willis. He would ask cricket correspondents. He would ask the man in the street if he had an opinion. I'm all for democracy, but you really have to draw a line and have the courage of your own convictions if you are chairman of selectors. I like David Graveney. He cares. He wants English cricket to do well. He makes the hard phone calls, and I'm afraid he's been on the receiving end of too many bollockings from me and others. Having Grav as chairman of selectors throughout my term as England captain was of great benefit because it provided a consistency that other captains didn't have.

But, again, I think he's too interested in protecting his own job, and in his case he does that by trying to keep everybody happy and being too quick to worry about what the press are saying. One of my favourite theories is that you always become a much better player when you are out of the England side than when you are in it, simply because your stock seems to rise in your absence, and what Duncan Fletcher and Geoff Miller have done is to stop us going round the houses and back to square one by trying to identify class and sticking with it. You have to decide whether a bloke can play or not. Like we did with Marcus Trescothick and like we did with Michael Vaughan. Others fall by the wayside, but most get a proper chance now, once they're selected. And once Duncan and Geoff have decided that someone cannot do it at the highest level, there's very little chance of them coming back.

Back then, the selectors decided Knighty was struggling a bit, was playing for himself a bit, and that I was in form. So I was in, even though they hadn't thought I was good enough for a place in the squad two months earlier. That's not to say I didn't think I could do it. It gave me the time at the crease to build an innings, and also the field being up for the first fifteen overs was a huge advantage. Later on in the innings my classic cover drive only earned me 1 run but opening, it got me 4, so although I felt for Nick I wanted to take my chance and couldn't believe I'd been handed it.

My role was to bat almost like I would in a Test Match, field at backward point and take some catches and pull off some run-outs. It was a clearly defined role and it was a straightforward one for me. I felt very comfortable doing it. And I ended up having a decent World Cup. But we didn't as a team. It had nothing to do with the Nick Knight situation or the contract debacle. It's just that we didn't win the key games. Getting through in the World Cup is all about peaking and winning the big matches, and we just didn't do that. There was also the issue of us not scoring quickly enough at Trent Bridge when we defeated Zimbabwe – but, to be honest, your first priority must always be to make sure you win the game, and we won that one in thirty-eight overs, so we didn't exactly cock that game up. It was more losing to India and being thrashed by South Africa that did for us. Not to mention Zimbabwe beating South Africa at Chelmsford. That was a killer.

There was also another little indication that all was not entirely well with our leadership regime. We were sitting there on the Saturday night at Edgbaston after our crucial game against India had been taken into a second day by the weather. Zimbabwe had just beaten South Africa, which shocked us all and threw our destiny into sharp perspective. We had to beat India the next day or go out. The lads were very quiet and we were looking for a bit of a talk or something from the captain or coach. But instead of Stewie or Bumble, Steve Bull, our psychologist, stood up to say something. Now, I am a big fan of Steve and I used him a lot myself and, as this book shows, I believe psychology has a huge part to play in cricket; but there is a time and a place for everything, and this wasn't it. A lot of people, me included, didn't even think Steve should be in the dressing room during matches, that his work should be done before the game.

Really, though, that wasn't a big issue. The next day we lost and were out of the World Cup at the first hurdle. A disaster for us. Eliminated the day before the World Cup song was released! The bottom line was that the trust between the ECB and Alec Stewart as captain of England had been eroded by the contracts dispute, and after that we really needed to have a good World Cup to make our point to the board in the best way possible. We didn't. So the search for a scapegoat was on.

This is when David Graveney came into his own as a political animal. The pressure was on him. He had to look after himself a little bit. The press were scenting blood and Stewie looked as if he might be the one to suffer. When you look at it, that is most unfair. Stewie had been captain when we had beaten South Africa in a major series a year before. We had done pretty well in the Ashes series and we should have progressed in the World Cup. So he hadn't done that badly, and we all thought he was a good captain.

I thought they should have stuck with Alec Stewart. I didn't think he had done anything wrong enough to warrant losing the England captaincy. But of course I thought about what any possible change meant for me. If they were going to get rid of him, I felt, then it would have to be me who succeeded him. There didn't really seem to be any other candidates.

As it turned out, both me and Mark Ramprakash were interviewed for the job, but I think to an extent the ECB went for me as what they saw as the lesser of two evils. I gather they thought both of us would constitute a gamble but that perhaps I was calmer than Ramps by this stage of our careers and was a bit more established in the team. If I could change my ways as captain, I'm sure Ramps could have done too and I'm sure he would have made a good captain. He certainly has a good cricket brain. But I felt confident that if a change was going to be made then it would be me, and I just waited before our Test series against New Zealand to see what would happen next.

One of the biggest plus points to come out of the World Cup was the large number of British Asian people who flocked to the grounds. And it was also hugely noticeable that the majority of them were supporting India or Pakistan, even the younger ones. This came as no surprise to me because I had seen at first hand at my dad's cricket school the vast numbers of Asian kids who loved the game, and I knew that there were thousands of them out there around the country. But now it seemed to dawn on the ECB that here was a whole new audience who wanted to watch the game and that maybe I could be a role model to persuade them that it might be a good idea to support England!

Now, having always considered myself to be totally English, while still being aware and proud of my Indian side, I have never thought of myself as a role model for British Asians. Didn't really think there was any sort of role for me to play in that regard. What I did feel – and it was something that I went public on a bit later – was that second- and third-generation Asians were still clinging to their sub-continental roots, whereas I felt that they should embrace their Britishness more and start swapping the Tendulkar shirts I saw them wearing at the Ilford Cricket School for Hussain ones or Stewart's or Gough's. Not quite Norman Tebbit territory, but similar, I guess. It is a delicate subject and one I haven't often got involved in. I can understand the mums and dads who have made their lives here still supporting the country of their birth and, of course, their children will have some interest in the fortunes of their parents' teams; but I do feel strongly that there's a huge amount to gain by the Asian community nailing their colours to England's mast, both as players and as supporters. It's good for them (and I speak from experience there!) but it's also good for England. No part of the English public follows cricket with more passion than the Asian community (and passionate support for England is always welcome!) and the potentially deep well of talent they provide is not something future England teams can afford not to draw on.

It was just that the ECB, perhaps a bit simplistically, had seemed to cotton on to the fact after the World Cup that I might be able to do some good simply because of my surname, and I was happy to go with that if they really felt it would make a difference.

I had my interview and basically I said the same stuff I told them the last time; and then I started to feel a little nervous because it really did seem as though I might get the job, and I had seen at first hand how it had affected Mike Atherton, Alec Stewart and Gooch and how it had changed their lives. I discussed the matter with Karen, discussing whether we wanted to or even could deal with the hassle that was involved, and the bottom line had to be that if I was handed the poisoned chalice, as the captaincy was regarded then, I really had to go for it. I had honestly never craved the England captaincy but I was not going to turn down the chance to lead my country if it came.

The phone call eventually came from Graveney and I remember being alone in the dining room of my old house in Little Leighs. There were the usual pleasantries and I just thought, 'Look, cut it out and get to the point,' because by that time I was desperate to know if it was going to be me. Grav then said, 'We'd like you to be the new England captain,' and it all started to sink in.

I thought I was prepared for the interest – but I really didn't know just how huge a story it was going to be. You try to play it down when you're the one involved and you try not to think about things too much, but clearly it was bigger than anything else I had experienced. Being an Essex player, going to university, getting married, these are all huge things, but also very personal things, whereas the England captaincy is public property. It dawned on me immediately that my life was going to change substantially.

My dad had been absorbing every word and hanging on to every one of them for weeks, asking me if I had heard anything, and after about a minute I knew I had to ring him first, even ahead of Karen. The first thing I said to him was, 'Dad, you'd better not read the papers for the next couple of years. I'm England captain.' But I knew he would never be able to do that. He was just so happy, almost thanking me for getting to the very top. I was trying to tell him that there would be some hard times ahead, because he feels any criticism of me so deeply; but this wasn't really the time for that. It was just a nice, brief moment on the phone, one that meant that all my dad's ambition and drive for me had reaped the ultimate reward. And it was quickly followed by a call to Karen at work. She was her normal matter-of-fact self, basically just saying, 'Captain. Are you? Well done.' Then it was back to her class of kids.

Then I didn't know what to do. I guess my thoughts quickly switched to who was going to be coach because Bumble had gone the same way as Stewie in the aftermath of the World Cup and we were going to have a completely new set-up. I remember going through the candidates, and it seemed to boil down to Bob Woolmer, Dav Whatmore or Duncan Fletcher, and I told people that it wouldn't be Fletcher simply because nobody really seemed to know much about him other than the Glamorgan players whom he had coached.

I was sure, the ECB would give it to someone they knew, and my money was on Woolmer. I thought he had all the chat and all the credentials, and Warwickshire had won everything going under him. Whether he turned it down or not I'm not sure, but I was surprised when it was announced that Duncan had got the job. At that stage I wouldn't have recognized him if he'd walked in the Chelmsford dressing room, and I thought to myself, 'Oh my God. Not only are you going into a job you know nothing about, but you are going to do it with a bloke you don't know at all.'

Another factor, to me, was that Glamorgan's England players, people like Robert Croft and Matthew Maynard, were not really favourites of mine back then, and I'd heard Duncan was close to Maynard. The word was, Duncan wanted to do the job with Maynard too, because Matthew is a very loyal man, and that appealed to him, so I think both of us were worried and apprehensive as we gathered at Lord's for our introductory press conference. I'd heard that Duncan was quite a disciplinarian and I wondered what he would make of me, but my dad's upbringing stood me in good stead and I arrived for my first meeting with Duncan, determined to respect him as an elder, and I would sit and listen to whatever he had to say.

He came across as a very gentle, knowledgeable man who spoke quietly about me and captaincy. Duncan said a couple of things I've always remembered since. In a nutshell, it was: 'Remember as captain everyone at all stages will be looking at you and your body language, bowlers, fielders, opponents, supporters and media. Keep that in mind.' Generally, it was an encouraging first meeting before we went out to meet the press and I thought, 'Well, why not? Why not work from a clean slate? He seemed a decent bloke. If it had been someone I knew well, like Graham Gooch or Keith Fletcher, it might have been harder for me, because it wouldn't have been easy to turn around and say I didn't agree with them on something.

In some ways I was very naive about Duncan. I thought that I would be starting off as the senior partner, with the perceived upper hand in our relationship because I was the one who had played a lot of Test cricket and he was denied that honour by Zimbabwe's lack of Test status in his playing days. I thought he would be coming to me, saying, 'What's he like?', 'What's that one like?' How wrong could I have been! I soon realized that Duncan knew everything about everyone!

So we did the photos at Lord's and I felt very proud. I was

wearing my England jacket, looking at the three lions, and people at Lord's were calling me captain. It was the start of the most eventful and wonderful times of my life.

20

One of the first things I did after being made England captain was to ring my agents, SFX, and say, 'OK, presume you've got another Atherton here.' By that I meant that I wanted to protect my privacy and that I wasn't interested in many of the commercial possibilities that would now come my way. I am not money-obsessed but I do need people to run my life at times; SFX, a well-regarded organization with some illustrious sporting clients, run in Britain by Jon Holmes, are perfect for me. I didn't want to be appearing in *Hello!* magazine and I didn't want to be opening supermarkets, and basically I needed their help to keep my life as close as possible to the way it was before.

Alec Stewart, typically, rang me straight after the announcement to say, 'No hard feelings, good luck with the job and I'll always be there to support you.' Stewie is a good man. He was definitely unlucky to lose the England captaincy. No question. And I had a huge regard for him. The number of sacrifices he made to play for England was enormous and there is no doubt that he was a world-class all-rounder. I don't know much about wicketkeeping but I think he was one of the three best in my time (along with Jack Russell and Keith Piper) and one of the best three batters of my time too, with Mike Atherton and Graham Thorpe. Together that's an awesome combination.

If Stewie had stayed as captain I think he would have developed us into another South Africa – a professional, hard-to-beat outfit. He was very well organized and he also sought and used other people's opinions well. He wasn't stubborn like Atherton, and I know that if I'd lost the captaincy with an identical record to Alec's I would have felt very hard done by.

It speaks volumes for the bloke that I had his full support every day of my captaincy, and at no time did he show any bitterness towards me for taking his job prematurely. If Stewie ever had those feelings, he never conveyed them to me and I think I would have detected any resentment he may have felt during the bad times on and off the pitch.

I am not as close to Stewie as I am to Atherton and Thorpe, but I do regard him as a friend. He was so different from me, both as a player and as a person. He was much more relaxed about the game, much more on an even keel. He never looked nervous and he had a stronger and more genuine love and enjoyment for the game than I did. I was tense and nervous all the time, and when you're like that about cricket for ten years eventually you feel a bit of dissatisfaction towards it.

Alec was so meticulous about everything, he was famous for it. Just look at our diets. He would have his glass of milk with his breakfast, chicken every night, and everything would be so military. Me? I would just like a curry and a glass of wine. For me, cricket was just something I was good at. For Alec, his whole life would be based around making him a better cricketer. And he was a damn good one, someone I wanted in my side – which, I was to discover, was far from automatic for the other selectors.

I found my first selection meeting as captain weird. There was Grav, who I knew from so many fraught phone calls, there was Gooch, who I knew very well, and there was Mike Gatting. Now, Gatt has never liked me. And I don't really believe he has any good reason not to like me. My first feelings towards him as a young player were of huge respect because he won the Ashes as I was growing up and because Phil DeFreitas had told me on my first full England tour that Gatt was a top bloke and a great captain. So in my early meetings with him I looked at him as someone to admire, and to learn from the way he did things.

But, as Gatt said in a newspaper article on my retirement,

he took huge exception to me not walking when I edged a ball from Simon Hughes when playing for the Combined Universities against Middlesex in the late 1980s, and he seems to have held it against me ever since. A bit odd from an ex-England captain to keep up a fifteen-year vendetta because someone didn't walk. From that day on he would sledge me in the field whenever our paths crossed, to the point where I believe some of his Middlesex teammates became a bit embarrassed by it. Here was this former England captain getting really worked up over this young lad, and I think some of them told him to cool it because he was making himself look rather silly.

So I found it strange to be in an England selection meeting with him; but, to be fair, he was fine and wished me well. It was only later that he had a go at me again, for taking my family to Australia so that I could be present at the birth of Joel, my second son, and for saying I would like to reach 100 caps for England. Maybe he just doesn't like me. Simple as that. And there's not much I can do about that.

I was amazed at some of the things that went on in selection meetings. At that time Ian Botham and Jack Birkenshaw were official observers who sat in on meetings, and Jack would say something and then Beefy would sit there with a big cigar, saying something very different, and more forcibly. So Jack would then agree with him! Botham was such an imposing character.

I went into my first meetings with my eyes open and a clear idea of who I wanted alongside me. To my mind, class was class and there were certain people I wanted, whatever their form was like, because to my mind they were world class. The ones I definitely wanted as we got ready to face New Zealand in a four-Test series in the second half of the 1999 season were Thorpe, Stewart, Atherton, Gough, Caddick and Tufnell. These were my people. It had nothing to do with any of them being mates. I just considered them, day in and day out, to be the best players in England. And I thought the other people in that first meeting ahead of the first Test would agree. Wrong!

Within an hour, each of those players was completely dismembered by someone in the gathering. Botham would say, 'Stewart? He's lost it. His eyes have gone. It's too late. Get rid of him now. He's gone.' Then Gatting sat there and said, 'Thorpe? What does he bring to the equation? What, apart from runs, does he bring to the party?' I was sitting there, thinking, 'It's your first meeting. Stay quiet.' But I couldn't contain myself when we got to the subject of Thorpe. 'What does he bring? Well he averages 40 runs in Test cricket, so that's all I want him to bring to the party. And he's a pretty good catcher. I know he's a quiet lad. But he's a little bloke who possibly was picked on at school, and he just keeps himself to himself. Just because he's not jumping up and down all the time doesn't mean he doesn't care.' To be honest, I was totally incredulous. I didn't know what had hit me.

There was a lot of support that summer for Botham to become a selector, but I'm glad it didn't happen. I was totally in awe of him at first, as anyone who grew up watching him would be. He was arguably the greatest cricketer England ever produced and he had such an aura and personality about him. So the moment he walked into the room as an adviser that summer I would listen, and listen and listen. On some points I didn't agree with him, and as I progressed that summer I grew more confident in my own opinions. I realized I could disagree with him, however much of a legend he was. It was a measure of how far I'd come that I no longer feared disagreeing with Botham. Yes, Ian Botham is a top man who cares passionately about English cricket, but there was never any consistency in his arguments. He'd say one thing one day and then suddenly he'd be saying that the same bloke he had been pushing for a year was now complete rubbish. The problem was that Beefy is such a legend, people do listen to him. Not only the David Graveneys of this world but also people in the street, so you would jump into a cab and the driver would say, 'That Ian Botham. He talks a lot of sense.' And I would always feel like turning around and saying, 'Well, in my opinion Ian Botham was a genius who could do things on a cricket pitch that no other man could before or since, but he couldn't really explain to you how he did them.' By the end of his time advising the selection panel, I was virtually listening to what he thought I should do and then doing exactly the opposite. Mind you, Beefy was adamant I should have batted first at Brisbane before the fateful first Test toss there in 2002. Enough said!

Then I was made quickly aware that the ECB wanted a cull. Lord MacLaurin was a prominent figure in this, as was Brian Bolus, who was very influential as head of the England Management Advisory committee. It was quite clear that they wanted all the senior people out and new, fresh figures in. It came to a head at a dinner at Old Trafford, staged to welcome Duncan, during the third Test of the series, when they virtually went through everyone over thirty and said boom, boom, boom, they've all got to go.

I'm just so relieved that Duncan was about to join us (he had to finish off his contract at Glamorgan and missed the New Zealand series) because I really was in need of some support. It's all very well, calling for younger players, but there has to be a balance and if Duncan hadn't come along when he did to support the claims of some of the players I still wanted to pick, then we could have seen a very premature end to some distinguished England careers, like Atherton's, Stewart's and Thorpe's. Not to mention Caddick, Tufnell, Hick and Ramprakash who were largely ignored during the Stewart–Lloyd regime and who I wanted to bring back.

Bolus was an extraordinary character; I think he's got a screw loose. He certainly liked to be the court jester. He used to throw ideas into meetings and then sort of giggle in the corner and you never knew whether he was being serious or not. It was quite weird; it had a destabilizing effect too. I felt that

Bolus was a total loose cannon. We were trying to analyse people properly and getting selection back on an even keel, and this bloke was running around telling everyone what was said in meetings. The press played him brilliantly. They knew he could be quite uninhibited about what he said, and they would ring him and nearly always get something out of him.

Duncan in particular hated that. He hated private things coming out. Which was why I always resented Grav insinuating that I leaked stuff and why in later times the Fletcher–Graveney axis has not always worked that well.

I didn't feel I had got my own way in our selection for the first Test at Edgbaston but, looking back now, they must have listened to me to a certain extent because Stewart, as a batsman, Thorpe, Caddick and Tufnell were all there. Atherton, meanwhile, was still struggling with his back injury and one paper said he had only a one-in-ten chance of playing for England again. He was back for the third Test! But I certainly needed help in assessing the qualities of the young players in England because by that stage I was playing a lot of international cricket and hadn't seen them enough to make a proper judgement. So in came Chris Read and Aftab Habib for debuts, and we had a reasonable balance of youth and experience that I liked.

The big thing for me was 'Please don't drop someone or leave someone out because of a perceived character flaw.' We have all got them and, to me, England weren't strong enough to leave out quality performers simply because Mike Gatting wanted Graham Thorpe to bring more to the party than an average of 40 in Test cricket, or because Ian Botham felt Alec Stewart's eyes had gone. You pick your best players and you sort out any problems there might be with them.

I don't remember too much about my first match as England captain. I remember little things, like sitting in the middle of the team photo and tossing the coin. I remember bringing on Tufnell for no apparent reason on the first day – and he immediately got a wicket, which eased my nerves. I remember feeling in the zone as a batsman and thinking that I should have got more runs. I also remember Stewie struggling to cope with their left-armer, Geoff Allott, giving more fuel to Botham's theory that he had lost his eyesight. He even got to Stewie, because after that match Alec went and had a secret eye test but the results showed he had 20/20 vision, which I think gave him the confidence to carry on.

Every match and series I have played against New Zealand has gone down to the wire and this Test was no different. We have been, in my time, two of the most evenly matched sides around, but we really should have beaten them more often than we have. It came down to a nerve-racking chase for us on the last day, and we needed 211 to win a low-scoring match. Enter Alex Tudor, who came in as nightwatchman and returned on the last day to play like an England number five. This is why I get so frustrated with Tudes. The boy could really play, and we haven't seen enough of him over the past five years – in fact, we've barely seen him at all.

If a Martian had come down to Earth that day, he would have been certain that Alex Tudor was a frontline batsman – if they know their cricket on Mars, that is. Alex Tudor won my first Test as captain with an unbeaten 99, playing brilliantly and turning what looked like becoming a nervous run chase into a convincing win for us. It is a great shame Tudes didn't score a century, particularly as he may never get that close again, but you can't mess with the game. You just have to get it won, and Tudes knew that, as did Graham Thorpe, who played a few shots at the end to hurry us to victory. At the time it wasn't a huge issue because we all felt that Tudes would have the chance again, but now it's a bit like Mike Smith not getting a Test wicket in 1997 when Thorpey dropped a chance off his bowling. It's a bigger issue now, but with our record of collapses we couldn't take any chances at the time.

It was nice, walking across the ground at the end to do TV

interviews with Tudes. We had won my first Test in charge, a young lad had done well to appease those who wanted radical change, and we had a nice balance in the side. It felt good. But what was annoying was that we didn't have a proper coach at that time, Gooch and Graveney were just filling in, and that would be a factor by the end of the summer. A chairman of selectors doing a coaching job? If that didn't put pressure on players, I don't know what would. Even the throwdowns become an ordeal because everybody would have to feel that they needed to middle every one. It was so, so not right. Can't blame Goochy and Grav. They carried on as usual. They would both do anything for England and were just helping out. Couldn't blame Duncan either. It says everything for the man that he wasn't prepared to walk out on Glamorgan before the end of the summer, because he wanted to finish that job properly before embarking on a new one.

Yet we went to Lord's for the second Test in good heart, and I really wanted us to end the hoodoo which seemed to affect England sides at the home of cricket in those days. The first thing that went wrong was that Tudes couldn't play through knee trouble. The worst possible time for him to pull out, after doing so well at Edgbaston, and there was a bit of trouble with Surrey because they didn't inform England that he needed a scan. Thank goodness, these sort of things happen more rarely in these days of central contracts. Dean Headley came in and Angus Fraser drove up from Taunton on the morning of the match to be on standby, only to be told just when he was arriving in London that he wasn't needed, and he had to go back again! I'm glad I didn't make that particular phone call to Gus, but sorry it meant that I never captained him in an England side. He was the sort of bloke I desperately wanted in my team, one who would always give it his absolute best, would play with passion and commitment and make no excuse or hide behind anyone or anything. He also (like me) came from a dressing room (Middlesex) where you said what you thought, had a few rows, got it out of your system, and then came back the next day with your differences sorted out and a team who went on to the field all fighting for each other. He was my sort of player and I wish I'd had the chance to captain him.

With Gus heading home, I won the toss but really I didn't know whether to bat or bowl. My instinct was to bowl but I was worried about the pitch deteriorating, and as the coin went up two lights came up on the light meter. I decided to bat because the forecast was for it to brighten up, but it stayed gloomy all day and the ball zipped around as we were bowled out for 186. It was the start of a terrible Test for us. Chris Read was famously bowled, ducking a Chris Cairns full toss, then I broke my finger in the field and we ended up being thrashed. The honeymoon was over. Welcome to the England captaincy.

Old Trafford was a right shemozzle. I had left Graham Thorpe in charge on the field when I had broken my finger at Lord's because I knew he had a good cricket brain, and I think at that time Thorpey was very keen to be my vice-captain and I could see little reason why he shouldn't be. But the selectors disagreed and a decision was made to make Mark Butcher captain for the third Test in my absence. I didn't know Butch too well at that stage, but certainly I had nothing against him and it wasn't his fault that, by the time I got there on the Tuesday before the game, half the team were upset for one reason or another.

Thorpey was upset because he had been my choice to take over at Lord's, but he had received a phone call from Grav, saying the selectors didn't want him to be in charge at Old Trafford, and he was questioning who was running the team. We had brought in Graeme Hick, but he was upset because Grav had told him it was only for one Test to stand in for me. Butch was upset because he had seen how dry the wicket was and he wanted to call up Craig White, but by that time it was too late. Mark Ramprakash was upset about something, but

I can't remember what it was, he was like that at times; and Brian Bolus was spreading it around that all the senior players were going to be ditched. Chaos!

The impetus was with New Zealand and they had the best of a rain-ruined draw; but more action was going on off the field. The ECB management, which included Lord MacLaurin, Grav, Brian Bolus and me, had a big 'welcome to Duncan' dinner on the fourth night and we just went through every player, deciding whether they had a future with England. It emerged that Gooch and Gatting were no longer going to be selectors, a move interpreted by many as them being made scapegoats because we had picked a few older players in that series, against the wishes of the ECB. Now I have already said that there were a number of senior players I absolutely wanted in the side, and I think the subsequent records of most of them post-1999 prove that I was right, so it's unfair to blame Gooch and Gatting for the selections of people like Atherton and Hick. But, again, scapegoats were needed, and probably it was their misfortune to have been around longest when the call was going up for change.

That dinner was the first time that I realized how impressive Duncan Fletcher was. He would comment only on people he knew and just listened to what other people had to say about those he didn't know. Grav was sitting on the fence, so I basically made the decision to take the initiative in picking the side myself for the final Test at the Oval. I thought, 'Sod it, I'm going to try to pick the players I want to go into war with me.' I wanted fighters. I didn't want any more squabbling. I knew Ronnie Irani was a real fighter, so I picked him. I knew Ed Giddins could swing the ball and I expected the Oval to swing, so I picked him. Chris Read had looked a little out of his depth at that stage of his career, so Stewie took the gloves again. I went for it. But the only problem was – and, however much I looked at it, I couldn't find a way round it – we had a very long tail. Basically three number elevens in Alan Mullally,

Phil Tufnell and Ed Giddins and a bowler in Andrew Caddick batting at eight who should really have been a nine or ten.

In those days I felt that your batters should bat and you should pick your four best bowlers, but I am now very much a disciple of Duncan's way of thinking, in that everybody in the team really should have two out of the three disciplines (batting, bowling and fielding) and that all bowlers really should be able to hold up a bat. Anyway, this game really gets my goat because we played bloody well, the selection had been almost solely mine and we should have won.

We had New Zealand at 39 for 6 and 79 for 7 in their second innings and it should have been Tufnell's moment, when he justified my faith in him by bowling us to victory, as he had done at the Oval in 1991 and 1997. But we came up against a formidable foe in Chris Cairns, who likes spin. What Cairns doesn't like is pace, because it gets his ticker going, but we didn't really have any real pace in our side, and Cairns changed everything by hitting 80 from 94 balls. He just kept on putting Tuffers into the pavilion. It wasn't a great wicket and it left us with too many to chase, and we ended up being bowled out for 162, to lose the Test and the series by 83 runs.

This was one of only four games in my time as England captain that really bugged me: losing the NatWest final game against India in 2002; the final Test in Auckland against New Zealand in 2002; being beaten by Australia at Port Elizabeth in the last World Cup, when we should have won; and this one. Very annoying.

I could understand it when people booed me when I went up on the balcony for the presentation at the end of the match. We had hit rock bottom. I knew they were not booing me; I was a symbol of what had been a terrible shemozzle of a summer. We started it by arguing about money before our own World Cup and then going out in the first round; then people wrongly perceived New Zealand to be a weaker side than us, and we ended up losing the Test series 2–1. The booing made me more determined. I knew how much the people cared and how it was up to me to try and turn things around.

The immediate repercussion for me was that it weakened me. If we had won that game (as we should have done), I could have gone in with a bit more confidence and said, 'This is the side I want.' And I had said before the game that I expected most of those players to tour, too. As it was, it now meant I had to give in to the likes of Brian Bolus as to the type of player England were looking to select, and that was not very good at all.

21

This was a good time to be a young player, ahead of the 1999–2000 tour of South Africa. I went into selection for my first tour as captain, knowing that the pressure was very much on us to pick as many new faces as possible. For me, that meant I had to fight to retain the senior players I still believed in, and it also meant that I had to find out as much as I could about the younger players who were challenging for selection.

One of the first things I did was to ring up David Byas, then the Yorkshire captain, because a lot of the candidates seemed to be from Yorkshire. Michael Vaughan's name kept on coming up, as did those of Craig White, Chris Silverwood and Gavin Hamilton. Byas, to me, seemed to have a downer on all of them! At least he was honest. So many people in cricket are one-eyed and always try to push their county people when you ask their opinions. Like I rang someone at Leicester, and they said, 'It's got to be Darren Maddy.' Then, when I spoke to someone from Sussex, they said, 'It's got to be Chris Adams.' At least Byas gave me the impression he was giving a proper judgement. For instance, he said of Vaughan, 'He's a good player and he always looks classy, but he always gets out.' He seemed to rate Gavin Hamilton and he played a big part in getting him on the trip; and we ended up going with a few people I barely knew, like Maddy, Adams, Hamilton, Vaughan, Swann and Read.

To me, it felt as if we were picking them just for the sake of it and that we were going round in circles, but I guess the policy was right when you think how far Michael Vaughan has come. I suppose if you find one world-class player out of five or six random selections, you haven't done too badly. We could easily have missed Vaughan, could easily have picked someone else instead – but thankfully we didn't!

It was just me, Duncan Fletcher and David Graveney making the selection, and that meant Duncan and I found it tough when we were talking about so many people neither of us had really seen properly. I do remember, though, Duncan mentioning a couple of young, barely known players who had impressed him even then. You may have heard of them: Marcus Trescothick and Steve Harmison. They didn't make the South African trip, but their time was to come. Spectacularly!

I agreed with Byas on Vaughan. He looked a very good technical player to me, a good bloke and a good team man, whose only fault at that time was not going on often enough to big scores once he had got a start. Chris Adams had always looked a good player to me in county cricket, so I had no problem with him, while Hamilton had had a good World Cup for Scotland, so I thought, 'Why not?' Maddy was someone Graham Gooch had always raved about, so he was worth a go, and senior players like Atherton and Stewart were there, so at least I had something of my own way. No Thorpe, however, as he wanted a winter off, and I could understand that, while people like Graeme Hick and Mark Ramprakash missed out.

I really imposed myself as England captain for the first time after we had lost the traditional tour opener to the Nicky Oppenheimer XI, the South African version of Lilac Hill in Australia or Arundel in England. Some of our younger guys seemed to be just going through the motions in the field, so I said to them afterwards, 'Look, some serious players (i.e. Hick and Ramps) have been left behind because of you lot. You've got your England jumper on for the first time and you're moping around as if you don't care. I won't stand for any of that. If you don't care that we've just lost to a social team, then you can get on the next flight home.' I really lost it with them. This was the young, vibrant side that was going to take England forward to a new era? It had to get better.

Meanwhile, Duncan and I were starting to build a good relationship. It helped having Dean Conway as physio. I knew Dean well from the 'A' tour I captained to Pakistan in 1995–6, and Duncan knew him well from their time together at Glamorgan. So Dean was able to go up to Duncan and say, 'Don't believe what people say about Nasser. I know everyone's told you he is an absolute arse with a bad temper, hot-headed and an accident waiting to happen, but really he's a nice bloke. It's just once a series that he explodes.'

Then Conway would come to me and say, 'Look, don't worry about Fletcher. He's not really a disciplinarian. He's just a big boring South African.' It was reassuring for both of us. And, if anything, Duncan went the other way. He was very keen on the social side of things. He formed a social committee which he put Conway in charge of; between the pair of them, they helped form a really good team spirit. So things were beginning to slip into place, even though neither of us had any idea what team we wanted to pick for the first Test. Mind you, I soon realized that Duncan knew his players. After just one net session he came up to me and said, 'Chris Adams. Something not quite right about his hands. I feel he's going to nick off quite a bit.' I told him that Chris did nick a few in county cricket but that he also scored hundreds, so we hoped that he would be all right. Then, during the Test series, Chris would constantly nick off to Allan Donald, pushing forward at back-of-the-length balls. It made me realize straight away that Fletcher really was a coach, not just a manager; he knew what he was talking about. The thing with Duncan that worried me until the day I retired was that you never really knew how highly he rated you. He would work one-on-one with a player, throw to him, have a net with him and talk with him, and never provide any clues as to what he thought about him deep down. Butcher, for example, is one who constantly asks me if the coach thinks he can play. He just tried to impart as much knowledge as possible without revealing his inner thoughts, except in selection. But I'm still not sure if he really felt I could play.

I knew this was a bloke who was really worth listening to, so when he talked about their players I devoured every word, trying to retain something that would help me in a match situation. Yet, however much things were progressing nicely, the selection for the first Test was still something of a lottery. We turned up at Johannesburg and the biggest problem for me was that I hadn't played on any of the big grounds in South Africa. So everything was new.

What was familiar was the rain that affected the build-up to the match, and the wicket looked like an old-fashioned sticky dog, a real club surface. I had made up my mind by this stage that, after batting when I shouldn't have done at Lord's, if in doubt I would bowl; but there was no doubt what needed to be done here. Win the toss and bowl. I lost it.

People had been talking up the return duel between Atherton and Donald, but I knew how hard it would be for Ath to go back to the scene of his unbeaten 185 and do something similar again. But I think we expected him to do a little better than record a pair! I was soon in the middle and, as I took my guard, I could feel water just below the surface, almost bubbling up. The soil was really dark and very moist and I thought, 'We're in a bit of trouble here.' Shaun Pollock quickly got one to bounce and I gloved it to gully. Soon we were 2 for 4 wickets and had two debutants together in Vaughan and Adams. It was the first Test Fletcher and I had been in charge of together; I sat in the pavilion, looked at him and said, 'Good start, Fletch.'

In many ways it was a perfect situation to make your debut. It was a total no-lose situation, with me, Atherton, Stewart and Butcher already back in the pavilion. And Vaughan responded to it very well. He's a relaxed character at the best of times, and here he was almost giggling when he went out to bat. He was very calm and his heartbeat would have been very low. Perfect.

The last thing we needed in that situation was someone with hard hands and, if you look at the careers of Hick and Ramprakash, you could say that that sort of temperament was the only thing they lacked. They had everything else; they really were the two most naturally gifted players I ever played with. They would have been the first two names on my team sheet for that tour if the pressure hadn't been on us to pick newcomers.

Sod's law applied on this tour. Soon after we picked the party, minus Hick, I played against him at Worcester for Essex and he scored hundreds in both innings, playing like God. I thought, 'Why haven't I got this bloke in my team?' Yet there had been a huge outcry when we brought him back to deputize for me at Old Trafford the previous summer.

If only Hicky and Ramps could have had the same mental attitude as Vaughny had in Johannesburg that day. If they had been able to relax, like he did on Test debut with England 2 for 4, then they would have been world-beaters, better than anyone of my generation, and probably right up there with Gooch and Gower. Michael only scored 33 that day, but it was an immense step forward towards establishing himself as a Test player. What it couldn't do was get us back in the match after such a poor start, and we eventually went down by an innings.

By the time we got to Port Elizabeth for the second Test, the position of Mark Butcher in the side had become an issue. Butch was really struggling on this trip. He was going through one of his dark phases, the most serious, I think, in his career. Butch had marital problems, he was very low, and at times during this tour he would be almost begging me to leave him out. I remember talking to Duncan about him and the whole package you got with Butch. We would ask each other how such a talented lad could get out cheaply too often. We recognized then that he was one of our finest players but we couldn't get it out of him often enough, and much of that at the time was due to problems he had off the field.

I think the person Butch looks up to most is Graham Thorpe. I think he would love, really, to be Thorpey. They both have this big on—off switch and when Butch is doing well he doesn't net as much and he switches off. When it's not going so well, he switches it all back on again and tries to regain form that way. What people sometimes don't appreciate is that sportsmen have personal problems, like anyone else. There was a spell recently when everyone was questioning the desire of golfer Phil Mickelson because he didn't seem to be putting everything into his game, until it emerged that his two children were ill and he had enormous problems to deal with. Sportsmen are not machines. On this tour Butch was going through it, and I think some of his problems were becoming public in the papers, which didn't help. It was something we had to monitor all the time.

Things went much better in Port Elizabeth. We played some good cricket but nearly lost the game through some bad umpiring at the end. For me, there was the bonus of scoring runs in both innings, something I had to do so as to feel comfortable with my contribution to the team. Remember, at this stage I had lost three matches as captain from my first six Tests, so I had to feel satisfied in my own mind that I was doing my bit for the team.

What I needed most of all, though, was my first hundred as captain, and that duly came in Durban. It was quite a feat of endurance because in high humidity and searing heat I ended up batting for 635 minutes for my unbeaten 146. All the time I was thinking to myself, 'Bat time, lead from the front,' and I wanted to know how long Atherton had batted for his 185 in Johannesburg a few years earlier. In the end I think he just beat me, but it was, I'm told, the third slowest hundred by an England batsman; at that stage, after my undefeated 70 in the second innings at Port Elizabeth, I had batted for almost 1,000 minutes without being dismissed. I couldn't tell you why it became such an attritional knock except to say that the conditions dictated it and we needed to put the runs on the board, however long it took, for us to have any chance of winning the game. At times like that I always used to try to motivate myself by setting little targets. In Durban it was simply a case of me saying to myself, 'I want to stay on telly today. I'll try and stay on telly all day.' And I did for much of the first and second days of the third Test.

We should, really, have won it. Caddick was superb in taking 7 wickets in South Africa's first innings as we made them follow on, and I'm sure it was the right thing to do in asking them to bat again, even though we were playing back-to-back Tests. As it happened, we ran into a brick wall in the form of Gary Kirsten, a player I admire immensely. Kirsten batted even longer than I had for his 275 to make the match safe – before, of all people, Butcher bowled him with the last ball of the match. By that time even I had bowled five overs, but I couldn't reproduce the bowling prowess of my youth!

This was the time when Fletcher's patience started to run out with Phil Tufnell. Phil had had a great shout for lbw against Kirsten when he was on just 33 but had overstepped the line; but more significant than that in Duncan's mind was that it was the last day at Durban and Tuffers went wicketless in 45 overs. He couldn't respond as we wanted him to on a last-day pitch and, from that moment on, Duncan's attitude was, 'Right, we might not be able to pick another English spinner as good as Tuffers, but we should look at others who can contribute in other areas.' I still wanted Tufnell in the side. I really wanted him to produce the goods for me and for England.

There was an incident on this tour which Darren Gough recounts in his book, when I shouted at Tuffers during a practice session that I had got him on this trip and he had better start repaying me. I don't remember it being as dramatic as Goughy recalls, but it is true that I started to feel a bit responsible personally for Phil and I still wanted him in the side. It wasn't a case of losing patience with him, because I was always happy for him to be the same as he always was. I just so wanted him to take wickets. I knew he was lazy. I knew he wasn't particularly fit. But I also felt he was our best bet on turning wickets. In the end it was his failure to live up to this belief of mine that let him down. In common with other sides, we were going in the direction of bowlers having to contribute with the bat, and if Phil couldn't do that or field particularly well, then he had to start taking 5-fors in Test cricket. And he wasn't doing it.

The reason was that spin bowling had moved on. Mystery spinners like Muralitharan and Saqlain were spinning it both ways, and orthodox spinners were under pressure as rarely before. Tuffers felt inadequate by comparison. This is when Ashley Giles started coming into contention. I do not mind admitting that at first I wasn't sure Ashley would make the grade at all but I was won over by him, not least because of what he contributes to the team as well as his share of tail-end runs and his reasonable fielding. He is also strong enough to cope with being an orthodox spinner in modern cricket.

Tufnell wasn't our only bowler who was not doing as well as we had hoped. Darren Gough was getting a lot of stick about his weight and he was struggling a bit with the Kookaburra ball, which was not swinging as much as he was used to. Gough was my trump card. He was our Botham. When I became captain I'd identified certain people from whom I had to have 100 per cent support, and Gough was right up there in our team. I love him to death and think he has been arguably our most influential bowler since Botham, but he was also dangerous in that he was such a magnet and such an influence in the dressing room that the young players took notice of anything he said. For me, that meant that if Darren Gough had chosen to criticize me over a drink to some easily influenced younger players, then it could have had serious repercussions for me and would have undermined what we were trying to achieve. If someone like Darren Maddy – nothing against him

– slagged me off, then it wouldn't really matter. But Gough was so well respected, so vociferous and he is such a character, I needed his support. And I knew him well enough to know that if he backed me and spoke highly of me behind my back, he would always think like that and I would always have him on my side.

So I decided that, even if he turned up weighing 35 stone, I would always back him, and it was on this tour that questions started to be asked about Gough and I told the press, 'Gough will be the first name on any team sheet I pick for England.' I meant it and I knew it had registered with Darren. I like to think it was one of the shrewdest things I said as England captain.

From that time on, I always had fantastic support from Darren Gough, and I think it played a big part in what we all went on to achieve with England over the next two or three years. In many ways it was an interesting about-turn, because the word was that he and Angus Fraser had not been slow in telling anyone who would listen on the West Indies tour of 1998 that Nasser would never have the support of the bowlers if he ever became captain.

I heard about that, and it didn't bother me in the least. For one thing, it would just have been Gus chuntering, and I loved that about him. That's why I would have loved to captain him. He would have a good moan, a bit like me, but he would always do it to your face and be big enough to admit it if he was wrong. Good on him. I love characters like him who try so hard, care and say what they think. Goughy was the same. And the same applied to Marcus Trescothick on our tour to Sri Lanka in 2003. We were in a management meeting, and Duncan asked Marcus who he would leave out for the third Test. I had been struggling with food poisoning but was fit again and Marcus said, 'I would leave Nasser out. Sorry, Nass, but you look out of nick, and I would play Paul Collingwood.' At first I was taken aback because Marcus was very much one of my boys when I was captain, but I respected him hugely for saying that in front of me, and I told him so the next day when it looked as though he was worried there might be a problem between us.

Gus and Goughy were the same. Darren had been up front about his reservations about what sort of captain I would be, but later he said I was the best captain he had played under. Remember, there is so much backchat and backbiting in cricket that a bit of honesty is very refreshing. I didn't even mind it when Graeme Swann, one of the other young players on that tour, had a bit of a go at me in front of the team one day. Swann was a bit like a young Tufnell; he had a bit of a swagger, gave you a bit of chat. I didn't mind him at all. It was just that he pushed it a bit too far one day, and all fell silent in the dressing room. Soon after, I saw Dean Headley taking him to one side, and when I asked what that was about Dean just said to me, 'I was reminding him who he was talking to when he had a go at you.'

We moved on to Cape Town for the New Year Test, where we started well but then collapsed. For me it was the start of my run of shocking umpiring decisions. I edged Lance Klusener through the slips for 4 in the second innings and was given out lbw by B. C. Cooray of Sri Lanka. We lost by an innings, but I think there was an acceptance that we had a young side and were going to lose a few matches before we started winning them. I knew deep down I was still in a bit of a honeymoon period as captain, but we were two down with one to play; and we moved on to Pretoria, looking to make sure we didn't end up on the receiving end of a 3–0 hiding. But the Test match at Centurion will be remembered for much more than the result.

22

The final Test of our series in Centurion, Pretoria, began like any other match. I was conscious of the need to avoid a 3–0 thrashing, but also content with the way we were performing in the series. Progress was being made, but we needed to earn some tangible rewards for our endeavours.

There was rain around and we reduced South Africa to 155 for 6 at the end of the shortened first day on a lively pitch. Nothing unusual so far. But the first of what was to become a highly controversial chain of events came when a huge thunderstorm hit the area overnight after the first day's play. Most of us stayed up half the night watching it, it was so spectacular.

And after that it was almost like Guyana revisited. The ground, remarkably, remained pretty dry, but around 3 p.m. each day the rains would come, water would keep surfacing around the footholes and it would be impossible to play. This pattern went on for three days.

A couple of things to note here. First, the inactivity led to some unusually late nights. Nothing untoward, but I mention it now because Darren Gough wrote about it in his book and confessed to getting drunk on the night before the final day's unexpected drama. I am not going to castigate him for that; nobody dreamed that we would have such an amazing last day's play. But the mere fact that I understood Darren's situation and refused to condemn him for having a few drinks would lead me into a bit of bother later on, when I was asked about it by Simon Hughes for a newspaper article. More on that later.

The other noteworthy thing also happened on the penulti-mate night of the Test. I was just going to bed at the Sandton

Sun Hotel, just outside Johannesburg, about 40 miles from the ground, at about 11 p.m. and thinking how late it was for me to be going to bed during a Test. Then I noticed Hansie Cronje going out of the hotel and I thought, 'I wonder where he's going at this time of night. He can't be expecting any play tomorrow.' And I left it at that.

Next morning, the ground had dried significantly and it was clear that we were going to be able to play, even if it would be just going through the motions of what would surely be a draw, with three full days lost to the weather. If nothing else, we owed it to the thousands of Brits who had dutifully turned up at the ground each morning to give them as much cricket as possible.

So we were doing our warm-ups and stretching on the ground when Alec Stewart walked by. 'I've just passed Cronje on the stairs,' said Stewie. 'And he asked whether we wanted to play a game.' I was both surprised and intrigued. But my first thought was negative. 'No, bollocks,' I said to Stewie. 'This is not Essex *v.* Hampshire during my youth, with Keith Fletcher and Mark Nicholas having a big old debate about targets. This is a Test. You don't mess around with Tests.' But my mind was wandering and I went up and asked Duncan Fletcher what he thought. 'No, I don't think so,' said Duncan. 'But find out what he's offering you.'

I made inquiries, and the first figure mentioned was for us to chase 300 in 70 overs, which seemed OK. But then I remembered that the wicket had done a hell of a lot on the first morning and I really didn't want to lose 3–0, so Fletch and I, both being conservative types, decided to just see how things went in the first session and be prepared to settle for a draw.

So out we went, and the first thing that was noticeable was that Gough bowled a pile of shite. I knew then that he had had a few drinks the night before. It was stinking hot, so I decided to punish him by keeping on bowling him. He knew the game was going nowhere, or so we thought, and he thought I was just going to let him bowl two overs and then rest up ahead of the one-dayers. No chance. Instead I said to Goughy, 'You've bowled a heap of crap. You've been out on the piss. You can bowl a few more overs and sweat it out of your system.'

It was also apparent now that the wicket had really flattened out. It was an absolute belter. So I wondered if Cronje still wanted to play a game. I pretended I needed to go to the toilet, left the field and went upstairs to see Cronje. We went into the back room at Centurion and, for the first and only time in my life, I prepared to negotiate a target for us. But it was nothing like what I expected, nothing like those old verbal jousts of my youth when I would watch Keith Fletcher, the master, some-how wangle Essex into gaining an easy target to chase with his expert bartering. Basically, Hansie just agreed with everything I asked for.

Phil Tufnell, who wasn't playing in the match, was in the room and he told me then that he found it a bit peculiar. I expected Hansie, at the very least, to still hold out for a target of 300 and, if anything, to go the other way and ask us to chase 320 now he had seen how well the wicket was playing. So I deliberately aimed low at first and said, 'How about us chasing 250?' Hansie just said, 'Fine.' I couldn't believe it. No haggling. No banter. No bartering. No mention of how many overs we would face. It was like that scene from the film *Life of Brian* when the salesman is all indignant because the guy has simply paid his first asking price without any argument.

I thought Cronje was going to hold out for 300, and we would settle for something like 280. But no. Tuffers came over to me and said, 'That was weird. You could have gone for even less there and he would have agreed.' For a moment I thought I had slipped up, but the fact was: this was a target which really should have been within our capabilities.

So we prepared for an unexpected run-chase by sending down a few lobs to get South Africa up to 248 for 8 declared.

I can honestly say that, at this stage, no one in our team thought that there could possibly be the whiff of corruption in the air. We thought Cronje was being generous towards us – and we just thought it must be the confidence, or arrogance, of the man in thinking he could roll us over. At the time he had a reputation for being a negative captain, so I just assumed that this was his way of proving to his detractors that he could be positive and make a gesture for the good of cricket. How wrong could we be?

So off we went. It was the usual roller coaster of a run-chase, with us, to be honest, making harder work of it than maybe we might have done. Stewie was in the runs, as was Michael Vaughan, and there didn't appear to be anything strange going on in the field. With hindsight, you look back on it and you remember that you thought it was a bit odd when Cronje brought himself on to bowl. But then again, I just thought that was the captain keeping the game alive and trying to make sure we kept on going for the win. As it turned out, that's exactly what happened, but only because Cronje had been paid to make sure there was a positive result. Yes, he was trying to make South Africa win, but it turned out that he would prefer us to win rather than the game ending in a draw because he had been paid to make sure that someone won.

Yet at no time did the words 'match' and 'fixing' ever come into our heads as we watched the drama unfold from the balcony. And the way it panned out was pure theatre. We were 8 wickets down at the close before Gough, the hungover hero, smacked a 4 off the first ball of the final over to give us victory, after I had told him earlier that he had better sober up because I had a feeling he would score the winning runs! Pandemonium broke out. Our supporters were hailing Cronje as the greatest captain in the history of the game for making such a gesture. I walked down the steps, shook his hand and said, 'Look, what you did today was brilliant. A lot of captains would have just said, "Two–nil up, sod it." What you did, you know, these fans really appreciate that.' He just nodded and walked off, to be met by more congratulations from Mark Nicholas who interviewed the 'gallant' loser for television.

It was clear that not everyone was hailing Cronje the hero. I could hear some of their players chuntering. They were saying things like 'What the hell's going on? We should have won the series 2–0, now it's 2–1.' God knows how many of them, if any, were in on the deal and knew what Cronje was up to that day. Surely some of them had their suspicions because of what was to come out later. Me? I just left, thinking what a great bloke Hansie Cronje was. How I had got it wrong about him all these years. How we now looked as though we had had a good series with a young side. How nice it was that our supporters' patience had been rewarded. Then, later, it transpired that Cronje had been given £5,000 and a leather jacket by a bookmaker to make sure there was a positive result, all the punters' money obviously having gone on a draw. It was clearly, it transpired, just the tip of the iceberg. What a mug I was! Mainly because Phil Tufnell was more astute than I was in smelling a rat!

I always thought of Hansie Cronje as a very good captain. It irked me, in fact, that Matthew Hoggard, who had played under Cronje at Orange Free State, once said to me, 'Apart from Hansie, Nass, you are the best captain I've known.' Cronje seemed a good tactician who did things in an organized, clear-cut way. A good pro who trained hard and who had an interesting personality. So he was right up there with people like Mark Taylor and Stephen Fleming as one of the most admired captains in the world. And he was one of those I looked at and tried to learn from when I first took over the job.

Others, notably Mike Atherton, thought he was a bit too righteous. This was a feeling, as I have said, that we had about the South African team in general, but Hansie epitomized it. Like the initials 'WWJD' on his bracelet: What Would Jesus Do. I can't imagine he would fix cricket matches. Cronje was known as a bit of a money man. At that time he was virtually running South African cricket and there was a suspicion that he was not averse to taking care of himself financially.

Perhaps he was a little defensive in his tactics, but only in a South African way. It's the way they play: you make sure you can draw a game before you think of winning it. Get it sealed up. That is not such a bad thing. So to my mind he was a decent cricketer and captain, and he would have been the last name I would have come up with as a potential match-fixer.

It amazes and pleases me that match-fixing never entered my career at any stage other than at Centurion. I'm amazed because, with a name like Hussain and with cricket corruption centring on the sub-continent, no one ever thought to try me out, to see whether I would be susceptible to an offer. They would, of course, have been told where to go in no uncertain terms; but nobody ever tried and there was simply no culture of match-fixing in English cricket. It wasn't something any of us thought about.

You have to differentiate here between the various forms of cricket corruption that have infiltrated our sport in the last twenty years or so. First, the 'crime' Shane Warne and Mark Waugh admitted and which Alec Stewart was accused of – and, it should be stressed, was completely exonerated – is not match-fixing at all in my book. Someone ringing them up and asking what the pitch was like or what the weather was like and then giving them some sort of cash gift because they are 'fans' of theirs is not the most serious crime on earth. You have to remember that, when that went on, there was no culture of corruption in the game, and I can imagine a lot of players saying, 'You want to give me five grand just for telling you what the weather's like, which you could find out on Ceefax? OK then.' I emphasize again: nothing like that ever happened to me, nor to any of my teammates as far as I'm aware, and it was only later, in the wider scheme of things, when it was viewed as a potentially serious 'offence'.

Match-fixing, which clearly has gone on, is altogether more serious; you are actually affecting an aspect of the game. If that means getting out deliberately, bowling wides deliberately, or doing anything that alters the course of the outcome, then that is heinous and the biggest sin in any sport. I'm sure some people who have fallen prey to the match-fixers try to justify their actions to themselves by saying, 'So what if I get a grand for bowling a wide off the first ball of the match. That's not going to harm my side.' But that is a delusion. It is affecting the match and it is mightily wrong.

Anyone caught doing anything like that should be banned for life by the International Cricket Council. Simple as that. Even if it is just one wide, or one innings when they have got themselves out for a particular score. Gone for life. But it hasn't happened. The ICC say they are fighting corruption, they set up their units and came to see me as captain and tried to ban mobile phones from dressing rooms. That's not getting to the crux of the issue. When I was asked to ban phones Karen was pregnant and I wanted my phone to be with me at all times. In any case, it's an empty gesture. We were expected to take some stance because the ICC didn't have the guts, for legal reasons or whatever, to ban the people they knew were guilty. They were not doing anything about the real culprits while they were trying to stop us ringing our families or finding out how Leeds United were getting on. So I refused. I told the ICC that, until they hold a few people up as match-fixers and ban them from the game, then I wasn't going to help them with their silly mobile phone gestures. So I didn't.

In the England dressing room we viewed the whole saga with disbelief. I became captain in 1999 when the whole thing had not yet erupted and, if Cronje was at it on our tour, I'm staggered that no one thought to ring me to see if I would do anything to help out their schemes. Thank God it never happened because, even if I had received a phone call and had gone straight to the authorities, my name would have been linked to the whole business somehow. Maybe they knew I wouldn't have been interested. I was lucky.

We were all very naive about it all. There was such incredulity about corruption in our dressing room, it was almost as if we felt that someone must have been making it all up. We'd heard about the cases in football and about accusations of players kicking the ball straight into touch to earn money at the time of the first throw-in or something like that, but never anything in cricket, other than the business of declarations to set up contrived finishes and much more innocuous stuff like that.

I think it's because we spent so little time on the sub-continent that bookies, on the whole, didn't try to involve us. That's where it was all happening. And because we are now fortunate enough to earn decent money from the game. Maybe the countries where the money is not so good have been the prime targets.

I do feel that the ICC have been lacklustre. They involve Lord Condon and seemingly take action, but all that's happened is that we are given some sort of security pass before we go into any dressing room – which everyone forgets anyway – and they tell us not to use our mobiles in front of the cameras. How is that going to stop match-fixing? I will tell you how you stop it: by getting two offenders up on the telly and saying, 'Right, these two have fixed cricket matches. They are banned for the rest of their lives.' We have all heard the rumours about who is involved. It's all speculation but clearly some of it is true. And that one measure would stop it dead in its tracks and ensure that it's not going to be a problem for future generations of cricketers and supporters.

Instead, the ICC are still obsessed with stupid, petty regulations. Like the time when I went to have a look at a pitch before a Test and was told by the match referee that I was not allowed to walk on it with my studs on or I might get banned. I felt like saying to him, 'Look, I made myself look bloody stupid in Brisbane when I hadn't looked at the pitch properly before a toss. I'm an honest man. I'm not going to do any harm to the pitch.'

Then there was the time when I got fined £500 for having piping on my pads. Apparently it broke some ICC regulation. In the end, Gray-Nicolls paid the fine because it was their fault for manufacturing a slightly wrong type of pad, but does it really matter? The ICC are very strict on small issues but they show no sort of leadership over serious, potentially ruinous things like match-fixing and our World Cup predicament over Zimbabwe.

In the end I gave up going to ICC captains' meetings. They used to ask us what concerned us in the game, we'd tell them, and then they would say, 'That's nothing to do with us. That's up to the various boards.' So what was the point? Like the issue of too much cricket. There was one meeting when every Test captain in the room voiced concerns over itineraries and the excess of international cricket diluting the product, but the ICC just said they couldn't do anything about it. Why not? They're the governing body. No one is accountable with them.

Certainly cricket has been taken into a very murky world by the match-fixers. When the whole Cronje and Centurion business eventually came out, I couldn't believe it. The victory had been tarnished. One of my Test wins as captain doesn't really count if we are being brutally honest, and that's very upsetting. Then, some time later, it became even more surreal when Cronje was killed in an air crash. Pursuing a life that he wouldn't have been involved in if he hadn't been banned from cricket. I have heard all the conspiracy theories, that he was killed off by the dark forces who managed to turn his head and got him involved with corruption. It seems totally far-fetched, but after the events of the last few years nothing can really be ruled out.

I will say one good thing about the ICC's anti-corruption unit. At least they talk to young players, warning them that, however attractive a one-off payment for some 'innocent' offence may seem, they must resist temptation at all costs, because once they are sucked in by these people it will get worse and worse and there will be no turning back. If people are genuinely held accountable, I see no reason why cricket can't rid itself of the bookies and the forces of evil and make sure the game is clean in future. Spread betting in cricket is incredible and you can bet on virtually anything, so it's clear that there will always be scope there for making money, but the players must not be involved in that in any way.

The bottom line is that people want to sit in front of any sporting contest and know they are watching a genuine game between two sides who are doing their utmost to win. If supporters sit there wondering if something is dodgy – and re-member, sport can throw up some incredible genuine happen-ings – then that defeats the object of the whole thing and makes it pointless. Let's hope the worst is very much behind us.

23

Our two-Test series against Zimbabwe at the start of 2000 was both the start of our successful run of four series victories and the beginning of my downfall as a Test batsman, for a year or so. I had played really well in South Africa both in the Test series and in one-day cricket and when we came back I seemed to be almost flicking a subconscious mental switch whereby I thought, 'Well, it's only Zimbabwe and someone else will get the runs for me anyway.'

I'm at my best when I need to get runs, when the team is in trouble or the match situation is crying out for me to take control. I am at my worst when everyone else is getting hundreds or when I know the opposition are weak and they are going to be bowled out cheaply anyway. I know that's completely the wrong attitude, but it's a mental thing that has stopped me cashing in on match situations where I really should have scored more.

Also, my technique against bowlers of the type that Zimbabwe possessed is not the best. I play pace well, I play spin well, but the medium-pace swing or seam bowlers can have my head falling over a bit and get me in trouble, like the way Graham Gooch always struggled against Terry Alderman. So this was not the sort of situation or attack I relished.

Ed Giddins was my pick for the first Test at Lord's. I wanted him because by now I had got to know Lord's and I knew that I needed swing bowlers. It's not rocket science. You look up on the honours board and it is littered with swing bowlers who have taken wickets. So I wanted Andrew Caddick and I wanted Giddins, even though Duncan Fletcher was worried that Ed was a bowler who might not be able to grow. This was a big thing of Duncan's and something that I grew to appreciate. At that time I was more of a 'horses for courses' man, but Fletch would say things like, 'OK, he might do well at Lord's, but what's he going to bring to the next game?'

I just wanted to cross that bridge when I came to it because I was convinced Giddins could bowl Zimbabwe out at Lord's. I still feel there is a place for that type of selection because there will be venues and conditions which suit certain bowlers, but I absolutely take the point that you are looking for continuity and the sort of bowlers who can prosper on most surfaces.

And things went very much as expected. Giddo bowled beautifully, taking 5 for 15 in the first innings with both in-swing and out-swing, as Zimbabwe were bowled out for 83. Ed proved everyone right in this instance. I was right in wanting him because he won the Man of the Match award in bowling us to victory, but Fletcher and David Graveney, who were not sure they wanted him, were proved right in the next match, when he struggled.

We won by a huge margin, but then we didn't have things all our own way in the second Test at Trent Bridge, where Giddins was more innocuous. He didn't look half the bowler there. I think there was a bit of an issue with chucking that was affecting Ed. Some people were saying that he chucked his bouncer, so he was wary of bowling it in a Test, even though I wanted him to. I should have said to him, 'You're innocent until proven guilty, let the bouncer go,' but he wouldn't, and you can't really have a bowler like that in your side.

So that was Giddins's lot in international cricket. He disappeared pretty rapidly, but that was because there were doubts as to whether he could grow in Test cricket, in the way that people like Trescothick, Harmison, Vaughan and Flintoff have, and those doubts were valid ones, to be honest.

We almost came a cropper in the second Test. At that time Zimbabwe had a few decent players, like Andy and Grant

Flower, Murray Goodwin and Neil Johnson. Meanwhile, we were having to accommodate players like Chris Schofield, who was being pushed forward by Mike Gatting after he had taken him away on an 'A' tour. OK, we needed a leg-spinner, so we gave Schofield a contract on the basis of Gatting saying he was ready for Test cricket, but he clearly wasn't and probably never will be. He didn't seem to be able to bowl a hoop downhill in my estimation, and wasn't a very pleasant lad either, so that particular selection wasn't exactly a roaring success.

The promotion of Schofield wasn't the only legacy of Gatting's 'A' tour to Bangladesh and New Zealand. The word had come back that we were never to pick Ronnie Irani again because he had clashed badly with Gatting on that trip. This wasn't the first time I had had to defend Ronnie. He had clashed badly with David Lloyd in New Zealand in 1997; but to me, at least at that stage, he was a real trier, a genuine bloke, and I was keen that Duncan and I judge him for ourselves. In any case, who hasn't clashed with Gatting?

So Ronnie was struggling to get back in the picture, Giddins was effectively written off as a Test player just one match after being Man of the Match, and we had won a low-key series against Zimbabwe. I wasn't in the runs and now felt in shocking form. The West Indies lay ahead, a series that really was the best of times and the worst of times.

West Indies still had a good side. We had not won the Wisden Trophy for donkeys' years, it was my first major home series in charge, and this was our big chance, but they had people like Courtney Walsh, who I always found difficult to play, Curtly Ambrose and Brian Lara, and they were well led by Jimmy Adams. We soon realized we were going to be in for a huge battle when they routed us at Edgbaston. I spent more than two and a half hours at the crease during that game, which was what I needed to try to regain my form, but I scored only 23 runs in that time so I didn't feel as if I had made any real progress at all.

My lack of runs was starting to become an issue. I went to Trent Bridge to play for Essex soon after the first Test, and I could see that Sky TV, who were covering the game, were featuring all my dismissals and focusing on me and my form in their debates. At that time I kept on getting caught at cover, leaning back and trying too hard, and the experts were quick to pick up on it. We were due to pick the team for the second Test at Lord's later that day, but by the time we got round to it I was already struggling to make the Test side because I stopped a shot from Chris Read in the covers and immediately felt the pain of a finger injury.

There I was, in the end, with my finger in ice, picking two teams for Lord's, one of them with me in it and the other led by Alec Stewart, to be selected if I didn't make it. I didn't. Not only was my batting form being dissected but my popadom fingers had struck again and I was to miss what turned out to be one of the best Tests in English Test history.

The story of that Test was Ambrose and Walsh versus Caddick, Gough and Cork. After a slow start it was a wicket that seamed and swung and did just about everything. There was no hint of the drama to come when West Indies scored 267 in their first innings, Gough again ending up with one of his Lord's 4 fors and a narrow near miss on getting on the honours board. When we slipped to 134 all out we looked dead and buried. West Indies only needed about a hundred in their second innings to make the game safe in those conditions. For the first (but not for the last) time, I wondered how secure my position was as England captain. I went for a run round St John's Wood and I remember thinking, 'God, we're going to go two down. Where do we go from here?' But what happened on that Friday night will stay with me for ever, even though I wasn't playing, and provided a buzz around Lord's that I had never witnessed before. It was also a major turning point in modern English cricket.

Andrew Caddick was in his element. He's at his best when

he's bowling from the Nursery End, slightly up the slope with the wind coming from sort of fine leg to the right-hander. And he just kept on hitting the West Indians on the pads or getting them to nick off. It was extraordinary. We bowled them out for 54, with Caddick taking 5 for 16 and, as I passed the ground later, at around 8 p.m., there were still people in the ground talking and buzzing about what they had seen. Normally the bacon and eggs just march off down St John's Wood Road as soon as play is over!

I still felt a huge part of what was going on, even though I couldn't do anything to help the lads or affect the outcome. I tell you, we may not have been the best side in the world in my time as captain, but I think we were the best to watch.

Then there was the chase. I just couldn't watch. We only had to get 190 to win, but in the circumstances it felt like 400 and I honestly think it was harder to reach than 400 on a flat one, batting last. I hate jogging. Always have done. But I went for another run that Saturday at Lord's, with my hand in a plaster cast.

When I came back, Atherton and Vaughan were putting on a stand of 92 that was just priceless; it was worth three times as much. While they were together we were always looking favourites, but there always has to be a twist in the tail and we steadily lost wickets until we were 149 for 7, and suddenly the West Indies looked on top. Then, in a perfect script, it came down to Dominic Cork and Darren Gough to try to win the game with the bat for us, with only Matthew Hoggard, on debut, to come. I was sitting next to Hoggy in the dressing room, having met him for only the first time five days earlier, and he didn't strike me at that time as the sort of batsman I wanted to go in with the task of scoring the winning runs for us! You could not ask for two better or worse players to have in that situation than Gough and Cork. They are the jokers of the dressing room. One of them has poked his tongue out while bowling a ball in a Test Match, the other has pulled his shirt over his head to celebrate a Test wicket. And we were having to rely on them to get us back into a series against the West Indies that we couldn't afford to lose.

Yet what character they both have in adversity! Again, in Cork's case, this was justification for Duncan's preferred policy of only picking bowlers who could contribute with the bat. When you're seven and then eight down, to have Corky, with all his idiosyncrasies, batting like a badger, flicking good-length balls outside off-stump into the grandstand for six and then sticking a few fingers up towards his missus, whatever that meant, and winding up Ambrose and Walsh with all his facial expressions and his stupid running between the wickets was just priceless. Not to mention damaging for my health. Imagine sticking fingers up to someone at Lord's! What could he have been thinking of?

It was ideal for England to have Coco the clown and his chubby mate out there for us at that time. The West Indies didn't know how to react. We couldn't breathe in the dressing room. Even with 4 to win it wasn't all over, with just Hoggard to come, but when the winning runs were struck it was an amazing feeling. There have been great Tests since, but that was the ultimate Test. I've got a print on my wall at home which proclaims just that, and it is true. Magnificent.

I was back for Old Trafford, now completely out of nick, having not batted because of my broken finger. And it was another terrible Old Trafford Test. It rained, Brian Lara played brilliantly, Alec Stewart got a hundred in his hundredth Test and I batted like a man with no arms or legs on the last day, edging Walsh to Ridley Jacobs and him dropping it, before the rain saved me from further embarrassment. Enough said. Except that there was also a notable debutant in that match. Marcus Trescothick had made an impact in the one-day series when replacing an injured Nick Knight, and now he had to show he could do it in the Test arena. Duncan had been talking about him ahead of that summer, and then Irani told me that the two players who had impressed him most on the 'A' tour to New Zealand were Tres and David Sales.

When Marcus was handed his chance, he never looked back. While I consider myself to be a good judge of character I'm not so good at judging players, so I was happy to leave that sort of task to the experts, and no one was better than the two Fletchers, Keith and Duncan. In Marcus's case Duncan was vindicated from the word go, and Michael Vaughan had already arrived as another inspired pick from county cricket. Both Tres and Vaughany had an aura about them from the start, the right personality to succeed at the highest level. They were immaculate, very professional people. They took to Test cricket like ducks to water. I didn't have to offer them much advice, but I did tell them that the two people in the dressing room they should look at and learn from were Atherton and Stewart and it would be nice if they both ended up like Atherton. Unfortunately for me, they both ended up as meticulous and organized as Stewie!

Neither was setting county cricket alight when they were picked for England – which makes you wonder just how many others like them there are out there. In the end that's why I stopped being a selector. It's just complete guesswork and I don't mind admitting I wasn't very good at it. As long as I could have my say in selection on the character of players, then I was happy to leave the finer points to others in the end.

Headingley was just as dramatic as Lord's. It was a good toss to lose because neither Jimmy Adams nor I knew what to do, but luckily he decided to bat and Craig White took 5 wickets as we bowled them out for 172, which was quite a good score on that pitch. We didn't take our chances as we should have done; we really should have got them out for less.

This was a period of dodgy wickets in England, together with hard Duke balls that were doing everything. Vaughan continued maturing with runs and Graeme Hick proved he was still valuable to us by playing really well, coming in at eight (because of the nightwatchman) to score 59. Around this time whenever Hicky came back into the side he seemed to be greeted less than enthusiastically by the press, but the guy really could still do a job and I just wish I could have got a little more out of him to help him fulfil his talent. I have already stated how highly I rated him and I hope Graeme Hick doesn't feel unfulfilled now. He did achieve an awful lot in the game.

In this Test, Hicky and Vaughan earned us a lead of 100, which was like gold dust on that pitch. So my hope was that we could bowl them out for around 200 maximum because I didn't want to be chasing 150 or more. As it turned out, we didn't have to chase anything at all! We got a couple of early wickets but then had a frustrating spell when nothing happened. Caddick was bowling at the Kirkstall Lane end and Trescothick walked past me and, casual as you like, said, 'You do know Caddy bowled better here for Somerset the other week from the Rugby Stand end.' I thought, 'Thanks for telling me, lads. No wonder Somerset are struggling!' So I switched Caddy to the other end and immediately you could tell it was going to do something. Again, it was swinging up the hill a little bit, the wind was perfect and the West Indies don't like the swinging ball because it is so different from their home conditions. Then Andrew Caddick produced the over of his life.

It was bewildering stuff. Jacobs went, lbw first ball of the over, then Caddy hit the stumps of Nixon McLean, Curtly Ambrose and Reon King in four legitimate deliveries. Amazing. Soon after, West Indies were all out for 61 and the match was over in two days. In the space of an over the situation changed from one where it looked as though we might have to chase 100 to it being all over. It was the weirdest feeling. Essex had started a county championship match on the same day as us, yet our Test was over and they still had two days to go.

We didn't know what to do with ourselves. Leeds United

were at home the next day. Should I visit Elland Road? No, still in too much of a daze to think about anything other than this extraordinary series. We got up and went to the ground to do a Channel 4 show when we really should have been taking the field for day three. Nobody could believe it.

I had always been a fan of Andrew Caddick. I just felt he needed careful handling. He had a self-destruct button, like Phil Tufnell, but in his case it surfaced in some of the things he said rather than what he did, like Phil. He had the knack of saying the wrong thing at the wrong time, like when he took the piss out of Gough for not getting on the Lord's honours board just when it was really starting to hurt Darren. I think when Caddy was younger, people used to take offence at what he said, but I wanted to get it into people's heads that he was a genuine bloke who didn't mean any harm and it was just his way of dealing with his insecurity.

It's all about man-management with Caddy. You have to back him up in front of people, never have a go at him in front of his teammates. I think he's had people have a go at him most of his life, and it's affected him. He's actually the most helpful, useful bloke to have in the dressing room, a real Mr Fixit, and he will do anything for anybody.

I relished the psychology involved in getting the best out of his rivalry with Gough. I remember asking someone what the truth was about the rivalry between Teddy Sheringham and Andy Cole at Manchester United, because they famously didn't get on but it never seemed to hinder their terrific relationship on the pitch. I'm not saying that Gough and Caddick didn't get on, but you could use their perceived differences to your advantage, and I think I did over the years.

I would go up to Caddy and say, 'Bloody Gough doesn't want to bowl into the wind. He's a prima donna, isn't he? Are you all right going into the wind?' and he would be fine. But if you went to him and said, 'Goughy's our main strike bowler, he wants that end,' then Caddick would have been furious and would not have been at his best that day. At the same time I would be going up to Gough and saying, 'I'm not having that big-eared twat running downwind. I want you to do it. You're our best bowler.'

Equally, there was always something Caddick wasn't happy with. Usually it was the footholes. But if I'd said, 'Oh, for fuck's sake, Caddy, just get on with it,' he wouldn't have responded. Instead it had to be, 'Yeah, bloody footholes. They're terrible, aren't they? Big lad like you as well. Bloody Gough won't bowl this end. I need you to do it. I'll go and have a kick at them, Caddy, you carry on trying your best, mate.' You just had to pamper him a little because he was a bloody good bowler, as he showed against the West Indies in 2000.

The only thing he couldn't do was bowl just an inch or two fuller from his natural length. Whenever he tried it, he'd be too full, become floaty and over-pitch it. That's why I found bowling him slightly uphill got his length that little bit fuller and made him a better bowler. He was very mechanical in his action and he just couldn't change it, really. Duncan and I talked about it and in the end we decided we were better off leaving him be. For instance, that summer we would write down clear plans for key people. Cork was the man to pitch it up to Adams to get him lbw, White was the man to try to reverse swing it at Lara to bowl him round his pads. Then, at the bottom of every team sheet, we would write 'Caddick bowl Caddick length'. He was happy with that. We didn't want to confuse him. We could never give him the impression he had done anything wrong. I was still a bit hesitant to ask him his opinion at a team meeting because he would invariably wind someone up. But there was a transformation both in him and in the way others viewed him during my time as England captain. As soon as Caddick was handled well and he started to feel part of the team, he became an incredibly popular member of the squad. Andy Caddick would do anything for anybody. If you wanted your bat-handle fixed or your DVD player plugged in at a hotel in Karachi, Caddick would always be there to help. We all soon found out that Andy Caddick had a massive heart and just wanted to feel wanted. Fletcher and I definitely wanted Andy Caddick. So did England. We missed him as a player, but, more importantly, as a person, when injury led to his not being there.

Caddick certainly knocked the stuffing out of the West Indies. All their batters were now looking in terrible nick. Brian Lara was out of sorts, Adams kept getting out lbw and no one else exactly looked a threat, yet I was feeling the pressure. Our long wait since we last won the Wisden Trophy was featuring prominently in the press. And I'd never heard of the Wisden Trophy! It was only that summer that I discovered there was a trophy, competed for by us and West Indies, and now we were in a position to win it for the first time in thirty years. In my mind I kept thinking of the 5–0 thrashings, the blackwashes experienced by my predecessors, Gatting having his nose broken by Malcolm Marshall, Tim Robinson batting with a broken arm. Revenge for the beatings inflicted on Gooch, Gower and Botham. The West Indian supporters all running on to the Oval after yet another series victory. All these things.

Everything about my life at that time was dominated by thoughts of us winning this series. I was brought up on drubbings by them. My first tour was to the West Indies. All I wanted to do was win it. It was the be-all and end-all of my life at that time.

So all my thoughts went on that and I didn't do any planning for my batting at all. I always had my elaborate plans and thought processes before I went in to bat, but on this occasion all I could think of was the team winning. I hardly bothered with nets. It was completely out of character for me. It was a period when I was batting from memory. For once I wasn't thinking about me and I wasn't thinking about my batting. In a way it was weak of me because I needed to get my batting right, but I didn't have enough mentally to focus totally on the team and then switch on to my batting. I got the balance wrong. It was a must-win match and someone else had to get the runs.

We made a good start at the Oval through Atherton and Trescothick before it was my turn. I had a long wait to bat and that's when I'm at my worst. It was the West Indies' new leg-spinner, Nagamootoo, who got me for o first time – but, to be honest, it could have been any bloody Japanese bowler. I was not going to score runs off anybody in that state. Luckily I still had my captaincy and my tactics, which was all-consuming, and we had the upper hand for much of the match without dominating them. Ath played bloody well, just at a time when people were beginning to question whether he was still good enough, and there was the added emotion of it being Ambrose's last Test and Walsh's last in England.

That may even have lifted us, the guards of honour and the rest of it, while it could have had an adverse effect on them. Our bowling plans were working and we had a good first-innings lead. Then I had to go in on a pair. I'd never bagged one before and I never have since, and as a batsman it's your worst nightmare, getting nought in the first innings and then having to think about bagging them. I was stuck there for a while, maybe I had the odd chance to kamikaze a single, but I just knew in my heart of hearts that I wasn't going to get a run. I could not see where my next run was coming from. In the end it was almost a relief when I was out lbw to McLean and there was complete silence around the Oval and in the dressing room. I think people were embarrassed for me. There was a deathly hush. It was then that I really started to question whether I should be captain of England.

It was just that I was putting so much into the job that my batting was shot to pieces and I didn't want to ask the boys to do something that I couldn't do myself. I was thinking to myself that the only way I knew how to captain a side was by fear and anger, and by having a go at people and not by putting my arm around them. I couldn't captain in a softly softly way. I had to captain by anger. I was bad cop. And how could I get angry with someone and ask them to do something if I was not confident in my own ability to do it myself? How could I have a go at Gough or Caddick for not stopping a 2 on the boundary after I had been out for two noughts? In many ways they were the lowest four days of my life, but the fifth was incredible.

Everything was hanging on the last day. The Oval was sold out. Hospitality boxes were opened to let more people in. Channel 4 had put up big screens in London parks so that more people could watch the cricket. My personal misery had to go to the back of my mind again because I was consumed once more with the prospect of doing something that a lot of great captains had never done, and that was leading England to a Test series victory over West Indies.

This was the beginning of the end for me as England captain. I know that now. It was affecting me so much, both mentally and physically, that even at that stage I didn't know how much more I had to give. When it gets to the stage that you can't sleep before any day's play, then something has to give. Until that point I had always been a worrier, an obsessive, but I knew deep down that it was only a game and I was able to keep it in perspective. I reckon, at the Oval, that my critical mass started going in the wrong direction. It was all becoming too much for me and too important a part of my life to be healthy. I sensed the whole country wanted us to beat the West Indies and it assumed an exaggerated importance.

When the moment of victory came on that fifth day, after we had bowled the West Indies out for 215 after setting them a formidable target of 373 to win and draw the series, I just sank to my knees on the outfield. It just happened. It's not something I usually do. I'm not a stump grabber. I'm a 'shake hands and walk off' merchant at times like that. But in my mind the famous words of Bill Shankly, 'It's not a matter of life and death. It's far more important than that,' were ringing true. I told Darren Gough soon afterwards that I was thinking of quitting.

24

As the captaincy enveloped me, so I tended to forget that all-important bit of advice Duncan Fletcher had given me when I first met him: that the eyes of the world will always be on me. Overlooking that, I tended to get a bit more extrovert in my reactions and started to have a go at people like Darren Gough and Andrew Caddick on the field.

Gough had told me not to be silly when I asked him if he thought I should pack up, and then he made a point of saying in a television interview that I was the best captain he'd played under, which was thoughtful of him. Gough said to me, 'Don't be stupid. Everyone in the team fully believes in you and wants you to captain us.' That was enough for me. I knew Goughy would call a spade a spade and would tell me if I had lost the dressing room in any way or if people were chuntering about my lack of runs. If Goughy had said one little negative thing, even if he'd joked that I couldn't have a go at him over anything now that I'd got a pair, I would have quit straight away. I carried on; but the first seeds of doubt had been sown and my perspective had changed for ever.

In a way, my over-the-top attitude helped because it made my players a little bit more scared of their captain and made us a more difficult side to beat, almost like Sourav Ganguly is with the Indian side, but I was doing nothing for show. It was just that every ball and every run and every day and every session had become more important to me than life or death. It meant everything.

Because we had beaten the West Indies with me this way, I got it into my head that this was the way to move forward, and so it became a bit of a vicious circle, with the next series just as important and then the one after that equally so. They were all close-fought series too, with Pakistan going down to the wire, and then Sri Lanka after that, so every night was a sleepless one, every morning a nervous one where I couldn't eat breakfast, I couldn't breathe properly, I couldn't so anything. I was just a nervous wreck every day and, although Karen was incredibly supportive, it affected my family and everything about my life. I so wish it hadn't in so many ways because I could well have carried on longer as captain, but the equilibrium had gone. My attitude made England a better side but me a worse person, and it affected me adversely both mentally and physically. By the time I resigned I'd driven myself into the ground. I was suffering from symptoms of depression and irritable bowel syndrome and no aspect of my life remained untouched by it.

We will go into all that later, but for now I was carrying on. I embarked on my most satisfying winter as captain, even though again it was torture at times and I can't say I enjoyed very much of it. The ECB were making a big to-do about our visit to Pakistan because it was the first full tour there since the Mike Gatting–Shakoor Rana business in 1987 and it was clear that there was a lot of bridge-building to be done. It helped me that I had been there as captain of an 'A' tour, but it was the first England tour of the sub-continent for quite a few years and not many of our players knew what it was like to tour there.

People talk about Pakistan being a difficult place to tour, but apart from the obvious things, like social interaction and stuff like that, it is actually fine. You notice things like the lack of bars in the hotels. Not that we're a bunch of pissheads, but it's not quite the same meeting up in a coffee shop at the end of a long day's play. The cities are interesting. Lahore is a beautiful city, really, with a lot of open spaces, and the temperatures can be quite pleasant. Then you have the supposed dangerous places like Peshawar, from where we always go up the Khyber

Pass, and Karachi, which is hot and busy. Faisalabad is a difficult place to visit, the sort of place you fly in and out of. Very industrial.

Dean Conway, our physio, had been on the 'A' tour to Pakistan with me, so I wanted him to make sure the boys had plenty to do socially. There was to be no sitting around moping. South Africa had just played Pakistan, which was handy, because Duncan was something of a father figure to people like Gary Kirsten and Jacques Kallis and he had got a lot of information from them about the Pakistan wickets and players.

The first thing that hit me in Karachi was the quality of the new bowlers provided for us. There were three or four lads in sort of Dunlop flip-flops who would run up and bowl like Saqlain Mushtaq, spinning the ball the other way with an off-spinner's action. I wondered why we couldn't have bowlers like that. How comes it those little Asian lads I see at my dad's cricket school are not encouraged to work on mystery spin all the way up to adulthood and professional cricket? Anyway, it was great practice for us. Saqlain was a big threat at that time and we needed all the practice we could get against bowlers of his type. These lads were perfect.

The tour started well. All the warm-up games were fine. We had to get used to the heat, the brightness, and the fact that they would throw pretty explosive bowlers at us at first and then spin would be on by about the fifteenth over. In the first game, the opposition threw us a Test fast bowler in Mohammad Akram, who was to later play for Essex and Sussex, which was a bit of a fright because it showed that there was some depth to their pace bowling resources. It also showed the sheer raw talent in the country. The quality of players they have behind the scenes is incredible.

Yet I quickly learnt that, even though they have all this talent, they don't utilize it quite enough. They either put themselves under immense pressure or they are quite selfish because of the politics of the sport in the country. Run-outs occur pretty readily because they are all looking after their own wicket. I know that sounds rich, coming from me, but then my surname is Hussain! My aim was to try to keep them under pressure because then they start to do stupid things and the papers and supporters get on their backs.

Duncan brought to us the necessity of a game plan and we had a very clear idea of the need to concentrate on playing Saqlain and Mushtaq Ahmed well and basically to play the game in a very different way than we would at home. There's no seam movement there. There's no point in picking English line-and-length bowlers. We needed Darren Gough's pace and Craig White's reverse swing. We had to play Pakistan at their own game.

First was the one-day series, notable for us successfully chasing 304 in the first but then losing the last two. For me, there was the encouragement of two fifties, which did not go amiss, and we played pretty well in the first Test, even though it was a turgid draw. The only thing I would say about my attempts to get back in the runs was that my batting had become a bit frenetic against spin. I ran down the wicket and hit Saqlain for 6, but it was chancy. I had always played spin well, but that was orthodox spin, when I knew which way it was turning. This new wave of mystery spinners was a different kettle of fish altogether, and I quickly holed out to cover, not what was needed. The second innings ended abruptly for me when Wasim Akram struck me on the elbow and I was forced to retire hurt. I had never been in such agony. Luckily an X-ray in darkest Lahore showed no break and both England and I emerged unscathed and showed that we could compete in Pakistan.

The second Test in Faisalabad proved to be a similar story. By this time Yousuf Youhana was starting to annoy us a bit. We called him the laughing hyena. He was a bit of a Javed Miandad type of character, chatting away to you and generally bugging us. He wasn't one of the players we had formulated a plan for, and he was proving a thorn in our side. We were all still learning on our feet, and my message to the boys was: just stay in the game and you never know what might happen next. It was a question of survival, getting to the last Test all square and trying to turn up the pressure on the home side.

I got two terrible decisions in Faisalabad: given out lbw in the first innings when I had hit it, and caught behind in the second when I hadn't. Between the two decisions the umpires had got it right, but in the wrong order! It got me back into a terrible state of mind over my batting and edged me ever more down the slippery slope. I was introspective away from the field. There were more sleepless nights, more nerves, more fears of not contributing to the team.

I calculated that I had gone eight months without a proper 'good day' in terms of my batting in Tests, which was just not good enough, and I thought back to my childhood and how I could possibly have coped with eight months without a good day when I was trying to impress my dad. There would have been some tension around the Hussain home back then.

It was like the bad old days when I lost my leg-spin. It was a traumatic time for me all over again, and I felt like a child utterly consumed with the game and its ups and downs. So I thought, who can I have a look at? What am I doing wrong? Why is it getting to me so much? It was now that I found help through a member of the press.

Scyld Berry is a cricket writer I have grown to admire both as a journalist and as a friend because of my time writing with him for the *Sunday Telegraph*. Scyld has always got a theory about the game, quite often coming from left field; but he really cares about the game and its players and he is quite an original, modern thinker. I was killing time in a coffee shop somewhere with Mike Atherton, as you do in Pakistan, and Scyld came up to us with his latest theory. 'I've been watching you two,' he said. 'Athers, perhaps because of his bad back, walked up to the table slowly. His heartbeat is low, his body language is calm and he seems relaxed. You, Nass, are like a bundle of energy. You whisked up to the table. It was like "What do I do next?" Why don't you just calm down, and get your heartbeat down.'

At the time I was like, 'Piss off, Scyld. What are you talking about? Low heartbeat and stuff? That's really going to help me against Wasim Akram!' But the more I thought about it, the more I felt he had a point. Scyld became a very useful shoulder to lean on as time went by and I started to take on board what he had to say. Atherton would read his *Racing Post* as a way of switching off. Thorpey would have his books on the SAS to keep him occupied. I kept on thinking of the words of Alan Knott: 'The knack is realizing what you're doing is important but trying to think it isn't.' It was all about mind games and trying to switch off on days off. I would sit there, have a cup of tea and get my heartbeat down. I would watch Ath, as Scyld recommended, and I noticed he was in a world of his own. He would hum to himself, whistle while he was getting ready to bat, and it would get on people's nerves, but it was Ath getting his heartbeat down and relaxing. He would sing the wrong words to a song in the dressing room and drive everyone mad.

I didn't go to those extremes, but I decided to give it a go. I would sit down the night before a game in Pakistan and write down the names of the opposition bowlers and what their strengths were. It became almost like a military operation. I wrote: 'Wasim Akram: can swing it in. Watch out for reverse swing later on. Has a good slower ball.' Then it would be: 'Waqar Younis: don't get your foot too far across. Always look for the in-swinging yorker. Saqlain Mushtaq: watch for the back of the hand. Mushtaq: sweep.' Things like that. Then I would write down a list of my shots and which ones I should play to each bowler. It was hardly switching off, I admit, but it was making me more organized and calmer about the task ahead. Then I would try, to quote our psychologist Steve Bull, to put all that information in a box and leave it there and try to have dinner without talking about cricket.

Then, when I picked up the paper the next morning, I would try to read about anything but cricket. There were some fascinating things going on in that part of the world and my eyes were opened to them. I'm not saying it solved all my problems, but it did do me some good because in the third Test in Karachi I scored 51 in the first innings, my first for months in Tests.

It made me believe that my new methods were working, even though I was disappointed I didn't go on to get a hundred. I felt I was back in the frame of mind I needed to be in, the beans weren't going when I went out to bat. I wasn't as frenetic. I wasn't thinking, 'What if I get out and I'm not contributing.' As I say, it was hardly perfect, but it kept me in the job for a little longer than my health would have allowed at one point.

As for the game, it was a typical sub-continental affair on a flat, old, sub-continental wicket. I put Marcus Trescothick on to bowl before lunch on the first day, and he got Imran Nazir out and then had Inzamam ul Huq absolutely stone dead in front, old heavy-headed Inzi, but it was turned down. Now I look back and laugh at how Marcus was bowling so early, but it just shows how different the game is there and we had to hang on in there as we had done all series. I knew if we could get to the last day all square, we could still have a chance of pulling something off. I know some people criticized the negative nature of the cricket on that trip, but what were we supposed to do? Hand victory to them on a plate by playing as if we were in England? I'm not saying I would have been totally satisfied with three turgid draws but, hey, that's not too bad in Pakistan, and I think we were helped in having a southern African coach in Duncan Fletcher, who backed me up in believing that, out there, it was important to make sure we could draw the game first before we thought of the possibility of victory.

By the penultimate day the press had started to get on our backs a bit, most unfairly, and people like Michael Henderson in the *Daily Telegraph* were chuntering on about how this wasn't attractive enough cricket. I like Hendo; he has both supported me and infuriated me over the years. He is an interesting character and I like his company. There have been times when my brother Mel has been furious about things Hendo has written about me and wanted to do something about it, but I have always told him and my dad that they would like him if they met him because he has a bit of Hussain madness about him. Maybe they will one day.

On this occasion, what he basically was saying was that he couldn't write anything flowery about three drawn Tests in Pakistan. I guess it was a bit like explaining to an American that you can have fifteen days of cricket and still end up with a 0–0 scoreline, but to be honest I didn't think it necessary to explain the complexities of the game in Pakistan to the cricket correspondent of the *Daily Telegraph*. He should have known that there might be a means to the end and that in this instance it really could have been an interesting 0–0. In any case, the time difference found Hendo out. By the time his piece criticizing us had landed on the breakfast tables in London on the final day of the series, we were well on the way to recording an extraordinary victory in Karachi.

A lot of it was down to team spirit. Take someone like Ashley Giles. People talked about negativity and, later in India, that he was bowling over the wicket too much, but he really spun the ball in Pakistan. I'm not sure he has spun it that much before or since. Absolutely brilliant. He was encouraged to do that by the depth of feelings we had in our side. I could go back to 1997, when the likes of myself and Irani, Cork, Thorpe and Tufnell were labelled the brat pack because we got on so well in New Zealand. Well, I wanted cliques in my side. I wanted close friendships. I wanted Ashley Giles and Craig White to spend time together so long as they enjoyed each other's company, because that meant they were pushing for each other all the more on the field. It was how I wanted my side to be, and it was working out brilliantly.

The last day in Karachi was amazing. It had been nip and tuck again for four days. It was still a pretty flat wicket. Our mantra of telling the boys that 'all three results are still possible' was still being repeated as Duncan urged the boys to practise all three disciplines, batting, bowling and fielding, before the final day's play. Everyone expected Pakistan to bat out the final day. But we kept on chipping in with wickets at valuable times. At lunch we had 6 wickets down but the draw was still the most likely outcome. But a clatter of wickets suddenly gave us a sniff of what we had been hanging on in there for over the last fourteen days. Pakistan had been bundled out for 158, leaving us with a victory target of 176 in a minimum of 44 overs. We had them exactly where we wanted them after fourteen and a half days of cricket. With the possibility of a home defeat, their team were under immense pressure. They had panicked, and now I was starting to think of my batting order and how we were going to have to go for this.

As each Pakistan wicket fell towards the end, I was revising my batting order as our likely target veered between 4 and 5 an over. Moin Khan was a real fighter, someone you'd like in your side, but now he was on the back foot and, as usual with Pakistan captains, fighting for his job. Now the go-slow tactics began. Pakistan's first 7 overs before tea took forty minutes to bowl, and in total they took three and a half hours to bowl 41 overs. Moin was warned to get on with it at tea by the match referee and we began to realize that only fading light could stop us.

Forget all this 'slow heartbeat' stuff and Scyld's switch-off mentality. My heart was going at three million miles an hour now and, as I still didn't really know which end of the bat to hold, I dropped myself down the order and offered Atherton the chance to do the same if we wanted to get Alec Stewart in straight away to try to get us off to a flyer. Typically of Ath, he said he was seeing the ball as well as anyone and went in with Trescothick to get us off to a great start.

Meanwhile, myself, Thorpe, Hick, Stewart and White were all padded up, ready to go in if necessary, and I vowed to try to keep the left/right-hand combination going to mess their bowlers up. We were always up with the rate, but the light was going and Moin was stalling. Maybe I would have tried to slow things down a bit if I was in his situation, but I don't think I would have done it to that degree because I don't think an England captain would have been looked on at all favourably if he had tried something like that.

As the light got worse and worse, some of the boys were questioning what we should do, but it was obvious to me that we had to keep on going. I felt we couldn't lose by staying out there because I could have always appealed successfully against the light if we had slumped to 8 or 9 wickets down. They appealed three times against the light but, to umpire Steve Bucknor's eternal credit, he turned them down, even though it was really dark by now; because Pakistan had been bowling their overs so slowly it was their own fault.

Thorpe played like a little genius, Hick was freed up to play really fluently, the reverse sweep being productive for him, and I ended up going in with 20 to win. It was farcical, really, because of the dark, but we were not going to budge. There was some great banter between Moin and Thorpey, with the Pakistan captain having a go at the umpire, pleading to come off, then turning to Thorpe and saying, 'Come on, Thorpe! You would be doing the same as me, wouldn't you?' and Thorpey would be turning back and saying, 'Yeah, yeah, Moin, we would be doing the same, but we're not. And we're going to have to finish this game, mate, to be honest. Time's not stopping still here. You're going to have to finish it. Come on.' Moin, who was under great pressure, was still able to laugh about the situation.

42. Celebrating in Sri Lanka – if anything, a better series win than against Pakistan.

43. Darren Gough, the first name on my team sheet, soaks up the applause.

44. Talking with Dad in Jaipur during our Indian tour of 2001.

45. A moment to ponder during our tour of India in 2001, the tour which completed me as a person and a cricketer.

46. The proud parents with Jacob, June 2001.

47. Karen and Jacob attempt to look impressed as I show off my ability at my other sporting passion, golf. Unfortunately the divot went further than the ball!

48. With my dad in his home city of Madras. Everything I have achieved in cricket is because of him, and going back to Madras as England captain was the ultimate.

49. I was truly humbled when so many relatives and friends turned up to a Hussain family reunion in Madras in 2001.

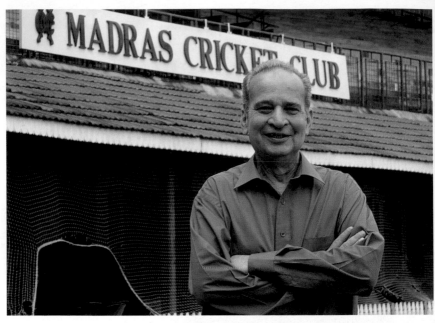

50. Dad returns home to the Madras Cricket Club.

51. A proud moment as my mum Shireen and dad Joe join me at Buckingham Palace when I receive my OBE.

52. My three-fingered salute to my one-day critics at Lord's in 2002. One finger each for Agnew, Botham and Willis!

53. Leaving for Australia with Jacob, late in 2002, where he was to be joined in our family by Joel.

54. A Test century at Lord's, against India in 2002. Getting my name on the honours board twice is a huge thing.

55. The fateful moment when Steve Waugh tossed the coin in Brisbane, I called 'Heads' and made the worst call of my captaincy.

56. The Australian media gleefully celebrate my mistake in inserting Australia after the fateful Brisbane toss.

57. Karen and Jacob came to Australia so that I could be present at the birth of Joel in November 2002.

58. Taking a walk in a Perth park with Jacob, soon after the arrival of Joel.

59. On the the field with Ben Hollioake. His death was a terrible tragedy. I wish I'd had the chance to get to know him better as a person and as a player.

60. Ben Hollioake's life and death are commemorated by us in a minute's silence in his honour at Wellington.

By now I couldn't see a thing. I edged my first ball, going for a big cover drive, and was almost caught by a diving Moin, and it was just pure reaction stuff. Thorpe was nurdling it around and then he went for a big hoik and got an inside edge. No one saw where it went except me, and we ran the winning runs. Just a couple of hours earlier we were thinking in terms of maybe having to bat a session to save the match, but now we had won on the sub-continent. As I ran back for a second run I realized quite how dark it was because I looked back at the pavilion and it seemed as though someone had left the lights on and gone home because it was pitch black, apart from our dressing room.

These are the moments I played the game for. Not the money. Not the quest for an average of 40 or a hundred caps. The scenes in the dressing room after that were priceless. Silly things that mean so much. Like, for some reason, the team song at that time was 'Who let the dogs out?' so there we were, all were singing it with this serious, middle-aged man in Duncan Fletcher in the middle woofing like a dog. The players I celebrated that victory with that night in Karachi, where Pakistan had never lost a Test, will always be special. To share those moments with people like Atherton, Thorpe, Stewart, Caddick, Gough, Giles, White and Hick made up for all the torment I had been suffering over my own position as England captain. It was lovely to see the ex-England captains clearly savouring the victory so much. There could easily have been some bitterness from Atherton or Stewart, a sense of 'Well, if I'd had Fletcher as my coach, things might have seen different,' or 'Well, Nasser's been lucky with his bowlers,' but there was none of that. They were as pleased as I was. After what I had been through during the previous few months it was one of the great moments. It was about now I started referring to this team as 'my boys', and they will always be that to me.

As ever at these times, I felt like ringing my dad and again saying to him, 'You were right. Thanks so much.' The side of my brain that had questioned why he had driven me so hard as a boy had again been silenced. I thought of him at his cricket school and of the Pakistani lads who went down there. Dad would have been giving them stick for not supporting England that night!

25

We did not have much time to bask in what we had achieved in Pakistan. After a brief spell at home at Christmas, it was off to Sri Lanka for the second half of our demanding winter. And how demanding it was. I remember Keith Fletcher telling me in my youth that Sri Lanka was the hardest place to tour, and he wasn't one for exaggeration.

It was the heat and the humidity as much as anything else. It was so oppressive and the wickets turn more there than anywhere else in the world. It's easily the hottest place where I have played cricket. There are so many areas that can affect you. Silly things, like gloves and bat handles and the amount you sweat and the fluids you must take on board. And how it affects the grip of the ball for the seam bowlers. And there are many more things. For such a small island, Sri Lanka has an incredible depth of talent. A much more gifted side than Pakistan, and one that was clearly going to test us even more.

We had formulated a plan again. We would all gather as a team to watch Muralitharan on the super slow-mo in the video room. Including Graham 'What else does he bring?' Thorpe. By this time Thorpe was on the management committee, proving again that if you treat someone properly they will respond. Thorpey, the man who would sit quietly fiddling with his bat handles, was by now running our net sessions and roughing them up to re-create the conditions we would have to encounter with Murali. The groundsmen would hate us!

And to simulate how far Murali could turn the ball, we would make people come up and literally throw it at our batsmen. Our spinners couldn't turn it that far – and, in any case, we didn't want to muck up their actions. However, we did want to completely focus on Murali and the threat he posed to us. He had, after all, taken 16 wickets in a Test when last we met, so we devised a method of playing against him and it was effective, much as it may have offended some people's sensibilities in that they seemed to expect us just to let him bowl at us and take cheap wickets.

We had all our bad luck, bad umpiring decisions and misfortune in the first Test at Galle. I lost the toss – I lost all three in the series – but we made them work hard in reaching 470 in two days. At one stage, our bowling coach, Bob Cottam, a good man, was giving everybody a master class in bowling cutters because he thought it would be more effective than our conventional bowling, and he was right. It was hard cricket but we stuck together as a team, at the end all going back to our fabulous hotel, the Lighthouse in Galle, and all just sitting round the pool with our families discussing what had happened and how we could improve.

We had great spirit. We found humour in our predicament. It was like 'We're not heroes any more' and 'We could lose 3–0 out here.' Meanwhile, my form was getting no better. I had fallen twice to Murali for next to nothing and I was confused about how to play him. In my youth I'd played on turning wickets, and had done well on an age-group tour of Sri Lanka, by playing off-spin late and generally on the back foot. But this bloke would spin it so quickly and from such an angle that if you played him off the back foot you were in trouble, especially with the umpires so keen to give you lbw on the back foot.

So, I went in at Galle having done my homework, having learnt, I thought, to get my heartbeat down and feeling a lot better about my batting. But I went on the back foot and was gone. It was clear that all my planning was in vain. The only way for a right-hander to play him was to get forward and kick it. I was back to square one. I had to go to these crappy nets in Galle and try to retrain my brain to try to get forward to him. He saw I was trying to do that in the second innings and was ready for me, so he bowled his other one, the one I feel he chucks, and he'd done me again.

We were beaten by an innings and I was now looking at just one Test fifty in around ten months. I thought I had turned the corner in Pakistan, but it appeared not. Karen was there and I just sat with her one night, not being able to explain how I felt. Everybody seemed to be backing me. Duncan was calling me an all-rounder, a captain and a batsman, and the boys were saying they didn't mind if I wasn't getting any runs, but I knew deep down that it did matter and I felt awful about not contributing. I was embarrassed.

Darren Gough had reassured me at the end of the West Indies series and the unlikely figure of Scyld Berry had helped me in Pakistan, but it was only glossing over my position. I decided I had to have further talks with someone I trusted, so I went to see Mike Atherton. I said to him, 'What do you think, Ath? I'm not getting any runs. I haven't got any for a long time. Do you think the side would be better off without me? I want to be picked on merit. I don't just want to play because I'm captain. I need to clear my head somehow. Should I just concentrate on batting?'

Ath listened. He didn't just butt in and tell me not to be silly. He could easily have just trotted out platitudes and told me that everyone was behind me and that I should just get on with it. Mike Atherton thought for a while before saying, 'Look, Nass, I know exactly what you're going through. I can't tell you what to do, but I can tell you that I've spoken to every single person in this team and there is not one that wants you replaced as captain.'

Again, I needed to know that I was going to be able to tick off people without any of them saying, 'How can he have a go at us when he hasn't scored any runs all year?' Ath reassured me about that. It was an important chat. And it was important that he was very honest with me and showed complete understanding. And I didn't choose him because I thought he would say what I wanted to hear. I chose him because I knew he'd give an honest appraisal of my situation. Which he did.

But I still had to make the decision as to whether it was right for me to carry on on my own. I went to bed but I couldn't sleep, so I got up around 1 a.m. and went to a little bar in the hotel that overlooks the ocean. The barman was just packing up but I managed to persuade him to hang on, ordered myself a rum and Coke, lit up a fag (even though I don't smoke), and sat there, going through everything. I said to myself, 'Right, what are you doing? What's this all about? Why the sleepless nights, and is it worth it? Are you a quitter? What's best for the team? Is it good for the team to quit halfway through a tour like this?'

I was very close to going. I was conscious of the fact that things often look better in the morning, so I wanted to make my decision that night while I was thinking clearly. People always say you should sleep on a big decision or give it time, but I'm not really a big believer in that. I like to go with my gut instinct. Most of the big decisions in my life have been taken on the spur of the moment. A couple of drinks helped. I discovered what I really thought about myself and where I was in life all coming out.

I decided there and then to carry on. I really wanted to turn over a new leaf. I wanted to play cricket without a care in the world, to lead a normal life. But I knew my failings too well. I vowed to try to be different, to work again on the slow heartbeat and the ability to switch off. I wasn't confident I would totally succeed in that, but I would try. I knew what Duncan Fletcher meant to me, what the team meant to me, and what the win in Pakistan had meant to me. I decided the team were better with me as captain. I carried on.

26

Mike Atherton said one other thing to me when we had our heart-to-heart chat. He reminded me that I had once scored a hundred at Kandy on an age-group tour we were both on and he said how nice it would be if I repeated the feat in the second Test. Well, yes, it would have been lovely, but I was never a great believer in history repeating itself and all I was concerned about was someone trying to unscramble my brain before a huge game. Yet history did repeat itself: I did score a century. Against all the odds. And it was one of the most important of my career. It was as if I had hit rock bottom as a Test batsman, and the only way now was up. It was the end of my bad run. It had lasted nearly a year.

It was quite a game. There was incident aplenty, poor umpiring decisions and a degree of edge between the sides that had basically been there ever since the infamous match at Adelaide early in 1999, maybe even since the Oval Test of 1998 when David Lloyd alluded to his belief that Muttiah Muralitharan was a chucker.

Sky TV must have loved this series; it had everything. Including a captain under enormous pressure. I have since watched a video of my innings in Kandy, and before I went into bat the TV cameras were homing in on me and highlighting the fact that I hadn't scored any runs. You can see me, aware of the cameras, laughing as I awaited my time in the middle. Very unusual for me. I can't remember whether I was feeling particularly relaxed but there was a sort of fatalism, I guess, about what was in store. Whatever will be, will be, I was thinking.

We had dismissed Sri Lanka for 297 and when I went in to

bat I immediately found myself feeling a lot more composed and playing a lot better, hitting a couple of 6s. Graham Thorpe was good for me. He could see that a couple of their fielders were struggling a bit, so he started playing tip-and-run cricket, which is often his game but has not really been my way of doing things. This time it helped take my mind off my troubles and enabled me to bat in an almost Dominic Cork-like way, the pair of us shouting 'Push him for 2' whenever either of us steered the ball into the outfield.

The gods were definitely on my side. I got away with hitting Murali to silly point, off bat and pad, but B. C. Cooray, the umpire who had started my bad run of decisions by giving me out when I edged it for 4 some months earlier, gave me a reprieve. Sri Lanka's chatty wicketkeeper Kumar Sangakkara started rucking and said, 'Bloody hell, Nasser.' I just turned to him and said, 'Yes, Sanga, I hit that. Shame, isn't it?' He smiled at me, I guess in acceptance that these things even themselves up. It was my day. I stroked the ball through the covers to reach my hundred, and my relief was palpable. 'Thank God,' I thought and I just went berserk because it was such a weight off my mind. I ran towards the pavilion, towards my boys. The hundred wasn't for me, it was for them. For ten months they had carried me with their performances. They had made me look like this great captain with the results they were earning for England and they had not said a bad thing against me or questioned my place at any time. I know it's a cliché, but the innings was for them as thanks for their support. My friend Sangakkara, who I enjoyed as an opponent, said, 'It's only a hundred. You haven't broken Lara's record.' But it was far more than a hundred for me. It was a career-saving innings.

My most satisfying hundred? Possibly. Certainly the most difficult. After that I never went three Tests without getting some sort of score for the rest of my career. It sometimes wasn't pretty after that, but I think that day in Kandy made me appreciate that it was possible to score runs by hanging in there when I wasn't playing fluently, that crease occupation meant runs. I had batted for an awful long time in Durban, but this was different because I was so out of touch.

In the short term it meant I could look my teammates in the eye again. And it was bad news for them too, because it meant I could come down on them like a ton of bricks again without fearing that they could say, 'What's he on about? He has no right to have a go at us when he's not contributing.'

I now knew that I should stay on as England captain for a while longer, and I would just have to put up with the mental torture that went with the job. I spent more time with Steve Bull, our sports psychologist, and Thorpey, and I often joked that we were giving him more information than he was providing for us, such was the amount of case-study material that was flowing from us. To this day Graham Thorpe says he has made Steve Bull a rich man with all his problems!

My innings in Kandy was about coming to terms with the seven days of stress that is a Test match, the two before it and then the game itself. I knew I would always feel the pressures but I was prepared to deal with them now, even though later they would almost make me ill. For the moment I had scored a hundred and England went on to win a Test: the dream double and a scenario that doesn't come along too often. There were incidents in abundance, disciplinary action and much controversy, but we had won in one of the hardest places in the world to win; and we went to Colombo for the third and final Test, knowing that a series victory which would even top the drama of Karachi was within our grasp.

Remarkably, I lost the toss again, provoking the players to start throwing things at me in the dressing room and serenading me with a full-blooded chorus of 'You useless tosser'. I was trying everything by this stage: wearing other people's jackets to go out for the toss; taking different coins out with me, and doing anything to break up a losing toss routine. Yet I always called 'heads'. Didn't want to change that, however often people told me to. The players kept on telling me to call 'tails' and I kept on quoting the law of averages and saying that it had to come down heads soon. Towards the end I think the law of averages did catch up with me and I won almost as many tosses as I lost, but there was a time, there in the sub-continent, when I was on an extraordinary run of toss failure.

No matter. One of the most notable aspects of what turned out to be a three-day thriller in the energy-sapping heat of Colombo was that Darren Gough was much more like his old self. He had been moody with me at times in Pakistan because I had had a go at him for saying that the wickets there didn't suit him. I said to him, 'Look, you're better than that. That's why you're Darren Gough. You've always been a short arse, but you've always got more out of your ability and shortness than anyone ever could, so don't give up on me now.' We had a bit of a heated discussion and he didn't really feature that much in Pakistan. But in Sri Lanka he found a much better rhythm and got the ball to swing in the humidity of Colombo. He ended up as the Man of the Series, and I think it was one of the highlights of his career. I don't believe any other bowler of his height could have bowled on those wickets as well as Goughy.

It wasn't the greatest of Tests for me. In Kandy I'd dived to stop a ball in the field and as I went over the rope I ripped my knee open. By the time we got to Colombo it had an enormous scab on it, which meant I couldn't stretch my thigh or my hip flexor without the scab cracking open. It was bloody sore. Then, early on in the third Test, somebody hit the ball past me in the covers, I chased it and I felt my hip flexor go. Besides the hernia, I'd never pulled a muscle in my life, but this felt as though I'd been shot in the hip. I stayed at mid-off and hobbled after every ball that came my way, and I know a lot of people were wondering why I didn't go into the slips. But I'd spent the last five Tests at mid-off, talking to the bowler occasionally, and it was becoming a productive way of doing things.

Also, I didn't want to go to slip because it would mean I would have Alec Stewart on one side of me and Mike Atherton on the other and, however much I valued their input, I didn't want two ex-captains that close to me. I didn't want to hear their opinions every ball. I wanted to be completely on my own at mid-off, near my bowler, formulating my own plans. I didn't want to be surrounded by thoughts because I could have ended up being too easily influenced by them. I wanted to be able to go to one of my ex-captains and ask his opinion when I thought the time was right.

If the injury affected my fielding, it certainly affected my batting. And I learnt later that this led to the one and only public disagreement between Mike Atherton and Duncan Fletcher. I called for a runner and Ath apparently said loudly that I should retire hurt because this was causing utter confusion in our batting. Later, Duncan took him to one side and told him not to question the captain and coach's decision in front of the players again, and I think Athers accepted that he had been wrong – unusual for such a stubborn bugger – and appreciated how Duncan had handled the situation.

There was parity after the first innings, thanks to a tremendous hundred from Thorpe, and then Ashley Giles, after an initial burst from Gough, bowled Sri Lanka out for 81 second time. We only had to chase 74 but we lost 6 wickets in getting there; one of them was mine, which was a huge disappointment because I had patched myself up and really wanted it to be me and Thorpey taking us to victory, as it had been in Pakistan.

Never mind. Pakistan might have been a remarkable win, but coming from behind to beat Sri Lanka 2–1 on their own patch was extraordinary, the best victory overseas, I reckon, since England won the Ashes. I had had my troubles, my periods of self-doubt, and I had been very close to resigning the captaincy on two or three occasions. But we had won four series in a row, two of them in the sub-continent in England's first visit there for years, and we had managed, to a large extent, to negate the influence of Muralitharan, the most dangerous spinner in the world. In my mind the positives were outweighing the negatives and we were building deep friendships within the team.

The anticlimax for me was that my injury kept me out of the one-dayers and it was awful having to come home ahead of the team. I arrived at Heathrow on my own with the trophy and people were starting to talk of me as the best captain since Mike Brearley, but I felt bad about that because I was getting all the praise while my team were still in Sri Lanka. Playing one-day cricket out there is even harder than Test cricket, so I felt bad that Graham Thorpe inherited a tough task as stand-in captain, and we lost 3–0. Mind you, they made sure they gave me some stick for not being there! One night a sarcastic message was left on my voicemail asking how come I was at home putting my feet up while my team were sweating in Sri Lanka. It had been left by a drunken Graham Thorpe and Duncan Fletcher!

27

I was feeling pretty good as we prepared for our mini-series against Pakistan in 2001. I was in the runs for Essex, England were going for their fifth series win in a row and there was a feel-good factor about the game in our country.

The series was billed as payback time for Pakistan after we had beaten them over there. There were also a lot of other issues swirling around, like the behaviour of the vast numbers of Pakistan supporters in the grounds at a time when there was a bit of racial tension in some towns in northern England. This was when I had to put my cards on the table: when I was asked at a question-and-answer session ahead of the first Test, I had to say that I thought young British Asians should be supporting England.

More than anyone else, I knew what a sensitive issue this was. It is one reason why I had largely tried to avoid it over the years. As a British Asian who had always felt English and supported England, it seemed to me the most natural and right thing in the world but I had enormous respect for those who felt differently. I just had to hope that people respected my viewpoint and understood where I was coming from.

On the pitch the major issue for us was the prospect of facing Shoaib Akhtar, now being billed as the fastest bowler in the world, properly for the first time in a Test series. I had come across Shoaib on my 'A' tour to Pakistan in 1995 but he was missing the previous winter and was clearly going to be a significant figure in our two-match series. Quite a character, old Shoaib. A real night owl. The original Pakistani prince.

I was relishing taking him on. I have always loved taking on fast bowling, have never been in the slightest bit apprehensive or scared by it. I do think there are professional cricketers who are scared of the ball (even some successful batsmen), but I have never been one of them. It is all about reactions when you face the quick men, and I backed mine.

But there was little I could so in the first Test when Shoaib got one to really fly at me, either by bending his elbow a little more or by hitting a crack at Lord's. I knew, the moment it hit me, that it had busted my right thumb. The physio came out, played with it a little bit, and I said, 'It's broken.' He said, 'No, carry on a bit longer,' which I did. But I could barely feel my hand when I nicked Azhar Mahmood to Rashid Latif on 64. Straight back to the hospital in St John's Wood I know so well, where they confirmed I had a clean break and would be out for around six weeks. Very disappointing. Particularly as we hammered Pakistan at Lord's and I wanted to be part of a fifth series win in a row.

There was, however, a considerable consolation: I would now be able to be present at the birth of my first child. Jacob was due to be born during the second Test at Old Trafford and, while I was going to try my utmost to be there, I knew that I couldn't guarantee it. Lord MacLaurin was talking about getting a helicopter to fly me to the birth if necessary, which was decent of him, but Karen and I were realistic enough to know that if he arrived in the middle of a Test when I was captain of England we might have to accept the reality of me not being there. When I look back now, I'm actually pretty pleased Shoaib broke my thumb because I was indeed at Jacob's birth, and later on I was at Joel's birth because Karen came out to Australia to have him, and they were two of the greatest days of my life. With hindsight, I would have hated to be present for one and not the other.

At the time, the Old Trafford game annoyed me hugely because we should never have lost it. We should really have won. Michael Vaughan scored his first Test hundred, the little genius Thorpe hit his ninth and the game was pretty even until the last afternoon when, chasing 285, we should at the very least have been able to hold out for a draw. But we collapsed on the last afternoon to Saqlain Mushtaq, which can happen; and poor David Shepherd was pilloried for missing a few no-balls, which, to be fair, can also happen. I wouldn't be an umpire for all the tea in China. It's incredibly difficult and while missing no-balls from a spinner is, I guess, pretty inexcusable we could only blame ourselves for letting the game slip. It would have been great to win five series in a row.

Jacob was actually born while a one-day international was going on soon after at Edgbaston. It was a hard labour for Karen, really difficult. He was born in St John's Hospital in Chelmsford and, while I was waiting for things to happen, I would pop out to the car and listen to a bit of the game on the radio. Nick Knight scored runs, the match was overshadowed by crowd trouble, which was a real problem that summer, and Pakistan won by 108 runs. A much better day, then, for me than it was for England.

Parenthood made me a completely different person. I know everyone says it, but it really does put everything into perspective. I came from an upbringing of major family values and I always wanted to be a parent when the time was right. We wanted to leave it relatively late, starting our family in our thirties after quite a few years together. I wasn't the only one with a career. Karen is a very successful teacher and we wanted to ready ourselves for parenthood, as we knew it would be the most important thing in our lives.

I believe that parenthood had the added bonus of helping my cricket. I have documented how much I have felt the pressure and the ups and downs of being England captain, but suddenly it wasn't the most important thing in my life any more, the matter of life and death I talked about earlier. Ever since Jacob and later Joel came along, the drive home after a Test has always been full of excitement at the prospect of seeing my family again. I have had less time to dwell on the duck or the bad decision. I'm not saying that suddenly my cricket was full of the joys of spring, and in the build-up to my resignation from the captaincy I had some seriously bad moments, but parenthood gave me a better balance in my life. It's the only thing that can give you so much satisfaction and pleasure but also so much pain and so many sleepless nights. We just liked the name Jacob, no other reason for calling him that. Karen's quite religious and liked having a biblical name. I am not at all, but I liked the name and also the fact that he could be called Jake, which is a good short form and nickname, I reckon.

It was significant that my dad didn't buy him a cricket bat. He had done that with his other grandsons. But I think he sensed that I was never going to be keen to push my boys into cricket the way Dad did and the way my brother Mel has been keen to do with his two boys. I have talked at length about my driven childhood and I am grateful for it now, but I want to approach things in a different way. If my boys want to play cricket and it's in the blood, then I will push them; but first I want to wait and see what they're like, what they like to do, what interests they have, and then maybe push them. Because I have explained that my dad's drive and pushing could easily have sent me the other way, made me hate cricket and rebel against it. I didn't really love the game when I was young, but I didn't have much choice as to whether or not I played it. I want Jacob and Joel to have a choice. Whatever they are interested in and whatever they are good at in life, then that's what I want them to do.

Jacob has an understanding that cricket is Daddy's job. He saw me on the telly and would start playing with one of my bats. But at the moment, if I have to be honest, I would prefer it if they didn't play the game because I know the pitfalls and the failings and what it can be like. Also, I don't really want them to go through what I had to in order to get to the top. Maybe it would be different if they played football or golf, but

I know cricket too well. The day after I retired from the game was the first day since I was about eight when I didn't wake up worrying about a cricket match. Do I really want that for my sons?

I think I'm a pretty natural parent. I would say it's even harder work than you think it's going to be. Before the boys came along I would see small children in the park and say to Karen, 'Oh, aren't they nice? That looks like a great age.' But what you don't see when you get all paternal over other people's children is the nappies, the sleepless nights and the endless colds and viruses they pick up. The end product, of course, is magnificent and I am truly blessed that both of them were born perfectly healthy. You sort of just assume that will be the case, but I have close friends who have suffered miscarriages and another whose little girl had to overcome serious problems.

The last couple of years of my career were particularly hard, having to leave the boys when going away on tour. It makes me realize how incredibly difficult it mut have been for the likes of Graham Gooch and Alec Stewart, who had their children young and spent so much of their children's formative years away from home. Because I'm away a lot I am the soft parent in our relationship. I don't like being strict with them when I'm trying to make the most of our time together. Karen is much firmer with them and it works well, the good-cop/bad-cop thing. Makes a change for me to be good cop! I was never like that with my other boys, the England team. And I remember how strict my dad was with me and I want to be a bit softer on them than that. As with anything, I am still learning to be a parent, but I know it's been the best thing that has ever happened to me. However, I wasn't given long to dwell on parenthood after Jacob's birth because 2001 still had a bit of cricketing drama to throw up, even though I wasn't playing. England were having a bad time in the triangular series against Pakistan and Australia, and halfway through it Alec Stewart went to Duncan Fletcher and said, 'I know I'm only doing the job while Nasser's injured, but I don't want to be captain any more. It's not working out.' Duncan and David Graveney rang me and told me that Stewie just wanted to concentrate on his own game, but I really wanted us to get through without further disruption until I was fit again because the Ashes were coming up and we didn't need any more turmoil.

It had to be an Ashes year, didn't it? I was injured, Thorpe and Vaughan were also hurt and Stewie was concerned that being stand-in captain was having an adverse affect on his game. We had had five bloody good series, apart from a late blip against Pakistan; but now, with the Aussies on the horizon, fate was dealing us a few cruel blows, as it always seems to when they are around. In the end we persuaded Alec to carry on for the triangular series, but the good news was that I was going to be fit for the Ashes. Whatever we had achieved before was now in the past. The ultimate cricketing test was upon us again.

28

I had only one game to get in some match practice before the first Test of the Ashes summer and that was for Essex against the Australians at Chelmsford. I was only able to have one brief knock because the Aussies batted on and on in their second innings, pretty much, I reckon, to stop me from having more time in the middle.

To be honest, form is irrelevant, going into an Ashes series. I remembered how poor my form had been early in 1997, and then I played the innings of my life in the first Test at Edgbaston. Playing Australia is unique because the Ashes have their own special pressures and nerves and expectations, and the Aussies are so much better and so much more professional than any other team in the world, so our five positive series before facing them didn't actually mean very much.

The build-up and the expectations were, it seemed to me, higher than ever. I sometimes think we'd have a better chance against Australia if we just tried to sneak up on them and catch them by surprise. But it is the biggest series in cricket and I guess it's inevitable that there will be a big old build-up each time it takes place. For me, on this occasion, it meant a television commercial with Steve Waugh for new Test sponsors npower, which was a terrific thing to do and drummed home to me how much interest there was in the country ahead of our battle.

He's a peculiar one at times, Steve. I have so much admiration for him, but in some ways I don't like him. He is mentally the toughest opponent I have ever come across and he was a particular role model for me because he didn't have the natural gifts of someone like a Sachin Tendulkar or a Brian Lara but he made himself into the best batsman in the world, and that is an example to all of us who could never just pick up a bat and dominate naturally.

Yet Steve kept his distance from me when we collaborated over an Ashes diary in 1997, and he was the same both now and when I did a further commercial with him when we were both writing for the *Sunday Telegraph*. I just think that, about this time, he had lost touch with reality a bit. When he did the press or talked to me, he gave me the impression that he had forgotten what playing cricket was like for everyone other than Australia. He became a bit of a preacher. A bit righteous. It was like he expected everyone to do it the Aussie way because their way was the only way. Well, yes, it's the only way if you have Glenn McGrath, Shane Warne, Jason Gillespie, Adam Gilchrist and the rest of them in your team, but we lesser mortals have to do things in a different way. It's like Manchester United telling Bolton they should try to do it their way. We were a bit like Bolton. We had to make our whole greater than its individual parts. It's the only way forward for us because our parts are not as great as Australia's yet.

In my time in the England team and as England captain, we did not, with the occasional exception of world-class performances from the likes of Gough and Caddick, have a world-class bowler (at the time of writing Steve Harmison looks as if he is becoming one, and that's great) and we only had a couple of world-class batsmen. So our success was based on plans, good coaching and, hopefully, good captaincy and at times sneaking past teams at the winning post. There is no point in Australia preaching at us to go out with all guns blazing like they do. Steve Waugh knows what it was like to be in a losing Australian team, and I just wished at times that he would remember that and how tough it was to turn that around.

Steve could also overdo the love of the 'baggy green cap' thing. He wore it at Wimbledon that year to support Australian tennis players, and I felt it was a bit of a 'look at me' sort of thing. I hated it when Australians would try to tell you they cared more or had a mental edge over us. No one cared about playing for his country more than me or most of the men I have played with for England. Australia had the edge over us because they were better, much better at times. That was the bottom line. My pride is in my heart. Yes, I showed it on the pitch; I showed my feelings and wore my heart on my sleeve. I didn't need any Australian telling me how I should play the game in order to get the most out of my team or that I should care more.

I don't have many good memories about my only home Ashes series as captain, I'm afraid. We lost Michael Vaughan for the whole series with his knee. Graham Thorpe was out for most of the summer. Then, to cap it all, Gillespie struck me on the finger during the second innings of the first Test and broke it. Broken digits in successive Tests for me. I couldn't believe it. As I sat in the Edgbaston physio room I was distraught.

Everything we had built up already seemed to be going pear-shaped. We were thrashed in the first Test and I was facing another spell on the sidelines. I couldn't believe how I kept on breaking fingers. I wanted to know if I could do anything about it. I had broken all the fingers of my bottom hand, and now I was suffering with my top hand too. Geoff Boycott sent me some stuff that he thought would help, and then I called on James Davis, our physio at Essex, to help strengthen my gloves. I hated them being too bulky but I knew I had to do something. I had double protection put on each finger of my favourite batting gloves and I kept using them for the rest of my career, even though they got old and worn. It worked, and I should have done it earlier – but that was no consolation to me at the time as I prepared to miss at least another two Tests.

I still wasn't fit, Alec didn't want to be captain any more and in the end a reluctant Mike Atherton agreed to make a return to the job. We were beaten convincingly again at Lord's, and then again at Trent Bridge. Now, however, I was fit and I wanted us to get something out of the series, anything. We met to select the team for the fourth Test at Headingley, and it became clear that something had happened with Mark Butcher at Trent Bridge. We don't have curfews, but people know they must be sensible and it appeared that Butch had been out late one night in the middle of the match and had been caught in the act.

Butch is a lovely lad and a player whose company I have enjoyed as a teammate and a batting partner. He is also a bit of a throwback in that he enjoys a good time and has very little will power, and he would have fitted in very well in the era of Botham, Gower and Lamb. There are times in the modern era when that leads him into trouble and there have been clashes with Duncan at times.

This time Butch was in trouble. He had been out too late one night in Nottingham and it wasn't the first time. But it wasn't a huge issue with me. I knew what he was like. I knew, too, that he was an insomniac who needed a couple of drinks to help him sleep. As captain, I didn't want Mark Butcher to just sit in his room from 8 p.m. every night, because that wouldn't have done anyone any good. So I didn't want him to stay in, but I also didn't want him to get caught out late, if that makes any sort of sense.

In selection Duncan spoke well about the need for senior players to set the right example and we talked about the whole subject in depth before ringing a few people who were there, like Alec Stewart, to find out exactly what had happened. Geoff Miller, by now an England selector, spoke most strongly about it. Dusty Miller was big on character and he felt that Butch was showing a lack of character by rocking the boat in going out. Graveney, being Graveney, was going round in circles and I wasn't saying very much as I wasn't there when it happened and, really, I wanted Butch in the side.

In the end it was decided that enough was enough, the Ashes

were gone and we were going to have to make an example of Butch. Then we had to decide who was going to replace him. We talked about Rob Key and a couple of others, before deciding to give David Fulton of Kent a chance. I'd played with him a bit and thought he had the character to do well at international level. So he was selected. David Fulton was going to play for England in the fourth Test against Australia in 2001.

Then, just as I left the room, Duncan said, 'Let's just make a few more phone calls on the Butcher thing so that we are absolutely clear on our facts when we tell the press why he has been left out.' With that in mind, I rang Stewie and told him Butch was going to be left out and talked it through with him. Then I spoke to Atherton. By the time I got home, I had come to the conclusion that we were shooting ourselves in the foot by leaving Butch out. So I rang David Graveney to talk about it again. It turned out that Grav had been having the same doubts. He agreed it was harsh and said, 'If that's what you think and what Ath and Stewie think, then let's reverse the decision.' I don't think David Fulton has ever known how close he came to playing for England. Until now.

Instead of dropping Butch we decided to haul him in and read him the Riot Act. Now I always find these sort of meetings funny. I have had a few of them, with the likes of Butch, Andrew Flintoff and Graham Thorpe, and they always amuse me. They amuse me because I'm usually sitting in judgement on mates and also because, a few years ago, I was the bad boy and this was happening to me. So I let Fletch do most of the talking. He told Butch that this wasn't good enough, that he was close to being dropped and that he was going to be fined £1,000. Duncan handled it brilliantly, telling Butch that no press announcement would be made about this and that only I and a couple of senior players knew about it, but that if he wanted to make it public he was within his rights to do so. I wish Essex had handled my problems in the same way when I was young.

Butch was taken aback. You could see how surprised he was at almost losing his place. Then I could see him calculating how many Jack Daniels and Coke £1,000 would buy, but after a bit of a protest he accepted the decision. You could say it was a narrow escape for Butch – and for England, because in this Test he played the innings of his life, not only to win the match for us but also to set up the rest of his career. It was the turning point for Mark Butcher and he so nearly missed it.

Adam Gilchrist, standing in as captain because Steve Waugh had damaged his calf at Trent Bridge, set it up. There was a bit of rain around, Australia were their usual selves, playing very well, and it could easily have been a draw; but by this time Australia were so determined to win every match they played in that the possibility of defeat never seemed to enter their heads.

Gilchrist declared on the fourth evening, leaving us 315 in just over a day, hardly the easiest of targets, particularly on the last day at Headingley. Afterwards Gilchrist was criticized for giving us a sniff, and it may even have counted against him when Steve Waugh packed up the captaincy, but you couldn't blame him for anticipating a fourth Australian victory in their quest for that 5–0 whitewash.

We lost Atherton and Trescothick early and the pitch seemed like a minefield. As so often, that reduced the pressure in my mind because I thought we would be doing well just to get a draw out of this. I joined Butch and we had a bit of a smile to each other at first, saying, 'It's doing a bit, isn't it?' We fought it out and conditions got noticeably easier as the ball got softer. I pulled Gillespie for 6 and when the ball came back it seemed to have lost a lot of its potency.

Meanwhile, Butch was playing like a god. I had never seen him play that well. It was like his version of my innings at Edgbaston in 1997. There are times in anyone's career when you just seem to be on a higher level. You play better than you have ever believed possible. This was Butch at his absolute best. It was incredible. The Aussies were completely taken aback. We put on 181 for the third wicket until I was given out caught down the legside when the ball had brushed my pocket. Venkat was the umpire. One of my dad's oldest friends. I have a theory about this: Venkat always asked me how my dad was and how my brothers were whenever I bumped into him, then he would invariably see me off! I have had more poor decisions from him than from any other umpire, and the only possible explanation I can come up with is that he was so worried about being seen to be biased towards his mate's boy that he went the other way. In later years I would try to avoid saying hello to him. I didn't want to talk about my dad and my brothers. I just wanted him to give me not out.

Luckily, nothing could stop Butch that day and he just motored to 173 not out as we won by 6 wickets. It was a great feeling, a 'get out of jail' sort of feeling, but I was realistic enough to know that they had still outplayed us for much of the game. The Aussies, typically, all shook Butch's hand and Gilchrist said it was one of the great Ashes innings, but they also made it clear that we wouldn't have won if they hadn't been so generous. And they were probably right.

We have made some bad decisions in selection over the years, but I'm delighted we got this one right. It's all about man-management and we were right not to shoot ourselves in the foot by leaving Butch out. I don't think the kick up the arse made him play any better. He was batting well that summer and he just carried on doing it.

We did not have long to enjoy the moment. Within seventy-two hours we were at the Oval, playing in the second of the first set of back-to-back Tests in England in the modern era. This is where I really must pay tribute to Steve Waugh. He was still badly injured from Trent Bridge and he had no right, really, to play. The Ashes had been won and he could easily have taken a holiday with his family. But whenever I saw him between Trent Bridge and the Oval he was having treatment on his calf. Literally squealing with pain as the physio was digging his hands into him. Just to be fit for one last Test in England. Waugh definitely fitted into the Gooch and Stewart category of having such a love for the game that they always wanted to be out there. No way did Steve Waugh ever take the easy option in any cricket match. Somehow he managed to play in the final Test on one leg. And scored an unbeaten 157 as the Aussies won again. The picture of him on the floor, raising his bat upon reaching his century, is one of the great images of Waugh.

I'm afraid it was the same old Ashes story. Groundhog day. One good game for us, four good ones for them. Lots of English injuries. Some basic mistakes. Not enough batters getting big runs and lots of dropped catches. In all honesty, though, even if everyone had been fit and we'd held our chances, we probably would still have lost because we're not producing enough cricketers of sufficient calibre to beat Australia.

We are now producing enough good cricketers to be third, maybe even second, in the world, but if the ECB are serious in their goal of being the best in the world by 2007 we still have to work at producing more fast bowlers and, most importantly, mystery spinners. One man lifted the England rugby team from being second- or third-best in the world to being world champions, Jonny Wilkinson. It is too simplistic to think the same could happen for us, but while the likes of Steve Harmison and Simon Jones have given us hope of achieving our goal there is still a lot of work to do. We can get enough runs against Australia. Can we take 20 wickets against them consistently on flat pitches?

29

I made my return to one-day international cricket, after quite an absence, in the autumn of 2001 in Zimbabwe. It was important to me because injury had kept me out of quite a bit of one-day cricket and I needed to prove I was still worth a place as the build-up to the 2003 World Cup in South Africa and, we thought, Zimbabwe began to gather momentum. There were a few mumblings about us going to Zimbabwe, but at that stage it wasn't a major issue and to be honest we were pretty naive about what was going to explode in front of us in a year's time. We were sheltered from it all, really. We had heard a bit about what was happening from Heath Streak and his family, but we were pretty much restricted to hotels and cricket grounds.

It was an important little tour on the pitch because we wanted to get our one-day cricket back on track after a pretty lean spell, so we decided to leave some senior players at home and find out about our next crop of young players, people like James Foster, Jeremy Snape and Owais Shah. We won all five internationals, there were rumblings about James Kirtley's bowling action being suspect and a funny little spat between Foster and Andy Flower which I got involved in.

I say it was funny because not long after that Andy was to join us at Essex, so the protagonists quickly became teammates and friends, but it caused a few headlines at the time because Fozzie was making his way in the international game and was taking on, verbally, a guy who had been rated the number one batsman in the world.

People took the mickey out of Fozzie when he first emerged on the scene because they said he was a clone of me, a sort of captain's pet. He had gone to Forest School, like me, Durham University and was even coached by my dad at the Ilford Cricket School. None of that bothered me because I thought he was a wicketkeeper-batsman of genuine talent and only injury has halted his progress so far. Let's hope even in that regard he has echoed me, because I broke my wrist soon after breaking into the England side and it held back my career by three years, and I hope Fozzie will get back on the international scene sooner or later when next an opportunity comes his way.

I believe he and Geraint Jones are the future of England's wicketkeeping simply because they are capable of scoring big runs at Test level. Chris Read may be a more natural keeper but I understood why, later, he was left out of the England side in Antigua for the final Test of the 2004 series against West Indies. It may sound controversial to the purists, but I believe it is easier to turn a player with real cricket talent into a wicketkeeper competent enough to perform at the highest level – for instance Marcus Trescothick could be England's wicketkeeper if we really wanted him to be – than it is to turn a natural keeper into a Test batsman. That's why I rang Duncan Fletcher and David Graveney when I first set eyes on Geraint Jones when he played for Kent against Essex. I said to them, 'I think I've spotted someone a bit special here.' And that had nothing to do with his wicketkeeping skills, which were perfectly adequate, but everything to do with his batting.

Anyway, in Zimbabwe Foster went up for a catch off Flower and Andy just turned round and started calling him a cheat, as if Fozzie couldn't appeal. He was trying to impose his authority on a young lad, and I was pleased to see James sticking up for himself because my only concern about him was that he was a bit too quiet and you need your keeper to be a bit of a leader in the field. Remember, this is the man who didn't appeal when he caught Steve Waugh later on in a Test in Melbourne, so I'd rather him having a go back at someone like Flower than be Mr Dopey.

I thought I'd better get involved here, so I had a go at Flower to show the team that their captain would always back them up and to show Fozzie that I was supporting him and giving his stance my stamp of approval. I remembered how the whole Australian team had got stuck into me in 1997 over that disputed Greg Blewett catch of mine and I wanted to show everyone that we were a team.

Of course, we all got dragged into the referee's room, which always makes me laugh. All you have to do is to be in some way apologetic and you get let off. Or start talking in legal terms; that normally scares them. Remember Arjuna Ranatunga in Adelaide in 1999? He basically made his team stop playing in a match against us, but as soon as he was up before the beak he just rang his lawyer and the toothless ICC backed down.

On this occasion, in front of the ref, I just said, 'Oh Andy, I'm sorry. You're the best batsman in the world. I shouldn't have got involved. I just wanted to back my young lad up.' He apologized back, the referee said that's fine, and Andy and I winked at each other as we walked out scot free. I like and respect Flower. Later, when he came to Essex, I found him to be one of the best captains I ever played under.

We may have been on good terms then, but there was generally a bit of bad blood between the teams. It was still there from the David Lloyd 'we flipping murdered 'em' affair. What concerned me much more than a verbat spat with Andy Flower was when their captain Alastair Campbell accused me of not going into their dressing room to shake hands with their side after one of the games. He was accusing me of not playing the game the way it should be played, which was absolute nonsense because I made a point of shaking hands with them as soon as I had congratulated my players on their victory. A silly little business but a productive little trip.

James Foster was there, really, because Alec Stewart had made himself unavailable for the forthcoming tour of India and we had to start looking to the future. Therein lies a tale. The seeds of Alec not going to India had been sown a year earlier when he was thrown into crisis during our tour of Pakistan. Alec had been accused of taking £5,000 from an Indian bookmaker by the name of M. K. Gupte during England's tour of India in 1993 in return for details about team selection and his opinion on how the pitch would play in a report that was published by India's Central Bureau of Investigation into cricket corruption.

It came as a hell of a shock to us at the time. We were in Rawalpindi during our successful tour, but I knew as soon as I found out that an England player – and a legend at that – had been named in this report that it would become a massive, massive story. I think the first thing to say is that Stewie was accused of things that to my mind did not in any way constitute match-fixing or even an action that was in any way bad for the game. You have to remember that in 1993 the idea of match-fixing never even entered our minds, and I can't imagine that any players in those days who passed on what was pretty innocent information actually thought they were doing anything wrong. But we have since discovered that these methods were used to draw people into much more sinister goings-on and, at the time we were in Pakistan, the affair had been given added spice by the fact that the ECB chairman had said publicly that anyone linked with corruption should be suspended forthwith. He, of course, meant Pakistan players. Our hosts were now wondering whether he included Alec Stewart in that.

The second point to make is that Alec vehemently denied passing on anything to this bookie, and none of us have any reason whatsoever to doubt him. Anyone who has played with Stewie knows all about the pride he has in wearing those three lions and the fact that he lives for his statistics. Alec Stewart would rather run over his own dog than give his wicket away, let a bye through or do anything else that might be to the detriment of his team or his own career. I've seen the man arguing with the umpires during a tea interval because they have given a bye while he was keeping and he felt it should have been a leg-bye. The man is not and could not ever be a match-fixer.

The bottom line for me was that Alec denied it and my job as captain was to support him in any way I could. Stewie's reaction, to be honest, was weird. To be linked with this whole murky business hit him very hard and I'd never seen him so quiet. He just locked himself away in his hotel room and became a recluse for about three or four days while the scandal swirled around him.

I left him alone at first but eventually I went to see him and he was on the phone to his dad, Micky, as he was every hour or so during that time. I just told Alec that he had my full support and I knew that he would never ever adversely affect the outcome of any England game. In the end he did the right thing and confronted the press to deny any involvement with bookmakers. Several months later his name was finally cleared, but it took its toll on Alec and I had never seen him that way before.

So when, the following year, we were due to tour India and the accusations against Stewie had come from an Indian bookmaker, I thought he might be reluctant to go there in case the whole business came up again. I had asked him early in the 2001 season whether he would be going to India and he told us all over dinner categorically that he wouldn't, but I didn't take it as his final word on the subject because I knew how people could change their minds. For instance, how often did I change my mind about when I would be retiring from the game?

We left it at that, and the matter of tour selection was obviously an issue as we approached the final Test of the summer at the Oval. The rumour was that both Stewie and Darren Gough were going to make themselves unavailable. There was also the possibility that Stewie might opt to join us in New Zealand for the second half of our winter programme, even if he ducked out of going to India.

But that was not something Duncan was keen to encourage. He was talking about the danger of precedents being set if we let someone at an advanced stage of their career like Stewie pick and choose which tours they went on. Duncan felt that any player should make himself available for all the winter's Test cricket or none at all. And the same applied to the one-day cricket. I was always going to stay loyal to Duncan on this one because I thought it was vitally important that I backed up a coach whom I believed in totally, even if I didn't have strong views on the matter either way. Duncan, to my mind, gets much, much more right than he gets wrong, and if he felt this was a necessary step then that was good enough for me and he had my full support.

So we ended up having a meeting in our team hotel on the last night of the Ashes series when we were preparing to go to a dinner in honour of Mike Atherton, who was to retire from cricket. My total admiration for Ath the player and man has been well recorded in these pages so I don't have to say anything more about him here, other than to say his exit was both low-key and dignified and I was looking forward to giving him a good send-off.

First the meeting, and it's fair to say it was tense. There was me, Duncan, Grav and Stewie, and right up until the last moment I was hoping Stewie would change his mind and declare himself available for the whole winter. I knew Duncan wasn't for turning. I had never seen Duncan angry about anything but he was close to it here, and Stewie was equally hot under the collar. He said he wasn't going to India for family reasons, no mention of the bookmaker, and he also needed an operation on his elbows. I knew Stewie's wife, Lynn, had had some health problems and I could sympathize with what he was saying. I felt for him and what he was going through. He hadn't had a winter at home for years. Supporters and commentators never see what a sportsman is going through behind the scenes, in his private life, and only judge him on the end product.

Fletch stayed firm, as he always does, and said, 'Sorry, Al. If you're saying you're not going to India we have to draw the line somewhere. You can't say you're not going to India but you are going to New Zealand.' Stewie was looking to Grav for some sort of intervention on his behalf, but it never came.

Stewie was very put out by the time he left that meeting and I was sad about that, but for me the most important thing was that we had a bloke in Duncan Fletcher who was going to run selection in a businesslike way and not be full of vagaries and half-promises. As captain I loved that. Geoff Miller came on board and was also a very good, strong selector who would always say things to your face and explain why he felt that way. The principle to me was more important than the characters involved. I think I was better than Duncan at man-managing the so-called difficult characters, but Duncan was much better than me at looking at principles, lateral thinking in selection, the setting of precedents, consistency of selection and how any decision would affect the long-term. We dovetailed well.

The decision was made that you could opt out of a whole winter in one form of the game, or retire from one form of the game, but you couldn't just pick and choose sections of tours to miss, and it affected Gough in the same way because he too made himself unavailable for the Test leg of India. So he could play in one-day cricket in India and New Zealand, but he couldn't stay on and play Test cricket in New Zealand. That was tricky because he would obviously be in the country for the one-dayers, which came first, probably excel in conditions that suited him, and would then have to leave while we prepared for the Test series. But those were the rules that Duncan set down, and he was right to do so. Every player knew where he stood.

I knew one thing: I was going to India. It was the only major country which I hadn't toured as a full England cricketer. It was also the country where I was born, and it was my dad's country. I wasn't sure how significant my heritage was going to be in advance, but it was to be the tour that completed me as a cricketer and enhanced me as a person because I learned so much about me and my family and I relished the country. Yet it so nearly didn't happen because of events far bigger, far more important and far more shocking than any trivial cricketing matter could ever be.

30

On 11 September 2001 I was in the South of France on a brief family break with Karen and Jacob. I had just come back to the hotel room after a morning out when, in common with people around the world, I switched on the TV, to be greeted by some of the most awful and astonishing pictures I'd ever seen in my life. At first I thought I was watching the movie channel. The atrocities in New York that day had an impact on everyone in the world, and my head was full of confusion on my return home. The world was on the verge of war, and the question of whether we would fulfil our tour to India was a complete irrelevance to those outside cricket. But it was an issue and it was an issue that was important to us and one that we had to discuss. Would we still go to the sub-continent when there was so much uncertainty in the world? The ECB were, for once, good and arranged a meeting at which we listened to security experts and were given a thorough briefing about what might be in store for us when we were due to leave for India the following month. Foreign Office advice to British people was to keep a low profile in India, which would not exactly be easy for the England cricket team.

I rang my dad up to ask whether he thought we should go, and he told me it was an incredibly difficult question for him to answer because he knew how much the Indian people loved their cricket and he couldn't imagine that they would attack a cricket team, but this was a situation the world had never encountered and no one was sure what might happen next.

This was India, the biggest tour for my dad I would ever embark on. The players were understandably concerned, not so much for themselves as for the families they would be leaving at home, worrying whether their husbands and fathers were safe. In the end we had further meetings involving Tim Lamb, who didn't seem to understand us at all, and Lord MacLaurin, who was a lot better; and they said it would be down to the individual over whether he wanted to tour, and that nothing would be held against anyone who didn't.

A lot of our guys were very emotional about the whole affair. We had a full and frank exchange of views at which Mark Ramprakash spoke very well and said that we were probably safer in India than we would be in London. Darren Gough was there, and he spoke very well on behalf of the boys even though he wasn't going on the Test leg of the tour. He asked Tim Lamb if the ECB had any contingency plans to get the players home, should an incident take place while we were there, and he got quite heated when he didn't get a satisfactory answer. That's what I love about Goughy: he speaks from the heart. Never afraid to take on authority, whether it was Tim Lamb or anyone else.

In the end it came down to me as captain to speak to each player individually, while the ECB kept on monitoring the situation and promised to keep us totally informed of any new development or Foreign Office advice. A few of the guys felt we should present a united front and I could understand the appeal of solidarity, but this was such a unique situation.

With it being India and my dad, I felt I had to go. And, being England captain, I felt it was my duty to go if my bosses were telling me it was safe. This was a different situation from Zimbabwe because that had always been about morality, whatever the ECB tried to say about safety; and this was purely an issue of world safety and whether we as Westerners would in any way be in greater danger being on the sub-continent than we would at home. No one knew for sure.

I got the distinct impression that the team were looking to see what I did. The England captaincy is a powerful thing at times like this. I think if I'd said I wouldn't go then the whole team would pull out, but as it was I had huge sympathy and understanding for those who had severe reservations about going. In the end I picked up two voice messages on my phone from Andrew Caddick and Robert Croft, saying they would love to be there with us but they were putting their families first. That was absolutely fine by me. They were my boys, part of the squad who had done so much for me as England captain and I rang them back to reassure them that this would never be a problem in future selection. What with Stewart and Gough already out of the trip, and now two more withdrawals, it was a difficult time. We were playing one of the hardest teams in the world to beat on their own patch, and now we were doing it with a virtual 'A' team. There were some members of our party whom I barely recognized!

No matter. As Atherton had once told me, you are never a complete cricketer until you have toured India; it is the soul of cricket. The heartbeat of cricket is in the streets of Bombay,* Calcutta and Madras. They live and breathe the game out there. All you see in the streets or on TV is cricket, cricket, cricket. The atmosphere and the wickets and the conditions are different from any place in the world, and above all it's fun out there. I went into the tour with a lot of trepidation, not least because of our absentees, but I left it with some of the best and fondest memories of my career and satisfied in the knowledge that I had enjoyed one of the finest times during my spell as captain. At the end of the third Test in Bangalore, which we could have won had it not been for the rain, Duncan Fletcher congratulated me on the way I captained the team. That meant as much to me as anything that has ever happened in my career.

It was a very emotional time for me, and luckily I was also batting well. I enjoyed the wickets, played spin well and enjoyed

---

* No matter how many of the names are changed, I shall always think of them – and will refer to them in this book – by their old names. Mumbai lacks the memories that Bombay evokes.

working with the young lads; there was no baggage with them. We were on a hiding to nothing, really, but the character they showed, with some of them barely out of university, was fantastic, and we all enjoyed it together. The player I need to single out here, though, is Matthew Hoggard. He really held his hand up. When as captain you lose both Gough and Caddick and are trying to bowl out a fantastic opposition batting line-up on flat wickets and in the heat of India, you need someone with a lot of character, someone who will do the hard yerds.

Matthew Hoggard was brilliant in India. He did everything I asked of him on that trip. He stuck to the unusual plans I gave him and at times he bowled incredibly long spells. I was beginning to value him as a real asset to our team. He would run through a brick wall for you as his captain.

In one of our first warm-up games I decided to try something different when we were in the field. It started off as a six–three offside field. Then I thought, 'Let's try a seven–two field and bowl one side of the wicket.' I put everyone on the offside and just got the lads to bowl there. I was simply experimenting at this stage because I thought the best way to approach India was to control their batsmen and the rate they scored at. I felt that if we could stop them scoring fluently we could exercise a degree of control over them. I told the lads we had to have very precise plans and then stick to them, being both obstinate and stubborn at times if it came to it. I didn't have the firepower to try to blast out the likes of Sachin Tendulkar and Rahul Dravid, so I needed to think of alternative ways of dealing with them. I asked the lads what they thought about it that night at dinner, and they were enthusiastic, so we worked at it in the nets and then went into all the warm-up games with packed offside fields. I didn't care if we were going to be boring. On England's last tour to India they had been thrashed and the home side had rattled up huge scores. I had no intention of letting that happen again, particularly as we were under strength.

There had been more controversy in the build-up to the Test, with a row going on between the ICC and the Indian board over whether Virender Sehwag was suspended or not following India's spat with South Africa and, more precisely, with match referee Mike Denness. For a while it looked as though the tour would be off again, so I was just grateful to take to the field at Mohali for the first game. We got off to a good start and I reached 85 before falling to Anil Kumble. This was really disappointing, because I so wanted to get a hundred in India, but worse was our collapse (because of our inexperienced middle order) to 238 all out. That's where we lost the game really; we didn't stay in it. My bowling plans had been partially successful but not totally so, and we lost by 10 wickets. It was what people expected of us but I felt we could do a lot better if we could just stay with them.

We didn't treat Tendulkar very differently from the others at this stage. All I knew was that I didn't want to feed his strengths, didn't want to make it easy for him to dominate. Yes, I wanted Matthew Hoggard to bowl a yard outside off-stump to him with an eight–one field. I wanted Freddie Flintoff to come round the wicket to him every now and then and try to hit him in the ribs, with two men out on the hook and a short leg to try to unsettle him. We hadn't talked about Ashley Giles bowling over the wicket to him, but it was a tactic we had used in the past and Duncan and I were certainly not averse to him doing it. To me it was not as negative as a lot of people made out. It was not like Phil Tufnell bowling into the rough outside the right-hander's leg stump. Ashley got much closer to the stumps than that and bowled wicket to wicket, so that if it spun you were looking for an edge and if it didn't you were looking for an lbw. People went on and on about it being a negative tactic and against the spirit of the game, that sort of stuff, and I think that affected Ashley's career for a while, but I think it was totally unfair and simplistic to call it a negative tactic. What did people expect us to do? Just lob it up to Sachin and then see him smack our inexperienced attack all over the place? What Ashley does at times is exactly the same as an off-spinner bowling over the wicket to a left-hander. And no one questions that.

We lost another player from our depleted squad before the second Test. During our short tour to Zimbabwe, before we went to India, I had discovered that Graham Thorpe was suffering from problems with his marriage. I went out with him and Ben Hollioake for a Japanese – Thorpey loves his sushi – and after Ben left we had a talk in the hotel bar. We were chatting about everything and we got on to the problems he was having with Nicky, his wife. Up until then I'd thought of them as inseparable. I thought they were a close family and that everything was rosy. At that time I think I was the only person he had confided in, and he told me he was going to try to sort it all out when he got home.

Well, when we arrived in India it was clear that it was all still raging on, and he became more and more worried and depressed about the situation and a lot more insular. He'd go back to his room every night after the match and play on his PlayStation. Then, very unlike Graham, he started to open up to everybody about what he was going through. Matters came to a head when we were playing a warm-up game in Jaipur. I went to see Thorpey and he told me he had had a terrible phone call and that he might have to go home because his marriage was falling apart. I don't want to go into detail because it's none of my business, but it was obvious that it was tearing Graham to pieces. The night before we started playing in Jaipur, he had been up all night, and it was clear he couldn't play in the game. I told him to stay at the hotel and that we would discuss it later, and after that Duncan and I would be talking to him on a regular basis. Fletch is very much the family man and so he was very supportive and understanding of Thorpe's predicament. In the end, after the first Test, we all thought it would be best for him to leave the tour. Graham found it so hard to compartmentalize at that stage of his life and he had to sort it out. I felt desperately sorry for him. It was to be some time before Graham Thorpe really came through the other side.

We played really well in the second Test in Ahmedabad and had the better of the draw, something that was beyond a lot of people's expectations for us before the tour. The impetus was with us and we actually started believing we could beat this side. Their batting line-up wasn't scoring at 4 an over, they were scoring at 2 an over, and I could see that our plans were working. We were playing their spinners well because of the work Duncan had done with them on things like the forward press, and our bowlers were pressurizing them and excelling within their limitations.

Then we moved to Bangalore for the third Test, where I noticed, when I was batting, that it was a very unusual wicket and was rock hard by Indian standards. They played three spinners, but none of them was turning it off the wicket. Yet the moment it hit the rough, it just exploded and Kumble, in particular, was devilishly hard to face when he landed it out there. So that night I thought to myself, 'I'm not just going to let Ashley run up and bowl on a perfect strip. He's not the biggest turner of the ball and they're going to love that on this concrete strip. I'm going to get him to land it in that rough.' When Tendulkar came in, I asked Ashley to land it out in the rough, with James Foster keeping in a helmet outside the leg stump and the ball exploding when it hit certain areas.

Sachin was a bit taken aback by this and didn't really seem sure what to do, the very object of our exercise. Sehwag went after Giles and succeeded to a large extent, but we were just picking wickets off at the other end while a confused Sachin was kicking it away and scoring very slowly. Meanwhile I wanted Freddie to get it into his ribs and shake him up a bit. I wanted Freddie to hit him on the head, encourage him to pull with two men in the outfield. It was an unusual plan, I grant you, but to this day I do not consider it a negative one. We were bowling on a flat wicket in Bangalore, for heaven's sake, against some of the best batsmen in the world, with a hugely inexperienced attack. And we bowled them out for 238. That, to me, is laudable. In the end Tendulkar had had enough, went down the wicket to try to hit Ashley out of the rough for the first time and was stumped for the first time in his Test career for a slow 80.

It got people talking. It was something new for cricket. Cricket is about challenges and we were meeting the next challenge put in front of us. I'd set one of the best batsmen in the world a new challenge, and he had come through it with 80. And I had come through it with my boys bowling out India cheaply around him, and I was very pleased with them and with myself. I certainly couldn't believe it when I was sent a letter by Ted Dexter, a former England captain and chairman of selectors, complaining about my tactics to MCC. He seemed to be saying that he went out there to watch Tendulkar bat and score at 4 an over and I'd spoilt his little trip. I really can't believe people expected me to just stand back and admire him. No, mate, you're the best player in the world and you're going to have to work for your runs out here – that was my attitude and I stick by it.

I don't think I did any harm to the game of cricket on that tour. In fact, I think I did it good because it was a new angle and it stimulated debate. It was all part of cricket's rich tapestry. I think it's great when people try new things. Like Stephen Fleming of New Zealand does. He's a good captain. For Damien Martyn once he had an eight–one field, with four people catching at deep point. He had thought about it and provided a new challenge for the bloke. That's what captaincy is about. Otherwise, why get paid the extra wonga? And why go through the extra hassle? If it hadn't rained over the last two days we would have had a great chance of winning that game, and if we had come back with a 1–1 series draw I think that would have topped anything we achieved in Pakistan and Sri Lanka and, later, in the West Indies.

This was the peak of my captaincy. I was enjoying it. I was thriving and I was scoring runs. The angst and the worries and the self-doubt were temporarily suspended. What made it even better was what happened off the field. People were so warm to me. Wherever I went I was recognized, and it made me feel humble. During the Bangalore Test I went for an early-morning walk, and this family of seven came up to me and asked if they could have their photo taken with me. Then it turned out they had driven three hours from their home, leaving at 3 a.m., just to try to meet me and have a photo done before I left for the ground. They didn't even have tickets for the game! I managed to find them some tickets. I was so touched. It was amazing.

My dad, who hates flying, turned up out there twice, first with the *Daily Mail*, who had brought him out to do a feature on the Hussain family roots, and then later during the one-dayers, when I finally played at the Chepauk Stadium in Madras, my home as a boy. That really was the ultimate.

They made me an honorary member of the Madras Cricket Club. I kept on seeing faces I recognized from my childhood, and I captained England in a one-day international on a ground where, as a boy, I had played on the outfield all day every day. My dad had organized a big dinner, with hundreds of family and friends, many of whom I didn't know and some of whom I don't think my dad knew; but they all came and they all seemed proud that I was coming back with England. There were people there telling me they'd changed my nappies, and everyone had a story about me. I made a speech, thanking my dad for everything, and I have never meant anything so sincerely.

I began to understand why I am how I am in India. I discovered who I am and who I was. I discovered that my passion and my fire came from the Indian side of me and their passion for the game of cricket. Funnily enough, I didn't feel nervous when I went out to bat in Madras with my dad in the crowd. It was as if I'd done it, done everything my dad could possibly have wished for. I scored 1, but there was no anger or tantrum in the dressing room. I was virtually smirking as I walked off because I was thinking to myself, 'Dad has come all the way home to see me out for 1. He could have stayed in Ilford to do that.' It was so emotional for both of us. I know he loved every minute of seeing people and I could tell that he was virtually saying to everyone, 'There you go. Now you can see why I left India.' People there had thought he was mad to give up his middle-class lifestyle to go to England with nothing, but he had come back with his boy as England captain, playing against India on his home patch. It doesn't get much better than that, for me or him.

31

It was not the end of our winter commitments. A great one-day series in India, which ended with the sight of Freddie Flintoff whirling his shirt around his head after leading us to a 3–3 series draw.

In between tours I received a letter from Buckingham Palace informing me that I was to be given an OBE in the New Year's Honours list. I was completely taken aback. I know it has happened to previous England captains, but it just wasn't something I thought could happen to me. I have had medals and stuff from cricketing sources of course, but to receive something from my country was the greatest honour of all. I received my OBE from Prince Charles at Buckingham Palace in front of my family. I couldn't have been more proud.

We left for New Zealand soon afterwards. They have never been the easiest of opponents. To me, it has always been a major series, almost more so than Australia. I was never involved in a close series against Australia and I went into each one almost with a feeling of 'here we go again'. But with New Zealand, as was emphasized in my last Test appearance, you always know that, come the last day of the series, the last over, there will always be something going on.

They're well led by Stephen Fleming, have a very similar side to us, with no superstars, and their whole is greater than their individual parts, which was always our aim. New Zealand just make the most of what they've got, and they're a little bit in your face at times, like we are. They play on similar wickets to ours, with similar cricketers. And they have always bugged me because they have proved so hard to beat, until summer 2004.

We should have won my first series in charge in 1999, and

we would have done if it hadn't been for an inspired assault by Chris Cairns at the Oval. I was very keen to put that right in New Zealand in 2002. The team was playing well, I was playing well, we had competed well against a much stronger team in India, and we were strengthened by Graham Thorpe coming back into the team.

New Zealand is a great place to tour. The one-day series was played on seamer-friendly pitches and ended with us losing narrowly. But the biggest issue was Darren Gough. He was due, as I have explained, to be with us for the one-dayers but not for the Tests, since he had made himself unavailable for the Tests in India; so there was always going to be talk about why he wasn't staying on. In the end the matter took care of itself because Goughy hurt his knee in his last over of the last international. It seemed pretty innocuous at the time and I remember us almost laughing about it because it had stopped the press questioning why he wasn't staying for the Tests. But if I'd realized at the time that this would be the end of Gough at his peak I would have been nearer to tears than smiles.

He didn't even go down. Darren just said to me, 'My knee's hurting a bit, I'll have to go off.' Yet it turned out to be so serious that he did well to ever play again, let alone play for England again. He was certainly never quite the same bowler again, the bowler who was probably England's finest of the last twenty years.

The novel aspect of the first Test in Christchurch was the drop-in pitch that New Zealand had introduced because of the damage done to the squares by the rugby at these dual-purpose Kiwi stadiums. Nobody had any idea what it was going to do. We turned up the day before the game and couldn't find the wicket, so green was it. They had done the same thing the year before and had cut too much grass from the pitch, ending up with a high-scoring match. So, for our Test, they decided to leave the strip damp and with some grass on it, and it was the most crucial toss ever. And I lost it.

We lost our first 2 wickets with no runs on the board and out I went for the sort of situation I relish. I was relaxed and hadn't had time to get nervous. Michael Vaughan was a good partner to have because he can always see the funny side of playing and missing, and I went on to make one of my best hundreds. It did a lot, they had some good seamers, but I was in good nick and I think our score of 228 was probably 70 more than par for that surface. I scored 106 of them.

For once I gave Matthew Hoggard the best end, with the wind at his back coming from mid-on to assist his outswinger, ahead of Andrew Caddick, and it really swung for him. He kept on getting the right-handers to nick it and it was still a great wicket to bowl on. After Hoggy had taken the fifth of his 7 wickets Caddy came into the huddle and said, 'You stay at the best end, Hoggy, with everything in your favour. I'll tie things up at the difficult end.' It was a typical Andrew Caddick comment, masking his insecurities. He couldn't just say 'well done' to Hoggard. He wanted to make sure everyone knew he was doing his job too. He wasn't being offensive. It was just his way. But I took my cue and walked back with him to his mark, saying, 'Yeah, Caddy, you're doing a great job this end, you can bowl at the worse end, you know. Let Hoggy have it easy.' New Zealand were all out for 147 and we were in the driving seat.

Thorpe was back with us by this stage, much to everyone's relief. I think his marriage was over, but he seemed able to deal with it and we all vowed to help him through his problems. We would all spend time with him listening to his problems. And it helped him to get everything off his chest. Now Thorpe came into his own. The wicket was getting better and better, and by our second innings was an absolute belter. So Thorpe, in company with Andrew Flintoff, hit what was then the third-fastest double hundred in Test history. For all of a day. I knew we needed to set them a big target because this was now one hell of a batting strip. People asked why I had batted on for so long before declaring and setting New Zealand a target of 550, but I didn't want to take any chances.

Even that total was nearly not enough, for Nathan Astle played the most remarkable innings. It looked as if it was going to be a routine victory for us when they slipped to 189 for 4, but then Astle started hitting our bowlers everywhere, and I knew they batted all the way down. I always worried when the opposition came after our bowlers. With the exception of Gough I always worried that they didn't really know what to do if a batsman came at them with all guns blazing. There was a limit to what I could tell them. At times during Astle's assault, both Caddick and Hoggard looked at me as if to say, 'What do I do now?' In Caddick's case it was his only failing. All I could tell them was to mix it up as much as they could, but that sort of thing came naturally to Gough. He had the 'dogfuck', as Duncan Fletcher would call it, the ability not to get fazed and to know what to do. I think Jimmy Anderson has that ability too – certainly he has the potential of Gough's capacity – for thinking on his feet. I hope Anderson proves me right on that one and goes on to have a great career.

Anyway, there were times when I really thought we might lose the Christchurch Test match. That really would have been terrible. I was nervous, especially when an injured Chris Cairns came in at number eleven and held one end up while Astle went ballistic at the other end. Thorpe's double hundred was quickly overshadowed. In all, Astle scored 222 in 168 balls, and the relief when he drove at Hoggard and edged behind was palpable. We were gone. Our bowlers were knackered. If they had started knocking it about for 1s and 2s, we would have lost that game and made history for all the wrong reasons. But Astle continued attacking. New Zealand had fallen, a hundred short of their monumental target, and we had won a Test.

Yet the tension got to me. I was relieved but also angry at our bowlers for not taking the right options. As we went back to the team bus afterwards, I threw my bag down on the floor and Malcolm Ashton, our scorer who went on to become our analyst, said something like, 'Oh, shall I put your bag on the bus for you then, Nass?' I must have been feeling the strain because I snapped at him and ended up having a big row with him. Now Malcolm was one of our most highly valued management men and he was very much one of the people I had a high regard for during my time as England captain. So I must have been on the edge to row with him. And I felt bad about it for about a week afterwards when the players would mischievously ask whether we were talking or not yet.

The second Test in Wellington was the most traumatic of my career. And it had nothing to do with cricket. On the third morning I was batting with Mark Ramprakash and we were building a partnership. We came in at lunch, to be met in the corridor by Duncan Fletcher. He stopped us and said that he had some really bad news. I thought it must be another injury or something, but he said, 'Ben's been in an accident, and Ben's died.' Ben was Ben Hollioake, one of the most naturally gifted English players in the game, who only a couple of weeks earlier had been with us, playing in the one-day internationals.

It was a stunning, shocking moment. It was the first time in my life I had been confronted with death. It was unreal, it was unbelievable. My head was swirling. My first reaction was to say to Duncan, 'We can't play on, Fletch. It's not possible. This is Ben. This is not someone we don't know. We wear black armbands for cricketers of the past who have died, and rightly so, but this is one of our teammates.' Duncan understood totally but he said he felt we were going to have to carry on.

Then I went into the dressing room, to be confronted by scenes I hope I never see again. Thorpey, one of Ben's closest friends in the team, was in tears. Everybody had their head in their hands. Mark Butcher was inconsolable. Ben was a very popular member of our team. I had got to know Ben very well in the previous six months, when he spent a lot of time in our one-day side, and I was just starting to really get to know him. I wouldn't say I was among his closest friends of the team because we were from different eras, but I always got on well with him and never had a single falling-out with him, which was unusual for me. He was so talented, so carefree, never had a bad word to say about anyone. Never a hint of malice in him, and he enjoyed life to the full, a great bloke to have around in a team. He made other people relax. Nobody said anything during the lunch break. We just sat there. It finished far too quickly.

In the end Duncan said, 'We've got to play on, fellas,' but he didn't want to and none of us wanted to. I subsequently discovered that everyone had known the terrible news earlier in the day and word had got around the ground, but there was no way anyone could send a note out to the middle for us or anything like that. Fletch just had to wait until lunch to tell me. How we got through the rest of the day I will never know. The cricket was completely irrelevant. Ramps and I went back out with black armbands on and the New Zealanders were very good, very sincere in their condolences and attitude on the pitch. Fleming expressed his sincere sympathy at what had happened and somehow we ended up with 280.

Coming off at the end of play was when it all really hit me. When we were on the field it was a question of trying to get through, but now the realization of the enormity of what had happened sank in. People were still just sitting around, not knowing what to do with themselves. The press wanted to know what was happening, so I had to go and face them even though it was the last thing I wanted to do. My biggest fear was that I didn't want the focus to be on us. I wanted everyone to be thinking about Ben, his family, and his girlfriend, who was still in intensive care, not the England cricket team. We didn't matter. I got through it somehow and hopefully said the right things. Next morning we had a minute's silence and people were in tears again. We carried on with the game and bowled them out for less than us. I remember feeling relieved when I held on to a catch because I had managed to concentrate on the cricket.

It has changed all our perspectives on life. There have been a few times since, if anyone is going through a bad run with the bat or whatever, that someone like Thorpey or Butch has said, 'Remember Ben. Remember how short his life was. Be grateful for what you've got.' He has been sorely missed ever since, as a player and as a man.

We got through the Test, which was drawn, but there were other tricky issues to deal with off the field. We had decisions to make about Ben's funeral which were proving to be more complex than they should have been because, for some reason, all the flights from New Zealand to Australia, where Ben had died, seemed to be booked. All the team wanted to go, and poor old Phil Neale, our manager, was working overtime trying to make it possible. The other factor to consider was that we were playing in back-to-back Tests and, with four flights involved in the return journey to Perth, it was clear that if we all went we would miss the start of a Test if any of those flights were delayed. We had a meeting about it, and while now it might sound a small thing it certainly wasn't at the time because everybody very much wanted to be there to pay their respects to Ben.

In the end it was decided that I should go as captain to represent the team and pass on their respects. Ben, being Ben, had left his England jacket behind when he had left New Zealand so we had it laundered and it was decided that I would present it to his family as a sort of gesture. Karen was out with me, which helped me, and she gave me her full support and said I was right to go as captain. I had been worried I was taking the place of someone who was closer to Ben than me, but what could we do in the circumstances? I left for Perth on my birthday. The only one I have not celebrated.

Butcher and Thorpe were particularly upset about not being

able to go to the funeral so Butch decided to stage a memorial service for Ben in New Zealand at the same time as the funeral. He wrote a song and played his guitar and all the lads attended, and by all accounts it was a beautiful service. I stayed in the same hotel in Perth as the Surrey team, who had all flown over together. God, I felt like an intruder. They were all together, they are a very close side, and Ben was at the centre of their closeness. I was with them, in their hotel, in their bus on the way to the funeral, but I felt like an impostor. He was their boy. I can't really explain the feeling.

I had Ben's jacket with me and I didn't know how best to give it to Ben's family. I asked Ray Alikhan, who was helping to organize things, what I should do, but he just said the moment wasn't right. I didn't want to make a big thing out of it, just to hand it over as a show of respect from the England team. In the end, just as I was leaving the church, I handed it to Mrs Hollioake and just mumbled, 'This is from the England team.' Adam Hollioake was immense. So strong. The way he was able to stand up and talk about his brother was extraordinary. I will never forget how strong he was that day in saying exactly the right things and keeping his composure in being able to say them. I left quietly, only to find there was a problem with my flights, and I missed my connection from Sydney to Auckland. In the end I got back on the night before the third Test started, to find everyone as low as when I'd left them. In my own mind, I just wanted to win this series now and go home.

Eden Park in Auckland is an odd ground, again a rugby stadium, with odd angles and odd winds. We had had a bad time bowling there in 1997 when David Lloyd had had one of his funny turns. Again, we couldn't find the cut strip this time after Fleming had gambled after winning the toss and decided to bat. It seamed and swung and we had Chris Harris caught at short leg and it wasn't given. I couldn't help but think back to what Keith Fletcher had told me about decision making in New Zealand. It was a crucial decision. He went on to get a horrible 71, and it was so annoying because we should have rolled them, and 202 was a decent score in those conditions. We were dismissed for 160, and then they batted in the dark in their second innings with floodlights on. Another great innovation from the good old ICC, this. Let's put the floodlights on in Test cricket. Only we are using a red ball and wearing white clothing, and the outfielders couldn't see a thing because a dark ball was coming out of a dark background. I remember Usmal Afzaal being under a high catch and I thought he was messing around in the way he was trying to locate the ball, because he could be a bit of a clown, but he just could not see the ball. They set us too many, it was now getting uneven, and I was very annoyed to lose that game. For all sorts of reasons: wanting to beat New Zealand so much; wanting to win it for Ben's memory. But we were frustrated again against the Kiwis, and I had to wait until the very last game of my career to put that right.

The other reason I remember that tour was for the end of Mark Ramprakash's international career. I was brought up with Ramps. Had always been a fan of his. In his youth he had everything. There was no reason why he shouldn't have played eighty Tests and averaged 40, but there was just something about him that stopped him fulfilling his potential. He over-complicated the game, I guess. I wanted him in my team, I desperately wanted him to succeed, and we batted him in various positions to try to get the best out of him. We tried him as an opener, now we were trying him in the middle order. We took him to India and he played reasonably well, but in New Zealand he just didn't seem to be the player I'd known. When I batted with him in Auckland, he just didn't seem to be with it at all. It had to be a mental thing.

Ramps was very like me. He was a better player than me, technically and shot-wise, but he had had a very similar upbringing, with an Asian-Guyanese father who put a lot of pressure on him. Ramps was a fiery character with a lot of pent-up

aggression. You had to stay out of his way when he was out –
again like me – but he was a nice guy and it was a great shame
he didn't do better than he did. The same applies to Graeme
Hick. Nice people who put too much pressure on themselves.
In the end the stats didn't add up with either of them. You can
do so much, but in the end it must be down to the individual.
Ramps had a big slog in Auckland when we were chasing 300
and Duncan and I decided that enough was enough. Our
decision gave me no pleasure. My career could easily have fallen
some way short like Ramps. He was better than me. I couldn't
go and say to him that it was the end. For one thing, you are
never absolutely sure there wouldn't be a time when he might
come back into the equation, but it was mainly because I
couldn't bear to say that to him. I never did say to Mark
Ramprakash or to Graeme Hick that their time was up. I wish
they had been more significant figures during my spell as
captain.

32

The pieces of the jigsaw were coming together – not enough to beat Australia, or even compete with Australia, but enough to feel optimistic against any other side in the world. Yet we couldn't please everybody. There was criticism of our decision to bring John Crawley and Dominic Cork back for the first Test against Sri Lanka at Lord's in 2002, and some sections of the press labelled us as Dad's Army. My point was that we were still not good enough to discard players of the calibre of Crawley and Cork just for the sake of bringing younger players in. The same goes for Alec Stewart.

Stewie may have made himself unavailable for the India tour, but when James Foster was injured in freak circumstances, struck on the arm by a ball from teammate Andy Clarke in the nets at Chelmsford, there was only one man who was going to come back for us and put on the gloves: Stewie. If Fozzie hadn't been injured it might have been an interesting decision. I know Alec has since said he was worried that his international career might be over when Duncan effectively ruled him out of the New Zealand tour, but such are the vagaries of fate that Fozzie's misfortune made the decision for us.

I have always been a fan of John Crawley. He's a good cricketer, a good team man and a good bloke, and I had a big part in bringing him back because, this being my captaincy and a new regime, I wanted to give him a final chance to show he could do it. John, I suppose, is the third great under-achiever in my generation who did not fulfil his potential, along with Hick and Ramprakash. In John's case it was a little bit more technical, rather than the mental problems of Hicky and Ramps. With John Crawley, opposing bowlers quickly realized that they should just not pitch anything up to him. Everything arrived above his waist because he was not a big cutter or puller and, while John had the mental strength to try to overcome that, he didn't quite have the technique to master his shortcomings.

Yes, there had been a lot of support in our selection meeting for Ian Bell and I'm sure his chance will come, but I was adamant that I wanted John to have one last opportunity under Fletcher and me. Cork was the same. For over ten years he had been a quality performer and had played a crucial part in the victory over the West Indies at Lord's in 2000, a turning point in modern English cricket history. People in cricket love picking various themed sides, like an ugly XI, a good bloke XI and a hated XI. Corky was always the captain of the hated XI. (I was in there too.) But when people played with Dominic they would love to have him on their side. Whenever his name came up in selection, I would ask whether he was swinging it; if he was, I wanted him in the side. On this occasion the selectors told me he was.

I was furious when I discovered that, in May, we had prepared a belting wicket for Sri Lanka again at Lord's. We do shoot ourselves in the foot at times. We drew the game, I was pleased to get runs and we moved on to Edgbaston, where the wicket did a bit and we won by an innings. Sri Lanka hate bounce, and Caddick and Hoggard had plenty of that.

Without blowing my own trumpet, I was pleased with my captaincy at this time. There were certain things that were going just right for me. I remember going round the corner to Aravinda de Silva in the third Test at Old Trafford and he hit it straight to me, and little things like that were going my way. Things like that make it all worthwhile. I was enjoying captaining the side and we were doing well. There was no friction. We had a good blend of youth and experience and we were going in the right direction.

Old Trafford ended up with a little run-chase for Marcus Trescothick and Michael Vaughan, where they scored 50 in

5 overs to win us the match and give us a 2–0 series victory. Again, I had seven of us padded up for that episode. It's a good job Duncan Fletcher stayed calm in those circumstances. Winning like that was great fun. Sanath Jayasuriya didn't exactly cover himself in glory: he just put everyone on the boundary and didn't captain his side very well at all in that situation. Mind you, he was positively Brearleyesque compared to Hashan Tillekeratne. I'll come to him later.

This was the game when Alec Stewart equalled Graham Gooch's record of 118 Test caps and celebrated the occasion with a first-innings century. He always had a sense of occasion. Some people were saying it would be his last game because James Foster was now fit again, but I wasn't one of them. To my mind, Stewie had proved all over again that he was worth his place in the side. Why are we so keen to throw away prime assets while they are still able to contribute so much? Alec seemed to be getting stronger and fitter, and his attitude was exceptional. He is one of only two genuinely great England all-rounders in my lifetime, along with Ian Botham. Why did people want to drop him when he was still as good as ever?

Our one-day cricket had been improving. Not as much as our Test cricket and not as much as I would have liked, but we were getting there. In fact, there were not too many topics for people to take issue with as we tried to build up to the World Cup. Except one: my position in the side. Was I worth my one-day place? Was I capable of batting at number three? Those were the questions being posed in the press. I felt I was. I believed I was an all-rounder because of my captaincy, but I could accept that my place in the order was something we had to think about. There were not enough hundreds coming from our batsmen in one-day cricket and we were not chasing down targets well enough. I include me in that because I had never scored a one-day-international hundred. But we had a good triangular series with India and Sri Lanka, and the best two sides reached the final in us and India.

The final, though, was one of my most annoying days in cricket. It was a game we should have won, and it would have meant so much to me after everything we had gone through. We played them in a Lord's final on a wicket that really suited our opponents – again – I wanted to keep Sourav Ganguly down because he didn't impress me as a captain and the whole number three thing with me had reached a climax. If you look at the stats around that time, I had a bloody good record in the top three for both England and Essex, but people were making out I couldn't bat there. I think you'll find I was averaging 40 at number three, with a strike rate of around 70, better than anyone else who had batted in the position for England in a one-day game. Now if people had said, 'Hussain's a decent number three, but his problem is that he doesn't score enough hundreds,' I would have fully agreed. Or if they had said my strike rate was a little low, I could have accepted it; but to blindly say I wasn't good enough at three and that someone like Freddie Flintoff should go there was too simplistic as far as I was concerned.

Freddie, as he has subsequently proved, is good down the order. To send someone like Freddie in against the new ball is a waste. Freddie is one of the hardest hitters of a cricket ball in the world and in my opinion it would have been suicidal moving him up the order when we were having trouble with boundaries and finishing games off. The whole thing had snowballed as far as I was concerned. Early on in the series Jonathan Agnew had asked me in a radio interview whether I felt I should be batting at three and I let that one pass, but then I turned on the radio later and he was still going on about it. Then one day I switched on Sky TV, and Ian Botham was going on about why I shouldn't be at three. Then it seemed to be all across the papers.

Whether I was exaggerating it or not I don't know, but at one point I even overheard one spectator saying to another, 'I agree with the media. I don't think Hussain should bat at three.'

I felt like running around to everybody and saying, 'Get the stats out.' I volunteered to move down the order if Duncan Fletcher wanted me to, but he was happy with me where I was – and, to be honest, I was better there than down the order when you needed people either to hit very hard or to improvise.

What I couldn't argue with was that I needed to score hundreds at number three. There were reasons why I hadn't. My fitness levels weren't good enough, to be frank, and I was always getting it into my head that there was someone waiting to come in after me who could score faster than me, so I tended to give it away a bit through fear of wasting any overs, later in the innings. Which was wrong of me. I should have seen the job through more often.

So, going into that Lord's final I was seeking some kind of incentive, some kind of motivation. That's how I work. I love to prove people wrong, it gives me an added reason to do well. We batted first, the conditions were good, and I got in and reached 40. That's when I thought, 'Right, prove these idiots wrong.' Then, when I was on 70, I again wondered whether it might be better for England if Freddie was now at the crease instead of me. But for once I said, 'No, don't be a lazy weak dick. You see it through. For once in your life in one-day cricket for England, you stay out here and you see it through. Don't leave it to anyone else.'

There and then I decided I had to get to a hundred and afterwards I was going to remind the three or four people who were questioning me what they had said. I was using this to get myself through to a hundred. When I reached three figures, I wondered if I should just stay quiet, but I thought, 'No, be true to yourself. A lot of what you are about is passion, fire and proving people wrong.' So I stuck up three fingers to the media centre, mainly to Agnew, Botham and Bob Willis, who had made a particular deal about it, not just to show that I thought they had got it wrong but to emphasize that I had used their doubts to motivate myself.

Not for one moment since have I regretted doing it. In fact, I'm going to have a picture of it put up in my study at home. Because it was me. It summed me up. I have always played with fire. I quite enjoy being Nasser Hussain. I don't want to be someone different, because it's led to me playing 96 Test matches. The boys in the dressing room thought it was humorous. Fletch told me he thought I was sticking two fingers up at them at first and that he feared he was going to be looking for a new captain, so I must have given him a bit of a scare. Then my brother Mel texted me and said that a lot of jokes were going round the City about three fingers and the number three, so it clearly caused a bit of a stir. No matter. I have no problems with it. That was the end of it for me. I never hold grudges. The next time I spoke to Aggers and Beefy, I just said good morning to them. I have no problem with them. They have their opinion; I have mine. I just used their opinion to lift my game.

We scored 325 from our 50 overs. Surely that would be enough. By about the eighth over of the Indian reply I was cramping up. I have always had problems with cramp and later on I would take some magnesium tablets for the problem, but here I had to go off and things went completely pear-shaped as Virender Sehwag started to hit us to all parts. But I quickly got back on and after a flying start we pegged India back to the point where they were 146 for 5. Never at any point did I think we had won – I'm not that sort of bloke – but I wasn't expecting Mohammad Kaif and Yuvraj Singh, two cricketers who have barely been heard of since, to bat so spectacularly.

I made one big mistake. Ashley Giles had bowled beautifully and I was thinking to myself, 'Take the pace off the ball,' so I asked Vaughan to warm up. Then Yuvraj hit Giles's last ball for 6 and I changed my mind, thinking that the Indian players were too good against spin and I had to go to my banker, Darren Gough. I didn't go with my gut feeling. Trouble was, Gough was not the bowler of old. He was incredibly stiff. He had just come back from the injury he suffered in New Zealand and he wasn't right. Goughy was half a yard short of pace and he went for a few; then Ronnie Irani, who had bowled well in that tournament, got a bit over-excitable and he went for a few too. We had lost an amazing game and for some time later, when I was on the treadmill or just doing something at home, I would remember when India were 146 for 5 and I should have gone with Michael Vaughan's off spin. Gut instinct is invariably the best way to do things. I failed to protect 325 as captain and I have to take responsibility for that. As Mike Brearley wrote in *The Art of Captaincy*, there's always something you can do as captain. I didn't do enough.

The Test series against India was also a bit disappointing because, while 1–1 was no disgrace, we really should have won it. Again it was as if we had gone up to the Indians and said, 'What sort of wicket do you want to play on, Sachin? How about you, Rahul?' Except Headingley, where we really should have won.

Lord's was good. Simon Jones came into the side and immediately proved a real asset on a flat pitch. Duncan knew him from his time at Glamorgan but was reluctant to push him too much – which I could understand, because you are always a bit wary of advocating those you know best, in case they are not quite up to the job. Fletch warned me that Simon was still raw but that he had real pace, and that was what we wanted to rough up the Indians. I liked him immediately. Jones wore his heart on his sleeve, was aggressive and fitted in well in our dressing room. Our tactics from the winter were working again. We had batted first and I had scored 155. Then in the second innings John Crawley hit a hundred, which I was delighted with as it justified my earlier faith in him that season, and we won and won well.

There was one big cloud on our horizon. Graham Thorpe was having problems again. He was terrible during practice in the days leading up to the Lord's Test and you could see his mind was elsewhere. He was late for things, he had been to see his solicitor and I think he was struggling to get in his house. I asked him if he was OK and he told me he was having problems, so I just left him alone, but it was so clear he was not right. Usually he is fiddling with his bat handle, but this time he was more interested in his mobile and whatever messages and texts he had on it. He failed twice in the match and it was the last we saw of him for a while. For a long time it looked as if it might be the end for Graham Thorpe, but I'm happy to say we were going to have some more happy times in the England team together before I retired, and at the time of writing Thorpey's still going strong. I'm delighted about that. The little man has sorted his life out, dealt with terrible adversity and is back on track. He remains one of my biggest buddies and one of the great England players.

It was right to put Dominic Cork in the team for the second Test at Trent Bridge because it swings at Headingley, but unfortunately Dom was a disappointment in this match. The conditions were perfect for him and it was like 'Over to you, Dom' but he didn't do it. Did he still have it? That was the question I was asking myself. Like when I went in, with us in trouble in both the first and second Tests in the West Indies later, I was saying to myself, 'Have you still got it, Nass?' You have to ask yourself that, towards the end of your career. I think I showed I did still have it. Just! But this was the beginning of the end for Dom.

It was Steve Harmison's debut game. We had been trying to get him involved for two years but had been frustrated by a combination of factors. Me and Duncan were very keen on him. He was a bit raw and a bit erratic but Harmison showed he had the tools to work with and that there was a lot more to come. You could see Ganguly didn't like facing him, and that was a good start! We had the better of the draw but we should have won. We got a big score and, amazingly, we were outplaying India on good pitches. But then we shot ourselves in the foot.

For the first time we got on a wicket that was made for us to play India on: Headingley. Overcast, damp, swinging conditions. They won the toss and, surprisingly, elected to bat, and we bowled terribly. Matthew Hoggard on his home ground couldn't control the swinging ball. By lunch Duncan was in despair and was drawing diagrams on the board in the dressing room about how Hoggard should be using the crease, changing his angle to contain the swing and to make them play more. But it was no good. Rahul Dravid, Sachin Tendulkar and Sourav Ganguly are class acts and they were too good for us that day. They got too many, and we were always chasing the game. I got a hundred in the second innings but we had missed a golden opportunity. This is one game that Duncan always looks back on with regret.

The Oval was played on a belter. It was a high-scoring match. Some people thought I could have been a bit more positive in my captaincy at times, but I'm not sure if there was much more I could have done.

A drawn series, spoiled for me on the last day, which was rain affected. I was watching Channel 4 in a little room at the Oval and the commentators were picking their sides for the Australian tour. I was interested, mainly because I wanted to see who Mike Atherton and Richie Benaud would go for. I'm always interested in what the commentators are thinking. Then Ian Smith's team came up. I was on it but I wasn't captain. He then explained that he thought I was too negative as a captain and he would have Mark Butcher in charge. This came as a shock to me. Ian Smith is a very fine commentator and has a good cricket brain, and I was upset that he didn't think I was the right man any more. I thought I had had an excellent year and a half as England captain, I had come through my barren time with the bat when I so nearly gave it away, and I thought England were progressing well. I know I shouldn't take things like this quite so personally, but a lot of what I'm about is being wanted and being loved. I do listen to everything that is said and I read everything that is written, however much I may have pretended I didn't. I wanted people to be saying, 'Nasser Hussain has gone a good job as captain of England. He gave his all.' Nothing gave me more pleasure than when I read people like Angus Fraser or Derek Pringle, former teammates, now cricket correspondents, writing, 'I had my doubts when Nasser became England captain, but I was wrong.'

Ian Smith shouldn't have bothered me, but he did. Graham Gooch and Alec Stewart had the ability to be thick-skinned in the face of criticism. So has Duncan Fletcher. David Lloyd was a bit like me. I sat there, thinking, 'I'm putting a lot of effort into this. We're trying to create something here. We're moving away from the bad old days. Don't say this when we've just beaten Sri Lanka 2–0, drawn with India and played some good cricket. I'm scoring runs too.' I was almost in tears. Butch came in and asked me what was the matter, and when I told him he just said, 'Shut up, Nass. Don't worry about it. Leave it.' But it made me think about packing it in yet again. I couldn't figure it out. Did I deserve comparison with Brearley, as some were saying, or was I too negative in my tactics to beat the best?

33

The comparisons in the press with Mike Brearley were extremely flattering and seemed to stick, but it was never how I viewed myself. I just wanted to be the best I could be. I never compared myself to other batsmen as a Test player and I never compared myself to any other captains. I just wanted to be true to myself and honest with myself.

Players quickly see through a captain if he is looking after himself, and it is easy to captain a side by committee or try to do what the media are telling you to do. What you have to avoid as an England captain is getting sucked into doing something because you perceive that this is what everybody wants you to do; if you do that, you end up going down a rocky road. You make decisions as England captain that will be with you for the rest of your life, like me at Brisbane with the toss or in Port Elizabeth in bowling Jimmy Anderson ahead of Andy Caddick in the World Cup, so you must make decisions that you are comfortable with and feel are right at any given time. Then you can't really go wrong because the players will see that you are doing it your way and are acting according to your gut instincts. If you are good tactically you will get more right than wrong, and you have to remember that you are where you are because influential people think you are good enough to be England captain, so you have to believe that and back yourself. Why do it someone else's way?

I captained England in a natural way. I was always happy to live with the consequences of my actions. Making a wrong decision wasn't something I feared. There were times when I knew I was making tactical decisions that would be criticized, like giving Anderson an attacking field for his first over in Test cricket at Lord's, but I was backing him to do well against an average Zimbabwe side and I was happy to put up with the odd leg-glance for 4 because I didn't give him a fine leg, rather than see the batsman edge through where a fourth slip would have been. There is often more than one way of doing something in cricket, especially when you are captain. On any given occasion you have two or three possible ways of achieving a goal, whether it be getting someone out or building pressure on someone. There is no hard-and-fast right and wrong as captain; you have to play the percentages. Your gut instinct might be telling you there's a sixty per cent chance of getting a wicket one way and only forty per cent the other. So you go with your gut instinct and, if you're right, you're a hero; if you're wrong, somewhere someone with hindsight will say you should have done it the other way. There is always the flip side in cricket. But if you are good tactically, you will get it right more often than not. Captaincy to me was all about percentages and flip sides. And, crucially, I had a coach in Duncan Fletcher who understood technique and tactics better than anyone else I have known in cricket. Duncan always knew so much about opposing batsmen's strengths and weaknesses and he was so precise in his advice to our bowlers. It made things much easier for me.

Man-management was my greatest asset as captain. I knew what it was like to be one of the stars of a side, but I also knew what it was like to be a villain and, being a nervous person, I understood the fear of failure. I could relate to almost any character in the England side, with the possible exception of Anderson, who was so quiet when he first came into the dressing room that I couldn't get into his head. In the dressing room I kept my eyes and ears open to any comment or behaviour from a player to help me understand what I was dealing with and how I could handle them.

When I became England captain it struck me that so many people were concentrating on what we couldn't do or what any particular player couldn't do. I wanted to get away from that. I wasn't too fussed about dress codes, shaving, stopping players doing things on their own or with the players they were particularly close to in the team. To me these were minor matters so long as someone was performing. It was one area where Duncan and I disagreed slightly, because he loved us all to look and act as professionals all the time. He often used to quote Ferrari and how immaculate and professional anyone connected with the motor-racing team always looked.

Duncan helped me develop, both technically and tactically, as my time went on. Angles meant little to me before I worked with him but I learnt so much about cricketing angles and how best to exploit them. When I retired, I wrote to Fletch to thank him for all he had done for me, in common with a few others I wrote to, and I concluded by saying, 'Thanks for making me look a better captain than I was.' That was definitely the case.

England needed someone like me when we hit rock bottom, not only to kick the players up the arse but also to kick the authorities up the arse. The authorities hated me, to be honest. The ECB certainly did, because I always said my piece. When I first started there was lots of interference from people who didn't understand the game, like Brian Bolus and Simon Pack. They tried to impose on us what they felt an England player should be, and I fear that if Michael Vaughan had become captain ahead of me he might have allowed himself to be influenced by these people. My biggest triumph was in not accepting their ways.

That disappeared in my later period as captain because I felt I'd kicked the establishment into touch. We'd had a bit of success, so they gave me my head and it was just what England needed at that time. It's impossible, though, to compare me with Brearley or with anyone else because you can look a great captain – but then along come Australia to thrash you, and suddenly you don't look so good any more. You can only go on results and who you have beaten as captain. We defeated West Indies and Sri Lanka and Pakistan but I was never anywhere near beating Australia. Brearley did, as did Mike Gatting, so they have to take an enormous amount of credit for that.

As I write, Michael Vaughan is doing tremendously well as England captain, and long may that continue. He's moved away from the tendency which he had at first to captain by committee, which was a worry. I also think he has overcome any initial worries he had about including people like me and Thorpe, the rebellious ones, in his side. My early fear was that he wanted a team of clones.

Vaughan is exactly what England needed after me, to move on to the next level. After bad cop has come good cop – but even though I had a reputation as someone who ranted and raved, I'm not sure the players thought of me as a bad cop. I would hand out bollockings, yes, but we would quickly move on and no bad feelings would linger, and I was also responsive to any suggestion that any player had and I felt they could approach me if they had something to say. We also put in place good management structures that brought us on a long way and really should have been around many years earlier.

Ever since I stopped being captain I have felt that the Brearley comparison was hugely unfair on the others. When you're England captain you throw your whole life into it, and all the captains did their absolute best and will be remembered in their own ways for the good they did. People like Willis, Botham, Gatting, Gooch, Gower, Atherton and Stewart are great cricketers and people, so for someone to say that Hussain was the best since Brearley, and for it to stick, is disrespectful to the others. It was a sound bite. It was nice to hear at the time, but since I resigned from the job it has bothered me because if I now heard 'Vaughan is the best since Brearley', I'd think, 'Hold on, what about me?' I'd be hurt because I know how much I've given to the game as captain, and I sometimes wonder if Atherton and Stewart felt hurt when they heard those words while serving under me.

We shouldn't compare captains from different eras. We should just celebrate our leaders and move on together in positive fashion. All that we all want is for England to do well and we can achieve that if we are all batting on the same side.

34

There was a bigger issue than the Ashes to consider as we approached our tour of Australia in the autumn of 2002. Karen was expecting our second child and I didn't want to miss the birth. So the decision was made that she would come out to Australia with me and have the baby there so as at least to give me a much better chance of being present at the birth and also so that I could spend as much time as possible with her and Jacob leading up to the great moment and with the new arrival afterwards. I couldn't bear the prospect of not seeing my baby for the first two months of his or her life. I couldn't play cricket while a child I had never seen was back at home in England. I'd seen it happen to Ashley Giles and I knew how much it hurt him.

We couldn't leave it any later than seven months, otherwise Karen wouldn't be allowed to travel, so we went out to Perth ahead of the team. It was a big decision for all of us, particularly Karen. It was a huge thing for her to decide she was going to have our baby in another country without her family around her and with every likelihood that I would be in another part of that vast land.

I have to say that the ECB and Medha Laud in particular were fantastically supportive. Lord MacLaurin, the chairman of the board, had a lot to do with it. He knew how people in business were treated in circumstances like this and he brought a modern, professional approach to what was a very personal and important time for us. To be fair, the ECB went way beyond what they had to do as a duty of care to one of their employees. Medha, who is a liaison officer between the board and the players and who has long been the ECB's most impressive and helpful employee, sorted everything out. I really do believe she holds the whole place together.

Obviously I was prepared to pay the additional costs, but the ECB ended up paying for virtually everything and that was extremely generous of them. Anything we needed, Medha sorted it for us. Karen and I chose the hospital and the medical care, and we had a great three weeks in Perth, mainly spent with my sister Benu, who lives there, before the team arrived and I had to go back to work. As the England team arrived in Australia, so did one of our best friends from university, Elizabeth, who came out to help look after Karen and Jacob when I had to leave them to return to business.

Anyone who knows me will tell you that I would let nothing interfere with my focusing on the Ashes battle ahead. Later on my friend Mr Gatting questioned my taking my family to Australia, but he was sticking his nose into my personal affairs and it really was none of his business. In any case I never switch off from cricket, and having my family around helped me concentrate on our monumental task. The biggest issue when the team arrived was the injury situation. We knew Darren Gough wouldn't be fit for the start of the tour, but, as far as I was concerned, having Goughy out there for any part of it would be worthwhile and it was worth picking him. Freddie Flintoff was a concern. He had had a hernia operation and had missed the last Test of the summer, but we were told he would be fit in six weeks' time, which would be fine for the Ashes. Only trouble was, it seemed by no means certain now that he would be fit. Word was, Freddie hadn't done his rehabilitation work at Lilleshall, but Freddie insisted that he had and that the medical people had been telling him he wouldn't be fit from an early stage. We were getting conflicting reports and it was worrying.

At that time I wished I had a Jiminy Cricket I could perch on Freddie's shoulder to tell him what to do all the time, because he didn't do himself any favours in the early years of his England career. His preparation was terrible. His netting was unprofessional. No wonder he wasn't fulfilling his vast potential at this stage. Freddie's attitude seemed to be that he would come out to Australia and work on his fitness out there, like Gough; but we expected Flintoff to hit the ground running. In the last two years the penny has finally dropped with Andrew. If he trains hard, practises properly and is more professional, he can be one of the great all-rounders of all time. He can do things no one else can. Mind you, it was probably me over-bowling him that had given him his hernia in the first place, so I couldn't complain about him too much and we just had to monitor what was already becoming an ominous injury situation.

We had lost Graham Thorpe before anyone, including my family, had set foot on a plane. Thorpey had been missing since the Lord's Test, but he had convinced the selectors of his readiness to take part, and a fit Thorpe is worth his place in any team, so we picked him. But his private life was still in turmoil and, I gather, after he had spent some time in a hotel on an away trip with Surrey he realized he just couldn't do it and withdrew before we left. To this day Thorpey thinks I was angry with him about that because I didn't ring him, but we have never been the sort of friends who are always on the phone to each other. We just catch up with each other whenever we see each other, so I felt no need to ring him. I didn't really know what to say to him, other than to sympathize. I would much rather Graham Thorpe had pulled out of an Ashes series to get his life right than be unhappy later in life. There are a lot of things in life that are more important than cricket; we have only to remember Ben to know that. So I had no problem with Thorpey pulling out before we left.

What did bother me was that the ultimate test was looming and it seemed we were going to be without our best batsman (Thorpe), our best bowler (Gough), and our best all-rounder

(Flintoff). A case of déjà vu? Things always seem to go wrong just before we play Australia.

Our first match was the original banana skin, the traditional tour-opener at Lilac Hill; when asked by reporters, I had said that our aim on tour was to compete and that we would need to be at 100 per cent to have any chance of beating Australia. This wasn't good enough for Glenn McGrath, who criticized me for not being positive enough. But what was I supposed to say? That we were going to thrash Australia? We were going to make them grovel? Not very wise, I would suggest, but it was a typical example of Australian mind games. Whatever I had said, McGrath or someone else would have found reason to have a go at me about it.

Steve Harmison's radar went on the blink at Lilac Hill, which was not the greatest start for him or us, and at this stage I was beginning to be concerned about our bowling coach, Graham Dilley, who was a lovely bloke but was just not hard, dynamic or imaginative enough to work effectively with our bowlers. I almost lost it with him a couple of times because he seemed more interested in having a fag and a drink with the bowlers than giving them the necessary motivation, and I started longing for the return of Bob Cottam, whom we had made the mistake of getting rid of because it was felt he was getting a little old for the job. As it turned out later, Troy Cooley was ideal and I wish I had had him in Australia in 2002.

We were struggling to get wickets in our warm-up games and, worse, it was now looking like Gough would not make any part of the tour. He had been due to play in a grade game but had broken down in the nets and had been told by an expert at the academy out there that he wouldn't be able to play competitively again, and he was distraught. This was all taking place in the build-up to the first Test, and my problems were mounting.

I was very worried about Darren and went to see him in his hotel room. Goughy was in tears and didn't know what he was going to do. He had done everything he could, he had worked his nuts off, but a seemingly innocuous knee injury picked up in New Zealand looked like ending his career. I rang Ronnie Irani up to ask him about the knee specialists he knew in America and Germany, and we all agreed that Darren should contact the man in America before he gave up. So low was Goughy's mood that I received a phone call from his wife Anna, asking me to keep an eye on him because she was worried what he might do. I did, but Goughy had to go home before the first Test, a huge blow to us. The Freddie situation, meanwhile, was rumbling on, with us having constant meetings with him and about him.

And so we turned up in Brisbane for the first Test – a little, you could say, under-prepared. I was getting very sceptical about our chances of ever bowling Australia out on their pitches but there was a good covering of grass on the Gabba pitch and the nets did a bit, so maybe, I thought, just maybe there might be some hope of getting early wickets. In the game before, against Queensland, they had batted first and got 500 for 3 on a flat wicket. Those figures terrified me, so that green grass seemed like a lifeline. Without my front-line bowlers I was clutching at straws. The day before the Test I was looking at the wicket and I bumped into Derek Pringle who, as if he was reading my mind, told me not to get suckered into bowling first and that I had to bat if I won the toss. What did he know?

We had a management meeting which was dominated by a variety of topics, none of them involving what we should do if we won the toss. Unusually for me, I didn't have a meeting with Duncan Fletcher either to see what he thought. Duncan was usually an 'if in doubt, bat' sort of bloke but because I was so pessimistic about our chances of bowling the Aussies out twice I wanted to give our bowlers any little assistance that could possibly be found in the pitch. And the only time when there might be anything in this pitch was on the first day. On the morning of the first Test I walked over to the nets and had a conversation that Marcus Trescothick which I laugh about to this day. He wasn't officially my vice-captain but he was very much my second-in-command and at that stage was being lined up to take over from me when eventually I packed up the captaincy. Marcus said to me, 'I've just had a net, and it did a bit. The wicket looks just the same as the nets to me. I think we should bowl first.'

I took that on board, but then I made my big mistake. I should have gone to the middle, had a good look at the wicket and then had a chat with Duncan, as I usually do. Instead, I went and had some throwdowns and then got embroiled in peripheral Ashes-type matters, like what coin should we use for the toss and other weighty concerns like that. I must confess I was looking for things that weren't there while trying to convince myself that we should bowl first. It was like we were in a crisis situation and I was trying to move the goalposts, do anything that could help us in our predicament against such a strong side. I was trying to be a bit clever, in the same way I had tried to be clever finding ways to get Sachin Tendulkar out in India. I learnt a harsh lesson that you can't muck around with cricket too much.

Before the toss I managed to grab a quick word with Duncan, who admitted he was in two minds and probably would bowl first, and I found out later that Steve Waugh would have inserted us, so I didn't exactly make the most surprising decision in the world. But when I won the toss I said we would bowl, and it has since been labelled the biggest mistake I made as England captain.

I went into the dressing room and I could see Andrew Caddick's face drop straight away at the prospect of being thrust into the spotlight. The ball swung a bit at first and I thought, 'Maybe this is going to work out,' but by the fifth or sixth over nothing was happening and I could feel the world closing in on me. I thought to myself, 'Oh God, Nass, what have you done?' and I was clever enough to realize, even in that first season, that the next twenty-five days of Test cricket were going to be absolute hell. The only consolation I had in my mind was that I hadn't taken the easy option. There are captains out there who never try anything unusual and always take the easy option, knowing that if it doesn't work it won't rebound so horribly on themselves. In my defence I was always looking to try things that might have won us a game even if it wasn't in the textbook way and I was always prepared to put my head on the block.

I threw the ball to Simon Jones, who had been missing since that encouraging Test debut at Lord's in our win against India. He immediately bowled well and I thought, 'Well, at least there is a silver lining to this dark cloud that has descended on me.' Then it happened. I was at mid-off; Jones was at mid-on, someone hit a ball past him and, as he chased it and slid to stop it, I heard the crack and the noise straight away. I'm terribly weak-stomached about things like that so I didn't even want to go over and have a look. I knew it was bad. It was the Brisbane outfield that was to blame. They play other sports on it and it was too soft underfoot.

Simon was in agony with what turned out to be a serious knee injury. He was writhing in pain and we all knew straight away that it was serious. I felt terrible; I couldn't believe what was happening to us. And it carried on in similar vein. Simon was carried off, we carried on misfielding, Matt Hayden provided some catching practice for Vaughany and he dropped it, and by now the Aussie crowd were laughing at us. Actually laughing at us. And I couldn't blame them. It was our worst day's cricket in at least five years.

We were very quiet that evening in the dressing room. Somebody said, 'Is it still doing a bit, skip?' but nobody laughed. I was embarrassed about what we had done. And we were all upset for Simon. We all went to see him and he had already been told that the injury might be career-threatening, so he was understandably at a very low ebb.

Going to bed, I couldn't have felt any lower. I'd got it wrong, simple as that. There were no excuses. A captain's life is all about decisions, and on this occasion I made the wrong one. You get a lot of compliments when you get it right, and you have to be man enough to take it on the chin when you get it wrong. I was quite pleased to get through the rest of that game. There were the usual 'Good toss to win, skip' type of comments from the Aussies when I went out to bat, and I was pleased to get 51. We didn't bat too badly first time, but I could see the pitch was deteriorating, just to rub it in, and it was all downhill from there. We got hammered.

I flew to Hobart with the boys for the post-Test meetings and to prepare for our game there against Australia 'A'. But I had other things on my mind too. My baby was due. At lunch on the first day of our tour match, which I missed, with Duncan's blessing I flew to Perth to be with Karen. I spent three days with Karen, hoping the baby would come but he didn't and then, with the second Test in Adelaide looming, we took the decision to have Karen induced, two days early, so that I could be at both the birth and the Test. This was not a decision we took lightly and we decided to do it only after consulting with people at the brilliant St John of God Hospital in Perth, who were totally happy with doing it that way. It wasn't just so that I could see Joel entering the world. I could also stay with him, Karen and Jacob for a day before I had to go back to Adelaide to work, and it was all those circumstances which made us think it was the best option. Joel arrived safely and everything was well.

I didn't miss a minute of anything connected with the Ashes series, not a moment of the build-up or any of the second Test. The boys were upbeat when I joined them in Adelaide, which was an encouraging sign; but much of the spring disappeared from our step when Ashley Giles was hit on the wrist by Steve Harmison in the nets and had to go home with a broken left wrist. Even then, people were reluctant to face Harmison in the nets. All the boys used to look with trepidation at the list of who was in who's net when Duncan used to compile it before practice. It is no surprise to me that his career took off so spectacularly in 2004.

The shame of it was that I think Ashley had bowled as well at Brisbane as I had ever seen him outside the sub-continent. Now he was on his way home – as was Andrew Flintoff, because his hernia was not getting any better. So we were down to the bare minimum, and then on the morning of the match Vaughan twisted his knee. We weren't sure whether he was going to be fit or not. Fletch rang up Ian Blackwell, who was at the ECB academy in Adelaide, and he was busily trying to find some kit to join us for what could easily have been his Test debut. It was like a club trying to find eleven fit players on the morning of a match after a big night out!

Steve Waugh, by this time, was waiting at our door for me to write my team down. I looked over to the nets and saw Michael rushing towards the dressing room, which I took to be a sign that he must be fit and wrote his name down on our list. Good job he was fit. He would have had to play then. As it was, he scored 177 and we batted pretty well but we didn't go on as we should have done and we didn't have the firepower to deal with the Aussies. We lost again and, to make it worse, Andrew Caddick went in the back.

We were completely outplayed in Perth. Brett Lee bowled really quickly and blew us away and I got a bad decision from Rudi Koertzen which led to me kicking over a pair of crutches in frustration in the dressing room! (I couldn't tell you whose crutches they were. By that time we had so many injuries they could have belonged to anybody!)

Later in that match I grew frustrated by Alec Stewart for the only time in my career. Alex Tudor had been hit on the head by Lee and he was stretchered off. It was a nasty injury which cut Tudes's face and made him look even more like Frank Bruno, but by that time the match and the Ashes were gone, so there was no point in trying to encourage him to stay out there. But Stewie was joined by Steve Harmison, who didn't really know which end of the bat to hold, and he proceeded to give our tailender the strike straight away. He exposed Harmy, one of our few remaining bowlers, to Brett Lee at his most fearsome and the only possible conclusion to reach was that Stewie was looking for a not out. Whether Alec was worried about his place by this time or whether he was trying to get his average up to 40 I don't know, but I was sufficiently annoyed to ask Duncan whether I should confront Stewie. The coach told me he felt I should leave it as we already had enough on our plate without me falling out with Alec Stewart; but the words that Steve Waugh had apparently said to Rob Key when he was at Kent came back to me. Steve had apparently told Key that England would never win anything while Stewie was in the team because he looked after number one too much, but I felt that was harsh.

In many ways I'm glad I didn't say anything to Stewie. I'm sure something would have been lost in our relationship if I had accused him of being too selfish. As I have said, everyone needs a degree of selfishness to thrive in this team game which is based around individual performances, and I was speaking as someone who had been accused of being selfish early in my career. So I gave Alec the benefit of the doubt, but I wasn't happy. We had been thrashed again and the Ashes were gone.

This was not, it is fair to say, the Ashes series I dreamed about or wanted. I was wondering what else could possibly go wrong. We switched into one-day mode for a couple of weeks before Christmas, which I will come to later, but the Ashes battle resumed in traditional Boxing Day fashion at Melbourne, where Hayden started bullying us from the start. We played some reasonable cricket, with Vaughan by this time playing like God, but lost again and my biggest concern then was to avoid a 5–0 whitewash. That would be just too much to bear.

The Sydney wicket looked as if it might help our cause. This was a wicket that did a bit, and I always felt we were in with a chance if that was the case. Mark Butcher scored a hundred and I got seventies in both innings – but that in itself was a disappointment because it meant I had never scored a Test hundred in Australia, and that was something I would love to have done. But this match wasn't about us, nor was it even about whether Australia would win 5–0. It was all about Steve Waugh and whether he was going to retire or be dropped at the end of the Ashes. The whole thing with him was building up to a crescendo. Waugh had looked fidgety all series, terrible by his standards, and for once it seemed as though he feared failure, just like us mortals.

He came in at 56 for 3 in reply to our 362, and from the first moment it all seemed set up for him. We bowled poorly at him at first and he was away, and it turned into an incredible day. It was just about whether Steve could score a hundred. Whatever I did, I couldn't seem to stop him. When he got to the nineties, people were still pouring into the ground, anxious to see the great man reach three figures. The place was buzzing. Steve was on 95 at the start of the last over of the day, which was to be bowled by Richard Dawson, and I was determined to keep him in the nineties overnight so he could sweat on it – if Steve Waugh ever does sweat. No room for sentiment here. We needed to get Steve out if we were to win this match.

Adam Gilchrist did well to get him on strike, and the last ball of the day loomed with Waugh on 98. I went up to Dawson and said, 'I have absolutely no advice to give to you. I just want to delay this for as long as possible to make him think about it. The only thing I'll say is that he will probably go for a big shot to get his hundred tonight, maybe the slog sweep, his favourite, so bowl it fast and straight and see what happens.' Dawson almost did it. He bowled pretty much the ideal ball. He only gave Steve about two inches of width outside off stump. I would have defended it, especially on 98, but Waugh, with his quick hands and sense of theatre, just pounced on it and rifled it for 4. An incredible shot, and the Sydney Cricket Ground erupted. I have never seen anything like it. The whole series had built to that point. Steve was such a strong competitor.

We all shook his hand and, looking back now, it was great to be involved in that moment, although I would have preferred it if Dawson had got him out! I felt this was the perfect time for Steve to retire; but he carried on for a while and that is his call and his business. I just feel that no one really remembers what happened in his career after that, but everyone remembers Sydney. Maybe he would have quit if they had won that match, but I'm delighted to say that didn't happen.

Vaughan was really blossoming by now and he scored another big century in our second innings. We were closing in on victory and the wicket was exploding by the time Australia batted again. Andrew Caddick found some holes in the pitch – he was always a world-class performer if he had something to work with – and took 7 second-innings wickets. It was a considerable consolation for us and I was pleased to have a rare beer with Waugh in the dressing room at the end of the game.

He didn't tell me anything I didn't already know. I knew how much injuries had affected us and I knew how hard we found it on flat surfaces. We were starting to develop some pace bowlers, a significant factor in later successes, but we were still far from finding a mystery spinner. My Ashes series had been as depressingly one-sided as ever, and I had to accept that and realize that, for all our progress, we were as far away as ever from being able to compete with Australia. When will it ever change?

35

It was when we were playing a one-day match against a Prime Minister's XI in Canberra during our Australian tour that I began to worry about our World Cup side, in particular our bowling. We were just getting smacked around and I sat there, not playing in the match, thinking, 'This is not good enough. We are never going to win the World Cup like this.'

So I asked Duncan Fletcher to hold an emergency meeting about our bowling and I called in Ronnie Irani as well. A few months earlier, during the course of a conversation with Ronnie's dad Jimmy, he had told me that a young bowler called James Anderson had particularly caught his eye, and on the back of that Duncan and I had found out more about him and had wanted him for our full Ashes party. It's amazing how players are picked at times! It turned out he wasn't fit enough then, so he went to the academy instead, but now I asked Ronnie to give me an update on Anderson. Irani was full of praise for the lad, so Duncan made the first of his (sometimes fraught) calls to Rod Marsh at the academy to see if the lad was fit, which he was, and a year after he was playing for Burnley we decided to put Jimmy Anderson into our World Cup squad. He was the one glimmer of hope for us in an otherwise indifferent build-up to the big tournament in the later stages of our tour of Australia.

There was one time when we were playing Sri Lanka in the triangular tournament and Sanath Jayasuriya was looking to get after Anderson. I could just sense that he was going to go after Jimmy's next ball and I wondered whether I should say something, but I left him alone. Then Jimmy bowled a slower ball which completely stuffed Jayasuriya, he went through with his big shot and lobbed it to me at the edge of the circle. I thought, 'We've got something here. We've got a Gough-like figure who thinks on his feet.' Some bowlers would have just kept bowling line and length and would probably have got slogged. Anderson sensed something was about to happen and changed his thought processes, which is something you just can't teach.

We had discovered a bowler who swung the new ball, had good pace, good options, a good head on his shoulders and was a nice lad, if incredibly quiet. That was my only worry: I couldn't get into his head, couldn't get anything out of him. If they gave you one sentence back when you asked them something, then you had something to go on, but Jimmy said nothing. David Lloyd told me that all the people from Burnley were like that, but Jimmy was a difficult bloke to captain because of that. No matter. I wanted Jimmy in the World Cup side.

We had other concerns. There were worries as to whether Ronnie Irani deserved his place. We all saw him as an incredible competitor who wouldn't shy away from the battle, but was he actually good enough? That's why I never really pushed Ronnie in selection, apart from that time in 1999 when I said I wanted him in my side for the final Test at the Oval. I wasn't sure about him. I knew his shortcomings – for instance, he wasn't very good against spin – but I knew he had character and I wanted to pick on that.

The inclusion of Nick Knight was even tougher. It was felt we were going back by selecting him, but I felt he had the right character and experience. Then there was Ian Blackwell, who had a lot of natural talent which was compromised by his poor physical condition, which wasn't acceptable. It was, in fact, a huge indictment of the county system because he should never have been allowed to come so far in the game in such a poor physical state. There are no excuses for young players not to be in prime fitness these days.

I wasn't massively confident, then, about the strength of our World Cup squad, but so totally overwhelmed were we by the whole Zimbabwe crisis that the cricket itself was virtually forgotten in the whole shemozzle. Mind you, I never actually believed that it had affected our cricket. We lost the points we might have won in Zimbabwe, but we played well against Holland and not so well against Namibia.

Then Anderson came to the fore against Pakistan. When it swings, like it did in Cape Town that day, the young lad has the ability to be a phenomenal bowler. Duncan had told him to bowl a yorker at Yousuf Youhana, which I'd forgotten, but Jimmy did it as soon as he came in, and got him out. We won and we won well, and I started to feel that we were getting it together, certainly playing better cricket than in the last couple of World Cups, which made the Zimbabwe affair all the more frustrating.

We had the worse of the conditions against India and lost, but they are a good side; then came our meeting with Australia, one of the games I will always look back on with angst. It was such an infuriating game. It was played on a terrible wicket at Port Elizabeth and I received one of the best deliveries from Andy Bichel I have ever had dismiss me. We did well to get up to where we did, 204, and bowled really well to have Australia 135 for 8 in reply. At the time it wasn't clear whether our qualification for the next stage depended on beating the Aussies, but what I did know was that we needed to beat them to make sure we took points into the next round under the complicated points system.

Earlier, however, I had noted that Bichel was coming in at ten, unbelievably low for someone of his class, and now that was to come back and haunt us. There were things I should have done against Bichel which haunted me for ages afterwards. First, I should have told Ashley Giles to go round the wicket to Bichel earlier than he did. Bichel and Michael Bevan were building patiently and things were starting to run away from us. All the time I kept looking up, to see Glenn McGrath sitting with his pads on, and I felt we were just one wicket away from the next stage. It just wouldn't come.

I brought Andy Caddick, who had bowled well, back on for one over but he looked innocuous. Then, with two overs left, Australia needed 14 runs to win and I had the choice of Caddick or Anderson to bowl the penultimate over. Yes, Caddy had taken 4 for 35, but I just didn't think he was the man. He has never been a great death bowler. For all his qualities, he just bowls a length, and in those situations his thought processes and ticker are not as good as Anderson's. So I decided to bring back the bowler who had the better slower ball and who varied his pace. The easy option was Caddick, the obvious thing to do was to bring back Caddick. But it's what you feel is the best option, your gut instinct in those circumstances.

Jimmy did what I wanted him to do. He bowled a good slower ball to Bichel, but the next bit didn't go to plan. Bichel saw it, met it perfectly and slogged it for 6. From that moment the game was over for us. If he had slogged it straight up in the air and been caught, we would have won, I would have been a hero and it would have looked like another of my moves had come off. As it was, it backfired and I was left wondering why I hadn't bowled Caddick. It ate away at me afterwards. Caddick was really upset I hadn't entrusted him with the job, and Anderson was distraught. Later, I went to look for Jimmy and found him playing pool with Blackwell at the hotel. He was even quieter than usual. I told Jimmy he had done brilliantly, he had a huge future in front of him and not to let it affect him. I know his career has stuttered a little at times since then, but I see no reason to change my view that he will be a major figure in English cricket for the next few years.

Now our fate was in other people's hands. Zimbabwe were playing Pakistan in Bulawayo, and a Pakistan win would have been enough to take us through. It never rains in Bulawayo. Never. And we had dismissed reports of a monsoon hitting

Bulawayo as rubbish. Yet when we turned on our TVs on the morning of the game, the start had been delayed by rain. We couldn't believe what was happening. A few of us went off to play golf and Steve Harmison was deputed to ring us with weather updates from Bulawayo. We got to the seventeenth hole when Harmy rang us and simply said, 'We're going home.' We walked straight off the course at that moment and prepared to come home. It summed up everything. We were hugely deflated. It was terrible that Zimbabwe had initially ruined our tournament, but we had had a chance to salvage it, and we hadn't been able to take it. I am destined never to have enjoyed success with England in a World Cup.

Even then there was one more little shambles to sort out. Before we came home Andrew Flintoff and Harmison had been out to some sponsor's day which involved, in their case, a fair bit of drinking. OK, we were out of the tournament, but the problem came when Freddie was late in fulfilling his obligation later that night to go to an official drinks party with Gulliver's, with whom we had an agreement to provide players for functions. Flintoff arrived back just as the players were supposed to be departing for the Gulliver's function but he was clearly drunk and in the wrong clothing. Phil Neale, our manager, told him he couldn't go; Freddie insisted he would and was trying to get on the bus. Phil hauled him off but was upset about it and felt that Freddie had made a fool of himself in front of everybody. Duncan got to hear about it and told me that we had a problem with Freddie. I asked Harmison what had happened, but he just refused to drop his mate Flintoff in it, denying that he was drunk, and I admired him for that. But Freddie had already had warnings that winter for various offences and we were trying to get the drink culture out of the team, so we had to take action. We ended up fining him £1,000, a suitably disappointing end to yet another disappointing World Cup.

But it was not quite over. I had a decision to make over my

future as a one-day player. I had been discussing with Duncan when would be the best time for me to go, and we both agreed that it was time for someone else to become one-day captain. I announced my retirement from the limited-overs game so that England could move on in the short form of the game.

I knew I was opening the door to my replacement as Test captain too, but that's what I wanted to do. I wanted someone to come in and prove that they were ready to take my job. But who was it going to be? I had long thought Marcus Trescothick could well be the man and there was no question that he was a brilliant vice-captain, who did everything I could have asked him to do and expected him to do as my right-hand man. But I also knew that as captain you have to be tough and be prepared to take shit. There was a feeling that Marcus might not be thick-skinned enough, or tough enough, for the top job. Whether he can develop those attributes and be the next in line time will tell, but Marcus is almost too nice for the top job. There is no such thing as a popular captain, Keith Fletcher once told me, but Marcus hates people having a go at each other in the dressing room. He is popular and he has a good cricket brain, but maybe the players would walk all over him if he was in charge. You have to be a little bit nasty, like me.

Make no mistake, Michael Vaughan has the ruthless, stubborn streak in him that a Test captain needs. He is a good bloke, don't get me wrong, but he'll go for the jugular when he needs to. The differences between them can be summed up by their reaction to Harmison's amazing spell of 7 for 12 against the West Indies in Jamaica in 2004. After the last wicket was taken, Vaughan immediately ran off to get padded up, as an opening batsman should, but Marcus was busy trying to get a stump for Harmy. That is typical of him, thinking of others.

I wasn't absolutely sure how Michael would do as captain because he never really said much in the field or at meetings, so I wasn't sure how tactically astute he was, but it has always been clear that he had something about him. Call it Yorkshire grit, or whatever, but he has done well as captain, possibly better than I thought he would. When I was asked my opinion as to who should succeed me as one-day captain, my heart said Trescothick but my head said Vaughan, and I am delighted it has worked out well. So well, indeed, that I was quickly thinking about the right time for me to go as Test captain too.

36

Once Michael Vaughan stepped on to the field at the head of the one-day side there were two captains of England and that felt strange. I'd always taken great pride in being England captain and, however much I tried to think otherwise, it took a little of the gloss off of what was always a special thing in my heart. It was always all or nothing for me and I knew deep down that it had gone. It had changed.

There isn't a problem having a separate captain of the one-day side if you are thick-skinned, but I found it hard. As Mike Brearley said in *The Art of Captaincy*, the only thing you miss about being England captain is the honour, and I already felt that the job was slipping away.

It was now that I wrote an article for the *Sunday Telegraph* which I now accept was a big mistake and showed me that perhaps Michael Vaughan was right when he decided at the end of the tour to West Indies in 2004 to stop doing newspaper articles while he was captain. I have already said how much I respect Scyld Berry and when he rang me to ask if I would do an article stating my remaining goals as captain, I saw no problem with it. I trusted Scyld's judgement implicitly and I thought I could use a bit of goal-setting to motivate me for the remainder of my captaincy. So I said it would be nice if I could earn 100 caps, captain the side more times than Mike Atherton's record and lead England to more wins than Peter May. I never meant it to sound selfish, I was just doing what I had always done in giving myself targets; but instead of keeping my goals to myself I shared them with the *Sunday Telegraph*, and perhaps it was naive. It certainly offered people a stick to beat me with. It wasn't Scyld's fault. It was mine for being too honest. But it rebounded on me because people made an issue of it for the remainder of my career, and quickest off the mark was my friend Mike Gatting, who said I should be thinking more about the team than about myself. Of course I was thinking about the team. It was just perhaps that it didn't come across that way.

We easily defeated Zimbabwe 2–0 in the Test series at the start of 2003, but that was not even a cause for great satisfaction because they were a shadow of their former selves without the likes of Andy Flower and others. The problems in Zimbabwean cricket had started to kick in and, while I had no problem in playing against them in this country – to me it was very different from playing them in their own country – the victory was a bit hollow because our opponents were a shambles.

Then Vaughan had considerable success with the one-day side, and his rather different style of captaincy was earning rave reviews in the press. I could see the tide turning. I had my eyes open. I wanted someone to prove that he was capable of replacing me, but in my own mind I now had to get the timing right for stepping down from the main job. I rang Duncan Fletcher to ask whether he thought I should resign ahead of our Test series against South Africa, but he felt that it was premature. Duncan, however, did admit that he had been impressed by Vaughan and told me that I would be under a lot of pressure at Edgbaston for the first Test. It was up to me to cope with that.

And I did feel under pressure when I turned up at Edgbaston. The key factor to me was that I now felt different with Duncan. In the past it had always been Fletcher and Hussain, but now, in the couple of days' build-up to the first Test, he would turn to Vaughan and ask how we got such-and-such a batsman out in the one-day series, or questions like that.

I felt the momentum had changed. I could feel emotions building up in me throughout the match. I actually felt depressed and had spoken to both the ECB medical officer,

Peter Gregory, and our psychologist, Steve Bull, about it. People were talking about Vaughan's young brigade and I felt, deep down, that I was done. My health was suffering, I had irritable bowel syndrome, the late nights and early mornings were catching up with me and I'd given as much as I felt I could give. It didn't help, of course, that South Africa piled on the runs after winning the toss. Their new young captain Graeme Smith put on the small matter of 338 runs for the first wicket with Herschelle Gibbs. I stood there in the field and thought, 'I've lost this side.' There were new players in the team and I had to find new energies to lead them, but I found I lacked enough energies in reserve to rise to the challenge.

Whatever I tried in the field failed to work. I knew I was under the microscope and I didn't want to do anything just for the benefit of the cameras. My captaincy had always been based on gut instincts and I still wanted to captain the side in my own way, but it just didn't seem right and Mike Atherton made the pertinent observation that I seemed out of sorts, not myself as captain.

When we eventually batted, I got a poor decision from Venkat and I just didn't think it was worth it any more. At that stage, before I revealed my true feelings to the world, I was seriously considering packing the game up altogether and I was feeling very low throughout that match. I normally loved Edgbaston and I have so many happy memories of the place, but I hated every second of the first Test. I felt the world was against me. I didn't read many papers that week but I did see the cheap shot from Peter Hayter in the *Mail on Sunday*, making fun of my momentary lapse in not remembering Graeme Smith's first name the week before when I went out of my way to give the Sunday newspaper journalists an interview.

I didn't know whether to stick or twist. I didn't know whether to captain the side in my own way or in the way that Vaughan did it, the way I now perceived, rightly or wrongly, the boys wanted me to do it. I knew they had been shown a different way by Michael and they liked that way, and it became clear to me I had taken the side as far as I could. I gave them passion and was very keen on character, but they were ready for the next step now. Vaughan and I were totally different in our approaches and I was sure it was now a question of 'when' and not 'if' I was going to resign from the job altogether.

I decided not to speak to anyone I was close to about my true feelings because I didn't want anyone to talk me out of doing what I thought was right for England. But when I woke up on the Monday morning, the last day of the Test, I had made up my mind to resign after the second Test at Lord's. Get the back-to-back matches out of the way, I thought, and then give Vaughan a bit of time to get ready to take over the job.

But then, as I prepared to leave the old Swallow Hotel in Birmingham for the final day of the match, I picked up a copy of *The Times* at reception. After the Hayter article I had decided not to look at any more papers, but I thought to myself that Christopher Martin-Jenkins was a safe bet to read, that he wouldn't be too hard on me, and that he would give a considered view of my and England's situation.

Journalists have a massive role to play in British sport; their words can have a huge impact on players and hence on the game. Players tend to read everything written about them and, even though when I was England captain I tried to read the papers only after a good day (to help build confidence), after bad days someone would inevitably call and say, 'Have you seen what So-and-so has written about you?' You would then have to read the piece and for a while it could really hurt you, lowering any player's confidence. The only proper options are either not to read it at all or to read it, then put it in your bag and use it later on to prove the writer wrong. But on this occasion I was so mentally low I didn't have the energy to prove anyone wrong any longer.

Even CM-J said that the pressure was well and truly building on me and that something had to give, and I thought, 'Bloody hell. If CM-J is saying that, it must be what people are thinking.' You only want to be captain if the people want you to be. I'd had comparisons with Mike Brearley as a captain, which meant a lot because it meant people believed I was doing a good job; but once that was lost, I wondered what I was carrying on for, especially as there now seemed to be such a valid alternative.

I could have held out for another five days and done the job at Lord's but I never ever wanted to captain England when my heart wasn't in it, especially at the home of cricket, and I felt that if I handed over to Mick now, it might even be to his advantage because the pressure would be off him in his first game and he wouldn't have time to worry about what lay ahead.

As I got in my car to drive to Edgbaston, I was at the end of the road. I rang David Graveney and asked him where he was. The chairman of selectors said he was at home in Bristol, so I asked him if he could come to the ground that day because I felt this was going to be it. I was going to retire from the whole game that evening. My mind was now made up. I was on the edge, physically and mentally. I couldn't bear to ring Karen or my dad, or talk to Duncan Fletcher. It was just something I had to do on my own.

As I led the team out, I listened very carefully to the announcer saying 'Captaining England, Nasser Hussain,' because I knew it was going to be the last time and I wanted to savour it. It was an on–off sort of day and an inevitable draw. Mark Butcher had a migraine so I had to go in at three in our second innings, which made it harder for me to tell everyone what I wanted to do. During one of the rain delays Duncan asked what this rubbish about me resigning was all about and that we had to have a chat; but for once in my life I had to avoid having a chat with Duncan Fletcher. I knew he would talk me out of it and I didn't want that to happen. Then I bumped into Alec Stewart in a back room at Edgbaston and he asked me what was the matter. I said, 'I've gone, Al. This is the end.' He said, 'I know how you feel, but don't pack it all in. Have a rest, take time off and see how you feel.' It was good of him and a big factor in my not going the whole hog and retiring from all cricket there and then, which I had intended to do.

Michael Vaughan was the only other player to be given any indication of what I was going to do. I made sure I had a quick word with Mick to run it by him and ask him if he felt the captaincy would affect his batting, because the last thing England needed was to lose his runs. He was a colossus with the bat at this time. He said he felt he would be fine and that it wouldn't affect him.

So, at the end of play, I sat with Duncan and Grav and asked Andrew Walpole, the media manager, to sort something out with the press. I looked at Fletch and he said, 'I can't help you with this one. There are one or two decisions in life that you either live to regret or which are right for you. This is one of those decisions a man has to make. Whatever you decide, we still need you as a player.'

Grav said much the same and I sat there for two minutes with my head in my hands. I knew it wasn't an ideal time to go, with just two days before the next Test, but in my mental state I didn't want to have to go through a Test in charge again. I couldn't. The walls were closing in. I told Fletch and Grav that I couldn't lead a team at Lord's in this state and then I went through and told the press my decision. It all happened so quickly that I wasn't able to sit down with the team and explain fully why I was doing this, which I regret, and I wasn't able to thank Duncan and the backroom staff properly for all their support. Karen and my dad and brothers were a little shocked, and upset, to learn the news without me telling them about it first, but I knew that they would urge me to sleep on it and I would end up going through it all again at Lord's.

Karen, though, had seen how much the stress had taken out of me over the previous year and she understood what I was doing. Dad's reaction was more of a worry because I knew how much it meant to him for me to captain England. I didn't ring him for a few days. I didn't want to speak to him, didn't want him to say, 'What have you done that for?' In the end I got my brother Mel to ring him first to test the water before I plucked up courage to speak to Dad, but he was fine. All he has ever wanted, really, is for me to be happy. The bottom line was that I didn't want to spoil what I had achieved as a captain by going on too long. It was so special to me and I was very proud of what I had achieved.

I was reassured by getting some good press after I stepped down, and one piece in particular, written by Simon Barnes in *The Times*, I will always cherish, and I can now say that it wasn't the press who got to me in the end, it was me. I couldn't give any more, and I couldn't fault myself for that. I knew I had made the right decision – but I knew Lord's was going to be a very difficult week, not least because I was still questioning whether I wanted to play the game at all. And, of course, it was a very difficult Test at times.

My mind wasn't right, I still hadn't spoken to my dad, and I found myself fielding at cover point now I wasn't captain, after we had tumbled to 173 all out in our first innings. Then Graeme Smith, with a huge double century at Edgbaston behind him, hit it straight to me on 8 and I dropped it. It proved to me beyond doubt that if you didn't respect the game of cricket and give it your full and utter attention, it will kill you. In some ways this helped me because it told me I had to buck up if I was to carry on, but in another way it was an absolute nightmare. He went on to make 259 and I had to live every moment of it.

I wasn't the only player with weighty things on his mind at Lord's. Darren Gough had been rushed back into the Test side at Edgbaston, but he had struggled and was now, like me, contemplating retirement. Goughy, who I had been through so much with, was asking me throughout the Test what I was doing and I told him this could well be my last game. I felt burnt out. He was saying the same to me and confessing that he couldn't bowl long spells any more with the knee injury that had seemed minor in New Zealand a year earlier.

Perversely, I felt relaxed the night before I was to bat in our second innings. Normally, before a batting day I would be in bed early, fretting about the day ahead, but because I felt I was a spent force I ended up having to go to dinner with Karen, Simon Hughes, Athers and a couple of other close friends. Very rare for me to socialize like this during a match, and I enjoyed being with people from a different walk of life but who still loved their cricket, and it chilled me to such an extent that I batted well and scored 61 the next day. But that and a great century from Andrew Flintoff were not enough to stop us going down by an innings.

My mindset had clearly been noticed by the new England captain. So, within a week of taking over, Michael Vaughan sat me down at the end of the game and read me the Riot Act. It didn't bother me that Vaughan had started to question my commitment; it was something I was doing myself. You have to remember, this was the time when I was probably the most tired mentally that I have been in my whole career, and what I needed was for someone to give me a wake-up call, a quick slap across the face: 'Are you with us or are you not?' He said he wanted me in his side but that I had to turn up for the next match at Trent Bridge fully focused, and that I couldn't play for England if I was going to be as distracted as I had been at Lord's. Vaughany said, 'I've heard that you and Gough want to retire, and you either want to play for England or you don't.' Darren did indeed decide that that was to be his last Test, but I decided to go away and think about my future. I needed that kick up the backside which was provided by Vaughan and my dropped catch, and I spent a lot of time on my own, thinking about what came next.

My brother Abbas told me not to be stupid and to carry on,

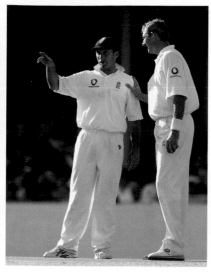

61. Trying to get the best out of Andrew Caddick was one of my biggest challenges as England captain.

62. The scene is Harare, 13 February 2003, and a World Cup cricket match is meant to be taking place. Instead, me and England are consigned to World Cup history.

63. With Tim Lamb. We never saw eye to eye – especially over Zimbabwe.

64. Leaving the Cullinan Hotel in Cape Town at the height of the Zimbabwe crisis. This was the venue for our dramatic meetings with Malcolm Speed and others.

ICC Cricket World Cup
SOUTH AFRICA 2003

MEDIA RELEASE

Quick news flash from East London:

Nasser Hussain dropped a bombshell at a lunch-time press conference here today with the news he would stand down as England cricket captain after the World Cup because he was so upset by the way the Zimbabwe situation had been handled by what he termed "the authorities".

He named the ICC as one of the culprits and, though he did not name them specifically, there was a very thinly-veiled reference to the ECB. "I'm very annoyed with the authorities." he said.

He was speaking in the wake of the ECB statement that the board would not appeal against the ICC rejection of the team's application to reschedule their game in Zimbabwe.

"Politics have shattered the dreams of some of my team members." he said. "members who have worked very hard to be in this tournament."

He added the press conference was the last time he would speak on the subject. Now he proposed to throw himself headlong into cricket. "I'm sick and tired of being messed around by the authorities."

ENDS

65. The statement issued on my resignation as England one-day captain. The World Cup debacle over Zimbabwe had been the final straw.

66. Leaving the field with two of England's next generation of players, James Anderson and Robert Key.

67. James Anderson was the hardest player to captain during my time in charge, I found.

68. Resigning as England captain at Edgbaston. So bad had the stress become that I believe I was actually experiencing symptoms of depression.

69. My nephew Reece, who is being given every encouragement to follow in my footsteps by his dad Mel.

70. Showing Reece how it should be done at home.

71. Leaving a disciplinary meeting after being accused of calling Muttiah Muralitharan a chucker.

72. Showing that the old boy can still do it: hitting a 6 in my last game for Essex at Cardiff.

73. A century for Essex against Glamorgan in Cardiff in 2004. I didn't know it at the time, but this was to be my last appearance for the county I have served for 17 years.

74. Catching Craig McMillan of New Zealand at short leg during my last Test.

75. Hitting out during my last innings, my hundred for England against New Zealand at Lord's.

76. Joy at completing a hundred against New Zealand at Lord's in my last appearance as a player.

77. The moment of victory, with a hundred under my belt at Lord's. Well, there are worse ways to go out, aren't there?

78. Walking off with my old mate Graham Thorpe after victory had been secured one shot later. It was the perfect way to leave the stage.

79. Ian Botham has at times been an outspoken critic of me. Now he is my
colleague in the Sky commentary box. Should be interesting!

80. Wherever we travel on a foreign field there are always thousands of England
supporters present. They never cease to amaze me. They are fantastic – the most
important people in the game.

and it helped that I was still scoring runs for Essex. Alex Wharf of Glamorgan chirped me about not being England captain any more, and that spurred me on to score a big century in a National League match and persuade me to give it a go at Trent Bridge, making sure I was totally focused. I also wanted to prove to the new England captain that I was still committed to my country and could still play at this level.

In many ways it was perfect for me. The wicket was poor and I went to the wicket with us in a bit of trouble. I remembered the ovation I had received at Lord's when I went out to bat and I used that as motivation for believing the people of England still wanted me. Emotion and adrenalin kicked in and I scored one of the most significant hundreds of my Test career. I got a great reception – Jacques Kallis had to abort his run-up before bowling the following ball because the applause was still ringing out – and I felt content that I hadn't gone out on a low, particularly as we won the match. I decided to behave as Atherton and Stewart had as ex-captains in the team with me in charge, offering advice if it was sought and keeping myself to myself so as not to undermine the new regime.

I couldn't help but reflect on the new captain's progress. It struck me that, in his early matches at least, Vaughan had a tendency to captain by committee, which was certainly different from me, but at the same time he clearly had his own ideas and was very keen on an enhanced fitness regime and overt displays of team spirit. For my taste there were a few too many huddles and demands that everybody must always be on the balcony showing their support for those in the middle. I thought it was a bit too much and that people cared about the team without having to see them clapping on the balcony for the benefit of the cameras. But that was Vaughan's way, and that was fair enough. And he might be right.

At Headingley my popadom fingers became popadom toes as I was hit on the boot and had my toe broken before falling stupidly to Jacques Rudolph. The press do love a story, however, and word got around that I had broken my toe kicking a door in the dressing room. Absolute nonsense. I later did an interview for Radio 5 Live and Jonny Saunders said, 'I hear you have broken a toe kicking a door.' For once in my life I almost aborted an interview before it had really started and I told him to stick to the truth if we were going to do this interview. We lost, and I was a serious doubt for the final match of the series with my broken toe.

If it had been left up to me, I would probably have played at the Oval with extra padding on my foot, but every fitness issue these days has to go to Peter Gregory and he rightly said that I shouldn't play because another blow on the same toe might put me out for the winter. Duncan asked me who I felt should play in my place and, even though a few younger batsmen had been tried that summer, I had no doubt who I thought it should be. I said, 'You've got to look to class, and that means only one man – Graham Thorpe.' I had wanted Thorpey in the side at the start of the summer, irrespective of whether he had pulled out of the previous winter's Ashes tour, and I was delighted that the selectors agreed with me and picked him to play on his home ground.

I went to stay with Abbas at his home in Brussels during the Test in an attempt to get away from it all, but I ended up listening to *Test Match Special* online, so that didn't work; and I was chuffed to bits when Thorpe scored a hundred and England pulled off an amazing victory to square the series. I knew the pressure Graham was under. He had hit rock bottom and to come back like that, show the willpower he possessed and play a fantastic innings, was proof of the strength of character the man has. Thorpey later told me he was tempted to retire there and then after that game, having proved to everyone he could still do it, in a similar manner to the way I bowed out at Lord's a year later. Luckily, he didn't and, at the time of writing, he is still going strong for England. I hope the little genius has a bit more left in the tank.

It had been quite a summer. It had been the end of me as England captain and almost the end of me as a player. I had battled back and kept going when my instinct had been to call it a day, but now I was keen to play on for a bit longer. Yet word reached me that the presence of my big mate Thorpey back in the fold might yet have serious repercussions for me. More interesting times lay ahead.

37

I had advocated the return of Graham Thorpe to the England side and I was delighted he had done so well, but now the whispers started. Occasionally in English cricket certain snippets of information which do the rounds appear well informed but nobody is totally sure where they come from. Now, it was being said around the England camp and in the press that Michael Vaughan did not want me and Thorpe in the same side.

The suspicion was that the leak had come from either David Graveney or the England captain himself, but now I felt I had done enough to tour and I wanted to tour. I had come through the spell of depression that dogged my last days as England captain, had scored a century in difficult circumstances at Trent Bridge and now felt that I had a bit of cricket left in me at the highest level. But did Vaughan really think that the two old campaigners would have a detrimental effect on his young side?

So concerned was I at this rumour that I buttonholed Ashley Giles at the England team's end-of-season dinner to ask him if he knew what his close friend Vaughan was thinking. I had had a few rum and Cokes and my tongue was sufficiently loosened for me to say to Ash, 'What's your mate thinking?' Giles told me that Mick was indeed concerned about the presence of an ex-captain and a senior pro in the same dressing room and had spoken to some business people about the psychology of the situation and how they would deal with it.

Ashley suggested that I have a word with Michael, but I didn't. I'd never had to beg for my place in my life and I certainly wasn't going to start now. I decided to wait and see what happened. Then I received a call from Graveney asking if I was still committed to the England cause. I was offended, but I guess I could see why the chairman of selectors had to ask the question, because all summer I myself had been questioning whether I wanted to carry on. I reassured Grav that I was very much committed (which was the truth), and I was duly handed a year's central contract, even though I knew my place was now an issue and that I had probably benefited in selection from Duncan Fletcher's support. Thorpey, meanwhile, was selected for the winter tours, so if Vaughan or any of the other selectors did genuinely have any doubts, they must have put them to the back of their mind.

So I was now due to spend my winter in Bangladesh, Sri Lanka and the West Indies, and deep down I knew that I would be finishing my England touring days in the Caribbean, where it had all begun some fourteen years earlier. I guess there was a nice symmetry in that.

Bangladesh was hard work. The weather was bad when we got there and the facilities were poor. I played OK in the two Test matches, which disappointingly were played in front of small crowds, finding my form in the second but also running Vaughany out – which wasn't the best thing for me to do in my new role as ex-captain and senior pro. I had earlier volunteered to go under the helmet at short leg in the field because I thought it was important to keep out of the way and let Vaughan captain the side the way he wanted to, but also because I could feel my body going and I thought I was a fraction of a second slower in the field than in my youth, when I had been one of the better fielders around.

Steve Harmison had a good game in the first Test but then had to come home injured – and little did we know at that time that his injury was the catalyst for him becoming one of the best bowlers in the world. Indeed, his setback was treated with a small degree of negativity in and around our camp. Harmy had suffered from homesickness earlier in his career and things like that stick, so when he had to go home from a country where touring life is difficult some people immediately thought he had made the injury up.

Harmison failed to recover in time for our tour of Sri Lanka and it was a time when I thought the team should have backed him up more. It's all very well having loads of huddles and making sure everyone is always out on the balcony during games, but the real test of a team and its team spirit is when one of your own needs your support. In Harmy's case there were some people going round in Sri Lanka saying that if he wasn't fit for that tour then he shouldn't be allowed to tour the West Indies later on in the winter, but I didn't buy that at all.

My view was that we are all human and if someone has an injury or any perceived weakness, then we just have to deal with that if the guy is worth having around the team. And Steve Harmison certainly was worth having around, as we knew ever since 2000 when we tried to involve him in the England scene for the first time. The guy had pace and bounce, attributes that were very well worth encouraging, even when he had some rough edges or problems with his run-up, which afflicted him in Perth in 2002.

What a lot of people didn't know at the time was that Harmy had worked hard on his fitness with his beloved Newcastle United while he was unable to be with us, and that proved a real turning point for him. Not only did it make him stronger physically but I think it dawned on him how hard even the most successful sportsmen (like his hero, Alan Shearer) had to work to reach and then, crucially, remain at the top of their profession.

I think it says everything for the professionalism of football in our country, and the lack of it which you sometimes find in county cricket, that it took three months with Newcastle to finally enable Steve Harmison to fulfil his potential, when Durham had had him under their wing for years. I really think it was fifty–fifty whether Harmison was picked for the Caribbean – but luckily he was and, at the time of writing, he has never looked back. I'm delighted for him. He is a top lad and I like to think I played a part in helping him develop from the raw fast bowler with all the potential in the world to the finished product England saw in 2004.

I was determined to work really hard in preparing for Sri Lanka. I spent day after day on the bowling machines at my dad's cricket school and at Chelmsford with Terry Charrington, one of my favourite coaches. I was trying to simulate the bowling of Chaminda Vaas, who I considered a key performer for Sri Lanka. I arrived there, I felt, in good nick and with great memories of our success in 2001. I managed to get only one knock ahead of the first Test and that saw me dismissed in freakish fashion for 0, so I arrived in Galle needing to spend some time in the middle. Unfortunately that wasn't going to happen.

A few of the guys had suffered from a really bad stomach bug while we were in Bangladesh, even the indestructible Duncan Fletcher had to miss nets once, and the day before the Test I started to feel really nauseous and dizzy and I was sweating buckets. By the morning of the game I was feeling really rough, so I thought I had better be professional and inform Vaughan and Fletcher. I told them I wanted to play but that I thought I had a touch of flu and Duncan immediately said, 'You won't be able to play with that if it's what I had. It really knocks you out.' Vaughan agreed, so I trudged upstairs in the dressing-room area until I thought to myself, 'I can't miss a Test because I don't feel well,' so I ran back downstairs and pleaded with Fletch to let me play. He said it was too late because Paul Collingwood had already been told he was playing – and, to be fair, this was absolutely right because I went back to the hotel and could barely move for three days. I just had no energy and couldn't even watch the cricket on TV.

I hated missing a Test through illness, but I was delighted when the boys earned a draw and we moved on to Kandy, where my family arrived for a holiday, and I was looking forward to putting Galle behind me. Yet things were hardly going to improve. This time my whole family, including my two young boys, fell ill with what was later diagnosed as salmonella poisoning, and I got out twice to Vaas despite all the practice I had put in at home! It was turning into a miserable tour.

There was, however, still the third Test in Colombo to go, and I turned up for our pre-Test management meeting in a better frame of mind as I now felt fully fit and my family were over the worst of their illness and were safely on their way home. Then I received the shock of my life. We were sitting there in the meeting and Marcus Trescothick, my right-hand man when I was captain, was asked who he would have in the team for the deciding match. He turned to me and said, 'I would leave Nasser out. Colly has come in and done well and Nass just doesn't look as though he's in any sort of form out here.'

I was taken aback. He was one of my boys. It hit me hard for a while, but the more I thought about it the more I thought, 'Good on him.' After I had recovered from my initial disappointment, I was really pleased that Marcus had had the courage of his convictions to say what he thought to my face rather than behind my back. He must have been a little concerned at my reaction, because later that day he came up to me and asked if I had a problem with what he had said, but I told Marcus that I respected him even more after that.

Paul Collingwood probably should have played ahead of me, because I was having a terrible time on that tour for all sorts of reasons, but I am never going to turn round to an England captain and say I don't want to play, so I said I disagreed with Tres and that I was fit and ready to play. I got the nod ahead of Colly but again fell to Vaas and, in the second innings, to Muttiah Muralitharan.

This wasn't my only brush with Murali on that tour. I had watched earlier how matey some of our players were with

Murali, particularly Freddie Flintoff, and I became concerned that this was having an adverse effect on the side. I even heard that Freddie had lent him a bat, only for Murali to respond by scoring far more runs against us than he had any right to!

Also, it was blatantly obvious to me that whatever anyone thought of Murali's bowling, he was definitely chucking his new ball, 'the doosra', which was turning away from the right-hander like a leg break. He was taking a lot more wickets against us than he did in 2001, but that was basically because, armed with his new delivery, he could bowl like both Murali and Shane Warne in one over. It was causing us all sorts of problems. So as I sat there, earlier in the tour, forced to endure his, it seemed to me, obvious cheating against us, I decided we didn't have to be matey with him. I decided to let him know he was in a battle.

As he came out to bat in Kandy we were in a huddle and, as we dispersed, I said, 'Let's get this fucking chucker out.' I didn't really do it because of his bowling, though. It was mainly because he was getting a few runs and I wanted him to feel he was in a hostile environment, not a friendly one. I didn't point at him or say it directly to his face. I was saying it to my teammates – but, of course, within his hearing. Things like that have happened countless times, like all the occasions when Steve Waugh or Shane Warne has said to me, 'Let's get dodgy technique out,' or 'Let's get Mr Popular out.' It is the game. But what happened next will always sour Murali's reputation in my eyes. Because he acted like a child, like someone who throughout his whole career had been given everything he ever wanted. He went straight up to the umpire and started whingeing and moaning, saying, 'Did you hear what he called me?' It was like being in a school playground.

Play was held up for a couple of minutes, and then at tea the match referee, Clive Lloyd, said that Sri Lanka had made an official complaint against me, which I couldn't believe. If I put in a complaint every time Waugh or Warne or Glenn McGrath chirped me, we would be at the ground until 9 o'clock every night. I would never dream of running to teacher.

To me it said everything about the man's character, as did his later refusal to tour Australia, where he has been called for chucking. The ICC have said that his new delivery is a chuck, but he won't accept that and Murali's attitude is like 'No, it's not, it's my ball and I'm not coming out to play in Australia. They don't like me there.' I was disappointed it had come to this.

So I was summoned to a disciplinary meeting and there seemed the very real possibility that I would be the first England player to be suspended for a Test match. One theory was that Sri Lanka were trying to get me banned from the third Test in Colombo – but, the way I was playing, I could hardly see why. I took Duncan in with me to face Clive Lloyd, and Murali was in there with a cast of thousands of supporters. Duncan immediately went on the offensive and said, 'Is this how the game is going to be played from now on? Every time someone says anything on the field, we are all going to be here in disciplinary meetings?'

It immediately got Sri Lanka on the back foot and I asked Clive to show me the evidence of what I had done wrong, saying to him, 'Let me see it because if there isn't any audio proof of me sledging him, then my legal representative will be in touch.' He played the video and there was absolutely nothing on it that incriminated me, apart from Murali looking startled. I wasn't even in camera shot.

Clive said to me, 'Did you say anything to Muralitharan?' I said, 'Yes, as we walked past I told my teammates to get this fucking chuker out.' So Clive said, 'You did say something,' and I replied, 'Yes, to my teammates. Am I not allowed to say to them "Let's get this bloke out"? Am I not allowed to swear to my teammates? Am I not allowed to say to my teammates that this bloke is a chucker?' Clive was scratching his head a bit by now; and all the time Duncan sat there, staring at Murali, until he was forced to look away. And that really was it. There was a warning but no fine or suspension, and we went back out the next day to find their wicketkeeper Kumar Sangakkara sledging everyone all day as usual. He was in my ear all the time, about me losing the captaincy, that I was one innings away from retirement, that I had dropped Graeme Smith and he had gone on to a double hundred. I didn't complain to the umpires. I just got on with it.

The funny thing is, I have often defended Murali when the subject of his action has come up. Even earlier in that tour, we had had a heated debate, with me saying he was good for cricket, and others – notably our spinners – saying he wasn't. I just think that if the ICC are happy that his bowling is legal, then we all have to accept that and not only let him carry on bowling that way but try to get our own kids bowling like him. We desperately need a mystery spinner in the England team, yet we are still coaching orthodox spin which, I'm afraid, has died in Test cricket on present wickets. If he is legal, then I would like to see all those little kids who run around my dad's cricket school in Ilford bowling or chucking it exactly like him because that's what you see in the nets or the streets of Sri Lanka.

My only concern is that the best spinner I have ever faced is Shane Warne and his action is 100 per cent legal. So when his stats are compared to Murali's in twenty or thirty years' time, the Sri Lankan will almost certainly have the better figures and that will do Shane a disservice because it is he who should really be the leading wicket-taker in Test history. Yes, Murali is good for cricket, but is he a better bowler than Shane Warne? I don't think so.

Sri Lanka should have beaten us in that series 2–0 or 3–0 but the main reason they didn't do that was because of their captain, who I never respected. I thought Hashan Tillekeratne truly was a terrible captain. His tactics seemed to be all over the place, but his side won 1–0 despite him. For me it was one of my most disappointing tours and I found myself on trial again before the squad was finalized for the West Indies leg of the winter touring programme. It seems that once you hit thirty-five years of age you only have to have a couple of bad Tests and you are being questioned again, and I got what was by now my usual phone call from David Graveney, asking if I was committed and saying that there was a feeling among the selectors that we needed to go with youth.

I interpreted this (rightly or wrongly) that Rod Marsh, by now an England selector, was pushing his academy boys and Duncan Fletcher would be backing me up because he wanted a blend of youth and experience in the Caribbean. Grav was probably stuck in the middle, and I am not sure what Geoff Miller, the other selector, would have been thinking. All I can say about 'Dusty' Miller is that I found him an exceptional selector during my time as captain. He would be very honest and trustworthy and would tell you what he thought.

I appreciated the way Miller went about things and I felt he was a very good addition to the panel. For instance, after I had resigned as one-day captain, he told me they would have replaced me if I hadn't jumped first, and I admired the straightforward way he would deal with bad news. It was like, 'We've got a difficult job to do but we just have to do it, make hard decisions and be straight with people.' Together with Duncan that was a good mix.

It's harder to provide a verdict on David Graveney. The first thing you have to say is that he cares deeply about the England cricket team and throws his heart and soul into the job. He has been a constant presence as chairman while I've been captain and I admired the way Grav kept things together. He is a good bloke, but he does have failings as a chairman which lead to problems every now and again. As I have touched on before, at times I feel Grav has too often sat on the fence. I think he can be a little indiscreet and that he worries too much about what people think of him. The good outweighs the bad in

David Graveney, but we have had some real ding-dongs over the years and he has left me exasperated on more than one occasion.

When Rod Marsh joined the panel at the start of 2003, I was asked if him replacing the captain as a selector was a problem, and I had no difficulty with it at all. All I asked was that I should have an input as captain, especially if they were thinking of jettisoning a senior player. But I think it has become a problem since then, because I believe Marsh is a bit one-eyed towards players at the academy. There is more to selection than just pushing for your own boys, and in my time (as I have said) the best people with an eye for a good player have been the two Fletchers, Keith and Duncan. It's such a lottery, picking people from county cricket, that I accept that I am not a good judge of a player, and I don't know yet whether Marsh is. Take the Chris Read situation. When I first rang Rod up to congratulate him on becoming a selector, I asked him who he particularly rated and he told me that Chris Read was one of the best wicketkeeper-batsmen in the world. I didn't have the heart to stop him and mention names like Gilchrist, Stewart and Boucher.

The wicketkeeping issue came to a head in the West Indies when Duncan and Michael Vaughan decided to pick Geraint Jones ahead of Read for the final Test in Antigua, and Marsh became upset that the selectors at home hadn't been told. That was an accident waiting to happen, but I believe it was absolutely right to go with Jones because of his clearly superior batting ability. I had, after all, excitedly rung Fletcher and Graveney a year earlier when I saw the Kent man making big runs against Essex.

In my case, I just had a hunch that Marsh wanted to see the back of me and I was quite angry when Grav rang me to say I was going to the West Indies but that it had been a fifty–fifty call. My form had been pretty impressive for nearly three years, but a small blip in Sri Lanka seemed to put me on trial again.

I had some strong words with Grav and also later with Geoff Miller, but I knew I was now very much in the Last Chance Saloon as a Test batsman.

Yet I like to think that Graham Thorpe, Mark Butcher and I proved in the West Indies that you do need experience in any side, that you can't jettison people and replace them with unproven youngsters just for the sake of having a young side. The trick is to attain the right balance and also to bring a young player into a successful side. That is a luxury that hasn't been afforded to many people in my era. I batted better than anybody in our warm-up games in the West Indies and I wanted to repay the people like Duncan who had stuck with me.

There was one incident that I didn't enjoy. When we were playing in our final warm-up game, a ball went down towards fine leg when we were in the field and I pointed lazily at Matthew Hoggard to field it. Hoggy, being the demonstrative type, started waving his arms around, reminding me that we had a policy of trying to protect the bowlers in the field as much as we could and that I should have run from short leg to get it. I told him to fuck off, that we only needed two more wickets and as soon as he and his bowler mates got them, we could all be off the field and putting our feet up. Next ball, Harmison took a wicket and as we were in a huddle my discussion with Hoggard as to who should have fielded that ball was in full flow. Then Vaughan came up, told me to shut up and said that I should have got the ball. It was a weird situation for me. I was back in the ranks and the England captain was having a go at me. I thought back to the time in Perth when I was tempted to have a go at Alec Stewart for not protecting our tail, but I didn't want to criticize an ex-captain in front of the boys. I wondered whether I should be my old rebellious self and tell him to piss off or realize that he was now the England captain and that I should accept it. I realized that Mick was only doing to me what I had done to other people, but I was also hurt because I couldn't imagine me doing anything similar to Stewart or Atherton. I was a bit quiet after that, and later Duncan asked Graham Thorpe if we had a problem because I seemed to be upset. Thorpey, knowing me so well, told Duncan to leave me alone, let me have my sulk and that I would be fine – which, of course, I was next day. I caught up with Mick on the square and said, 'Good on you, skip. Well done for giving me a bollocking. I was out of order.' It showed to me that I had grown up because I knew if I had fallen out with Vaughan it could have been hugely detrimental to the team.

It was great to be back in the Caribbean. I knew that the West Indies had a couple of really quick bowlers in Fidel Edwards and Tino Best and I was looking forward to them getting my ticker going and providing me with the sort of challenge I needed at this advanced stage of my career. Tino. What a character he is! He started by coming round to each of the England players at a drinks reception before the series and introducing himself to us. He was so small that I thought my old mate Brian Lara was having a laugh with us by sending some nutter round to pretend he was Tino, before unleashing some seven-foot paceman on us on the first morning at Sabina Park. But it really was him.

Then Tino told me I was his hero. Bemused, I asked why. He explained that I had played against his uncle, Carlisle Best, on my first West Indies tour in 1990 and that he had been a young kid, playing cricket on the outfield with Desmond Haynes's son. Apparently I had applauded when the young Tino played a good shot at the Kensington Oval and encouraged him, but I have no recollection of that. 'If I am your hero,' I said to Tino, 'I hope you won't be bowling anything short at me.' Fat chance.

The bowling at times in that series was as quick as anything I had faced, certainly since my youth when I came up against the likes of Malcolm Marshall and Patrick Patterson. I found it really stimulating, being hit, being in a real battle. We were in trouble in both Jamaica and Trinidad when I joined Butcher at the crease, and both times we put on crucial stands to help England to victory.

Harmison's spell of 7 for 12 at Sabina Park as we bowled the West Indies out for 47 was the stuff of dreams and proof, if any were needed, that it would have been madness to have left him at home for missing the second Test in Bangladesh and the Sri Lankan tour through injury. Our third win on the trot in Barbados, mainly due to an amazing Thorpe hundred and a Hoggard hat-trick, gave us the series, and not even a draw which featured Lara breaking the world record again in scoring 400 in Antigua could take the gloss off the tour. What an effort that was. Almost ten years to the day since I had stood there, as a substitute fielder, seeing Brian stack up 375 in Antigua, here we were again, with him doing the same thing again. It made me smile.

The only time I really felt my age in the Caribbean was off the field when it became clear to me that things had changed. The team were moving on. There was a major concentration on fitness that was alien to me. Hardly anyone went out for a meal and a couple of glasses of wine. They were too busy training or stuck in their rooms with their PlayStations.

It was the buddy system which confirmed to me that I belonged to a different era. The idea was for people of similar ages and body shapes to be full-time buddies on tour, and Thorpe was the obvious partner for me. Trouble was, you were accountable for your buddy's behaviour and this was the only time I understood what Mike Gatting had meant when he asked, back in selection in 1999, what Graham Thorpe brought to the party. Fact was, he was always ten minutes late for the party. I love Graham to bits and he is one of the great players of my time, but it was incredible how forgetful he was and how he was late for everything. Ask him to shave or wear the right gear, and he won't do it, he is just so anti-Establishment. It would really annoy Duncan, even though he had a huge respect for Graham as a batsman and, I think, saw himself as a similar sort of batsman. If Duncan Fletcher played in the modern era, I'm sure he would like to be Graham Thorpe, but that respect was tested at times by Thorpey's insistence on paying lip service to punctuality. I knew all this of course because I had toured with Thorpey for years, but the trouble now was that I kept on being fined because my buddy was late or wearing the wrong clothes! So that was the real reason why I retired in 2004: I couldn't afford to carry on being Graham Thorpe's buddy.

38

Throughout my later years taking part in international cricket, my time as England captain and beyond, county cricket – and Essex in particular – became a smaller part of my life. The advent of central contracts and the work done by Richard Bevan and the PCA was a tremendous step forward for English cricket, but the inevitable consequence of that was that players would have fewer and fewer ties with their counties. And rightly so.

While there are a lot of people in our game who are still not entirely happy about this and the fact that England players are, first and foremost, just that: England players first and county players second, it is a development that has played a huge part in the progress of the England team. The simple fact is that England players will move further and further away from their counties, and that is both inevitable and right.

But this is not to say that my last few years with Essex didn't throw up more than their fair share of incident and drama, and whenever I was involved with the only county I played for since I was eight years old there was always something going on. The first thing to say is that when I look back on my time with Essex I am hugely positive about the club and what they did for me. They have been a successful, well-run family club with a lot going for them. They have produced more than their fair share of England players – which is surely the whole point. I do believe, however, that they have taken their eye off the ball in recent years and they still employ the methods and personnel that brought them such success in the 1980s and early '90s. The fact is, the game has moved on, and Essex need to move on with it.

I only spent the one season as captain of my home county in the end, 1999, but even that ended up being a part-time thing because I was made England captain the same year. After that, when I had recommended Ronnie Irani for the job and he had become Essex captain, I became club captain but that, really, was more of an honorary thing. It didn't, in practice, mean much at all.

The first year after Ronnie took charge, 2000, went well for Essex. They were promoted into Division One of the championship, with Ronnie at the forefront of things and Stuart Law once again proving he was one of the best overseas players in the country, if not *the* best. The following year was worse, much worse. I had plenty on my plate with England, so I was only a peripheral figure in all the chaos, but I got dragged into it often enough and usually ended up trying to sort out some disaster or other when I could have done without the aggravation.

The reason I recommended Ronnie as captain in the first place was that I thought he would lead by example. He was never going to be a great tactician, I felt he didn't have a great understanding of the game, he was just Ronnie Irani. He gave his all. He was a fighter. I respected him. And he lived up to that in 2000, leading by example and playing a big part in the county's success.

But the problems began when he started to think he was something he wasn't. He spoke a lot with Frank Dick, the old athletics coach and psychologist. Ronnie would come into the dressing room and say things like, 'Snowdrops will fall in your hand and unless you grasp them they will melt away.' Other times he would quote Alex Ferguson. It could be quite humorous. But you could see Stuey Law, this straightforward Queenslander with two Sheffield Shields as captain to his name, sitting there, thinking, 'What the fuck's he going on about?' When Essex were doing well, it was funny. When the wheels started to fall off, it was anything but.

They started to have a bad season in 2001 and the camp became split. Stuey was still an incredible player, right up there with people like Allan Border, Mark Waugh, Ken McEwen and Salim Malik as the best to have played for Essex, but he was always abrasive and that was to contribute to the anarchy that descended on what used to be the happiest dressing room in English cricket. Instead of involving him tactically, and realizing that there were certain big characters in the dressing room whom you had to keep onside, Ronnie and the coach Keith Fletcher would do it their way, apparently ignoring Law and his views. They never got the best out of him.

Stuey, meanwhile, was far from blameless. An overseas player needs to score runs (and Law got them by the sackful), but he also needs to be an influence on the younger players, help with team spirit and help the club move in the right direction. It's fair to say that those weren't obvious strengths of his. So, when I went back, I just tried to keep my gob shut. When I did try to give Ronnie advice he usually wanted to do it his way and I became more and more aware of this huge split in the dressing room. The younger players and people like Paul Grayson were right behind Ronnie and Fletch because of their reputations and their standing in the game and because they wanted to be loyal to their captain. The other camp was dominated by Law and Paul Prichard, the captain before me.

Prich was a follower of people, not a leader, so he would be with Stuey; other members of their 'camp' included Ashley Cowan, Darren Robinson and Stephen Peters. And it was a disgrace that it had come to that. I can't exaggerate how bad it was. I would turn up, looking to switch off from the demands on me as England captain, but they would all be there, slagging each other off. There was no loyalty. For me, Keith Fletcher was my mentor and Ronnie was our captain and someone I had always believed in, so if I was going to be in any camp it was theirs, but the truth was I wasn't in anyone's camp because it was so wrong and was doing so much damage, and I always ended up trying to sort out the mess when I was with them.

I was stuck in the middle and I could see the rights and wrongs of both sides. I would always say to the young lads, 'Look, Ronnie is your captain and Fletch is your coach. Remember who you're dealing with here. Don't bite off the hand that feeds you. It's all very well Stuey Law having a moan, but he's going out there getting hundreds every day. Maybe you lot can moan about your captain and coach when you're performing to that level.'

At this time I was probably the most popular member of the Essex dressing room because half of them were anti-Irani and Fletcher and the other half anti-Law and Prichard, so I was the only one everyone got on with! It was like, 'Oh good. Nasser's back from the Test. We can take the piss out of him. He's just lost to Australia again.' I somehow seemed to lighten the mood without doing anything.

Then Darren Gough wrote his autobiography. Not, on the face of it, a development which had much to do with the problems of Essex County Cricket Club. But Goughy wrote about the fateful game at Centurion a couple of years earlier when he had got drunk the night before the final day's play, thinking that it would be rained off, but it wasn't and he ended up scoring the winning runs. And Simon Hughes wanted to do an interview with me for the *Daily Telegraph* about captaincy and man-management, and he asked me what I thought about the Gough revelation that he had been drunk. I said, 'Look, I've played a lot of cricket, been brought up in the Essex culture, and you've got to know what you can and cannot do, what's best for your game and when to do it and when not to do it.' Then I decided to give Hughes an example. I said, 'If I'm captaining Robin Smith or Stuart Law or Paul Prichard, the last thing I would want is for them to go to bed early because I've seen how they play and I know their methods.

I've seen Law and Prichard have a couple of beers and go out and score hundreds the next day, and it works for them. Others, like Graham Gooch and Alec Stewart, go to bed early and are completely different. So each to their own, and as long as they're performing let them do it their way.' A perfectly normal interview and one that, I thought, summed up my views on the subject pretty well.

Then I was at a Test match and Prichard rang me up. Now Prich is a really nice bloke. I've always got on well with him. But he was quite irate. He said, 'Nass, what is this piece you've done. Me and Stuey need to speak to you about it.' I didn't know what he was on about. He went on to say that I'd done a piece which said he got pissed when he was playing cricket and that he was at a stage in his career when he was thinking about his future and it didn't reflect well on him to possible employers. I said, 'Hang on, Prich. Let me have a look at this piece and I'll speak to you.'

When I read it, I saw that Hughes had changed it. Instead of 'going out and having a couple of drinks', it now read 'people like Law and Prichard go and get pissed and can still score runs the next day'. Yosser Hughes, being Yosser, had wanted to make it more dynamic. Before I could get back to Prich, Stuey was on the phone, saying much the same thing: 'What's going on here, mate? Me and you had a mutual respect. Why are you slagging me off to the papers?' Luckily, I was at an awards dinner when he rang and standing not ten yards from me was Simon Hughes. So I put Simon on the phone and he said to Stuey, 'It's my fault. Nasser didn't mean anything. He was actually being complimentary and saying he had a great respect for you and Prich and doesn't want you to change.'

I thought that would be the end of the matter. I was wrong. When I next went back to Essex, full of the stresses and strains of another losing Ashes series, the players not in the Law–Prichard camp were saying to me, 'Oh, you should have seen it last week, Nass. They were slagging you off. Stuey and Prich were taking photocopies of the article round the dressing room, saying to the lads, "What are we going to do about Nasser?"'

I had had enough now. So I said to Fletch, who was running nets that day, 'Can I have a word with the boys?' I sat them down and went for it. I said, 'Look, you lot can sit here and you can have your rows with each other and you can have your county backbiting and bitching and you can avoid looking at yourselves and what you're bringing to this team. But don't fucking sit there while I'm away, playing for my country, taking a fucking photocopied article around the dressing room, taking what I'd said out of all proportion and using it in your stupid internal war.' Prich tried to interrupt me but I said, 'Sorry, Prich, you had your say bad-mouthing me when I was away last week. I've tried to stay out of this whole shemozzle. You lot want to drag me into it. My piece in the *Telegraph* was complimentary. If you can't see that, that's your problem. You do what you want now. I'm out of here.' And I left.

Stuey never really spoke to me much after that. My relationship with Prich recovered because he's not the sort of bloke to fall out with you for good, but I couldn't believe how a couple of innocent comments which were supposed to praise the way they did things could lead to so much trouble. I'm afraid it was typical of the Essex dressing room at that time. It was a shame, because after that I guess by definition I was in the pro-Ronnie camp and Stuey started to feel very isolated. My view was that we should have tried to find a solution to the differences. The bloke scored 2,000 runs a season. Let's keep him and work it out. But a regular comment from Ronnie at that time was 'Cut out the virus'. Both Law and Prichard left at the end of that season, a season in which we finished bottom of Division One in the championship.

They were not the only casualties. Keith Fletcher, such a big figure in my career, was replaced by Graham Gooch as coach, an equally big figure to me, and Fletch began a new scouting role for the club.

David East by this time had become chief executive of the club after the sad death of Peter Edwards the previous year. Now Peter had his detractors and was something of a county dinosaur, but he did a tremendous amount for the club. I'm not sure people fully appreciated just how much until after he died, particularly as Peter's strong right hand, Malcolm Field, sadly left the club too soon afterwards. Things have never been quite the same since.

East asked me what I thought about Gooch taking over from Fletcher, and as I was loyal to both I didn't really have strong views, except to say that I thought it a bit harsh on Fletch. I was worried about how Gooch would react to some of the different characters in the side, but in the first season, 2002, everything went like a dream. I wasn't around much because of my England commitments, but the difference in atmosphere and achievement was stark. Andy Flower was Law's replacement and he was a tremendous influence on the dressing room, one of the best captains I've played under. After Stuart Law, he was exactly what Essex needed. I never really knew him when I had played against him in the past, but I soon found out everything about the bloke, on and off the field. He is thoroughly likeable. He hates losing and never gives his cricket less than one hundred per cent. Gooch was calm and enthusiastic, Ronnie played really well and we were promoted in both championship and National League. He went back to his first year as captain, where he took a more quiet role and let Graham do all the talking. Ronnie just played and led by example. We still managed to lose in the final of the last Benson & Hedges Cup.

But things were changing between me and Graham Gooch, the man who had done so much for me, going back to when he picked me for his England team as a raw youth in 1990. I made a conscious decision to move away from Gooch's style of coaching. He still felt that when you were not playing for England you should be playing for Essex – and fair play to him for being able to do that so spectacularly well in his own career – but he didn't appreciate that things had changed; there was so much more international cricket now. I had become aware of the benefits and need for quality rest between international commitments. Above all, I had become influenced by Duncan Fletcher and I felt that his way was the best way for me and for the England team.

As things got on top of me with England I needed my periods of rest and to get my heartbeat down. I needed a bit of breathing space. I needed Duncan Fletcher. And this led to a bit of friction between me and Graham. If you stay on the right side of Graham Gooch, he will love you to death but strike out on your own and things are less happy. I had gone in another direction from Graham and I never thought he could really understand my point of view.

And the cracks slowly started to appear at Essex in 2003. Graham was indeed struggling to deal with different personalities within the team, making me think back to his clash with David Gower all those years ago; at times it seemed to me that Flower was holding the team together. Ronnie's tactics and fitness record were being questioned and Graham's only answer to any setback was naughty boy nets or yet another meeting. The boys were bringing their problems to me but my attitude, with my England future in the balance, was 'Not now, not me.'

I was having my own problems with Gooch. At the start of 2003 it became clear he was becoming increasingly antagonistic in his dealings with England and me, strange for someone who was such a proud England captain. At one point he questioned why Phil Neale, the England manager, was e-mailing him details of how my central contract worked rather than phoning him. In the end Duncan Fletcher rang Graham to explain and said, 'This is why Nasser's going to miss three matches.' Graham's reaction shocked me. He said to Duncan, 'Fine, I'm not sure Nasser is going to feature in our one-day side anyway.' This got back to me and I couldn't believe it because my form had been good when I went back to Essex, but I just decided to get my head down and carry on. The fact was, I was considering my whole future after standing down as England one-day captain, so the last thing I wanted was a row with Gooch.

Earlier in the summer I had intimated to Essex that I didn't want to play in Twenty20 cricket, the new shortened form of the game, which struck me very much as a young person's game. But with my England future in the balance I decided the best way to see whether I still had an appetite for the game was to throw myself into county cricket and play as much as possible. So I asked for a meeting at Chelmsford and talked to Gooch, his assistant John Childs and vice-captain Paul Grayson. Ronnie wasn't there. I think he could have been away, doing something for his benefit. I explained to the three guys that I knew I'd said I didn't think I should play in Twenty20, but now I felt I needed to play as much as possible so I was available if they wanted me.

Next day Goochy left a message on my voicemail, saying he didn't want to go with me in Twenty20 cricket. I felt, as England captain, I could still do a job for the team, but if he wanted to go with young players, which had always been the Gooch way, then I respected that and went with it. I didn't have a problem with Gooch, Childs or Grayson. But I did have a problem with Ronnie. And that problem was his silence and the total lack of support he was showing me when, for the first time in my life, I needed it from him. Just six months earlier, he had been crying on my shoulder over the World Cup and also telling me I should be opening the batting for England in one-day cricket. Just three months earlier I had possibly saved his job as Essex captain by talking him out of staying away from a game against Lancashire after a row with Gooch. During the whole Stuart Law situation I had stood by Ronnie's side. When I stood down as Essex captain, I recommended the job be given to Ronnie. I had backed him in New Zealand in 1997 when David Lloyd had a downer on him, and I had backed him when Mike

Gatting came back from an England 'A' tour with him and said, 'Don't pick Irani at any cost.'

The very least I expected was an explanation as to why Essex were leaving me out of Twenty20 cricket. After all, he was captain. I was his close friend, and I was still the England captain; surely I deserved a little respect. All I wanted was an explanation. As I have stated throughout this book, all I have ever wanted is openness and an upfront conversation of the type Vaughan had with me in the back room at Lord's. You have your say, you agree or disagree, it doesn't matter, and then you move on. All I got was a message two days later in which he just said, 'Nass, it's Ron. Have you left the country? Speak soon.' No one could question my county record at first-class or one-day level, and when I did play in 2003 I produced some of the best county form of my life, but I was being left out and I felt I deserved a lot more from Irani. When he eventually rang me again, I was on my way to the Rose Bowl to do a bit of commentary for Sky as I wasn't needed by Essex, and he was surprised that I wasn't more communicative. It turned out that he had only rung me because I had promised to get him a signed David Beckham shirt for his benefit from my agents, SFX. Ronnie asked me why I was angry, and I lost it with him. I went through all the times I had supported him and explained that all I wanted was a phone call telling me whether it was him who didn't want to pick me, or Gooch or whoever. He told me he had backed me in the meeting, but the trust had gone. Two stubborn people were not giving an inch.

Then it got worse. In the middle of Twenty20 there was a National League game against Warwickshire and I turned up for it, not having heard that my place in that form of the game was in jeopardy. Ronnie read out the team when we were in a huddle after practice on the outfield. I wasn't mentioned. I felt like a seventeen-year-old waiting to see if I'd made the team. It was embarrassing for me. He hadn't even thought it worth warning me that I wasn't playing or explaining why, before he read the team out. Again, I thought I was deserving of a little bit more respect than this.

I just went home. As I was driving, I turned on Essex Radio and heard David East being asked why I wasn't playing. 'Graham has picked his best one-day side and we don't think Nasser is in it,' he said. I was so hurt. After everything else that was going on in my life, I didn't need this. It felt like a dagger in my heart from my county.

When, later on, they did decide to pick me, I always rewarded them with runs, but things were never the same between Ronnie and me. We were at Arundel a few weeks later and he said, 'Are we over our little tiff now?' I said, 'No, Ron. We will never be over that.' Ronnie Irani looked after number one too much in 2003. My experiences were far from atypical. When Darren Robinson was sacked, he didn't receive a phone call from the captain, even though a couple of weeks earlier Ronnie had made a point of singling out Robbo for praise during our match against Kent. James Davis, our former physio, had been with Ronnie through the bad times over his knee, had travelled to America to seek treatment with him and had always been there for him. When James Davis left the club there was not a single word of explanation or thanks from Ronnie. He even bumped into James in a bar soon afterwards but didn't even say hello to him.

People in cricket like David Lloyd and Mike Atherton had always told me to be wary of Ronnie, but I've always considered myself a good reader of people and I thought they were wrong. I would always say he was a fighter, that he was similar to me and that he inspired people. But he is the one person who changed his attitude towards me since I stopped being England captain. It was as if I was no use to him any more. Even now I hope I'm wrong; I want to give him the benefit of the doubt. Maybe Ronnie had a lot on his mind. I don't want to think of him as a bluffer. There are too many of them in county cricket already and I don't want to think my old mate Ronnie is another. But the end of my Essex career was soured by what happened between me, Gooch and Irani.

I've played cricket with Essex since I was eight years old, however, and nothing can change the immense fondness and pride with which I'll always view my time with my home county. Essex have been an enormous part of my life. As for county cricket, I get accused of being a detractor but I don't feel I am. I just feel the game needs to change, and the counties must recognize that. We need less cricket played on better wickets and the England team, which pays the bills, must be at the forefront of any decision that is taken, but this is still not the case at times. Essex have provided more England players than most counties, so in that way I can only praise my county. The good has definitely outweighed the bad, and I owe Essex an awful lot.

39

There was one final arm ball that Graham Gooch bowled at my career at the start of 2004 and, I must confess, it trapped me plumb in front. Before our return from the West Indies, just ahead of the start of the domestic season, Phil Neale rang Graham up, asking for me to be rested from the first championship game and opening one-day games. Phil wasn't expecting the rather sharp reply he got. 'If that's what England want, then fine, but we run a professional club here,' said Graham. 'If our young players score runs, Nasser won't be in the side.' Phil relayed this to Duncan Fletcher in the England dressing room in Antigua. The other lads, whose counties appeared to be being much more supportive, could hear this and they were looking at me. Not for the first time in recent years, I felt hurt by Essex. I had scored consistently well for them when I played in 2003 and, while I am all for giving young players opportunities, you must have a blend of youth and experience in any side. We had been through all this the previous season, and I thought I had proved that I was still deserving of a place. I thought I was going to have to return home and have it all out with Graham – but other, far more important things happened to make my latest little upset with Essex seem irrelevant.

At the end of the final Test in Antigua I received a phone call from my brother Mel telling me that Dad had been taken very ill and had been rushed to hospital with a pancreatic problem. He was in a very bad way. It hit me really hard, and on the flight home I was thinking terrible things and was extremely worried. When eventually I got to see Dad in hospital in Ilford, he was in a very poorly state. The stomach problem had led to other complications and he had a mild heart attack on his way to hospital. The doctors were talking in a serious way; everything I had been mulling over, about my cricket and whether I should retire, just disappeared from my mind.

My mum doesn't drive, so I started taking her to hospital every day, and in a funny way it brought us all together again. Dad was as ill as he had ever been, we were all extremely worried and I was talking at length to Mel about the right time for me to retire and how the news would affect Dad's health. Would it have an adverse affect on him if I retired before reaching 100 caps, which he so wanted me to do, or would it actually make his condition worse if I battled on and then was at the mercy of the selectors? I knew, if it was down to me, that I would go either at the end of the New Zealand series or at the end of the summer; but all I could think of was Dad, and I couldn't imagine having to concentrate on my cricket and one last push before I retired.

Thankfully his health has improved enormously and, as I write, he has made a virtually full recovery and there was some good to come out of it; good in that I felt I was doing something for my mum and dad for the first time in years by spending time with them and ferrying Mum to and from hospital. I hadn't done enough for them over the years other than playing cricket. I guess the whole incident made me realize there was much more to being a Hussain than playing cricket. The simple things, like watching Dad getting better over a period of time, meant so much more, I realized, than trying to reach 100 caps.

When I eventually did speak to Goochy about my situation, it was in the context of my dad's illness, and I was much more restrained about what I wanted to say. I said to Graham, 'I hope you understand what England are trying to do. I need those games off.' We had a give-and-take type of chat, and in the end we agreed, with Duncan's blessing, that I would play for Essex in the one-day games I had been scheduled to miss. It was the new non-confrontational Nasser Hussain, and it worked because I came to an amicable arrangement with Graham and I then scored runs in virtually every early-season game for Essex that I played in.

Some of the press had bothered me at the end of the West Indies series. I'd had a good series, following on from some other good performances against South Africa the previous summer and Bangladesh in the early part of the winter, with only Sri Lanka proving a disappointment; but people like Simon Wilde in the *Sunday Times* and Colin Bateman in the *Express* were writing thank you and goodnight. I guess deep down I could understand what they were saying because I myself was questioning my future. I knew that I was starting to run on empty. The fire was burning out in my belly, even though I was still batting well. I knew inside that I didn't have the energy to cope with any more ups and downs in form; but, as things stood, my form didn't warrant people writing me off just yet.

I thought it had all died down – but then, just before the squad for the first Test against New Zealand was due to be picked, Ian Botham was quoted as saying he felt I should be dropped, and the whole issue was reignited. At Cardiff with Essex and at breakfast Andy Flower sympathized with me and said it looked as though I was going to be on trial again, which was exactly how I felt. Aged thirty-six, getting runs and still on trial. Enough was enough. Botham later tried to drag it back and said he was misquoted, but the damage was done. David Graveney again asked me if I was committed and whether it was right that I intended retiring at the end of the season, but while that time-scale was very much in my thoughts I found it impossible to say for sure when I intended to go. In any case, I didn't feel I could be presumptuous enough to assume at my age that I would still be around to make that call at the end of the summer, so I just told Grav I was as committed as ever, which was true, and I just had to see how things would go in terms of my retirement. I said to him, 'I'm thirty-six.

How can I know what's going to happen in six months' time?'

I was angry because it was about the fourth time I had had to reaffirm my commitment to England, something that has never been in doubt as far as I'm concerned, and you can only do so much in proving people wrong, but I do understand that the selectors were only doing their job and were trying to plan for the future.

Lord's, as it turned out, was the final hurdle. It was an incredible week. I started by writing an article in the *Daily Mail* in which I said I knew I had only a limited number of Lord's Tests left and that I was determined to enjoy every second, but I honestly didn't know at that stage that this was to be my last game before retirement. As it turned out, I played the game as if it was going to be my last one – and how I wish I could have approached every game in my career like that. It relaxed me. It made me play better.

I suppose the first key moment in the whole business had nothing directly to do with me at all. A routine net practice saw a young MCC bowler by the name of Zac Taylor bowling at England captain Michael Vaughan. An innocuous delivery ended up with Mick crumpling in a heap on the floor, having injured his knee and straight away looking doubtful for the match. Up stepped a young batsmen called Andrew Strauss for what was to be his debut and, as a direct result, my last game in cricket.

I loved the game. I got a couple of catches at short leg, executed a direct-hit run-out straight from my youth, and even enjoyed my streaky 30-odd in our first innings. But it was somebody else's innings that really set me thinking. Strauss played beautifully, to become the first batsman to score a century on Test debut for England since a certain Graham Thorpe. He did it on his home ground and he made me think that my time was up. It was up, I reasoned, because Vaughan would be fit in time for the second Test at Headingley and I just couldn't see who, other than me, would be required to stand down. I had never wanted to outstay my welcome as an England player. I have always wanted to go when someone was presenting an unarguable case for taking my place, just as I did when it was clear Vaughan was ready to replace me as captain; and here was Strauss playing as if to the manner born.

On the Sunday night, with an intriguing final day ahead of us is the first Test, I did a lot of thinking in my room at the Landmark Hotel in Marylebone Road. I asked Duncan Fletcher to come round for a glass of wine because I wanted to find out how he felt about the possibility of me retiring. I told him I thought the time might have come for me to call it a day. If he had said straight away that he felt I should carry on, as he had done in the past, I would have done so. But he didn't. I think both he and I knew that I was right. He never said 'Go' or 'Stay', he just told me that I should try to go out at the top on my own terms and that I should make sure I was neither bitter nor twisted when I went. He also told me to get some runs on the board the next day!

Then I rang those closest to me, while still putting off, for the moment, the conversation that would be the hardest: the one with my dad. I rang Karen, my brother Mel, Mike Atherton, Richard Bevan and Paul Newman, my close friend and collaborator on this book. I also rang Jon Holmes, my agent, and asked him to keep his phone switched on for the next couple of days because I might need some career advice from him! I told them all I was planning to retire the next day, and they were all a bit worried whether or not I was doing the right thing. Karen said that, knowing me so well, she realized my time was up, but she felt that it was a decision I had to make myself. Athers said, 'I can see what you are saying, but I don't think you should go now because it would look as if you were going because of the press.' I said, 'It's not that, I just feel completely done, and a young lad has come in and shown he is ready to play for England. How can I stand in his way?' Mel said he would speak to Dad, as he has often done in my career, to sound him out and find out how that decision would affect him, while Paul said, 'What if you score a hundred tomorrow and England win? How could you go out then?' I told him that would make it even more right for me to go – but little did I know that that was exactly what would happen!

If that net bowler hadn't bowled that ball to Michael Vaughan and Andrew Strauss had not got his unexpected call-up for England, it would all have ended differently and I'm pretty sure I would have played another couple of Test matches before I retired; but my mind was made up. It was fate. Duncan's reaction was the key for me. I trusted his judgement implicitly, and he seemed to be backing my decision to go now without having to say so in so many words.

When Strauss scored his hundred, I felt a calmness descend over me. I knew it was time to go. Later that day, I was one of the last players to leave the changing room and I saw Andy, sitting on the balcony at Lord's and going through hundreds of congratulatory messages and ringing his dad. I listened quietly to him talking to his dad, saying it was the best day of his life, that it was like a dream. It made me smile. I realized that it was somebody else's turn now; I'd had my go. I don't want to put pressure on Andrew Strauss. I know he will have his ups and downs in his career, but the bottom line to me was that I would be holding him up if I stayed on at a time when both my gut instinct and my head were telling me it was time to go.

I felt very relaxed on the Monday morning as we prepared for our fourth-innings run-chase. I bumped into Alec Stewart at Lord's and asked him how he was. 'Not as stressed as you,' Stewie smiled, but I wasn't and I dearly wanted to tell him why. It was my last day as a Test cricketer and I was sure I was doing the right thing. That decision and the mood I was in made me play the innings I did in a winning cause for England. I was just savouring every moment. I knew it was going to be the end.

But was it? Because fate was to take another twist. I ran Strauss out at a time when he looked certain to become the first Englishman to score hundreds in both innings of his debut and at a time when we were well placed for victory. I couldn't believe it. I had run out the local hero at a crucial moment. I felt like Geoff Boycott running out Derek Randall.

Yes, we had had a talk the previous over about the need to take singles, and yes, I had told him I thought there was an easy run to Chris Cairns in the covers, but I have no excuses. It was my fault. I have felt, over the years, that this reputation I had for running people out has been grossly exaggerated, but I hold my hand up to this one. I tried to get back when I realized what was happening, but for some reason the idiot ran past me and was run out. To be honest, if we'd not won that match Andy would have been at fault for doing that because he was batting so much better than me, but I can understand him thinking he should sacrifice himself as the junior partner, and I'm also very grateful that he did it because it enabled me to go on and experience the perfect farewell. Now my head was spinning. I thought, 'God, I can't go now. If we don't win this game I will be the villain of Lord's and will always be remembered as such if it's my last game.'

Luckily a familiar face was coming to join me in the middle. Graham Thorpe could clearly see the turmoil I was in; I had talked to him earlier in the match about my feelings. He took control straight away. He said, 'Look, you miserable git, stop behaving like a pork chop. Let's win this game.' I must have had an inner strength or something, because I played much better after that. No way was I going to let this Test slip. I just kept saying to myself as the bowler ran in, 'Be here at the end. Be here at the end!' Then I had an argument with Thorpey. When I had reached 80, he started blocking them, trying to make sure I could get to a century before we reached our target. I told him not to be stupid and to hurry up and win the game, and he said, 'I've been crucified for five years for not letting

Alex Tudor get a hundred like this at Edgbaston. I'm not going to do that again.'

I was having none of it and I told Thorpey to get on with it, but then I realized I was just going to have to get on with it myself and I started playing more fluently than I had done for some time. My last three shots went to the boundary – but the last one only counted as the winning single – as I went to a hundred and then hit the winning runs. It does not get much better than that. I raised my bat to all corners of the ground and I couldn't have written the script any better. It was like someone upstairs was saying, 'You are doing the right thing and this is your reward.' The whole week summed up my career in microcosm. As I walked off with Thorpey to the acclaim of Lord's, my teammates came down to congratulate me and the MCC members in the Long Room patted me on the back as I walked through to get to the dressing room. It was the most amazing time of my career, and it confirmed my decision for me.

I know people said that I couldn't have been left out after that, but who would have been left out to make room for me at Headingley for the second Test? Whoever it was, it would have been wrong. And anyway, if the decision had been fudged, it would only have been a matter of time before it became an issue again. I didn't want to go through it all again. As I said earlier, you can only prove people wrong so many times. It was a selfish thing for me to do, as well as an unselfish one. I'm a proud person and if it had reached the point where the selectors had had to tell me they didn't want me to play cricket for England any more, it would have been hard for me to take. And it would have been impossible for my dad to deal with that sort of rejection.

I just wanted to finish my career on my own terms and have something tangible to take into retirement with me. For a while I thought that the tangible reward I sought was a cap to signify my hundredth Test, but I realized that this was much, much better. I went on ninety-six caps because there was no better way to go. The only thing that confused the issue was the run-out. If we hadn't won, I might have had to play on and fight back one last time after that. I wanted to make sure everything was complete. Closure of my career in this way was the substantial gift I wanted to be able to give to my dad, to look back on as a thank-you for all the sacrifices he made.

I told the press and TV that I was considering retiring after the game and then I went away to put the finishing touches to my decision. I rang my dad on the way home, and it was clear he was content with my decision. He told me that not even Bradman had been able to retire like that. Then I spoke to Mum, to make sure Dad was telling me the truth, and she confirmed that he was happy. If Dad or Duncan Fletcher had asked me to stay, I would have done so, but their blessing was all I needed to know that I was doing the right thing.

The only decision left was whether to carry on playing for Essex, but I just felt that everything after that would have been an anticlimax. Why finish with a duck at Derby when you can finish with a hundred to win a Test match for England at Lord's? I don't think I would have had the fire to carry on, and I have never done anything unless I wanted to do it to the best of my ability. In any case, I had scored a century in what turned out to be my last innings for Essex, at Cardiff, and there was a nice symmetry in that. Graham Gooch and Essex were very understanding, and there has not been a moment since when I have questioned my retirement or thought that I had done the wrong thing. I rang up Jon Holmes, and within two hours he had a great offer from Sky TV to be a commentator for them and that, together with writing for the *Daily Mail*, is to be my future for at least the next four years.

Everything I have done in my cricketing career has been for my dad, and nothing has given me greater pleasure than to see us spending time as a family, with Dad back to good health and able to reflect on my goodbye at Lord's. England went on to win the series 3–0 – which was important because I didn't like going in the middle of a series – and look in a great position to build on what we have all achieved over the last few years and, maybe, even challenge for the Ashes in 2005. I will be looking down with pride from the commentary box at my part in that and hope for and expect continued progress from the England team. I hope my dad is proud of me too. I think he is.

Epilogue

Well, there you have it. It's been quite a journey just being Nasser Hussain, let alone an England cricketer and captain. It's been full of conflict. What people have seen on the outside and made judgements on was not always how it was, though.

Throughout my career, I have been full of self-doubt, nerves and the fear of failure. But those fears have meant that I've led the most incredible life and they have provided me with fantastic opportunities. I will be forever grateful for the sacrifices my father made in order to instil in me a belief that being the best you could be mattered so much.

My upbringing did, however, also create a complex character. I'd be the first to put up my hand and say that I've been a contrary, restless man. Thank goodness I was lucky enough to have that final, wonderful Monday at Lord's to give me a sense of closure. It was the kind of ending I couldn't have scripted and, most of all, it was one that I wouldn't be beating myself up over. It means I can now move on with the rest of my life without looking back with any kind of negativity in my head but instead look forward to the future with enthusiasm and satisfaction.

I took to the title of this book immediately because it summed up everything about me. I always played cricket with plenty of fire in my belly and I never wanted to play or to captain England or Essex once that fire had eventually burned out. And because of my single-minded nature I guess there are some in the game who find that being in the same team has forced them to play with fire too.

In the end, undoubtedly, the positives outweighed the negatives. I have been in an incredibly fortunate position and my life has been enriched by the game of cricket and by the people in it. Both have made me a better person than when I first started, and for that reason again I will always be grateful to my dad for seeing so clearly the life he believed I could live.

When I became England captain, people told me I was taking on a poisoned chalice, but they turned out to be the greatest four years of my life. I absolutely loved the job and walking out on any cricket ground in the world and hearing the guy on the Tannoy saying, 'And leading out England is Nasser Hussain,' was one of the biggest thrills I have experienced. As was sitting in the dressing room after winning a Test, a beer in hand, looking at all the faces around me, listening to what they were saying, taking it all in. Sitting with someone like Graham Thorpe (whom I have known since I was fifteen and with whom I have shared so much) in Barbados after he had scored a century and we had won a Test series in the Caribbean and just sharing the moment. Unforgettable feelings that just can't be replicated in any walk of life, I reckon.

The pride I felt when a young player came in and did well, people like Marcus Trescothick and Michael Vaughan and, latterly, Jimmy Anderson, fresh out of club cricket and playing well for England, will stay with me. Having a hand in making it happen for lads like that was a privilege.

But most of all I'll remember walking around the ground, after a win like we had in Barbados, and seeing the thousands of England fans, feeling what it means to them when the England cricket team do well. It makes you realize the real reason why you want England to do well. Much more than any individual player and his career, it's about them.

So many rich, exciting, sometimes humbling experiences around the world, and lasting friendships that I've made with those with whom I shared them – and still it's the warmth of the cricket-loving public that seals it all!

I fully admit to being an introvert, an insular person and an abrasive man. For reasons I've tried to explain in this book, my whole early life was geared simply towards cricketing success. Nothing else mattered. Consequently, people weren't sure about me; they were wary of me, steered clear of me. I don't think I was particularly well liked or popular with the public early in my career (and who can blame them!), but back then it just didn't seem important. I'm not sure I'd have appreciated being popular anyway, I was simply too obsessed with trying to be as good at cricket as I possibly could be. If it meant stepping on people's toes or, to quote Paul Nixon again, being 'Mr Unpopular', then I was prepared to live with it.

That changed when I became England captain, though. I remember the exact moment when it changed: when we defeated West Indies at the Oval in 2000 to clinch our first series win against them in over thirty years. I realized then that the cricketing public were beginning to value my efforts and, more importantly, I began to realize what it meant to me to enjoy that support – not given lightly.

The number of letters I received on giving up the captaincy – and later, when I retired – was extraordinary. Shedloads of them. Letters from friends, from people in the media, and others just making cheering comments or thanking me for what I had tried to achieve. But, more significantly, letters from people I didn't know, just ordinary cricket fans wanting to say, 'Well done' or to wish me well for my future. I was over-whelmed. I don't think it would have happened when I was younger – and again, if I'm frank, I probably wouldn't have cared much then. But now it means everything. I was grateful for every single one.

Duncan Fletcher had a lot to do with my change of attitude, my coming to understand the wider context of what I did for a living. At an early stage of my England captaincy he drummed into me how much it all mattered to people, that ultimately what we were doing meant more to other people than it did to us. He taught me, by the way he did things, that there was a way of being successful different from the one I had always aspired to: the team way, the right way. And he made me a better person. That is one of the many reasons why I respect him so much and why I have spoken so positively about the England coach in this book. He is a special person.

I was petrified, by the end of my career, that I would lose that goodwill which had seemed to build up around me. That's why my time as captain and ultimately as a player ended so abruptly, perhaps earlier than many people might have imagined. I couldn't bear the thought of outstaying my welcome, of throwing away the goodwill that I'd been so slow in taking to heart. I felt that the public had seen me play with pride, passion and dignity, and because of that I wanted to go out with those qualities intact. It was vitally important to me. Better to go prematurely than to outstay my welcome and ruin all the hard work and all the achievements I'd gained. I have talked in the book about some of the many clashes I have had with people during my career – run-ins with people who mean a great deal to me, people like Graham Gooch and Ronnie Irani. I can only conclude that I somehow must have needed confrontation in order to motivate me and to get the best out of myself. It was the only way for me. If I had a point to prove I was a better player. I was Nasser Hussain.

The clash at Essex, in the latter stages of my career over my exclusion from Twenty20 cricket and a National League game, was a classic example. I was really hurt by it, but it was no coincidence that in my three matches for Essex after they had left me out I scored 150, 150 and then a double hundred. That just sums me up as a player, and I can see that now. Being the joker, talking easily with the umpire at square leg or chatting to the members around the boundary edge just didn't work for me. I wasn't the same player when I attempted to be nicer. Maybe that's why I had a spell as England captain when I couldn't score a run: I was trying to live up to the image that I perceived an England captain should be, and it just wasn't me. It was Ronnie Irani who said to me, 'This is not you,

Nass. Get back to playing with fire, get angry again.' And he was right.

My career has been littered with occasions when I have been written off. I've always used it to my advantage. I make no excuses for that, but I can see now that I was in the wrong at times (and that's not an admission I can imagine myself having made even a few months ago!). I was definitely wrong when, as a younger player, I was twice disciplined by Essex for speaking out of turn. As a captain I know I wouldn't have liked a youngster coming in, like I did, and questioning what I was doing and the way my team was preparing. I can understand now why it rubbed people like Graham Gooch and Neil Foster up the wrong way. Who was I to do that? But there were times when I questioned the ICC and the ECB when I still believe I was right to do so. I'd do it again, without hesitation.

I don't really look back with any regrets, but if there's one thing lacking that I could seize on, it's that I didn't enjoy myself more. Before that last Test at Lord's – when I knew it would be my last – I took a conscious decision to relax and smell the roses. And it was amazing. Should I have tried to take a similar approach to the rest of my career? Deep down, I think I know that if I had tried to play it differently, to be calmer and more philosophical, I wouldn't have been the player I was. Would it have made me a better sportsman if I'd been fearless and carefree, like Darren Gough? I doubt it. I fed off the angst.

The thing to remember on reading the last few pages of this book is that I have tried to convey the thoughts and emotions I was experiencing at the time – a more revealing approach, I believe, than writing with the benefit of hindsight or even with the perspective I have gained, even in the short time since I retired. If I sat down and started writing my autobiography now, it would probably be a very different book but I believe it would also be a less interesting one.

If I've been critical of people and situations, it's because at the time I felt I was fighting the world; it was always me against the rest of them. On one of my earliest appearances in the Sky commentary box I sat there, thinking back to my three-fingered salute to the very same box in 2002, and I wondered, 'Was it such a big deal?' The guys in there were probably only saying things about me that I have already said about somebody else. Well, I have to say that on that particular occasion, it was a big deal. While I can see many other incidents in a different light now, I don't regret for a second my defiance on that day and I never will. But at least the thought had occurred to me!

Nothing that I say in this book is set in stone. I am not saying my way is the best way and certainly it is not the only way, but it had to be my way, the product of the full-on, driven, confrontational character I am and all that this entails. As I've been at pains to stress, the good far outweighed the bad. I can even recognize now that my supporters and my critics have helped me in equal measure, the supporters to give me self-belief and the critics to give me my motivation and desire to prove them wrong. I thank them all!

I also know that I've been extremely lucky. I look around at cricketers whom I've played with – some of whom I'd count as friends – who never enjoyed the same breaks. Even if I had been given out (as I should have been) cheaply by Darrell Hair at Edgbaston in 1996 and my England career had fizzled out then, I would still have had a better run than a whole host of talented players on whom fortune hasn't smiled in the same way.

So if anyone thinks it a shame that I played 96 Tests instead of 100, I would urge them to think again. I am delighted with my lot and at peace with myself over what I have achieved.

The abrupt nature of my departure as captain and then as player meant I never properly thanked the people around me who had done so much for me. Hopefully I have redressed the balance here; but in case I haven't, a quick mention again of people like the two Fletchers, Keith and Duncan, Graham Gooch and the key people around me when I was England captain, not just the players but the fantastic management team of Phil Neale, Nigel Stockill, Dean Conway, Malcolm Ashton and many others. And my thanks to the selectors, mainly David Graveney and Geoff Miller. We were all in it together, despite our ups and downs. And the supporters. Those who I came to realize were the most important people of all.

But thanks mainly to my family. To Karen and the boys, a fantastically supportive unit whom I am delighted to be seeing more of now; to Mum for all her quiet support and sacrifice. To Mel, Abbas and Benu for always being there. But, above all, to Dad. He played with fire in the way he brought me up and in his own life by giving up so much. Was it all worth it? I'd say so. It has been a pleasure. Thank you.

Appendix: Text of the letter from the Sons and Daughters of Zimbabwe

HARARE
6 January 2003

Dear Mr Lamb

This letter is coming from Harare, Zimbabwe, but it is going to be posted in Britain. Congratulations on your decision to come and play cricket in Zimbabwe.

We were interested to be informed that a spokesman of the Department of Culture stated: '*We are pleased the ECB has made it clear players will not take part in Mugabe's propaganda.*' What a cynical piece of crap! By coming to Zimbabwe in the first instance, your Players *ARE*, wittingly or unwittingly, taking part in Mugabe's propaganda.

Our message to you is simple: COME TO ZIMBABWE AND YOU WILL GO BACK TO BRITAIN IN WOODEN COFFINS!

Mugabe's thugs and a huge opposing group are like two chemicals waiting for a catalyst to spark a violent reaction. Your visit to Zimbabwe will provide precisely that catalyst and there's going to be one mighty bang. The England Players and a load of Zimbabweans will die in the carnage.

Of course, Mugabe and his henchmen will assure you that they will protect you, and if you seek and accept that assurance are you not, in actual fact, conniving with his murderous regime? And all for what? Money? One Black Zimbabwean's life is worth a damn sight more than £5M.

So, all you can think of is money when Black men, women and children are being tortured, murdered, beaten up and starved on a daily basis. Did you know that there is a facility at Goromonzi, a few miles outside Harare, which looks like a covered public swimming pool? The only difference is that the pool is covered with concentrated Sulphuric Acid. Anybody who opposes Mugabe ends up in there – dissolved and with no trace left behind. A bit like the Concentration Camps in Nazi Germany, or is your memory so short that you have already forgotten?

Anyway, we know your Team. Come to Harare and you will die. And how safe are your families back there in the UK? Even if you survive, there are foreign groups who are prepared to hunt you and your families down for as long as it takes, and they will do that in your own very country.

Our advice is this: DON'T COME TO ZIMBABWE OR YOUR PLAYERS WILL BE LIVING IN FEAR FOR THE REST OF THEIR LIVES.

Yours sincerely
Sons & Daughters of ZIMBABWE.

A Statistical Appendix

by Paul Dyson

Brief Chronology

28 March 1968: born in Madras (now Chennai), India

2 May 1987: debut in senior cricket – in Benson & Hedges Cup for Combined Universities against Hampshire at The Parks, Oxford, with a score of 62 not out

5 July 1987: debut for Essex – against Sussex in the Refuge Assurance League at Chelmsford

8 August 1987: first day in first-class cricket – Essex v. Northamptonshire at Northampton

1989: awarded county cap

1989: elected Young Cricketer of the Year by the Cricket Writers' Club

24 February 1990: first day in Test cricket – England v. West Indies at Kingston, Jamaica

11 May 1995: first experience of captaincy in a first-class match – Essex v. Cambridge University, Fenner's

November/December 1995: captain of England 'A' team on tour of Pakistan

1999: benefit season

1999: appointed captain of Essex

1 July 1999: first day as England Test captain – against New Zealand at Edgbaston

2000: awarded ECB contract

2002: awarded the OBE

2002: one of Five Cricketers of the Year, *Wisden Cricketers' Almanack*

28 July 2003: final day as England Test captain – against South Africa at Edgbaston

24 May 2004: scored match-winning century in Test Match at
   Lord's against New Zealand
27 May 2004: announced retirement from all cricket

NOTE: All figures in the following pages are correct as on 31 May
2004
* = not out

First-class Cricket

BATTING AND FIELDING

In each season

	M	I	NO	Runs	HS	Avge	100	50	Ct
1987	2	3	0	32	18	10.66	–	–	2
1988	9	13	3	486	165*	48.60	1	2	5
1989	15	24	3	990	141	47.14	3	3	23
1989/90	6	10	1	260	70*	28.88	–	1	2
1990	16	23	3	752	197	37.60	1	2	16
1990/91	5	8	1	391	161	55.85	1	3	9
1991	25	33	8	1354	196	54.16	3	8	38
1991/92	1	2	0	32	27	16.00	–	–	2
1992	20	26	3	866	172*	37.65	1	5	24
1993	20	35	5	1604	152	53.46	7	7	16
1993/94	3	5	2	144	103*	48.00	1	–	3
1994	19	31	2	922	115*	31.79	2	5	34
1995	19	35	1	1854	186	54.52	6	10	34
1995/96	6	8	1	370	89	52.85	–	3	5
1996	18	31	1	1386	158	46.20	3	7	18
1996/97	10	16	0	583	139	36.43	2	2	13
1997	16	28	0	1081	207	38.60	4	3	17
1997/98	10	17	3	529	159	37.78	2	1	5
1998	10	19	0	591	105	31.10	1	4	9
1998/99	9	18	1	724	118	42.58	1	5	8

	M	I	NO	Runs	HS	Avge	100	50	Ct
1999	12	20	1	988	143	52.00	2	8	13
1999/2000	9	14	3	559	146*	50.81	2	2	5
2000	10	16	1	166	33	11.06	–	–	7
2000/01	10	18	3	379	109	25.27	1	2	6
2001	6	10	1	306	64	34.00	–	3	–
2001/02	9	16	1	723	106	48.20	1	6	9
2002	8	12	0	483	155	40.25	2	2	8
2002/03	7	13	1	534	117	44.50	1	4	3
2003	11	19	2	783	206	46.05	2	3	3
2003/04	10	17	1	517	95	32.31	–	6	8
2004	3	5	1	309	103*	77.25	2	1	5
TOTALS	334	545	53	20698	207	42.07	52	108	350

For each team

	M	I	NO	Runs	HS	Avge	100	50	Ct
Essex in County Championship	171	272	25	11054	206	44.75	29	56	225
Essex in other matches	18	26	1	928	118	37.12	2	6	12
England XI	34	54	7	2021	159	43.00	6	7	26
England 'A'	13	20	2	847	161	47.06	1	6	18
Other teams	2	2	2	84	47*	–	–	–	2
ENGLAND (Test matches)	96	171	16	5764	207	37.19	14	33	67
TOTALS	334	545	53	20698	207	42.07	52	108	350

Against each opponent

(minimum two matches, excluding Test Matches)

	M	I	NO	Runs	HS	Avge	100	50	Ct
Derbyshire	11	14	1	690	152	53.08	2	3	13
Durham	5	8	0	406	10	50.75	1	4	8
Glamorgan	11	19	2	730	103	42.94	2	6	18
Gloucestershire	5	8	0	277	85	34.63	–	3	9

	M	I	NO	Runs	HS	Avge	100	50	Ct
Hampshire	9	16	2	799	145	57.07	3	4	9
Kent	12	15	1	971	206	69.36	3	3	18
Lancashire	12	20	7	697	172*	53.62	2	3	7
Leicestershire	13	19	2	902	196	53.06	5	–	20
Middlesex	11	16	2	642	104	45.86	1	4	9
Northamptonshire	15	25	2	848	141	36.87	1	5	18
Nottinghamshire	10	17	0	653	143	38.41	2	3	17
Somerset	6	10	2	221	88	27.63	–	1	9
Surrey	11	17	1	795	197	49.69	3	2	14
Sussex	13	18	1	654	118	38.47	1	4	19
Warwickshire	9	16	2	722	141	51.57	2	5	11
Worcestershire	11	19	0	591	78	31.11	–	5	16
Yorkshire	9	16	1	503	158	33.53	1	1	11
Cambridge University	4	5	0	258	111	51.60	1	2	5
England 'A'	2	2	0	118	118	59.00	1	–	–
Australians	3	5	0	150	57	30.00	–	1	1
Indians	2	3	1	129	85	64.50	–	1	1
New Zealanders	2	2	0	72	71	36.00	–	1	1
West Indians	3	6	1	184	56	36.80	–	1	1
Queensland	2	3	0	92	40	30.66	–	–	2
Victoria	2	3	0	38	28	12.66	–	–	2
Western Australia	2	4	1	270	118	90.00	2	–	1
Pakistan 'A'	3	4	0	133	52	33.25	–	1	2
Sri Lanka 'A'	3	4	0	239	161	59.75	1	1	7
Sri Lanka Board President's XI	2	3	0	90	81	30.00	–	1	2
Barbados	2	2	1	115	70*	115.00	–	1	1
Jamaica	2	3	0	53	24	17.66	–	–	1
Leeward Islands	2	4	1	81	42	27.00	–	–	2
West Indies 'A'	2	4	0	194	159	48.50	1	–	3
Other teams (one match each)	27	44	6	1617	139	38.50	3	9	26

	M	I	NO	Runs	HS	Avge	100	50	Ct
English teams	180	282	26	11531	206	45.04	31	58	233
Overseas teams	58	92	11	3403	161	42.01	7	17	50
Tests	96	171	16	5764	207	37.19	14	33	67
TOTALS	334	545	53	20698	207	42.07	52	108	350

On each ground

a) in England, listed by county

	M	I	NO	Runs	HS	Avge	100	50	Ct
Derby	5	6	0	149	81	24.83	–	1	6
Chester-le-Street	3	4	0	163	70	40.75	–	2	2
Stockton-on-Tees	1	1	0	101	101	101.00	1	–	3
Chelmsford	62	109	7	4044	206	39.43	8	23	85
Colchester	12	16	2	771	145	55.07	3	2	13
Ilford	11	20	5	879	172*	58.60	3	3	14
Southend-on-Sea	15	22	3	947	127	49.84	2	5	22
Cardiff	5	8	1	217	102	31.00	1	2	6
Swansea	2	3	0	191	103	63.66	1	1	4
Bristol	2	3	0	70	67	23.33	–	1	4
Cheltenham	1	2	0	150	85	75.00	–	2	–
Gloucester	1	1	0	8	8	8.00	–	–	–
Bournemouth	1	2	0	93	63	46.50	–	1	1
Portsmouth	1	1	0	19	19	19.00	–	–	–
Southampton	2	4	1	219	115*	73.00	1	1	4
Canterbury	1	1	0	186	186	186.00	1	–	–
Folkestone	1	1	0	72	72	72.00	–	1	2
Maidstone	1	1	0	41	41	41.00	–	–	–
Tunbridge Wells	1	1	1	75	75*	–	–	1	1
Lytham	1	2	2	119	105*	–	1	–	1
Old Trafford	8	13	3	174	65*	17.40	–	1	6
Leicester	7	10	0	299	196	29.90	1	–	14
Lord's	15	22	2	943	155	47.15	3	5	11
Uxbridge	2	3	0	119	86	39.66	–	1	–

	M	I	NO	Runs	HS	Avge	100	50	Ct
Luton	1	2	0	27	27	13.50	–	–	2
Northampton	6	10	1	304	77	33.77	–	2	8
Trent Bridge	13	23	2	1017	143	48.43	4	4	12
Taunton	1	1	0	43	43	43.00	–	–	2
Weston-super-									
Mare	1	2	0	41	28	20.50	–	–	2
The Oval	11	20	0	839	197	41.95	3	3	10
Arundel	1	2	0	117	95	58.50	–	1	1
Eastbourne	1	2	0	61	61	30.50	–	1	–
Horsham	2	3	0	75	32	25.00	–	–	4
Hove	4	5	1	295	118	73.75	1	2	6
Edgbaston	13	22	3	718	207	37.79	2	1	10
Kidderminster	2	2	0	88	78	44.00	–	1	–
Worcester	4	8	0	146	68	18.25	–	1	5
Headingley	11	19	1	869	158	48.28	3	2	5
Middlesbrough	1	1	0	6	6	6.00	–	–	1
Fenner's	4	5	0	258	111	51.60	1	2	5

Summary

	M	I	NO	Runs	HS	Avge	100	50	Ct
In Essex	100	167	17	6641	206	44.27	16	33	134
In rest of Britain	139	216	18	8312	207	41.98	24	40	138
TOTALS	239	383	35	14953	207	42.97	40	73	272

b) overseas, listed by country

	M	I	NO	Runs	HS	Avge	100	50	Ct
Adelaide	3	6	1	261	89	52.20	–	2	3
Brisbane, WACA	2	4	0	168	59	42.00	–	2	2
Brisbane, ABF	1	1	0	28	28	28.00	–	–	–
Cairns	1	2	0	64	40	32.00	–	–	2
Melbourne	3	6	0	149	50	24.83	–	1	1
Perth	4	8	1	346	118	49.43	2	1	1
Sydney	2	4	0	242	75	60.50	–	3	2
Chittagong	1	2	0	171	95	85.50	–	2	–
Dhaka	1	2	0	17	17	8.50	–	–	1

Ahmedabad	1	2	0	51	50	25.50	—	1	2
Bangalore	1	1	0	43	43	43.00	—	—	1
Hyderabad	1	2	0	84	46	42.00	—	—	—
Jaipur	1	2	0	99	59	49.50	—	1	1
Mohali	1	2	0	97	85	48.50	—	1	1
Auckland	2	3	0	92	82	30.66	—	1	1
Christchurch, LP	2	4	0	162	106	40.50	1	—	5
Christchurch, HO	1	1	0	69	69	69.00	—	1	2
Hamilton	1	1	0	7	7	7.00	—	—	—
Palmerston North	1	1	0	139	139	139.00	1	—	1
Wanganui	1	2	0	71	57	35.50	—	1	2
Wellington	2	3	1	143	66	71.50	—	2	2
Bagh-I-Jinnah	1	1	0	23	23	23.00	—	—	—
Faisalabad	1	2	0	28	23	14.00	—	—	1
Karachi	2	3	1	146	89	73.00	—	2	2
Lahore	4	6	2	182	83	45.50	—	2	4
Multan	2	2	1	94	52	94.00	—	1	1
Peshawar	2	4	1	76	29	25.33	—	—	—
Rawalpindi	1	1	0	43	43	43.00	—	—	1
Bloemfontaine	1	1	0	41	41	41.00	—	—	2
Cape Town	2	4	1	73	33*	24.33	—	—	—
Centurion	2	3	0	28	25	9.33	—	—	1
Durban	2	2	1	249	146*	249.00	2	—	—
Johannesburg	1	2	0	16	16	8.00	—	—	—
Port Elizabeth	1	2	1	152	82	152.00	—	2	2
Colombo, MC	1	1	0	0	0	0.00	—	—	1
Colombo, PSS	2	3	0	160	81	53.33	—	2	1
Colombo, SSC	3	5	0	188	161	37.60	1	—	2
Galle	1	2	0	4	3	2.00	—	—	—
Kandy	3	6	0	152	109	25.33	1	—	6
Matara	2	3	0	90	56	30.00	—	1	2
Basseterre	1	2	0	52	42	26.00	—	—	—
Bridgetown	6	10	3	233	70*	33.29	—	1	4
Georgetown, B	3	4	1	119	103*	39.66	1	—	2
Georgetown, ECC	1	1	1	7	7*	—	—	—	—
Kingston, SP	4	5	0	110	58	22.00	—	1	3
Kingston, SFWCG	1	1	0	86	86	86.00	—	1	1

	M	I	NO	Runs	HS	Avge	100	50	Ct
Montego Bay	1	1	0	15	15	15.00	–	–	–
Port-of-Spain	3	6	1	152	61*	30.40	–	2	2
St Catherine	1	2	0	162	159	81.00	1	–	1
St George's	1	2	0	12	6	6.00	–	–	1
St John's	4	8	1	300	106	42.86	1	1	4
Bulawayo, AC	1	2	0	78	40	39.00	–	–	–
Bulawayo, QC	1	2	0	113	113	56.50	1	–	1
Harare	2	4	0	58	39	14.50	–	–	3
TOTALS	97	162	18	5745	161	39.90	12	35	78

In each batting position

	I	NO	Runs	HS	Avge	100	50
1	3	0	107	68	35.66	–	1
2	15	1	825	206	58.93	3	4
3	185	12	7543	186	43.60	18	46
4	190	17	6771	207	39.14	18	33
5	103	15	3930	196	44.66	11	17
6	35	6	1194	165*	41.17	2	5
7	12	1	281	71	25.55	–	2
8	2	1	47	47*	47.00	–	–
TOTALS	545	53	20698	207	42.07	52	108

Scores of over 150 (12)

207	ENGLAND V. AUSTRALIA	Edgbaston	1997
206	Essex v. Kent	Chelmsford	2003
197	Essex v. Surrey	The Oval	1990
196	Essex v. Leicestershire	Leicester	1991
186	Essex v. Kent	Canterbury	1995
172*	Essex v. Lancashire	Ilford	1992
165*	Essex v. Leicestershire	Chelmsford	1988
161	England A v. Sri Lanka 'A'	Colombo SSC	1990/91

159	England XI v. West Indies 'A'	St Catherine	1997/98
158	Essex v. Yorkshire	Headingley	1996
155	ENGLAND V. INDIA	Lord's	2002
152	Essex v. Derbyshire	Chelmsford	1993

Two consecutive centuries (three times)

a) in 1993	118	Essex v. England 'A'	Chelmsford
	111	Essex v. Cambridge University	Fenner's
b) in 1994	115*	Essex v. Hampshire	Southampton
	101	Essex v. Durham	Stockton-on-Tees
c) in 1997	105	ENGLAND V. AUSTRALIA	HEADINGLEY
	128	Essex v. Leicestershire	Colchester

NOTE: The instances in 1993 and 1994 both occurred in the first two games of each of the two seasons concerned.

A century and a half-century in the same match (three times)

70* & 118	Essex v. Sussex	Hove	1993
103 & 80	Essex v. Glamorgan	Swansea	1995
141 & 56*	Essex v. Derbyshire	Chelmsford	1999

Six consecutive half-centuries

85 & 65 v. Gloucestershire at Cheltenham

145 v. Hampshire at Colchester

103 & 80 v. Glamorgan at Swansea

56 v. West Indians at Chelmsford, for Essex, in 1995

Most consecutive innings without a half-century

27 – from 2 January to 3 December 2000

NOTE: This sequence contained NH's only **pair** – ENGLAND V. WEST INDIES at THE OVAL

Significant landmarks

10,000 runs	24* (out of 43)	England 'A' v. Pakistan 'A'	Rawalpindi	1995/96
20,000 runs	42* (out of 58)	ENGLAND V. WEST INDIES	KINGSTON	2003/04
50 centuries	116	ENGLAND V. SOUTH AFRICA	TRENT BRIDGE	2003

Best English seasons

Highest positions in national averages	7th in 1999, 10th in 1988
Highest positions in leading run aggregates	2nd in 1993, 3rd in 1995

NOTE: NH was in first place in the averages for each of the following tours: 1999/2000 and 2001/02.

Methods of dismissal

Caught	305	62.0%
lbw	91	18.5%
Bowled	76	15.4%
Run out	11	2.2%
Stumped	8	1.6%
Hit wicket	1	0.2%
TOTALS	492	100.0%

Bowlers with most dismissals

11	S.K. Warne (Australia)
8	G.D. McGrath (Australia), S.M. Pollock (South Africa)
7	C.A. Walsh (West Indies)
6	J.N. Gillespie (Australia, Australians), P.C.R. Tufnell (Middlesex)

Double-century partnerships (13)

347*	3rd	M.E. Waugh	Essex v. Lancashire	Ilford	1992
317	3rd	S.G. Law	Essex v. Leicestershire	Colchester	1997
316	5th	M.A. Garnham	Essex v. Leicestershire	Leicester	1991
314	4th	Salim Malik	Essex v. Surrey	The Oval	1991
290	4th	Salim Malik	Essex v. Derbyshire	Chelmsford	1993
288	4th	G.P. THORPE	ENGLAND V. AUSTRALIA	EDGBASTON	1997
287	4th	G.A. Gooch	Essex v. Northamptonshire	Colchester	1991
230	2nd	M.A. ATHERTON	ENGLAND V. INDIA	TRENT BRIDGE	1996
221	2nd	P.J. Prichard	Essex v. Nottinghamshire	Trent Bridge	1999
213	2nd	D.D.J. Robinson	Essex v. Middlesex	Chelmsford	1997
208	3rd	M.E. Waugh	Essex v. Surrey	The Oval	1995
207	2nd	M.P. Vaughan	England XI v. Canterbury	Christchurch	2001/02
206*	4th	A.J. Stewart	England XI v. New Zealand Selection XI	Palmerston North	1996/97

NOTE: The stands of 347, 316 and 314 are all records for Essex in all first-class cricket for each of the wickets concerned.

Two century partnerships in one innings (five occasions)

129	4th	B.R. Hardie	Essex v. Surrey	The Oval	1990
194	6th	J.J.B. Lewis			
114	5th	G.P. Thorpe	England 'A' v. Sri Lanka 'A'	Colombo, SSC	1990/91
138	7th	P.J. Newport			
176	2nd	G.A. Gooch	Essex v. Hampshire	Colchester	1995
186	3rd	M.E. Waugh			
118	4th	G.P. Thorpe	England XI v. West Indies 'A'	St Catherine	1997/98
110	5th	A.J. Hollioake			
114	1st	D.D.J. Robinson	Essex v. Kent	Chelmsford	2003
174	4th	A. Habib			

Summary of century partnerships (99)

For each wicket

1st – 3 2nd – 24 3rd – 32 4th – 22 5th – 12 6th – 3 7th – 1 8th – 1 9th – 1

For each team

Essex – 56   ENGLAND – 30   England XI – 9   England 'A' – 4

Against each team (four or more)

7 AUSTRALIA
6 Kent
5 Derbyshire, Hampshire, INDIA
4 Middlesex, SOUTH AFRICA, Surrey, Warwickshire, Worcestershire

With each partner (five or more) – for Essex unless otherwise stated

11 G.A. Gooch
9   G.P. Thorpe (ENGLAND, England XI, England 'A')
8   P.J. Prichard, M.E. Waugh
7   M.A. Butcher (ENGLAND)
6   A.J. Stewart (ENGLAND, England XI)
5   M.A. Atherton (ENGLAND, England XI), Salim Malik

On each ground (four or more)

16 Chelmsford
6   Lord's
5   Colchester, Headingley, Ilford
4   The Oval, Trent Bridge

Bowlers from whom NH took most catches

(for Essex, unless otherwise stated)

55 J.H. Childs
42 P.M. Such
18 N.A. Foster
17 M.C. Ilott

12 S.J.W. Andrew

11 A.F. Giles (ENGLAND, England XI), R.C. Irani

10 A.P. Cowan, R.D.B. Croft (ENGLAND, England XI), P.C.R. Tufnell (ENGLAND, England XI)

BOWLING

Season-by-season

	O	M	R	W	Avge
1988	9	0	47	0	–
1989	1	0	1	0	–
1990	12	2	62	0	–
1991	8.3	0	50	0	–
1992	4	0	38	1	38.00
1993	10.3	0	108	1	108.00
1994	1	0	1	0	–
1999/2000	5	1	15	0	–
2001	1	0	1	0	–
TOTALS	52	3	323	2	161.50

Test Cricket

BATTING AND FIELDING

Series-by-series

	Opponents	M	I	NO	Runs	HS	Avge	100	50	Ct
1989/90	West Indies	3	5	0	100	35	20.00	–	–	1
1993	Australia	4	8	2	184	71	30.66	–	1	2
1996	India	3	5	1	318	128	79.50	2	–	3
1996	Pakistan	2	3	0	111	51	37.00	–	1	1
1996/97	Zimbabwe	2	4	0	130	113	32.50	1	–	2
1996/97	New Zealand	3	4	0	117	64	29.25	–	1	6

	Opponents	M	I	NO	Runs	HS	Avge	100	50	Ct
1997	Australia	6	11	0	431	207	39.18	2	–	8
1997/98	West Indies	6	11	2	295	106	32.77	1	1	2
1998	South Africa	5	10	0	347	105	34.70	1	2	2
1998/99	Australia	5	10	1	407	89*	45.22	–	4	4
1999	New Zealand	3	5	0	164	61	32.80	–	1	3
1999/2000	South Africa	5	8	2	370	146*	61.66	1	2	2
2000	Zimbabwe	2	3	0	31	21	10.33	–	–	0
2000	West Indies	4	7	1	61	22	10.16	–	–	2
2000/01	Pakistan	3	6	2	92	51	23.00	–	1	3
2000/01	Sri Lanka	3	6	0	136	109	22.66	1	–	1
2001	Pakistan	1	1	0	64	64	64.00	–	1	0
2001	Australia	3	6	1	177	55	35.40	–	2	0
2001/02	India	3	5	0	191	85	38.20	–	2	4
2001/02	New Zealand	3	6	1	280	106	56.00	1	2	2
2002	Sri Lanka	3	4	0	163	68	40.75	–	2	2
2002	India	4	6	0	315	155	52.50	2	–	4
2002/03	Australia	5	10	0	382	75	38.20	–	4	3
2003	Zimbabwe	2	2	0	37	19	18.50	–	–	1
2003	South Africa	4	8	1	293	116	41.85	1	1	0
2003/04	Bangladesh	2	4	0	188	95	47.00	–	2	1
2003/04	Sri Lanka	2	4	0	46	17	11.50	–	–	0
2003/04	West Indies	4	7	1	197	58	32.83	–	3	5
2004	New Zealand	1	2	1	137	103*	137.00	1	–	3
TOTALS		96	171	16	5764	207	37.19	14	33	67

NOTE: NH came top of the England averages in each of the following series – v. India 1996, v. South Africa 1999/2000.

Against each opponent

	M	I	NO	Runs	HS	Avge	100	50	Ct
Australia	23	45	4	1581	207	38.56	2	11	17
Bangladesh	2	4	0	188	95	47.00	–	2	1
India	10	16	1	824	155	54.93	4	2	11

	M	I	NO	Runs	HS	Avge	100	50	Ct
New Zealand	10	17	2	698	106	46.53	2	4	14
Pakistan	6	10	2	267	64	33.37	–	3	4
South Africa	14	26	3	1010	146*	43.91	3	5	4
Sri Lanka	8	14	0	345	109	24.64	1	2	3
West Indies	17	30	4	653	106	25.12	1	4	10
Zimbabwe	6	9	0	198	113	22.00	1	–	3
TOTALS	96	171	16	5764	207	37.19	14	33	67

On each ground in England

	M	I	NO	Runs	HS	Avge	100	50	Ct
Chester-le-Street	1	1	0	18	18	18.00	–	–	1
Edgbaston	9	16	2	537	207	38.35	2	–	7
Headingley	8	14	1	621	110	47.76	2	2	1
Lord's	11	18	1	861	155	50.65	3	5	9
Old Trafford	4	7	1	55	16	9.16	–	–	4
The Oval	7	13	0	243	52	18.69	–	2	5
Trent Bridge	7	12	2	498	116	49.80	2	2	4
TOTALS	47	81	7	2833	207	38.28	9	11	31

In each overseas country

	M	I	NO	Runs	HS	Avge	100	50	Ct
Australia	10	20	1	789	89*	41.52	–	8	7
Bangladesh	2	4	0	188	95	47.00	–	2	1
India	3	5	0	191	85	38.20	–	2	4
New Zealand	6	10	1	397	106	44.11	1	3	8
Pakistan	3	6	2	92	51	23.00	–	1	3
South Africa	5	8	2	370	146*	61.66	1	2	2
Sri Lanka	5	10	0	182	109	18.20	1	–	1
West Indies	13	23	3	592	106	29.60	1	4	8
Zimbabwe	2	4	0	130	113	32.50	1	–	2
TOTALS	49	90	9	2931	146*	36.19	5	22	36

In each batting position

	I	NO	Runs	HS	Avge	100	50
3	65	7	2352	155	40.55	6	13
4	82	5	2877	207	37.36	8	17
5	11	1	275	61	27.50	—	2
6	4	1	72	35	24.00	—	—
7	7	1	141	71	23.50	—	1
8	2	1	47	47*	47.00	—	—
TOTALS	171	16	5764	207	37.19	14	33

Centuries (14)

128	v. India	Edgbaston	1996
107*	v. India	Trent Bridge	1996
113	v. Zimbabwe	Bulawayo	1996/97
207	v. Australia	Edgbaston	1997
105	v. Austalia	Headingley	1997
106	v. West Indies	St John's	1997/98
105	v. South Africa	Lord's	1998
146*	v. South Africa	Durban	1999/2000
109	v. Sri Lanka	Kandy	2001/02
106	v. New Zealand	Christchurch	2001/02
155	v. India	Lord's	2002
110	v. India	Headingley	2002
116	v. South Africa	Trent Bridge	2003
103*	v. New Zealand	Lord's	2004

NOTE: The score of 207 contained 38 boundaries and this is a record for England against Australia (see under MISCELLANY).

Three consecutive half-centuries (twice)

82 v. New Zealand at Auckland, 2001/02

57 & 68 v. Sri Lanka at Lord's, 2002

82 & 70* at Port Elizabeth, 146* at Durban v. South Africa, 1999/2000

5000th run

59 (out of 61) v. South Africa, Lord's, 2003

Methods of dismissal

Caught	100	64.5%
lbw	34	21.9%
Bowled	20	12.9%
Run out	1	0.6%
TOTALS	155	100.0%

NOTE: NH holds the world record for the most innings without being stumped (see under MISCELLANY.)

Bowlers with most dismissals

11	S.K. Warne (Australia)
8	G.D. McGrath (Australia), S.M. Pollock (South Africa)
7	C.A. Walsh (West Indies)
5	A.A. Donald (South Africa), J.N. Gillespie (Australia), M. Muralitharan (Sri Lanka)

Partnerships of over 150 (11)

288	4th	G.P. Thorpe	v. Australia	Edgbaston	1997
230	2nd	M.A. Atherton	v. India	Trent Bridge	1996
189	3rd	M.P. Vaughan	v. Australia	Sydney	2002/03
181	3rd	M.A. Butcher	v. Australia	Headingley	2001
168	4th	G.P. Thorpe	v. West Indies	St John's	1997/98
167	3rd	G.P. Thorpe	v. Sri Lanka	Kandy	2000/01
166	3rd	M.A. Butcher	v. Australia	Sydney	2002/03
159	3rd	M.A. Butcher	v. Sri Lanka	Lord's	2002
156	4th	A.J. Stewart	v. South Africa	Durban	1999/2000
155	2nd	M.A. Atherton	v. South Africa	Port Elizabeth	1999/2000
152	2nd	M.A. Atherton	v. South Africa	Trent Bridge	1998

NOTES:

a) The partnership of 288 is the record for the fourth wicket for England against Australia.

b) The partnership of 167 is the record for the third wicket for England against Sri Lanka.

c) NH holds two partnership records for England against Zimbabwe: 68 for the third wicket with A.J. Stewart and 148 for the fifth with J.P. Crawley – both made at Bulawayo in 1996–97.

Two century partnerships in the same match (three occasions)

| 106 | 3rd | M.P. Vaughan | v. Sri Lanka | Lord's | 2002 |
| 159 | 3rd | M.A. Butcher | | | |

| 116 | 3rd | M.A. Butcher | v. Australia | Sydney | 2002/03 |
| 189 | 3rd | M.P. Vaughan | | | |

| 116 | 5th | R. Clarke | v. Bangladesh | Chittagong | 2003/04 |
| 138 | 3rd | G.P. Thorpe | | | |

Summary of century partnerships (30)

For each wicket

2nd – 8   3rd – 10   4th – 8   5th – 4

With each partner

7   M.A. Butcher

6   G.P. Thorpe

4   M.A. Atherton, A.J. Stewart

3   J.P. Crawley

2   M.P. Vaughan

1   R. Clarke, M.R. Ramprakash, A.J. Strauss, M.E. Trescothick

Against each opponent

7   Australia

5   India

4   South Africa

3   Pakistan, Sri Lanka, West Indies

2 Bangladesh, New Zealand

1 Zimbabwe

In each country

12 England (including 6 at Lord's and 4 at Headingley)

4 Australia

3 West Indies

2 Bangladesh, India, South Africa

1 New Zealand, Pakistan, Sri Lanka, Zimbabwe

Bowlers from whom NH took most of his catches

10 A.F. Giles

8 R.D.B. Croft

6 S.J. Harmison

5 D.G. Cork, D. Gough, P.C.R. Tufnell

BOWLING

Career record – 5–1–15–0

AWARDS

Man of the match: v. India, Edgbaston, 1996

v. Australia, Edgbaston, 1997

v. India, Lord's, 2002

Man of the series: v. India (3 Tests), 1996

One-day Internationals

BATTING AND FIELDING

Season-by-season

	M	I	NO	Runs	HS	Avge	100	50	Ct
1989/90	2	2	1	17	15*	17.00	–	–	1
1993/94	2	2	0	26	16	13.00	–	–	1
1996/97	8	8	3	112	49*	22.40	–	–	3
1998	6	6	1	101	39	20.20	–	–	1
1998/99	10	10	0	293	93	29.30	–	2	8
1999	5	5	2	194	88*	64.66	–	2	2
1999/2000	9	9	0	189	85	21.00	–	2	7
2000	3	3	1	46	34	23.00	–	–	2
2000/01	5	5	0	228	95	45.60	–	3	4
2001/02	15	15	1	504	73	36.00	–	3	4
2002	7	7	1	244	115	40.66	1	1	3
2002/03	16	15	0	378	79	25.20	–	3	4
TOTALS	88	87	10	2332	115	30.28	1	16	40

Against each opponent

	M	I	NO	Runs	HS	Avge	100	50	Ct
Australia	13	13	0	394	93	30.30	–	3	3
Bangladesh	1	1	0	95	95	95.00	–	1	2
India	13	13	1	410	115	34.16	1	1	4
Kenya	1	1	1	88	88*	–	–	1	–
Netherlands	1	–	–	–	–	–	–	–	1
New Zealand	10	10	2	185	50	23.12	–	1	3
Pakistan	5	5	0	138	73	27.60	–	2	2
South Africa	10	10	1	173	85	19.22	–	1	2
Sri Lanka	14	14	0	291	79	20.78	–	1	11

	M	I	NO	Runs	HS	Avge	100	50	Ct
West Indies	4	4	1	44	16	14.66	–	–	3
Zimbabwe	16	16	4	514	75	42.83	–	5	9
TOTALS	88	87	10	2332	115	30.28	1	16	40

In each country

	M	I	NO	Runs	HS	Avge	100	50	Ct
Australia	20	20	0	571	93	28.55	–	4	10
England	21	21	5	585	115	36.56	1	3	8
India	7	7	0	179	49	25.57	–	–	2
Kenya	2	2	0	100	95	50.00	–	1	2
New Zealand	10	10	2	185	50	23.12	–	1	3
Pakistan	3	3	0	128	73	42.66	–	2	2
South Africa	10	9	0	207	85	23.00	–	2	5
Sri Lanka	2	2	0	76	75	38.00	–	1	–
West Indies	3	3	1	41	16	20.50	–	–	2
Zimbabwe	10	10	2	260	73	32.50	–	2	6
TOTALS	88	87	10	2332	115	30.28	1	16	40

In each batting position

	I	NO	Runs	HS	Avge	100	50
1	14	2	383	88*	31.92	–	4
3	27	1	1036	115	39.85	1	8
4	26	0	604	93	23.23	–	4
5	11	4	194	49*	27.71	–	–
6	8	2	87	34	14.50	–	–
7	1	1	28	28*	–	–	–
TOTALS	87	10	2332	115	30.28	1	16

Century

115 v. India at Lord's, 2002

Methods of dismissal

Caught	40	51.95%
Bowled	18	23.38%
lbw	9	11.69%
Stumped	8	10.39%
Run out	2	2.60%
TOTALS	77	100.00%

Century Partnerships (12)

190	3rd	G.A. Hick	v. Australia	Sydney	1998/99
185	2nd	M.E. Trescothick	v. India	Lord's	2002
175	2nd	A.J. Stewart	v. Bangladesh	Nairobi	2000/01
165	1st	N.V. Knight	v. South Africa	Bloemfontaine	1999/2000
159*	2nd	G.A. Hick	v. Kenya	Canterbury	1999
141	2nd	M.E. Trescothick	v. Zimbabwe	Colombo	2002/03
128	1st	N.V. Knight	v. South Africa	Kimberley	1999/2000
123	3rd	G.P. Thorpe	v. Zimbabwe	Trent Bridge	1999
117	2nd	N.V. Knight	v. India	Delhi	2001/02
114	3rd	G.A. Hick	v. Pakistan	Karachi	2000/01
112	2nd	N.V. Knight	v. Zimbabwe	Harare	2001/02
102	3rd	N.V. Knight	v. Australia	Sydney	2002/03

Bowlers from whom NH took his catches

9	D. Gough
5	C. White
4	A.R. Caddick, R.D.B. Croft, M.A. Ealham
3	J.M. Anderson
2	A. Flintoff, A.D. Mullally

E.E. Hemmings, A.F. Giles, M.J. Hoggard, B.C. Hollioake, A.J. Tudor, P.C.R. Tufnell,
V.J. Wells

Domestic limited-overs matches

(main competitions only – minimum 40 overs)

BATTING AND FIELDING

Season-by-season

	M	I	NO	Runs	HS	Avge	100	50	Ct
1987	9	7	2	178	62*	35.60	–	1	3
1988	12	10	1	234	76*	26.00	–	1	6
1989	15	13	2	424	118	38.55	1	2	6
1990	8	8	4	163	66*	40.75	–	1	7
1991	23	19	4	416	97	27.73	–	1	10
1992	21	18	2	400	108	25.00	1	1	8
1993	14	13	2	272	50	24.73	–	2	3
1994	20	20	2	666	76	37.00	–	5	11
1995	24	24	2	915	83	41.59	–	9	10
1996	19	18	2	753	103	47.06	1	6	7
1997	20	19	5	511	89*	36.50	–	3	8
1998	16	14	1	612	101	47.08	1	6	11
1999	9	9	0	413	114	45.88	1	3	8
2000	10	10	0	336	60	33.60	–	3	3
2001	6	6	0	200	63	33.33	–	2	3
2002	8	8	2	446	136*	74.33	1	2	3
2003	7	7	2	437	161*	87.40	2	1	2
2004	3	3	1	149	85	74.50	–	1	2
TOTALS	244	226	34	7525	161*	39.19	8	50	111

For each team

	M	I	NO	Runs	HS	Avge	100	50	Ct
Combined Universities	13	12	2	450	118	45.00	1	3	5
Essex	231	214	32	7075	161*	38.87	7	47	106
TOTALS	244	226	34	7525	161*	39.19	8	50	111

Against each opponent

	M	I	NO	Runs	HS	Avge	100	50	Ct
Derbyshire	9	9	3	172	47	28.66	–	–	2
Durham	4	4	1	75	57*	25.00	–	1	3
Glamorgan	17	14	7	610	161*	87.14	2	1	7
Gloucestershire	11	11	0	377	98	34.27	–	2	6
Hampshire	25	23	3	611	73	30.55	–	5	9
Kent	12	12	0	443	83	36.92	–	4	8
Lancashire	15	14	1	362	83*	27.85	–	2	5
Leicestershire	10	9	0	314	88	34.88	–	3	5
Middlesex	18	17	1	636	101	39.75	1	5	6
Northamptonshire	12	12	1	353	74	32.09	–	4	4
Nottinghamshire	11	11	1	358	89*	35.80	–	2	4
Somerset	12	10	3	386	118	55.14	1	2	7
Surrey	15	14	1	481	68*	37.00	–	5	6
Sussex	13	11	2	490	97	54.44	–	4	6
Warwickshire	14	14	5	394	81	43.77	–	3	8
Worcestershire	15	15	1	290	67	20.71	–	1	4
Yorkshire	14	12	3	551	136*	61.22	2	2	8
Other teams	17	14	1	622	108	47.85	2	4	13
TOTALS	244	226	34	7525	161*	39.19	8	50	111

On each ground

(minimum four innings, listed by county)

	M	I	NO	Runs	HS	Avge	100	50	Ct
Derby	4	4	2	69	41	34.50	–	–	–
Chelmsford	88	82	11	3091	161*	43.54	5	20	41
Colchester	10	10	1	279	66	31.00	–	3	5
Ilford	9	9	3	314	63*	52.33	–	3	3
Southend	12	10	1	210	57	23.33	–	1	4
Cardiff	7	6	4	291	144*	145.50	1	1	3
Southampton (NR)	10	9	1	275	73	34.38	–	2	4
Old Trafford	6	5	0	132	73	26.40	–	1	–
Leicester	4	4	0	88	40	22.00	–	–	3
Lord's	8	7	1	220	88	36.66	–	2	2
Northampton	5	5	0	60	38	12.00	–	–	2
Trent Bridge	6	6	1	231	89*	46.20	–	1	1
Taunton	4	4	1	227	118	75.66	1	1	1
The Oval	7	7	1	206	68*	34.33	–	2	4
Hove	5	5	1	265	97	66.25	–	2	3
Edgbaston	6	6	1	170	81	34.00	–	1	7
Worcester	6	6	0	118	67	19.66	–	1	1
Fenner's	4	4	1	114	81*	38.00	–	1	1
Others	43	37	4	1165	114	35.30	1	8	26

Summary

	M	I	NO	Runs	HS	Avge	100	50	Ct
In Essex	119	111	16	3894	161*	40.99	5	27	53
In rest of Britain	125	115	18	3631	144*	37.43	3	23	58
TOTALS	244	226	34	7525	161*	39.19	8	50	111

In each competition

	M	I	NO	Runs	HS	Avge	100	50	Ct
GC/NWT/C&GT	34	32	4	1190	108	42.50	2	7	23
Benson & Hedges Cup	57	53	9	2136	136*	48.54	3	17	23
Sunday and National Leagues	153	141	21	4199	161*	34.99	3	26	65
TOTALS	244	226	34	7525	161*	39.19	8	50	111

In each batting position

	I	NO	Runs	HS	Avge	100	50
1	27	2	1192	136*	47.68	2	9
2	8	2	550	161*	91.66	2	2
3	98	10	3383	105	38.44	2	28
4	45	9	1281	118	35.58	2	7
5	37	7	938	97	31.26	–	4
6	7	3	144	38	36.00	–	–
7	4	1	37	22	12.33	–	–
TOTALS	226	34	7525	161*	39.19	8	50

Centuries (8)

118	Benson & Hedges Cup	Combined Universities v. Somerset	Taunton	1989
108	NatWest Trophy	Essex v. Cumberland	Chelmsford	1992
105	NatWest Trohpy	Essex v. Devon	Chelmsford	1996
101	Benson & Hedges Cup	Essex v. Middlesex	Chelmsford	1998
114	CGU National League	Essex v. Yorkshire	Headingley	1999
136*	Benson & Hedges Cup	Essex v. Yorkshire	Chelmsford	2002
144*	National League	Essex v. Glamorgan	Cardiff	2003
161*	National League	Essex v. Glamorgan	Chelmsford	2003

Four consecutive half-centuries

62	Benson & Hedges Cup	v. Sussex	Hove
71	Benson & Hedges Cup	v. Ireland	Chelmsford
101	Benson & Hedges Cup	v. Middlesex	Chelmsford
73	AXA League	v. Hampshire	Southampton

NOTE: These scores were all made for Essex in the period from 2 May to 10 May 1998.

Five consecutive half-centuries in one competition

73	v. Lancashire	Old Trafford
55	v. Warwickshire	Ilford
68*	v. Surrey	The Oval
58	v. Leicestershire	Chelmsford
57	v. Somerset	Southend-on-Sea

NOTES:

a) These scores were all made for Essex in the AXA Equity and Law League in the period from 25 June to 23 July 1995.

b) NH scored a total of seven half-centuries in the 1995 season in this competition and this remains the record for Essex.

Over 400 runs in three consecutive innings

144*	v. Glamorgan	Cardiff
98	v. Gloucestershire	Chelmsford
161*	v. Glamorgan	Chelmsford

NOTE: These scores were all made for Essex in the National League in the period from 13 July to 5 August 2003.

Methods of dismissal

Caught	117	60.9%
Bowled	42	21.9%
lbw	22	11.5%
Run out	7	3.6%
Stumped	3	1.6%
Hit wicket	1	0.5%
TOTALS	192	100.0%

Bowlers with most dismissals

4 – M.W. Alleyne (Gloucestershire) and M.V. Fleming (Kent)

Partnerships of over 150 (6 – all for Essex)

189*	3rd	G.A. Gooch	v. Comb. Univs	Fenner's	BHC	1995
176	1st	A. Flower	v. Glamorgan	Chelmsford	NL	2003
167	2nd	S.G. Law	v. Sussex	Chelmsford	AELL	1996
163	2nd	W.I. Jefferson	v. Scotland	Edinburgh	CGT	2004
161	1st	S.G. Law	v. Surrey	Colchester	NUNL	2000
153	2nd	D.D.J. Robinson	v. Sussex	Hove	BHC	1998

NOTE: The stand of 163 is the Essex 2nd wicket record for the Gillette/NatWest/C & G Trophy.

Summary of century partnerships (31)

For each wicket

1st – 6   2nd – 14   3rd – 5   4th – 4   5th – 2

For each team

Combined Universities – 2   Essex – 29

Against each team (three or more)

4	Sussex
3	Glamorgan, Lancashire, Leicestershire

With each partner (four or more)

7	D.D.J. Robinson
5	G.A. Gooch, P.J. Prichard
4	S.G. Law

On each ground (two or more)

11	Chelmsford
2	Colchester, Hove, Old Trafford, Southampton, Taunton

Bowlers from whom NH took most catches (all Essex)

17	M.C. Ilott
11	P.M. Such
10	R.C. Irani
9	T.D. Topley
6	A.P. Grayson
5	A.P. Cowan, J.K. Lever, M.E. Waugh

MATCH AWARDS (8)

Comb. Univs v. Somerset	Taunton	Benson & Hedges Cup	1989
Essex v. Cumberland	Chelmsford	NatWest Trophy	1992
Essex v. Middlesex	Chelmsford	Benson & Hedges Cup	1996
Essex v. Devon	Chelmsford	NatWest Trophy	1996
Essex v. Nottinghamshire	Trent Bridge	NatWest Trophy	1997
Essex v. Yorkshire	Headingley	Benson & Hedges Cup	1998
Essex v. Yorkshire	Chelmsford	Benson & Hedges Cup	2002
Essex v. Lancashire	Chelmsford	Cheltenham & Gloucester Trophy	2002

Captaincy

RESULTS

First-class matches

	Played	Won	Lost	Drawn
County Championship	12	5	3	4
Other matches	23	10	0	13
Test Matches	45	17	15	13
TOTALS	80	32	18	30

Analysis of test results against each country

	Played	Won	Lost	Drawn
Australia	8	2	6	0
India	7	1	2	4
New Zealand	6	2	3	1
Pakistan	4	2	0	2
South Africa	6	1	2	3
Sri Lanka	6	4	1	1
West Indies	4	2	1	1
Zimbabwe	4	3	0	1
TOTALS	45	17	15	13

One-day internationals

	Played	Won	Lost	No result
Australia	7	0	7	—
Bangladesh	1	1	0	—
Holland	1	1	0	—
India	12	4	7	1

	Played	Won	Lost	Tied	No result
New Zealand	6	3	3	—	
Pakistan	4	2	2	—	
South Africa	5	1	4	—	
Sri Lanka	7	5	2	—	
West Indies	1	0	1	—	
Zimbabwe	12	11	1	—	
TOTALS	56	28	27	1	

Domestic limited-overs matches

	Played	Won	Lost	Tied	No result
NatWest Trophy	2	1	1	—	
Benson & Hedges Cup	8	4	3	—	1
Sunday & National Leagues	20	10	9	1	—
TOTALS	30	15	13	1	1

Miscellany

BATTING PERFORMANCE AS CAPTAIN COMPARED WITH WHEN TEAM MEMBER

First-class matches

	As captain			As team member		
	M	Runs	Avge	M	Runs	Avge
Test Matches	45	2487	36.04	51	3277	38.10
County Championship	12	952	47.60	159	10102	44.50
Other matches	23	1427	47.57	44	2453	34.07
TOTALS	80	4866	40.89	254	15832	42.45

Limited-overs matches

	As captain			As team member		
	M	Runs	Avge	M	Runs	Avge
One-day internationals	56	1598	31.33	32	734	28.23
Domestic matches	30	1162	43.04	214	6363	38.33
TOTALS	86	2760	35.38	246	7097	36.96

COMPARISONS

Players who have captained England in most test matches

		P	W	L	D	% Won
M.A. Atherton	1993–2001	54	13	21	20	24.07
N. HUSSAIN	1999/2000–03	45	17	15	13	37.77
P.B.H. May	1955–61	41	20	10	11	48.78
G.A. Gooch	1988–93	34	10	12	12	29.41
D.L. Gower	1982–89	32	5	18	9	15.63
J.M. Brearley	1977–81	31	18	4	9	58.06
R. Illingworth	1969–73	31	12	5	14	38.71
E.R. Dexter	1961/62–64	30	9	7	14	30.00

Players who have captained England in most one-day internationals

		P	W	L	Tied/ no result	% Won
N. HUSSAIN	1997–2002/03	56	28	27	1	50.00
G.A. Gooch	1988–93	50	24	23	3	48.00
M.A. Atherton	1993/94–97	43	20	21	2	46.51
A.J. Stewart	1991/92–2002/03	41	15	25	1	36.59
M.W. Gatting	1986–88	37	26	11	—	70.27
R.G.D. Willis	1978–83/84	29	16	13	—	55.17
J.M. Brearley	1977–80	25	15	9	1	60.00

Most runs scored in tests by England captains

	M	I	NO	Runs	HS	Avge	100	50
M.A. Atherton	54	98	4	3815	185*	40.59	8	22
G.A. Gooch	34	63	2	3582	333	58.72	11	16
P.B.H. May	41	65	8	3080	285*	54.04	10	15
N. HUSSAIN	45	77	8	2487	155	36.04	5	17
E.R. Dexter	30	49	4	2427	205	53.93	4	17

Most runs scored in one-day internationals by England captains

	M	I	NO	Runs	HS	Avge	100	50
N. HUSSAIN	56	55	4	1598	115	31.33	1	12
M.A. Atherton	43	43	2	1392	127	33.95	2	8
G.A. Gooch	50	48	2	1378	112*	29.96	1	7
M.W. Gatting	37	37	7	1013	82*	33.76	–	5
A.J. Stewart	41	41	1	924	88	23.10	–	6

NH's Test career compared with two other contemporary players

Mike Atherton was born just five days before NH and made his Test debut six months before NH; Alec Stewart made his Test debut in the same match as NH. All three captained England.

NOTE: All figures are correct as on 30 April of each of the years stated in the first column.

	Atherton				HUSSAIN				Stewart			
	M	Runs	Avge	Tests as capt	M	Runs	Avge	Tests as capt	M	Runs	Avge	Tests as capt
1990	2	73	18.25	–	3	100	20.00	–	4	170	24.28	–
1991	13	1087	45.29	–	3	100	20.00	–	12	541	24.59	–
1992	18	1166	35.33	–	3	100	20.00	–	17	1096	37.79	–
1993	23	1374	32.71	–	3	100	20.00	–	26	1705	38.75	2
1994	34	2437	38.68	7	7	284	25.81	–	37	2560	39.38	2
1995	45	3324	40.04	18	7	284	25.81	–	45	3055	40.19	2
1996	56	4202	41.19	29	7	284	25.81	–	54	3489	38.34	2

	Atherton				HUSSAIN				Stewart			
	M	Runs	Avge	Tests as capt	M	Runs	Avge	Tests as capt	M	Runs	Avge	Tests as capt
1997	67	4986	42.25	40	17	960	36.92	–	63	4433	42.62	2
1998	79	5442	38.87	52	29	1686	36.65	–	75	5153	41.22	2
1999	88	6045	38.50	52	39	2440	37.53	–	86	5968	41.15	13
2000	95	6403	37.88	52	47	2974	39.13	8	95	6525	40.78	13
2001	108	7409	38.58	52	59	3294	34.67	20	108	7084	39.35	14
2002	115	7728	37.69	54	69	4006	36.09	30	115	7469	39.31	15
2003	115	7728	37.69	54	81	4866	37.14	42	126	8187	40.13	15
2004	115	7728	37.69	54	95	5627	36.53	45	133	8463	39.54	15

Most boundaries in an innings in ashes test matches

4s	6s	Runs	Score				
46	–	184	334	D.G. Bradman	for Australia	Headingley	1930
43	2	184	304	D.G. Bradman	for Australia	Headingley	1934
38	–	152	207	N. Hussain	for England	Edgbaston	1997

A century in last Test for England since 1945

W. Place	107	v. West Indies	Kingston	1947/48
R. Subba Row	137	v. Australia	The Oval	1961
C. Milburn	139	v. Pakistan	Karachi	1968/69
N. HUSSAIN	103*	v. New Zealand	Lord's	2004

NOTE: Although all of the above instances represent each player's last innings in Test cricket, only that of NH was played in a Test that England won. The last batsman to achieve this feat was M. Leyland with 187 against Australia at The Oval in 1938.

Most Test innings in a complete career without being stumped

171 N. HUSSAIN (England)
154 Salim Malik (Pakistan)
137 N. Harvey (Australia)
134 R.J. Hadlee (New Zealand)
131 K.F. Barrington (England)

Most consecutive Test innings by an England captain not to include a half-century

28	R.G.D. Willis	1982–83/84
20	I.T. Botham	1980–81
19	M.J.K. Smith	1964/65–65/66
17	N. HUSSAIN	1999/2000–00/01
16	N.W.D. Yardley	1946/47–50

NOTE: An unfair table in some respects as Willis was a genuine tail-ender and never scored a half-century in Test cricket. However, for him, Botham and Yardley the sequences referred to above coincided with the ends of their careers as England captains. Smith led England in four more Tests but NH in as many as 29.

Most consecutive Tests as captain without winning the toss

10 N. HUSSAIN (England)
9 S.M. Gavaskar (India)
8 A.C. MacLaren (England), L. Armanath, S.C. Ganguly (both India)

NOTE: NH's world-record sequence ran from 2000/01 to 2001/02 and included two Tests in Pakistan, three in Sri Lanka, four at home (one against Pakistan and three against Australia) and one in India. NH had won seven of his first nine tosses, then lost five and won one before the above-mentioned sequence.

10,000 runs in first-class matches at highest average

		M	I	NO	Runs	HS	**Avge**	100	50
G.A. Gooch	1973–97	391	650	57	30701	275	**51.77**	94	143
N. HUSSAIN	1987–2004	189	298	26	11982	206	**44.05**	31	62
K.S. McEwan	1974–85	282	458	41	18088	218	**43.37**	52	82
C.A.G. Russell	1908–30	379	628	51	23610	273	**40.91**	62	117
D.J. Insole	1947–63	345	574	54	20113	219*	**38.67**	48	97

Most runs in Sunday/national leagues

		M	I	NO	**Runs**	HS	Avge	100	50
G.A. Gooch	1973–97	274	268	23	**8573**	176	34.99	12	58
K.W.R. Fletcher	1969–88	262	238	39	**5726**	99*	28.77	–	37
B.R. Hardie	1973–90	236	219	21	**5621**	109	28.38	3	34
K.S. McEwan	1974–85	180	178	19	**5531**	162*	34.78	9	31
P.J. Prichard	1982–2001	197	178	10	**4328**	107	25.76	4	19
N. HUSSAIN	1987–2004	153	141	21	**4199**	161*	34.99	3	26

Most runs in Benson & Hedges cup

		M	I	NO	**Runs**	HS	Avge	100	50
G.A. Gooch	1973–97	115	114	15	**5176**	198*	52.28	15	30
K.W.R. Fletcher	1972–88	83	78	15	**2111**	101*	33.50	1	15
B.R. Hardie	1974–90	86	80	16	**1943**	119*	30.35	2	8
K.S. McEwan	1974–85	63	60	6	**1925**	133	35.64	3	10
N. HUSSAIN	1991–2002	45	41	7	**1698**	136*	49.94	2	14
P.J. Prichard	1985–2000	59	56	8	**1542**	114	32.12	2	8

Most runs in C & G Trophy (including Natwest Trophy and Gillette Cup)

		M	I	NO	**Runs**	HS	Avge	100	50
G.A. Gooch	1973–96	57	56	4	**2547**	144	48.98	6	17
N. HUSSAIN	1989–2004	34	32	4	**1190**	108	42.50	2	7
B.R. Hardie	1973–90	34	34	1	**1143**	110	34.63	1	9
P.J. Prichard	1985–2000	36	35	5	**1138**	94	37.93	–	9
K.W.R. Fletcher	1963–88	47	45	4	**1036**	97	25.26	–	5
K.S. McEwan	1974–85	27	27	3	**836**	119	35.08	1	5

NOTE: Again it may be seen that NH's average compares very favourably with other batsmen in each of the three above tables.

Most catches by a fielder in domestic limited-overs matches

	C&GT	BHC	Sunday/ National Leagues	Total
G.A. Gooch	26	68	100	**194**
K.W.R. Fletcher	16	21	87	**124**
R.E. East	13	16	85	**114**
B.R. Hardie	13	27	66	**112**
N. HUSSAIN	23	23	65	**111**
S. Turner	5	16	82	**103**

Most match awards in limited-overs matches

31	G.A. Gooch
10	K.W.R. Fletcher
8	R.C. Irani, K.S. McEwan
7	N. HUSSAIN
6	J.K. Lever, D.R. Pringle

Most test caps

118	G.A. Gooch
96	N. HUSSAIN
61	T.E. Bailey
59	K.W.R. Fletcher
30	D.R. Pringle

Most one-day international appearances

125	G.A. Gooch
88	N. HUSSAIN
48	N.A. Foster
44	D.R. Pringle
31	R.C. Irani

. . . and to conclude

Edgbaston is the ground where NH:

1. scored his first Test century;
2. made his highest Test and first-class score;
3. first captained England in a Test match;
4. captained England for the last time in a Test match.

Bibliography

Mike Atherton: *Opening Up*

Bill Frindall: *Limited-Overs International Cricket – The Complete Record*

The Wisden Book of Test Cricket

Rajneesh Gupta: *One-Day Internationals – The Complete Record Book*

Stephen Samuelson, Ray Mason & David Clark: *One-Day International Cricket*

Keith Walmsley: *Mosts Without in Test Cricket*

Jason Woolgar: *England's Test Cricketers*

Various editions of: *ACS International Year Book, The Cricketer Quarterly, The Cricket Society Newsletter, Essex CCC Yearbook, Playfair Cricket Annual, Wisden Cricketers' Almanack*

www-uk.cricket.org (Cricinfo)

Index

487

491